VERLAG DER BUCHHANDLUNG WALTHER KÖNIG
2011

ELMGREEN
& DRAGSET

1995 - 2011

PERFORMANCES

Break a leg!

BY ROSELEE GOLDBERG

When it comes to theater and performance art, it all comes down to this: the art world and theater world don't have much time for each other. There is little in common between those who view performance through a visual lens and those who pay attention primarily to the text. The visual group wants images that they can sort and store in their minds, with gaps in between for inserting their own meanings and associations into the mix. The text-based group, those sitting in the theater, prefers a story well told, with some sort of resolution at the end of a well-conceived evening. Their fare is logical, affecting, and articulate. The visual crowd will have no such thing; they resist the very thought of such qualifiers—too didactic, too obvious, too specific. Even backstage, the scene couldn't be more different. In theater, there is a long line of collaborators: playwright, actor, director, producer, stage designer, costume designer, lighting designer. In the visual art world, all roles merge into one. There is a clear division of labor on one side and a fiercely singular vision on the other.

—

Michael Elmgreen, Danish artist and poet, and Ingar Dragset, Norwegian actor and mime, came together more than 15 years ago—one with art aspirations, the other with dreams of acting—and began a process that would, in a variety of ways, merge their two sides. "It was a time, in 1994-1995, when the contemporary art scene in Denmark was underground," Elmgreen says of their early days in the art world, allowing them to experiment with a range of approaches in alternative spaces around Copenhagen. *The End of Natural Behavior* (1996) could be thought of as a live play in a theater without walls: it comprised Elmgreen & Dragset dressed in sailor's uniforms playing the "gay sailor," eating, sleeping, talking into a microphone. Simultaneously filmed from different angles and shown on multiple small monitors set up on the floor, *The End of Natural Behavior* was an inventive blend of theatrical devices and art world license to break them apart. Dragset describes his introduction to that world, "I was fascinated by how fast you could go from an idea to what you present for an audience in art compared to theater, which has such a heavy production apparatus, and takes so many people and such a long time to get there. Also, performance in the art world is much more revealing about identity and telling about who the person is behind it than most theater."

—

With the proverbial overview of outsiders, each looking over the other's shoulder, they made work that scrutinized the acts of making art and looking at art, with a theatrical flare for dramatizing both. They turned the white cube of the gallery inside out and upside down, buried it below ground, and suspended it above, examining the history of objects, and the language and theory used to describe the various parts. They questioned the context of art and the collectors' endgame, and managed to interject each project with disarming humor. "Our job is to be critical," says Elmgreen, in regard to an art world where they have the good fortune to be recognized as significant players. "We do the wrong thing." Their approach is not ironic. "That would be misanthropic," he adds.

—

Their early material has the bantering quality of lovers at play; clever, fast, each outpacing the other, performing over the other, for the other. The choreography of partnering is central to their style, content, and imagination. At their most conceptual (in the early years) or their most architectural (more recently) their ideas are literally staged; they are set-ups, passageways for the viewer, with every footfall measured and accounted for. Missing is a script—enter stage left, bow, turn, now, exit stage right—although not entirely. "The Collectors," their double installation in the adjacent Danish and Nordic Pavilions at the 53rd Venice Biennale in 2009, came with its own guide; an actor playing a real estate agent toured visitors through the spaces, a grand old house and an airy modern one, which the artists had pieced together, window frame by doorway, dining room by teenager's bedroom. "Now look at this, now look at that," said the broker, pointing out the many clues that the artists had left behind for all to see—a fly collection on a wall, an exploded staircase, a porcelain table setting, a "drowned collector" in the form of a life size dummy face down in a pool—providing a detailed iconography of their intellectual highways and byways, about aesthetics and the machinations of the art market which absorbs it.

—

Born raconteurs, each work that they produce is in its own way a three-dimensional model of their latest obsession. Though it may begin, "Once upon a time in the art world," it quickly spills outside the box so that the rest of the world may get it too. For *Happy Days in the Art World*, their Performa Commission, script doctor and playwright Tim Etchells was on call to watch their language at all times. "Out" went anything obscure or arcane. "Out" went anything that smacked of too much insider information. "In" remained the relentless style of questioning of Samuel Beckett's existential duels, pairings that allowed the twosome of Elmgreen & Dragset to play out their own double headed version of the world: high and low, gay and straight, masculine and feminine. "There is a lot of talk about the market, the gold rush, and the desperation once the recession kicked in," they say. "This experience is not exclusive to the art world; it is in all parts of society. Everyone can identify. Everyone can relate to the conflicts of two people having gone through ten years together and splitting up. How do you maintain all the good things of the relationship? How do you continue in a respectable way?"

—

Happy Days in the Art World is a double self-portrait; intimate and exacting. The idea of it being so personal came from Sarah Thornton's book *Seven Days in the Art World*. "Sarah's book was an inspiration for us to speak about the art world and to do it from a very personal point of view," both explained. It is also a prime example of the "singular vision" of the artist. Though in every way it resembles a piece of formal theater, it is entirely made by the two of them, from script to set design, to stage direction, even to directing the director. All the players and all the parts of their production are material in the hands of Elmgreen & Dragset. This was apparent at the first reading of the play in London, as, mournful eyed, Michael, sitting behind the director, instructs an actor on the character "ME" (for Michael Elmgreen), whom he is playing: "No, you have to be really, really depressed. I mean really depressed. Like it's the worst day of your life." The actor nods, not realizing that his character is indeed the man in the blue checked shirt who is talking to him. "No," Michael groans again, "not depressed enough. And don't listen to ID (for Ingar Dragset). He's just too happy for words. Treat ID as though he is completely irrelevant." How might Mark Rothko have written himself in *Red?*, I wondered. How different is that earlier play about the life of the artist in mid-century America, from this one about the global art world of 2011?

—

They chose Beckett, whom they have both read extensively over the years, as a template for their own script, because the grumbling twosomes in Beckett's plays sounded just like them, and they chose to work in legitimate theater for their Performa Commission, because, they explained, they wanted to skate on thin ice again, to step into the long traditions and the form of theater, but without the safety-net from years of experience. "How can we put ourselves in a situation where we will bite our nails and sweat? So we thought, why not make a play about the artistic process? How difficult it is, over time, to refresh yourself and keep up your excitement so things don't turn 'business as usual.' How difficult it is, over and over, to question yourself; how difficult it is to cope with pressure when you get more in the spotlight."

—

These questions and this play led Elmgreen & Dragset to look back over more than a decade and a half of work, to realize that many of their projects, directly or not, have been performance based. Their method for staging ideas, close up and within eye contact of an audience, has provided them with endlessly complicated ways to think about art and the lives of artists, amidst the big picture of life, and to making their art accessible through performance. Hence, this retrospective, which comes in two versions: a publication that is a record of their performances to date, and a one-time only evening of selected highlights from their repertoire. ______

Elmgreen & Dragset's Theatrical Turn

BY SHANNON JACKSON

"In my dream we were SUCCESSFUL artists, we had something BIG coming..." — Happy Days in the Art World

—

On a blustery late morning in Rotterdam in 2011, a group of people assembled on a stone sidewalk in front of a defunct city post office. In front of this "deaccessioned" civic space, an exquisite plinth and glass vitrine had been installed. Members of the group began to circle it. Some meandered; some laughed with each other; some photographed; some took video footage of people taking photographs. Inside the vitrine, a perfectly smooth metal cone shone in the available light, reflecting and refracting the images of viewers who peered at it. Near the top of the cone, a metal handle was attached, evoking the shape of a designer tool or household fixture fabricated for the Alessi consumer. More cameras and a larger crowd of Rotterdam's civic figures came forward to welcome assembled guests. As the clock approached noon, they formed an expectant circle around the plinth. A bespectacled wiry gentleman in khaki and gray adjusted his flat cap and stepped forward to unlock the vitrine; he pulled out the cone by the handle, transforming the sculpture into a megaphone by raising it to his mouth. As the noon bell began to toll, the gentleman called out in international English, "It's never too late to say sorry." He spaced his words evenly and enunciated clearly, as if he wanted to make sure that all Dutch citizens within earshot were appropriately reassured. He then carefully replaced the megaphone, re-locked the vitrine, and walked out of the crowd and down the block. His gait and costume blended into the moving landscape of the city street as the bell tolled behind him.

—

To reckon with performance in the work of Michael Elmgreen and Ingar Dragset means reckoning with performance itself. Having collaborated together for over fifteen years, their projects have been contextualized within a variety of vocabularies, including terms such as theatrical, spectacular, exhibitionist, active, live, camp, durational, performative, and performance art. The use of this eclectic performance-based vocabulary has also coincided with other artistic vocabularies drawn from Minimalism, institutional critique, public art, relational aesthetics, and queer theory. What does it mean to extract performance-based work from the long arc of this duo's career? To what extent is this "p-word" referring to a discrete genre of practice? And to what degree does it coincide with other structures deployed in their many sculptural, institutional, and public projects?

—

Such questions are particularly opportune at a moment when a "performative" terminology circulates in so many art world contexts, one with a vexed and sometimes opaque relationship to words like theater, acting, or theatricality. Performativity—with its distinctive suffix—is used to describe all varieties of contemporary art practices that seek, in Dorothea von Hantelmann's rephrasing of J.L. Austin, "to do things with art."[1] The term derives from a philosophical school of speech act theory that focused on the world-making power of language. Its application in contemporary art expands upon the classical etymology of the word "perform," stemming from a root meaning "to furnish forth" or "to carry out." While all art practice arguably has the capacity "to furnish" the world it simultaneously describes, some contemporary art is more self-consciously aware of its world-making actions. In J.L. Austin's *How to Do Things with Words*, such actions depended upon what he called the "happy uptake," that is, enabling conditions for "felicitous" reception that allowed the performative act to affect the thing it sought to do. A piece such as *It's Never Too Late to Say Sorry* fits nicely into this capacious frame, employing, as this piece does, a durational and spatial structure that simultaneously seeks to reach, and potentially absolve, an unspecified

---

1 _ Dorothea von Hantelmann, *How to Do Things with Art* (Zürich: JRP| Ringier, 2010).
See also J.L. Austin's classic, *How to Do Things with Words* (reprinted, Cambridge: Harvard University Press, 1975).

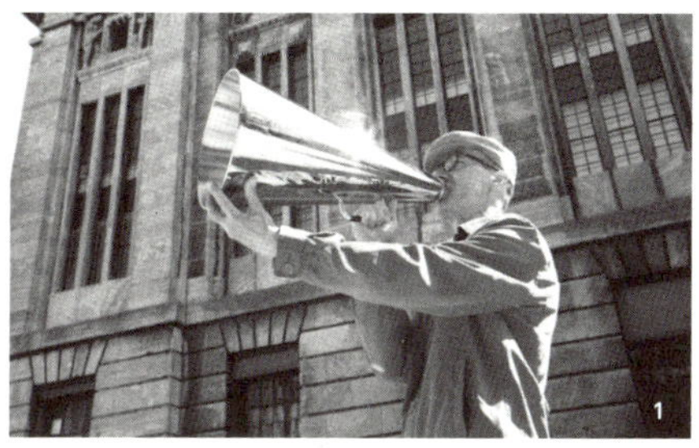

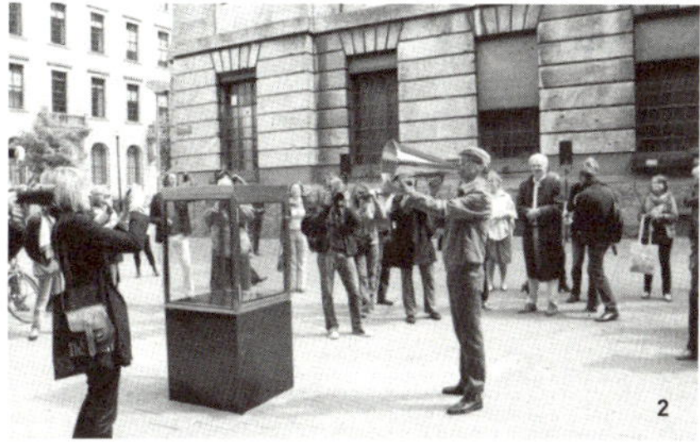

addressee. We might then ask a follow up question: How would the performative aspects of such a work interface with its theatrical aspects? A theatrical frame would focus, not only upon the audience's "uptake" of a particular speech act, but also upon the *casting*, the *costuming*, and the *blocking* of the performer who raises a *prop* to express a *script*. Such a focus would align with the etymology of "theater" as a term, one that derives from a root meaning "a place for viewing." The theatrical focus would emphasize, not only what is viewed, but how the act of viewing itself becomes a subject for reflection. Odd as it may seem, the fact is that the vocabulary of performativity and that of theatricality are only occasionally brought into the same space. However, precisely because Elmgreen & Dragset have experimented so widely, the interpretation of their work requires an open and inclusive vocabulary. Indeed, the span of their work across genres of performance art, live installation, public sculpture, theater, and even opera provides occasion, not simply to document their hybrid practices, but more interestingly, to reflect upon the conventions we use to understand them. In what follows, I invoke different projects to track varied types of intervention, noting that structures of the performative and the theatrical appear in projects labeled performance art and in projects labeled institutional critique or public art. I then turn to what might be an especially radical cluster of performative projects, precisely because their focus is so traditional: the theater. I conclude with a return to *It's Never Too Late to Say Sorry* and with an anticipation of *Happy Days in the Art World*, positioning them as integrations and expansions of Elmgreen & Dragset's performative performances.

—

Fig. 1 & 2 _ *It's Never Too Late to Say Sorry*, 2011-2012, daily performance on the Coolsingel in Rotterdam as part of Sculpture International Rotterdam's (SIR) public art program.

EXPANDED PERFORMANCE ART

"Such instant complicity...we were cross-peeing in a cruising park. Two steaming golden diagonals..." — ME, Happy Days in the Art World

—

In many ways, performance was the form that brought Michael Elmgreen and Ingar Dragset together in the first place—well, perhaps the second place. Born in Denmark and Norway respectively, the two had varied backgrounds when they met in the mid-1990s. Elmgreen had some art training, wrote poetry, and had odd jobs as an interior decorator. Dragset studied the Lecoq tradition in theater school and also worked as a theater instructor for children. After spending the first year "doing nothing together but being boyfriends," they decided to begin collaborating. Dragset recounts:

> Since we had so many other things in common, and were getting along so well on most matters, we thought that we would try to combine my theater experience and Michael's visual art experience ... I started helping Michael with preparing a show in Stockholm. That was because I could knit, and he wanted to do these knitted pieces. Some abstract pets, that the art audience could hug and nurse and feel confident with ... but in Stockholm nobody feels relaxed at openings, so we had to show the audience how to feel confident and how to use these knitted pets, and then everybody thought it was a performance—so it became our first performance... by coincidence.[2]

—

The coincidental turn to performance thus came about through an act of demonstration, a primary action aimed to provoke more actions in others. Whether or not viewers were moved to "hug and nurse," Dragset's recounting shows objects being transformed into performance. The involvement of the artists'

2 _ Hans Ulrich Obrist, "Performative Constructions: Interview by Hans Ulrich Obrist," in *Powerless Structures* (1998), 27. Online at http://www.nicolaiwallner.com/artists/micing/text1.html.

gestures before a group was enough to transform beholders into theatrical spectators. Because these beholders decided to receive the demonstration, not only as a performative invitation to act themselves, but also as an extroverted display, a lesson about the objectworld became "a place for viewing;" the attempt to "furnish forth" became a time-based piece of theatrical art. If the action "was a performance," a shift in perceptual convention made it so.

—

Elements of this origin tale reappear in other early performance art work by Elmgreen & Dragset. Dragset's knitting skills came in handy in a piece at the Institute of Contemporary Arts in London in 1996, a kind of craft-based endurance performance where the artists unraveled and re-knit a 100 meter piece of white cloth for hours on end. (Appropriately, the piece was remounted in Paris in 1998 during "Nuit Blanche.") Incorporating the subtext of "being boyfriends," the unraveled knitting was given an erotic transcontextualization in another piece where the pair donned knitted skirts while performing in public toilets and soccer clubs; the unraveling of the skirt thus coincided with a camped-up act of seduction (1996). Other pieces made use of different theatrical elements. *Human Rights, Funky Hair* (1996) parodied the normalization of gay parenting by dyeing a child's hair orange, positing the boy's hair as the non-bio inheritance of the yellow and red lacquered into the hair of his temporary "parents," Michael and Ingar. This kind of self-transformation and self-costuming also appeared in *Untitled* (1995), which documented the two artists cross-peeing in a stream. Wearing identical clothing and sporting bleached hair, the geometry of the "golden diagonals" anticipated the doubled geometry that would undergird later sculptural projects such as *Powerless Structures, Fig. 255* (a transparent glass pavilion with two urinals installed back to back, 2003) and *Boy Scout* (metal bunk bed with the top bunk upside down, 2008). Most importantly, the captivating twinness of the duo isolated one of queer theory's central theoretical challenges to psychoanalysis. Responding to the heterosexism of a Freudian model that separates those whom we desire from those with whom we identify, the boy-boy

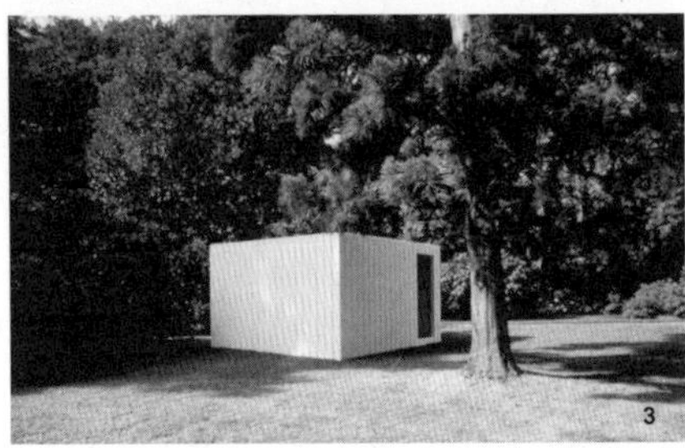

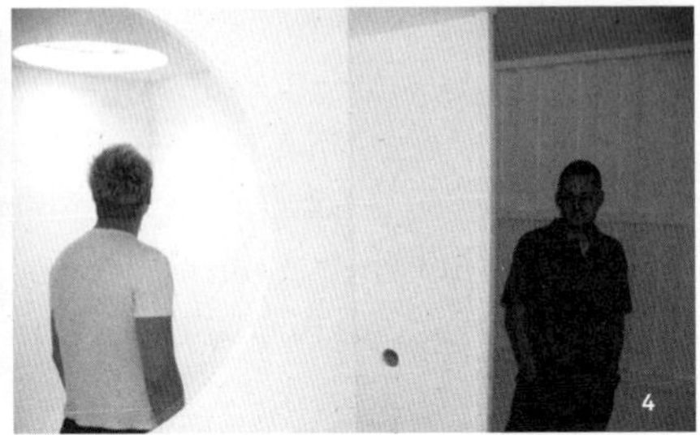

structure aligned an object of identification with an object of desire in a single figure.[3] In this piece, the person one wants *to be* is simultaneously the person one wants *to have*; "liking" and "being like" coincide in "instant complicity." Finally, the camera documented the event for us to recall decades later, a visual capture that reciprocally heightens the fleeting quality of the action. If the event "was a performance," the camera retroactively made it so.

—

Early pieces such as *TRY* (1996) and *The End of Natural Behavior* (1996) reused but also extended this nascent theatrical vocabulary. Arranging beer and walkmen invitingly upon comfy rugs, *TRY* asked three men to bring in favorite books and to relax in the setting. Titling the piece with a verb made the invitation clear, obviating the need for demonstration. It is worth recalling that this piece took place around the same time that Nicolas Bourriaud curated his famous exhibition "Traffic" in Bordeaux, an event that coincided with the French publication of *Esthetic Relational* and the attempt to gather a variety of performative, interactive work within a relational art movement. *TRY* echoed Bourriaud's characterization of relational aesthetics, for here, "intersubjectivity" is the "material substrate" of the art event.[4] In this case, however, that substrate had a queer erotics, one that gave the abstract "relational" a heightened specificity, anticipating later works such as *Cruising Pavilion/Powerless Structures, Fig. 55* (1998) and *Untitled (Home is the Place You Left)* (2008), in which relational encounters have a distinct sexual politics. At the same

3 _ For a queer critique of this psychoanalytic frame, see Diana Fuss, *Identification Papers: Readings on Psychoanalysis, Sexuality, and Culture* (New York: Routledge, 1995).

4 _ Nicolas Bourriaud, *Relational Aesthetics* (Dijon: Les Presses du Réel, 1998).

Fig. 3 & 4 _ Exterior and interior views, *Cruising Pavilion/Powerless Structures, Fig. 55*, 1998, Marselisborg Forest, Århus.

time, the fact that those who "try" will also be "watched" joined participation and theatrical display. As a place for viewing that is also a space for connecting, *TRY* exposed the fine line that separated the extroversion of the theatrical from the relative introversion of the relational. Finally, *The End of Natural Behavior* brightened the line between the theatrical and the relational more intensely, returning to identical costumes and to semi-choreographed activities placed squarely on display. As the boy-boy duo performed their sailor routine, Art and Life playfully revised each other. Interestingly, the placement of this performance inside "The Ark"—the name given to the Arken Museum of Modern Art's evocatively designed museum building—gave the piece a degree of site-specificity. By surfacing a queer sailor subtext within the museum's seafaring metaphor, *The End of Natural Behavior* exposed and questioned the naturalized structures of the art institution. In other words, it was a performance that took a step toward institutional critique.

INSTALLATIONS, INSTITUTIONS, THEATRICALITY

"We used to discuss Foucault and his 'Powerless Structures,' the 'smooth spaces' of Deleuze and Guattari...We used to talk about important stuff." — Happy Days in the Art World

—

By the late nineties, Elmgreen & Dragset's interest in "performance art" diminished. With the launch of a new series of works under the title *Powerless Structures*, they began to develop a reputation as practitioners of institutional critique, albeit a mode that expanded publicly and often entered into the territory of queer politics. Inspired by Felix Gonzalez-Torres's practice, their connection to institutional critique came primarily from a fairly self-conscious decision to turn to the post-Minimalist geometries and formal interventions of an object-based practice.

—

"We were always curated to be the funny guys in the corner. If some curator wanted to have a more light activity in a very stiff exhibition ... very much like becoming a stereotype of yourself ... So it was fun suddenly to do installation works, cause that was a big surprise for everybody, 'oh they can do art objects.'"[5] Indeed, they worried that the gestic world of performance interacted with their sexual identity to fix them inside queer stereotypes. "I mean the performances we did were very important on a personal level and also on the level of artistic development for us; but you felt you were becoming too much of a gay icon, and that's where our *Powerless Structures* series started. That was also an emancipation from this stereotypical image of gay people or being a gay couple. So we opened up our own artistic expression to include all kinds of material, historical and cultural."[6]

—

The "all kinds of material" meant developing a stronger relationship with the traditional materials of visual art but using them to explore the material structuration of powerful public spaces. It was at this point that they also decided to move to Berlin to reorient their careers. In 1997, *Powerless Structures* launched a series of related spatial interventions where the autobiographical bodies and identities of the artists were placed at a remove. Acknowledging that the title "is derived form our misreading Foucault,"[7] Elmgreen & Dragset began to explore the reciprocal structuration of selves and institutions, creating formal interventions within institutional structures in order to propose new alternatives for inhabiting the world.

—

Even as we acknowledge the turn *from* "performance art" *to* "art objects" in *Powerless Structures*, it is worth noticing that performance-based techniques—both the constitutively "performative" as well as the explicitly "theatrical"—still animated many of these projects. *Twelve Hours of White Paint/ Powerless Structures, Fig. 15* (1997) oriented itself toward the white cube of the gallery; like many institutional critique projects in the late 20th century, it

---

5 _ Hans Ulrich Obrist, "Performative Constructions: Interview by Hans Ulrich Obrist," in *Powerless Structures* (1998), 30.

6 _ Ibid., 31-33.

7 _ Brian Sholis, "Interview: Michael Elmgreen and Ingar Dragset," *Ten Verses* (June 1, 2003). Online at www.briansholis.com/interview-michael-elmgreen-and-ingar-dragset/.

questioned the presumed neutrality of the visual art space by exposing its construction. In this case, Elmgreen & Dragset painted, rinsed, and repainted the white walls of the gallery, positing "neutrality" as a construction that could be layered and removed. Interestingly, that construction and that layering required the action of a laborer. Whether performing as artists who mimicked the house painter in 1997 or, with *Zwischen anderen Ereignissen* (Between Other Events, 2000), hiring professional house-painters instead, a critical stance on the museum gallery came about by exposing the labor required to produce it. Most importantly for the purposes of this essay, the attempt to expose the contingency and structure of the museum required performance. In fact, performance-based turns would animate several spatial interventions, including their well-publicized decision to place an aesthetic umbrella over the construction and rehab process of the Kunsthalle in Zürich with *Taking Place* (2001-2002). Consider Daniel Birnbaum's extended account:

> When the crowd walked through the doors, they encountered a construction site in which two men were busy demolishing a concrete wall with sledgehammers while another pair of workers were erecting a new one. Still another duo was removing the rubble and emptying the director's office of its furniture. The wreckage was everywhere and the noise was deafening. What was going on? Had there been an accident? Was it all a misunderstanding concerning address or date? In fact, everything was proceeding according to plan. What the crowd was experiencing and participating in was a performance piece, *Taking Place*, 2001-2002, involving six men restructuring an art center in the largest city in Switzerland. Why not put the office at the entrance to the building instead of hiding it in the back? the artists asked. Why not open up the reading room and make it more welcoming? ... The construction work, carefully choreographed by the artists, took place only when the museum was open to the public. After the first few days' din of sledgehammers and concrete smashing,

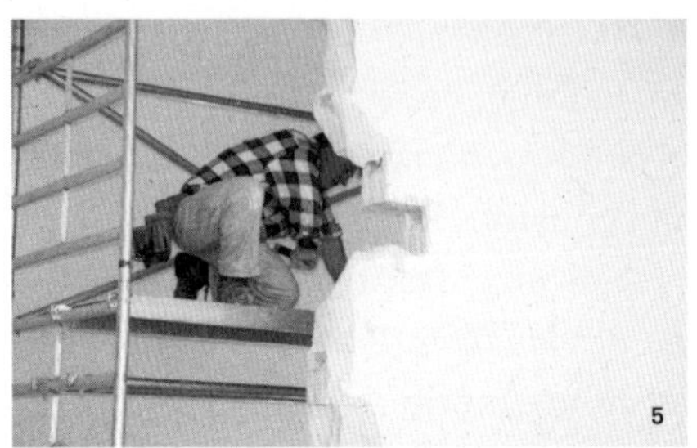

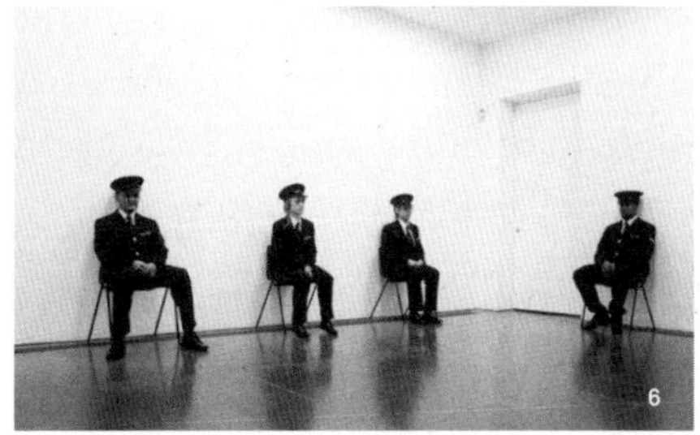

> things quieted down. The show grew calm, approaching the solemn state we associate with the experience of art: The last weeks were about white paint, primarily; the very last days exclusively about degrees of whiteness and the fine-tuning of light.[8]

—

This project—like others by artists ranging from Hans Haacke to Mel Bochner to Andrea Fraser to Daniel Buren to Santiago Sierra and more—sought to expose the apparatus of the art world, sometimes through explicit revelation, sometimes through spatial re-organizing, and sometimes by withdrawing, destroying, or rebuilding elements of a gallery structure. Interestingly, *Taking Place*'s act of infrastructural avowal created a temporal experience. The exposure and reordering of the material space became a "performance piece," one that was not simply fabricated but "choreographed." The dismantling of the supporting apparatus of object-based art simultaneously opened the door to a new kind of time-based art.[9] A certain kind of cross-medium encounter thus enabled an anti-medium-specific gesture. For Elmgreen & Dragset, this gesture was another way to combine "his visual art experience" with "my theater experience."

—

Other projects exemplify a latent theatricality within practices of institutional critique and expanded public art. Several projects focused, not only on representing the laborers behind the construction of a public space, but also on the people responsible for maintaining it. The museum security guard is a constant

8 _ Daniel Birnbaum, "White on White," *Artforum* (April 2002): 98-101, 99.

9 _ For more examples of how labor performance coincides with institutional critique, see "Escape Artists" by Jens Hoffmann in this volume.

Fig. 5 _ *Taking Place*, 2001-2002, Kunsthalle Zürich.

Fig. 6 _ *Reg(u)arding the Guards*, 2005, "The Welfare Show," Serpentine Gallery, London.

if functionally invisible figure in most venues of artistic display. In *Reg(u)arding the Guards* (2005), Elmgreen & Dragset decided to call attention to this figure by defining a group of guards as an art installation. In a move that provoked reflection on employment practices within post-Welfare State nations, they hired unemployed citizens to be cast as uniformed "guards," seating them in chairs within a single room of the museum gallery.[10] These performers both watched over the artwork and occupied the place of the artwork itself. Meanwhile, receivers faced sentient sculptures who looked back at them in return. *Reg(u)arding the Guards* thus conducted an institutional critique via a theatrical enactment, one that itself troubled who was beholding who in this place for viewing. The exposure and deployment of an institution's latent theatricality appeared in several other projects that involved the creation of new character-laborers. *Tate Modern Walks—A Power Station Revisited* (2004) redefined the performance of the docent tour by giving spectators an alternate tour of the Tate Modern's backstage and repressed history as a power station. The *Butler* of "Celebrity—The One & The Many" (ZKM | Center for Art and Media, Karlsruhe, 2010), the *Amigos* of "Amigos" (Galería Helga de Alvear, Madrid, 2011), and the *Real Estate Agents* of "The Collectors" (53rd Venice Biennale, 2009) all adapted an existing labor performance to the needs of an artistic experience, choreographing gestures and rehearsing monologues that commented upon the classed experience of work and the classed experience of art in the same breath. Finally, other works heightened the theatricality of the viewing relationship to reflect upon the menace and pleasure of seeing and being seen. The infrastructural intervention of *Taking Place* took a more intimate turn in *How Are You Today?* (2002) when the artists constructed an enlarged peephole between Galleria Massimo De Carlo in Milan and the personal apartment of a neighbor above it. The female neighbor's everyday actions thus "became a performance" by virtue of being watched. At the same time, the viewer's head appeared inside a large bubble visible to the neighbor, providing the opportunity for her to watch the viewer watch. Once again, an institutional critical gesture partook of a theatrical structure:

10 _ For a fuller analysis of visual art and performance issues as well as this work in the context of Elmgreen & Dragset's "The Welfare Show," see Chapter Six of Shannon Jackson, *Social Works: Performing Art, Supporting Publics* (London: Routledge, 2011).

> You popped into her domestic setting like an alien ... And you looked into this stranger's private life from a floor level perspective as if you were a bug or a frog ... After having talked so much about "the missing link" between the exhibition space and the everyday life taking place right outside its walls, it was such a great satisfaction suddenly being able to drill this hole into the ceiling—and by this simple gesture making a very concrete connection between the art space and its immediate surroundings.[11]

—

While some projects created surveillance schemes in which viewers remained relatively anonymous, several projects installed this kind of reciprocal surveillance into their structure. In *Paris Diaries* (Galerie Emmanuel Perrotin, Paris, 2003), for instance, young men were each seated at desks in a gallery and asked to write in their diaries for hours on end. When visitors entered, they could peer over the shoulders of the writers to read the journal, deciding at the same time how far to tread into private territory. Eventually, however, the diary writers began to record the behaviors and experience of the gallery itself; hence, when visitors peered over the shoulders of the writers, they suddenly realized that they themselves were being surveilled.

---

11 _ Ivanmaria Vele, "Elmgreen & Dragset: Boiler's Choice" (includes interview with Elmgreen & Dragset), *Boiler* (Issue 1, 2003): 112-119, 117.

THEATRICAL RETURNS

"As far as I can see, there is only a big black void like an endless darkened auditorium filled with a bored, exhausted, and invisible audience." — Happy Days in the Art World

—

After several years of proving that they could "make art objects" with *Powerless Structures*, Elmgreen & Dragset began to recall but also expand some of their earlier performance art and theatrical interests. Of course, as the above section argues, such interests never entirely receded. Even as they were critically undoing and reassembling museum structures, they also took such infrastructurally critical practices to the space of the theater. At the Odense Performance Festival in 1998, they created a piece that involved the de-installation of the theater's stage and lighting equipment before an expectant audience. In *Erste Reihe* (Front Row) of 2001, they removed seats from the Schauespielhaus in Hamburg, replacing them with a large velvet replica that put the act of theatrical viewing on display. Meanwhile, *Safety Curtain* (2002-2003) positioned a huge Vinyl Eye on the safety curtain of the Komische Opera house in Berlin, questioning concepts of security and surveillance with its counter-gaze. In fact, in an art world context, this kind of engagement with the theater building was unusual. Most institutional critiques positioned "the museum" as the institution in need of critique, a habit that paradoxically legitimated the museum as the custodian of "Art," even if the espoused desire was to question it. But if there remains some ambivalence toward the theater as an institution—even if we are in the midst of a self-consciously performative moment in contemporary art—some curators and commissioning bodies began to offer new opportunities to stage a theatrical return. Elmgreen & Dragset jumped at the chance to do a set design for the Opéra de Lyon for *Faustus, The Last Night* (2006) and also tried out filmmaking in *L'amour de loin* (2008).

—

A far more explicit foray into theater making came about in their creation of *Drama Queens* (2007), a play that used a theatrical stage to comment upon the conventions and quirks of visual art world behavior. Conceived by Elmgreen & Dragset, with text by Tim Etchells of the British theater troupe Forced Entertainment, the play premiered at Skulptur Projekte Münster in Germany and then moved to The Old Vic Theatre in London with a celebrity cast performing the voice-overs. The play embodied as characters seven iconic artworks: Alberto Giacometti's *Walking Man*, Hans Arp's *Cloud Shepherd*, Barbara Hepworth's *Elegy III*, Sol Lewitt's *Four Cubes*, an untitled granite sculpture by Ulrich Rukreim, Jeff Koons's unstoppable *Rabbit*, and a cameo appearance from Andy Warhol's *Brillo Box*. The text alternates between group dialogue and caricatured soliloquies that repeat art critical statements as the internalized monologue of a sculpture. Says Koons's Rabbit, "They said I was nothing, an empty gesture, a superficial if kind of clever decoration. Others said that I embodied a devastating critique of the economy of the superficial."[12] The play thus puts a first person "I" behind each sculpture who narrates his or her fraught history, loves, losses, and merits as an art object with excessively egoistic subjectivity. In the text, Walking Man speaks with old-world weariness. Elegy III and Four Cubes flirt; Rabbit runs about the stage, recounting critiques of himself and occasionally getting the other figures to disco dance with him. The play ends with a silent cameo from the Brillo Box that brings an end to art-celebrity jockeying.

—

If "performance" was something that Elmgreen & Dragset felt that they had to give up in order to be taken seriously as gay male artists, then the creation of *Drama Queens* marked a different kind of return to the form. This performance piece was wholly different from their knitting pieces, not only because it took place in a storied theater rather than a "gallery corner" but because it conformed to the conventions of a "play" rather than "performance art." As a play, it used techniques similar to those recognized by theater makers: script, proscenium stage, actors, movement, and lighting. At the same time, it also

---

12 _ *Drama Queens*, a play by Elmgreen & Dragset with text by Tim Etchells, 2007.

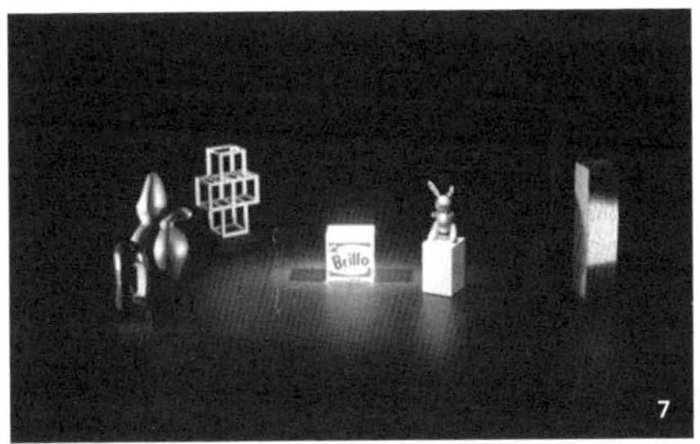

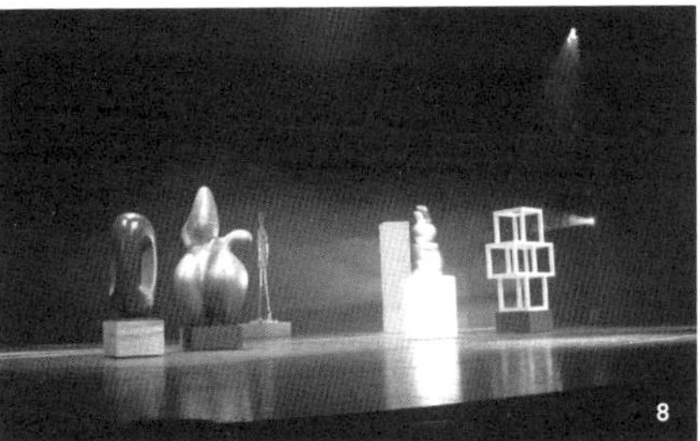

recalled modernist art definitions of theatricality, sending up Michael Fried's anxious response to the theatricality of Minimalist sculpture. Fried famously articulated his anxiety with Minimalist sculpture as the scandalized encounter with "the silent presence of another person."[13] *Drama Queens* heightened the threat by imagining that figure loudly talking to him. Meanwhile, other modifications made these sculptural interventions durable within the time-space contingencies of the theater. The sizes of the sculptures were adjusted slightly to give them proportional stage presence as an ensemble. In order to provide a mechanism for motorization, every one of the sculptures appeared on a plinth, with the exception of Untitled (Granite) who incorporated his own. With such plinths, the production both conformed to some quite traditional sculptural rules and broke those rules by making those plinths move. At the same time, the moving plinths neutralized whatever gravitational statement each had made in its time by equalizing each artwork's relation to the raised ground plane of the Old Vic stage. While Cloud Shepherd had appeared onstage in the Münster production, it was cut by the time it reached London due to "sightline and space issues."[14] Apparently, its bulbous bulk could not be tracked mechanically by the remote or tracked visually by the hyper-frontality of a proscenium stage. What Tim Etchells called a "a preposterous object-drama," another critic called "The 'Robot Wars meets Samuel Beckett,'" expressing relief that it was "not serious or snobbish, not political or peripheral, but clever and entertaining."[15]

13 _ Michael Fried, "Art and Objecthood," *Artforum* 5 (1967): 12-23.

14 _ Etchells, "More Drama," *timetchells.com* (August 12, 2008). Online at http://www.timetchells.com/notebook/august-2008/more-drama/.

15 _ Ossian Ward, "Art Shows in Kassell and Munster," *TimeOut London* (June 27, 2007): n.p. Online at www.timeout.com/london/art/features/3089/Art_shows_in_Kassell_and_Munster.html.

Fig. 7 & 8 _ *Drama Queens*, 2007, Städtische Bühnen Münster.

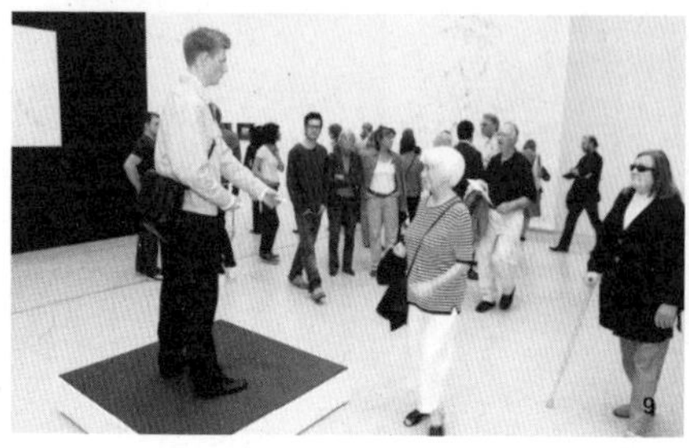

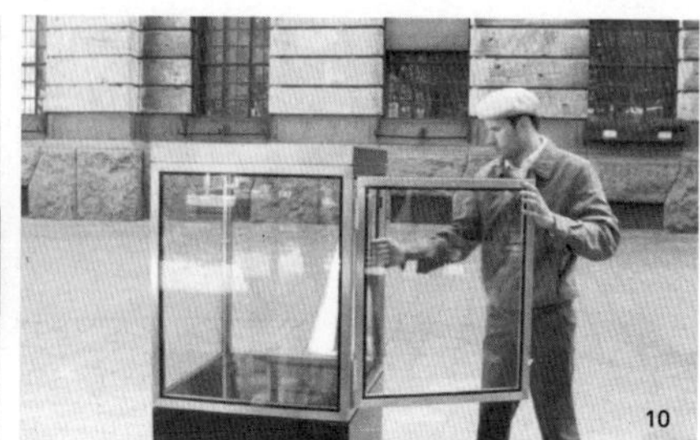

The extroversion of *Drama Queens* came into higher relief for some critics who contrasted it with quieter "living installations." During the premiere of *Drama Queens*, Elmgreen & Dragset installed another piece nearby entitled *Have You Come Here for Forgiveness* (2007). The piece consisted of a young man, perched on a short and squat plinth inside the Sprengel Museum in Hannover, reverently and compassionately handing out business cards with the title of the piece imprinted upon them. While in another context, such a piece might have been perceived to be excessively "live" or "theatrical," the comparison with *Drama Queens* prompted critics to perceive it as "placid and dry," a response that shows that the assessment of introversion and extroversion is highly relative.[16] In fact, the relative calm of *Have You Come Here for Forgiveness* was an intended component of the piece. Elmgreen & Dragset hoped that this living sculpture would provoke questions about the values and affective affirmation that many seek when visiting an art institution, especially in situations where organized religion no longer provides a potent spiritual service.

—

The theme of forgiveness brings us back to where this essay began, standing before an unassuming Dutch citizen who boldly offered the possibility of forgiveness to anyone who decided to listen. Compared to the larger and more stylized *The One & The Many* which opened the same day in Rotterdam, *It's Never Too Late to Say Sorry* might also have seemed relatively "placid" or even "dry."[17] However, the piece's site-specific and temporal parameters created (and

---

16 _ "Michael Elmgreen and Ingar Dragset have hired an attractive young man to stand composed on a pedestal at the same venue, handing out cards to viewers that read (in English) *Have You Come Here for Forgiveness*. The duo's living sculpture is placid and dry when compared with *Drama Queens*, their profoundly funny, parodic theater work staged for Skulptur Projekte Münster." Michelle Grabner, "Made In Germany," *artforum.com* (August 15, 2007). Online at http://artforum.com/archive/id=15678.

Fig. 9 _ *Have You Come Here for Forgiveness*, 2007, "Made in Germany," Sprengel Museum, Hannover.

Fig. 10 _ *It's Never Too Late to Say Sorry*, 2011-2012, Rotterdam.

as I write, are still creating) a performative structure with an intriguing durability and transformational capacity. After extensive auditions, Elmgreen & Dragset selected Wim Konings to play this role, an individual with a dual career as an artist and a postal carrier. As a piece installed before a de-accessioned post office, the casting could not be more apt: "The city had to close down the building," said an assistant in Rotterdam's sculpture project, "because all of the mail systems are becoming privatized. Some think it might be made into a mall for high end shops."[18] As Konings finished his announcement and walked down the block, heading firmly in the direction of city hall, the piece begged the question: who needs to say sorry? And for what? Do civic leaders need absolution? Prospective retail owners? Dutch anti-immigration activists? Or the citizens of Rotterdam who are reckoning with their own relationship to imperiled public and civic systems? Interestingly, there will be ample time to consider different answers to such questions. The city of Rotterdam has committed to constant public reminding, authorizing Elmgreen & Dragset's piece to be repeated each day at noon for 365 days. What might come of this ongoing act of public penitence? We can imagine that its content and its addressee will transform throughout the year, subject to more and less felicitous forms of uptake by the people who choose to listen and those who choose to ignore. The city and its citizens will contend with the happiness and unhappiness of "saying sorry" as the conditions of performance change each day.

—

ID: We'll wait.
ME: Nothing more to add.

—

The premiere of *Happy Days in the Art World* at the Performa 11 biennial (2011) provides the occasion for this essay, and an occasion to survey a range of performative and theatrical work. The play itself is its own survey, told from the biographical position of two-middle aged queer male artists who wonder what, if any, sense their lives have made. The title, of course, cites Sarah Thornton's

---

17 _ For a lengthier account of *The One & The Many*, see "Scenario Planning: Elmgreen & Dragset Queer Agitprop" by Aaron Betsky in this volume, and Peter Weibel and Andreas F. Beitin, eds., *Elmgreen & Dragset: Trilogy*, exh. cat., ZKM | Center for Art and Media, Karlsruhe (London: Thames & Hudson, 2011).

18 _ Author's Interview, June 2011.

widely-read *Seven Days in the Art World* while also corralling the central metaphors and figures of Samuel Beckett, a reliable go-to resource for existential reflection.[19] The play does not so much recall *Happy Days* and its buried female monologist as it does plays like *Waiting for Godot* and *Endgame*. Elmgreen & Dragset expose a queer male subtext in Beckett's familiar male pairings, transforming Vladimir and Estragon into ID and ME who occupy *Boy Scout*'s bunk bed and anxiously "wait" for a new round of curatorial interest. Meanwhile, Beckett's classically contextless visitor is contextualized as BI, a "SpedEx" mail carrier; BI is perpetually in need of a "signature" and erupts into a jargon-ridden theoretical monologue that recalls the run-on monologue of *Waiting for Godot*'s Lucky.

—

Samuel Beckett became famous as a playwright who broke theatrical tradition. However, relative to the performative offerings usually commissioned by Performa, this piece is quite strikingly "a play." More than any knitting-based performance art, more than the talking sculptures of *Drama Queens*, Elmgreen & Dragset's contribution is not simply theatrical, but quite shockingly "theater." It is a script written by the artists, edited by playwright Tim Etchells, and directed by Toby Frow. It has a set with props. It casts actors who play characters, wear costumes, memorize lines, exchange witty dialogue, and move about a stage space with rehearsed blocking night after night. Elmgreen & Dragset have, of course, been creating sets, employing actors, devising costumes, exchanging witty dialogue, and re-blocking the art world for their entire careers. With *Happy Days in the Art World*, they seem to be asking us whether "a play" can be "performance art." In pondering the question, we might find ourselves realizing that Elmgreen & Dragset have been making theater all along. ———

19 _ Sarah Thornton, *Seven Days in the Art World* (New York, London: W.W. Norton & Co., 2008).

1.

EARLY PERFORMANCES

1

EARLY PERFORMANCES

1.

WORKS

TEXT

ATERIALS: *C-print*
RFORMERS: *the artists*
OTHING: *indentical cargo shorts, belts, and boots with red shoelaces*
MENSIONS: *180 x 118 cm; edition of 5 + 2*
HIBITED AT: *"Art Against AIDS," Galleri Nicolai Wallner and Galleri Michael Andersen, Copenhagen, 1995; "Into Me/Out Of Me," P.S.1 Contemporary Art Center, New York, 2006; KW Institute for Contemporary Art, Berlin, 2006; Museo d'Arte Contemporanea di Roma (MACRO), Rome, 2007*

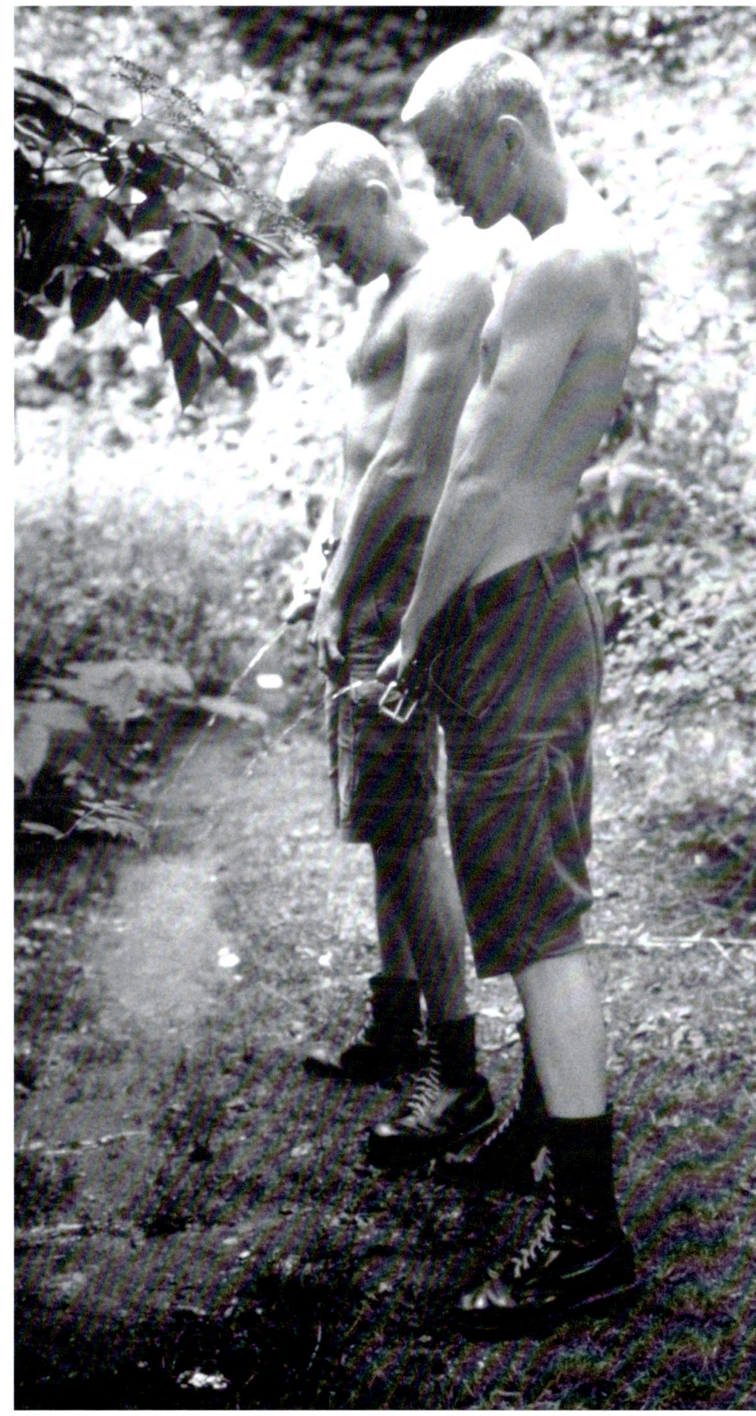

NTITLED
95

—

oto of the artists cross-peeing, taken for magazine contribution called "Homo vins." The photographer documented rious stylized scenes in the everyday vironment of the artists, all of which picted the two men dressed in identi-l clothing. The work addresses issues of mosexual lifestyles, identical looks, and rcissism.

MATERIALS:	*oversize knitted white cloth, slide projector*
PERFORMERS:	*the artists*
CLOTHING:	*army green pants, sneakers or boots, white T-shirt, light pink shirt*
DIMENSIONS:	*variable*
DURATION:	*three to four hours*
PERFORMED AT:	*"The Spring Exhibition," Kunsthal Charlottenborg, Copenhagen, 1995; "The April Sessions," Institute of Contemporary Arts (ICA), London, 1996*

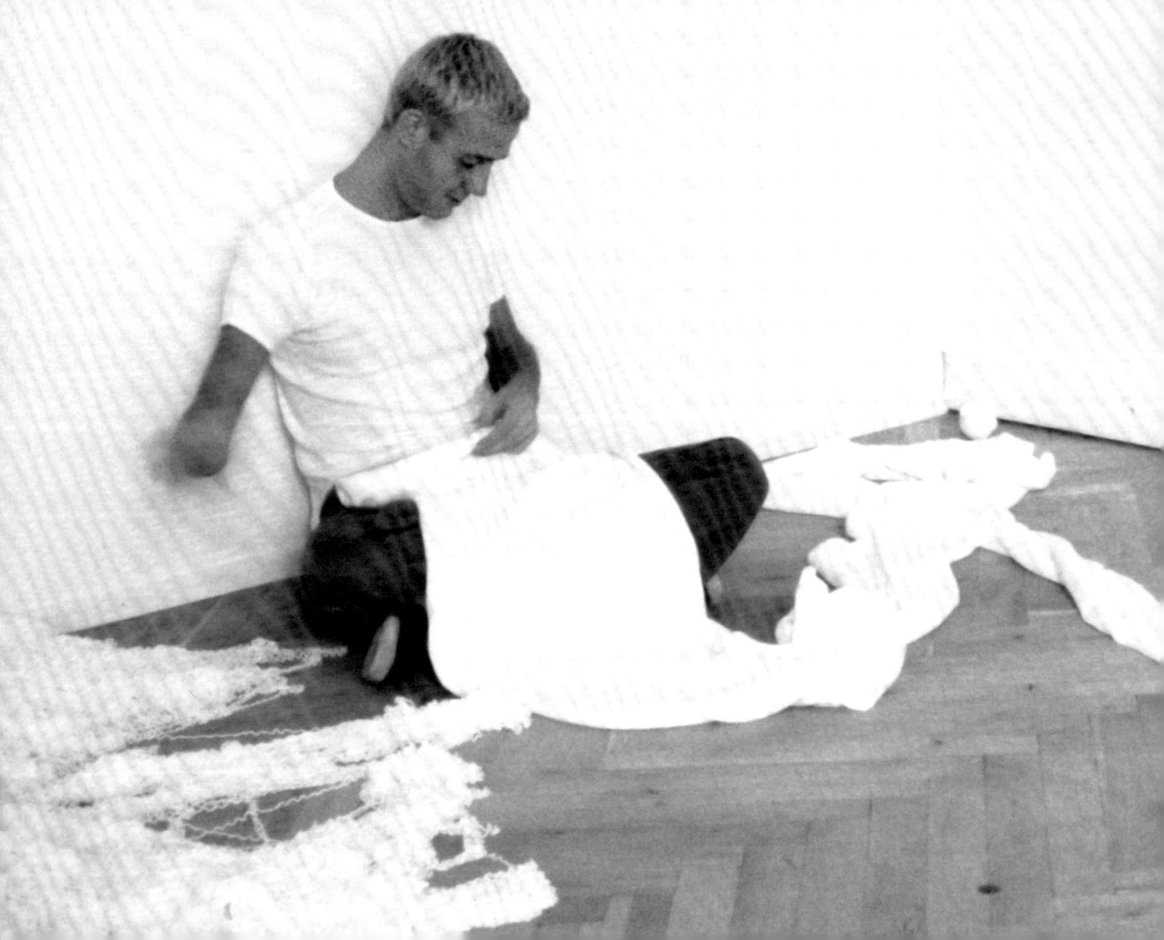

UNTITLED
1995

Performance in which the artists engage in knitting and unraveling a 100 meter long piece of white cloth under a slide projection of the two artists cross-peeing (*Untitled*, 1995).

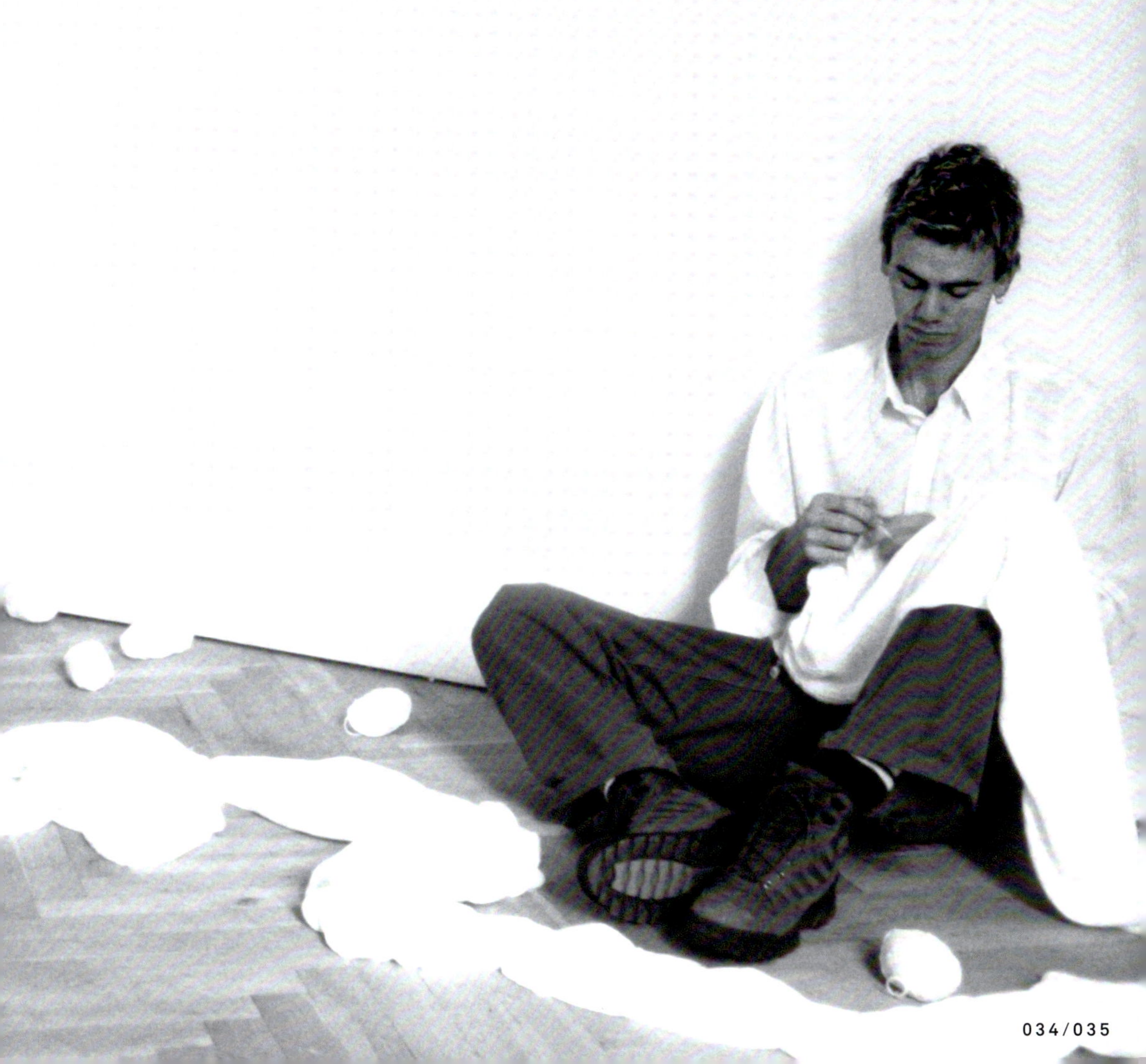

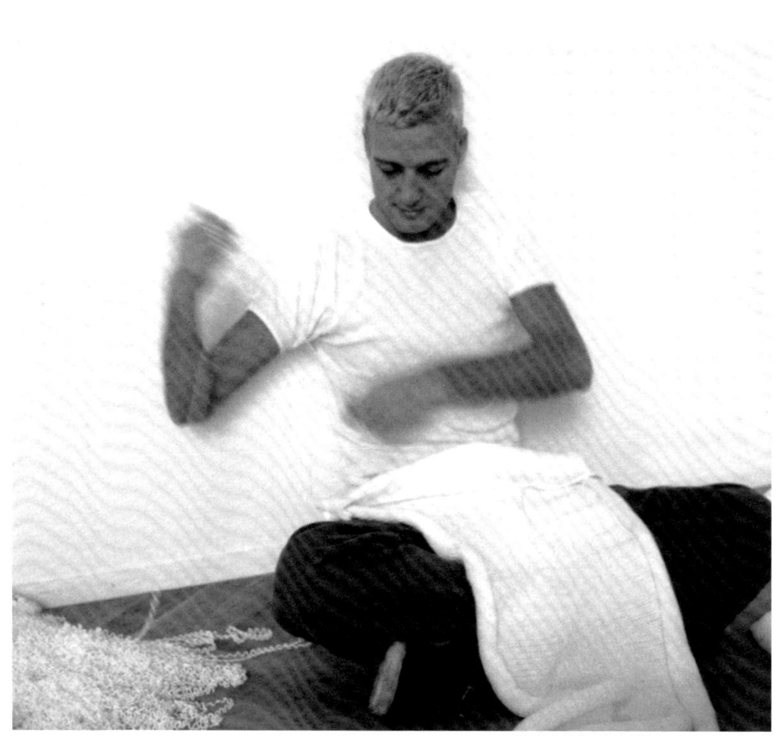

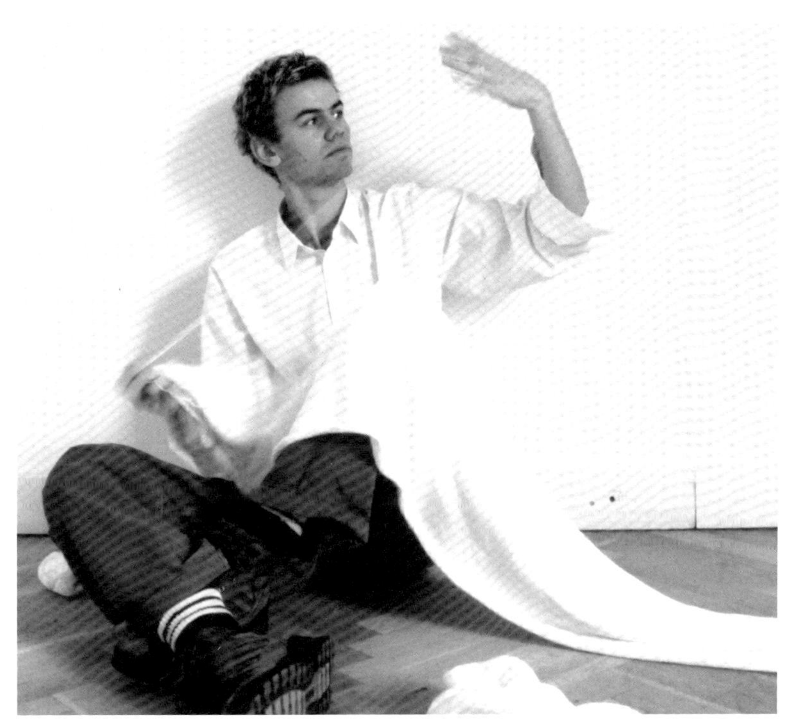

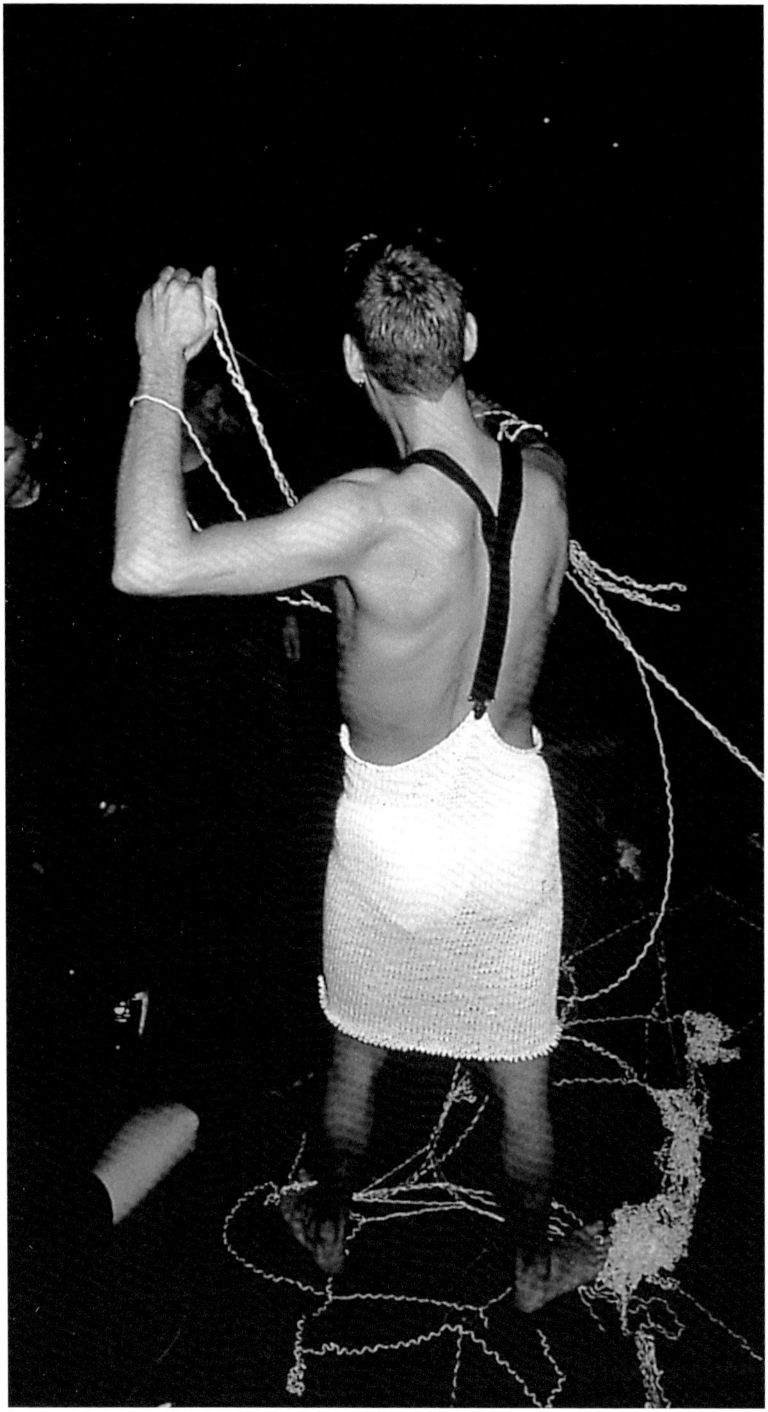

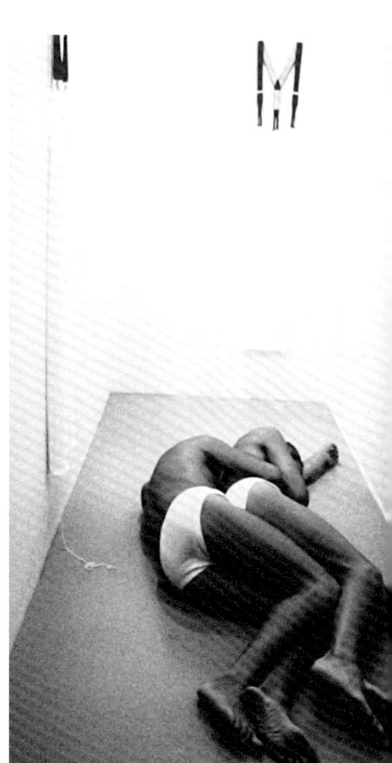

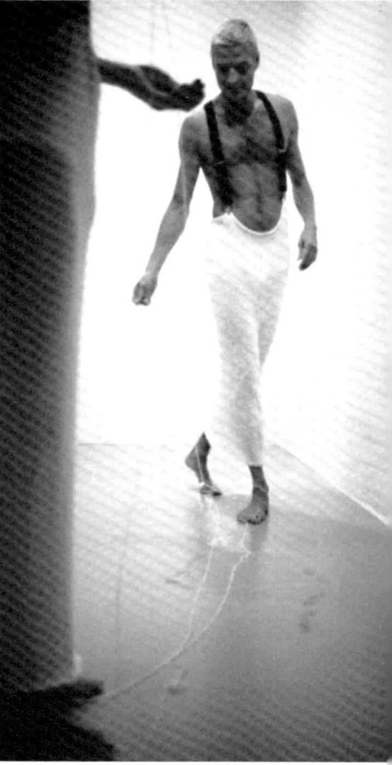

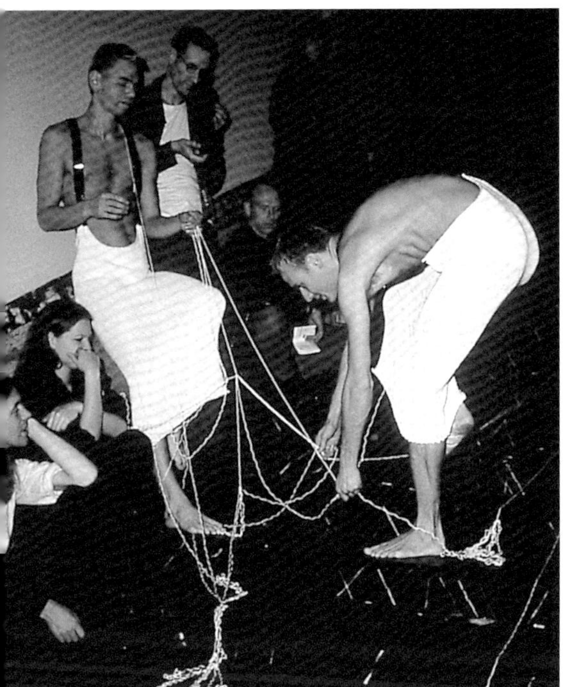

PERFORMERS:	*the artists*
CLOTHING:	*knitted skirts, black suspenders*
DURATION:	*approximately thirty to forty minutes (as long as it takes to unravel the skirts at a slow pace)*
PERFORMED AT:	*"One Night Stand," Kunstnernes Hus, Oslo, 1996; various other locations, such as a public toilet in Copenhagen, a soccer club changing room in Helsinki and the men's room at Kulturhuset in Stockholm*

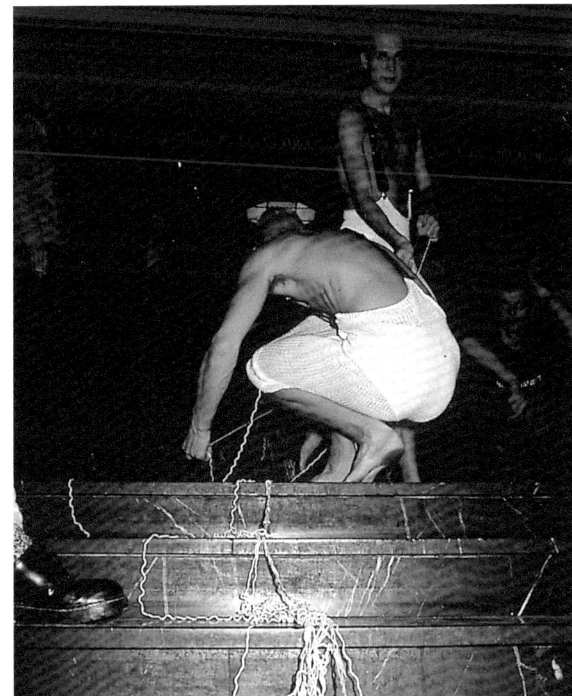

NTITLED
996

erformance in which the artists unavel two long white knitted skirts off ach other.

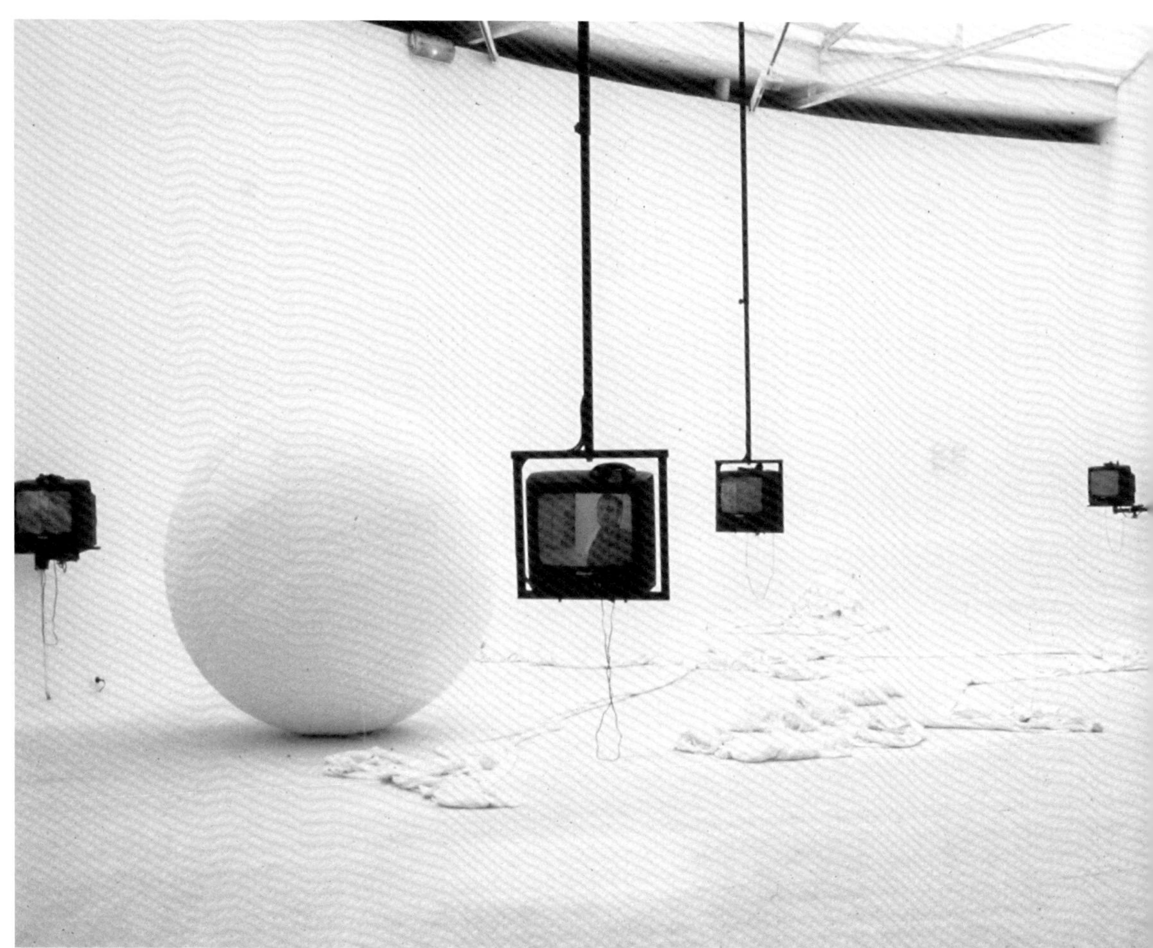

MATERIALS:	*white carpet, oversize knitted white cloth, ball of yarn*
PERFORMERS:	*the artists*
CLOTHING:	*white T-shirts, black pants, white socks*
DIMENSIONS:	*variable; oversize knitted white cloth: 100 m,* *white oversize ball of yarn: 1.7 m diameter*
DURATION:	*throughout the opening reception for the exhibition*
PERFORMED & EXHIBITED AT:	*"Nuit Blanche," Musée d'Art moderne de la Ville de Paris, 1998*

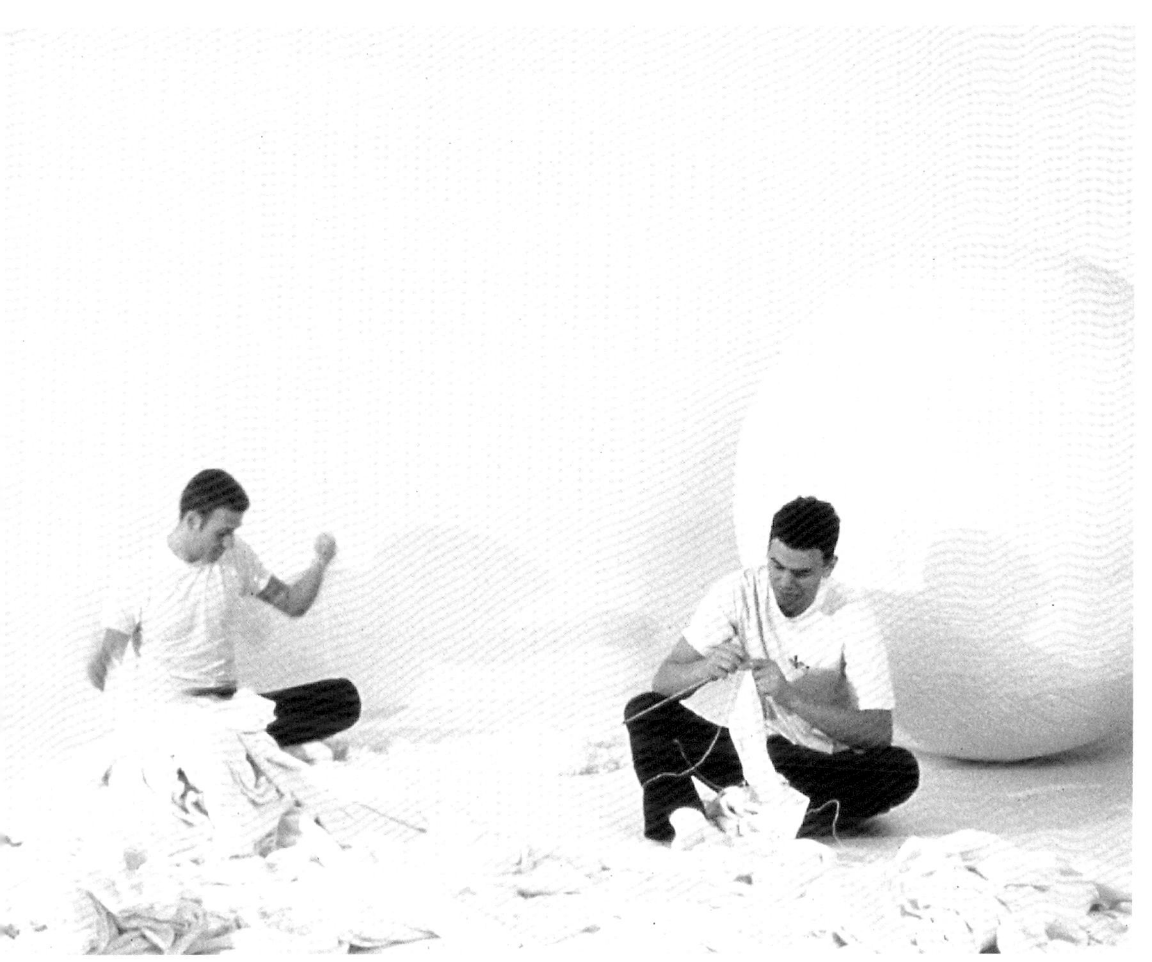

OWERLESS STRUCTURES, FIG. 22
998

erformance, as part of a video art display, where the artists ngage in knitting and unraveling a 100 meter long piece of hite cloth, using yarn from a ball of white yarn 1.7 meters diameter. The multiple small televisions hanging down om the ceiling show work by contemporary Nordic video tists.

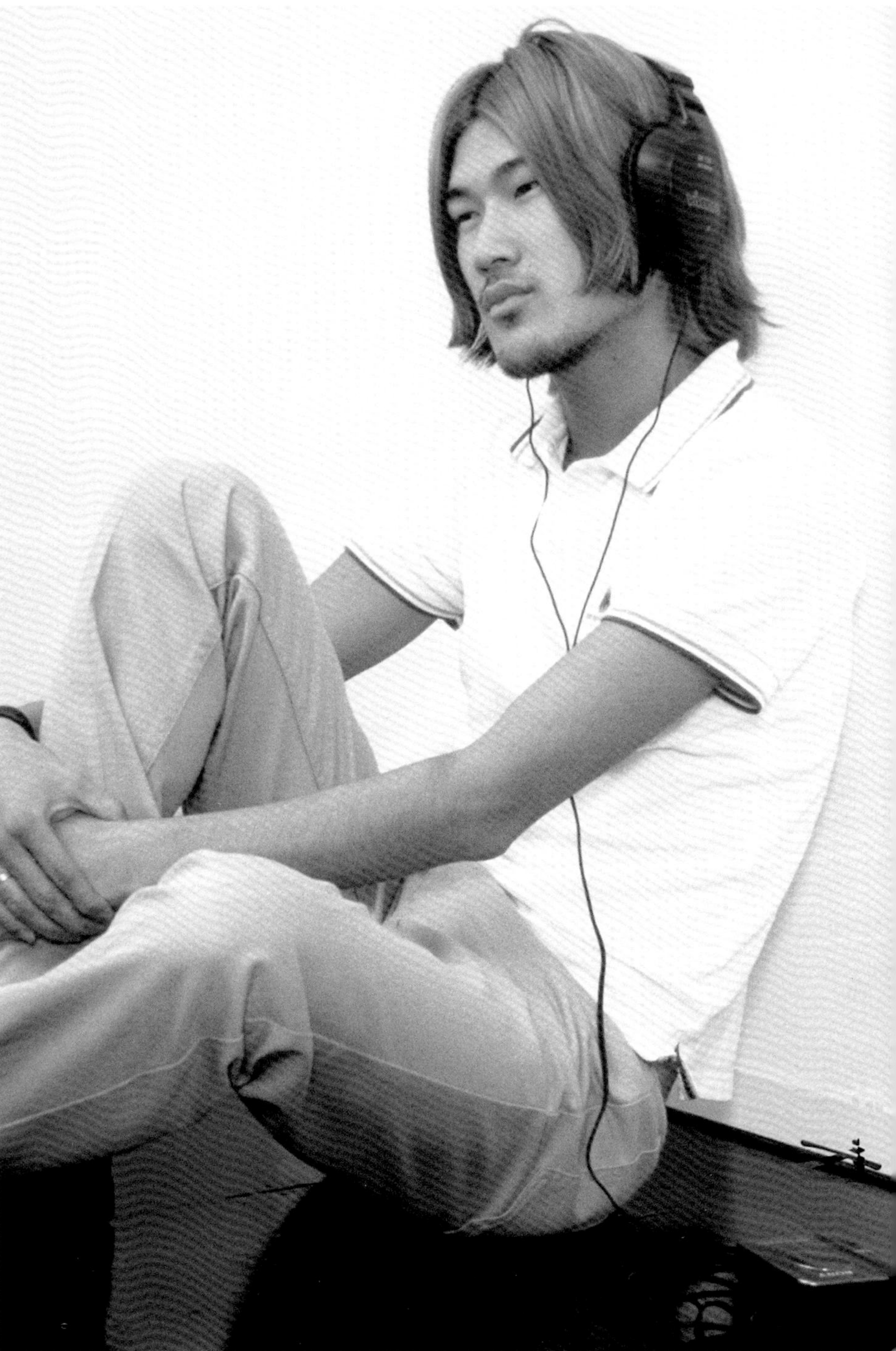

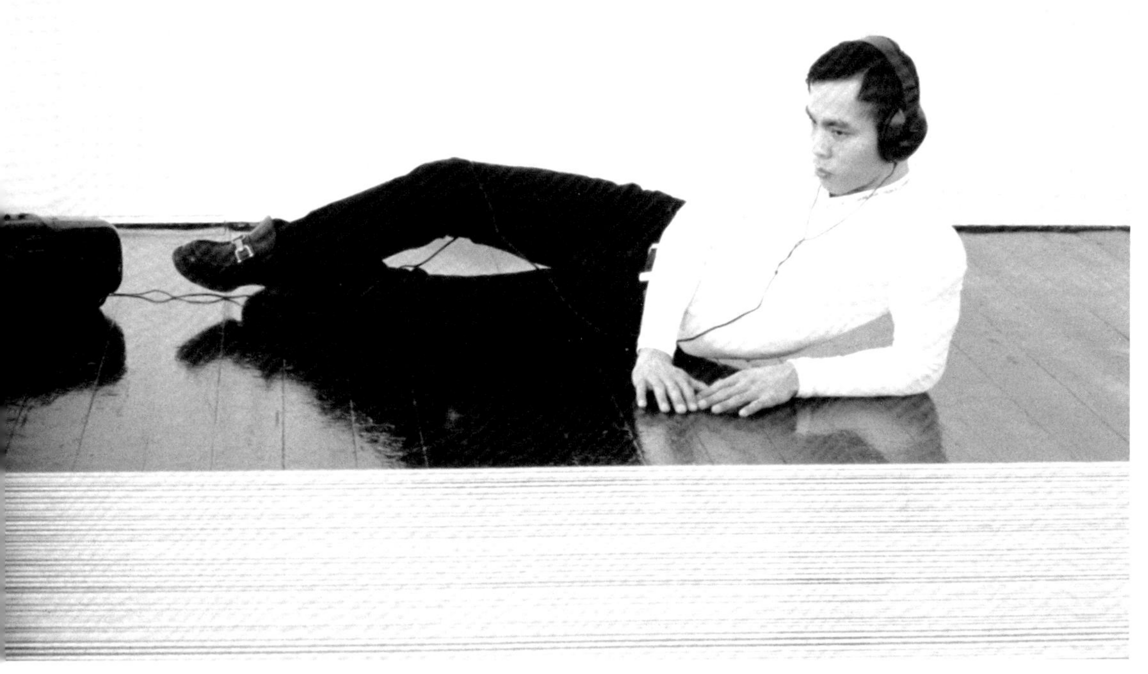

TERIALS:	*CD players, headphones; nails, white and blue yarn; paint, aluminum paint cans without labels*
RFORMERS:	*two young males, early 20s*
OTHING:	*their own*
MENSIONS:	*variable*
RATION:	*approximately three hours (throughout the opening reception for the exhibition, then occasionally during the exhibition period)*
RFORMED & HIBITED AT:	*"To Ken Ishii," Galleri Struts, Oslo, 1997*

TO KEN ISHII 1997

Performance installation: Two performers silently listening to Ken Ishii's music on headphones, one in each room of the exhibition, accompanying *Powerless Structures, Fig. 8* and *Fig. 9* (both 1997) respectively. Ken Ishii is a critically acclaimed "minimal techno" music DJ from Japan. The work *Powerless Structures, Fig. 8* is a horizontal loom strung across the gallery floor on nails attached to the skirting board. The work *Powerless Structures, Fig. 9* is nine aluminum paint cans filled with paint and circular spots painted on the floor in colors not matching the paint in the adjacent cans.

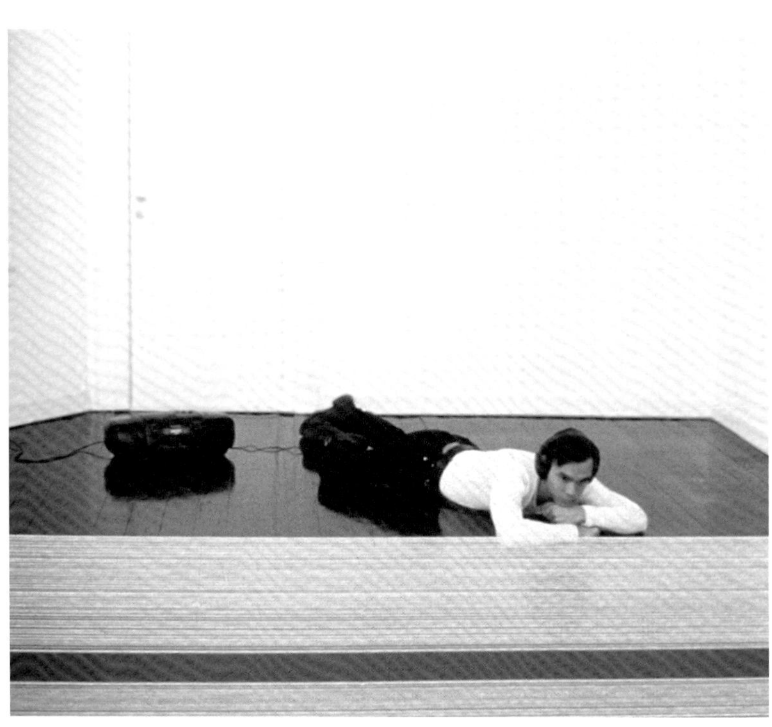

Artwork as World

BY INA BLOM

With the live installation "To Ken Ishii" Michael Elmgreen and Ingar Dragset establish the conditions for a work of art to function as a world of its own.

—

Not all music serves as a means of communication. At least not if by communication one means that a message is passed on from one individual to another, from sender to recipient. Some forms of music do, on the contrary, attempt to establish a world of its own; a space or territory in which one may immerse oneself, and take on a number of different roles or perspectives. In such cases the listener might claim the music as his or her territory and therefore be the one playing the role of "communicator."

—

This phenomenon often occurs within genres such as techno or ambient music, where a relatively anonymous DJ compiles sounds that principally function as a social framework in which audiences anticipate and produce the potentialities of the music. In *To Ken Ishii* music takes on a similar role. The sound itself is barely heard; instead you are confronted with two live performers wearing headphones, laying withdrawn on the floor in a listening-position. The body wrapped up in headphones serves as the living image of the idea of music as a world of its own, where the body and the music have become one single entity.

—

In this installation, music comes across as such a world, since as a spectator one is placed on its exterior. People wearing headphones disconnect from you—they can or will not share their experience. Their facial expressions become impenetrable surfaces, creating a boundary towards the outside since you know that something is happening that is inaccessible to you. Still, this installation does give us some possibilities for involvement. Although you are excluded from the sensation of hearing, the gallery rooms are utilized in a way which directs us towards similar worlds in which one can immerse oneself. In fact, they evoke the sense of infinity articulated by certain forms of abstract painting, although in this case such articulation expands beyond the ordinary confines of the canvas. Precise geometrical fields of thread are stretched across the room slightly above the floor, only interrupted by small intersecting fields where the threads are woven tightly. In the adjacent room, small, circular two- and three-dimensional fields of color have been painted on the floor. A number of "color-cylinders" are placed next to these circles, represented by open paint-tins filled with paint differing in color from the fields on the floor.

—

The rooms transmit the coming into being of a new world, an emergent structuring and organization of an area through points and lines, impres-

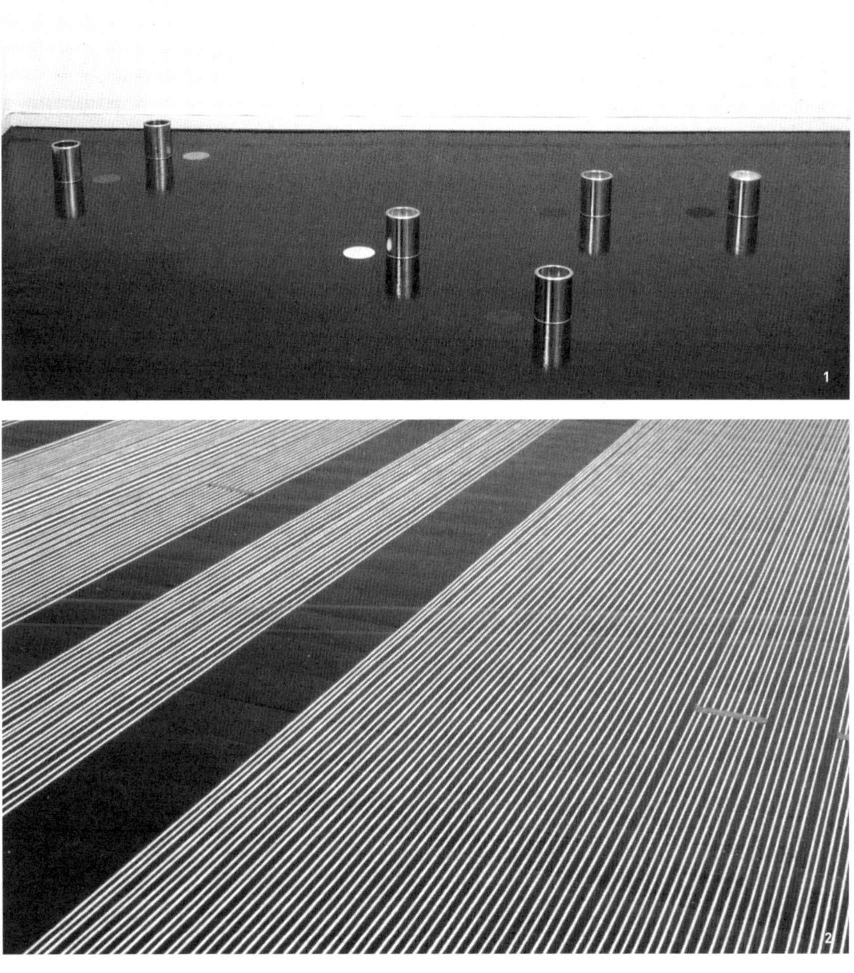

Fig. 1 _ *Powerless Structures, Fig. 9*, 1997, Galleri Struts, Oslo.
Fig. 2 _ *Powerless Structures, Fig. 8*, 1997, Galleri Struts, Oslo.

sions and expansions. As a spectator, I appreciate this work because of the way in which it resists simply enclosing you within a world where you are more or less hypnotized into participation. This is the potentially fascist aspect of the rave-culture—when the organization becomes too monotonous, and the response too potentially totalitarian. By enclosing oneself and refusing to pass something on, while at the same time introducing you to elements that seem to suggest further development, the installation opens onto something far more essential. It connects to the desire for such immersive environments and the fantasies that surround such free rooms or alternative spaces of experience. (As we know, ecstatic pleasures are generally the object of strict governmental supervision.) And it alerts us to the fact that such worlds—far from being banal phenomena—are rare and valuable events that are only rarely accessible. ———

Translated from the Norwegian by Hanne Lippard.

This article was previously published in the Norwegian newspaper *Aftenposten:*
Ina Blom, "Kunstverk som verden," *Aftenposten*, March 24, 1997.

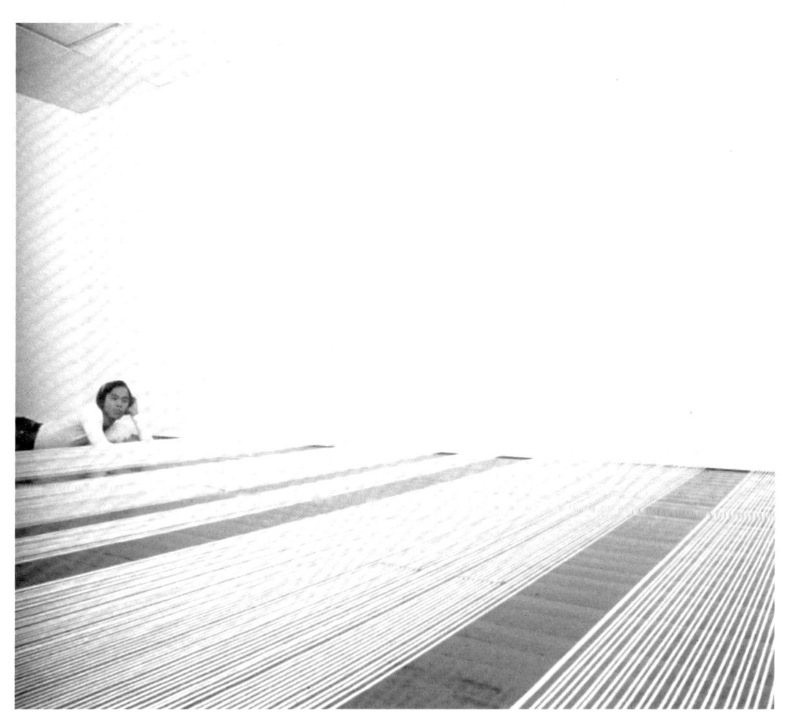

MATERIALS: *rugs, stereo, walkman, headphones, white counter-height refrigerator, beer*
PERFORMERS: *three males, ages 18 - 25*
CLOTHING: *their own*
DIMENSIONS: *rugs: maximum 2.5 x 2.5 m; space variable*
DURATION: *approximately three hours (throughout the opening reception for the exhibition, then occasionally during the exhibition period)*
PERFORMED & EXHIBITED AT: *"Between You & Me," Overgaden, Copenhagen, 1996*

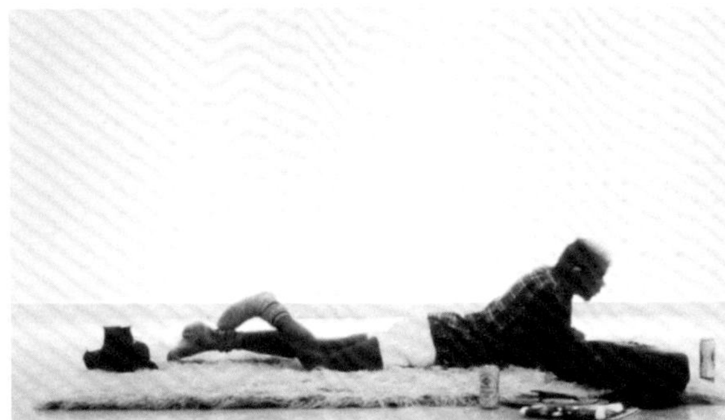

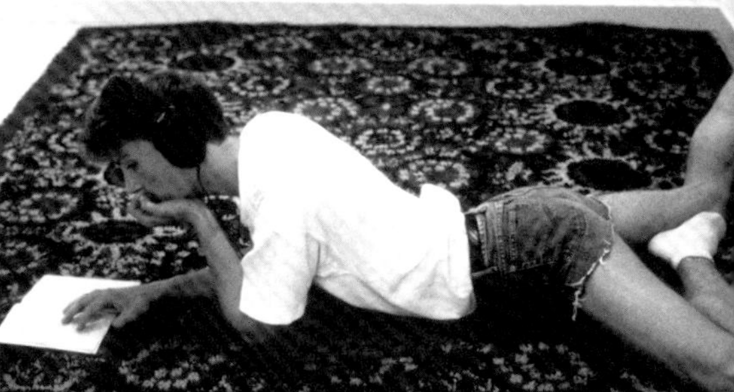

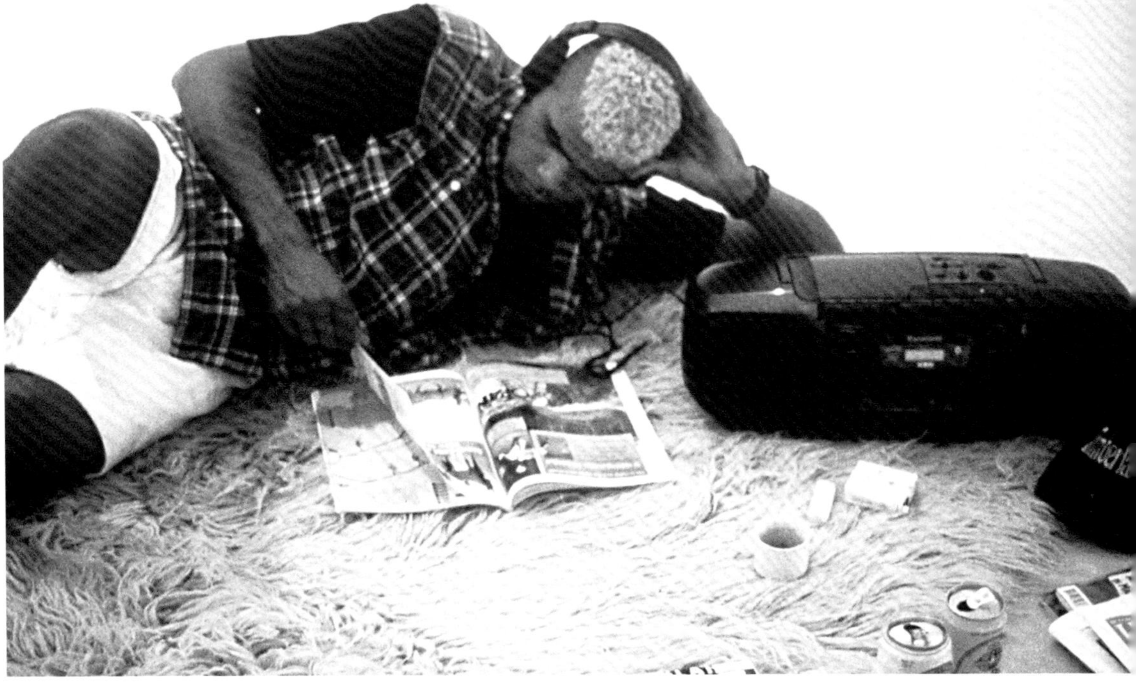

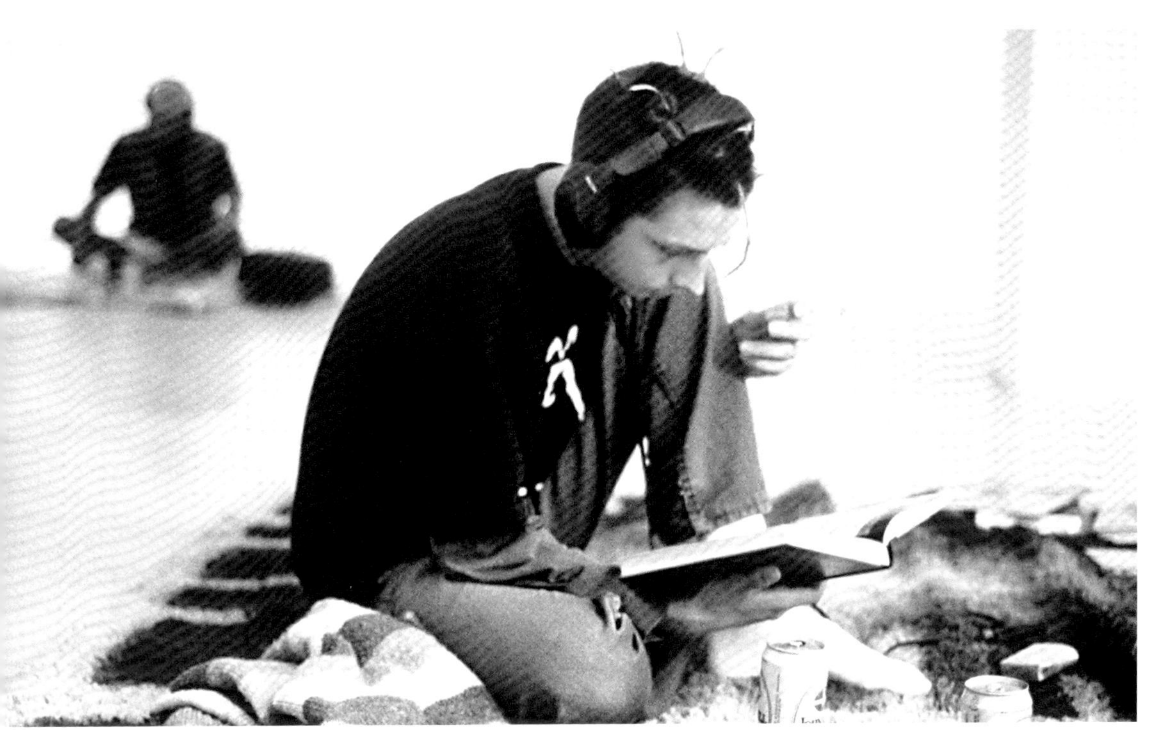

TRY
1996

Performance installation: a space with three rugs, each with a stereo or walkman and headphones, and a fridge stocked with cans of beer, to which three men were invited to bring their favorite books, magazines, and CDs, and hang out on their individual rugs during the exhibition. The performers, each from different social backgrounds, were approached on the street and asked to participate. They become engrossed in their own worlds on the three rugs and do not interact with visitors.

MATERIALS: *hair dye*
PERFORMERS: *the artists; boy, age 7*
CLOTHING: *T-shirts with prints*
DURATION: *one day*
PERFORMED AT: *Prosjekt Hårsalongen, Malmö, 1996*

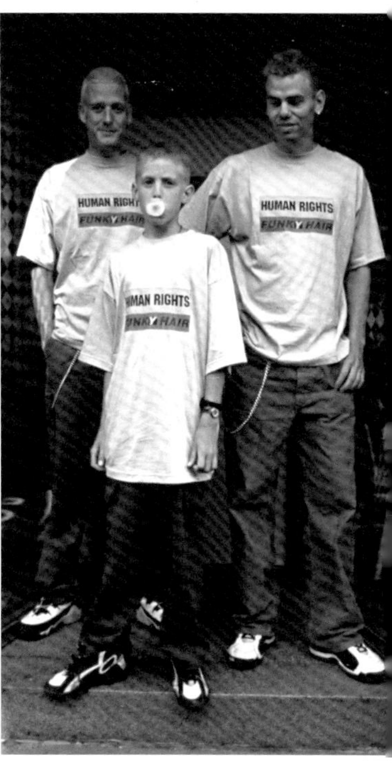

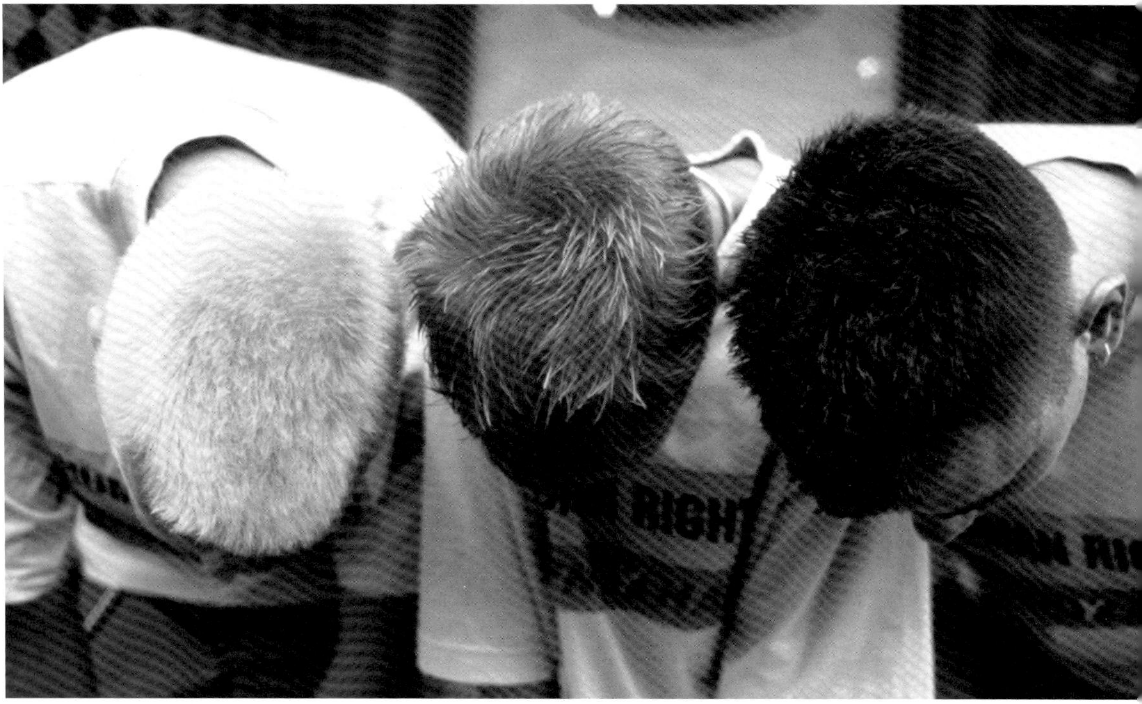

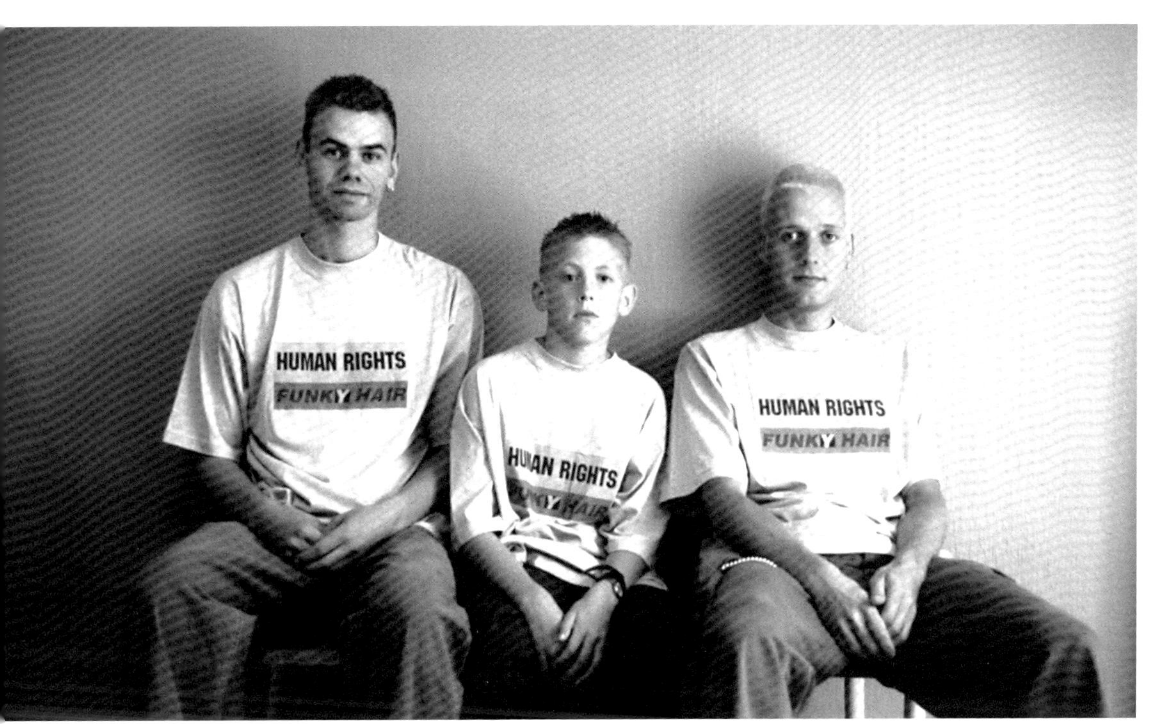

UMAN RIGHTS, FUNKY HAIR
996

erformance: Danish Elmgreen and Norwegian Dragset adopt-
d a Swedish "son" for a day. The new family had their hair dyed,
ed and yellow for the "parents" and orange for their "son." The
ansformation at the hairdressers was open to the public, as
as the following "birthday party" for the boy.

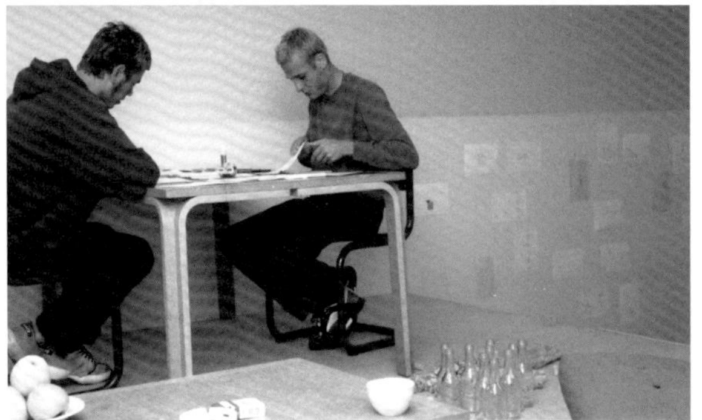

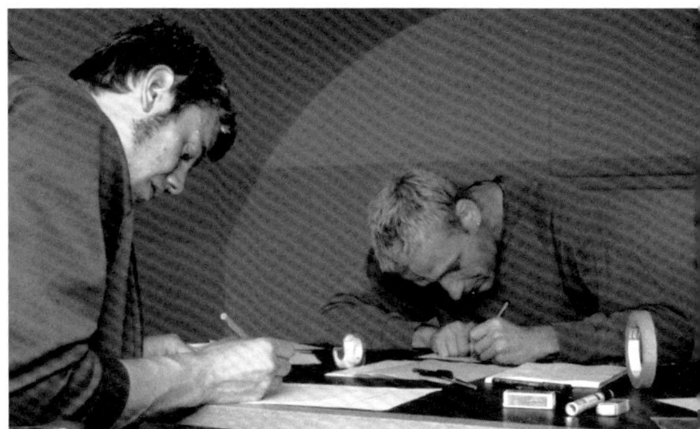

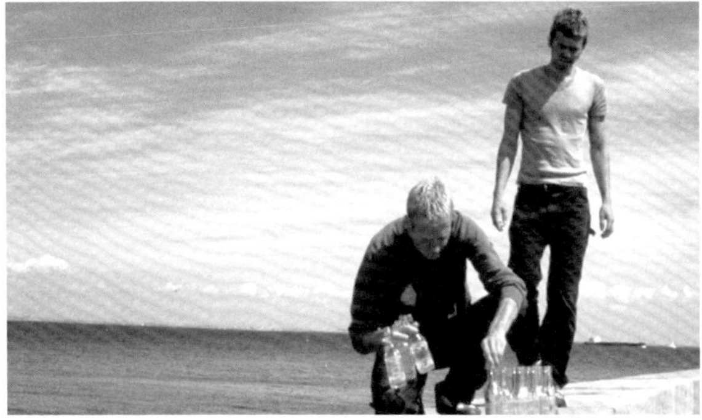

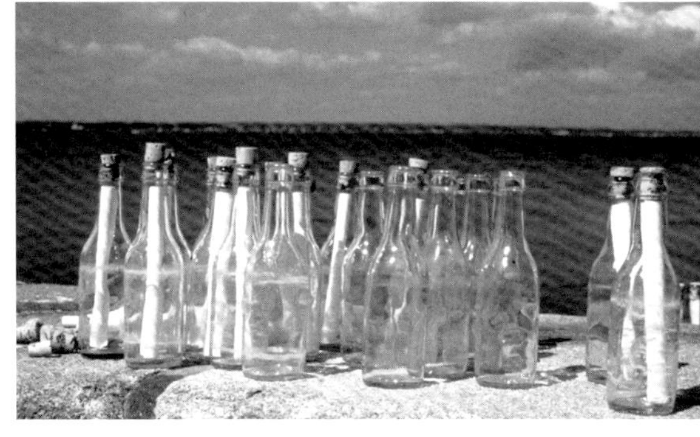

MATERIALS: *bottles, paper, pens*
PERFORMERS: *the artists*
CLOTHING: *the artists' everyday clothes*
DURATION: *one week*
PERFORMED AT: *"What is a Guy from Leicester, a Swedish girl, a Family Father and a Gay Couple Doing on a Deserted Island between Denmark and Sweden?," Middelgrundsfortet, 1997*

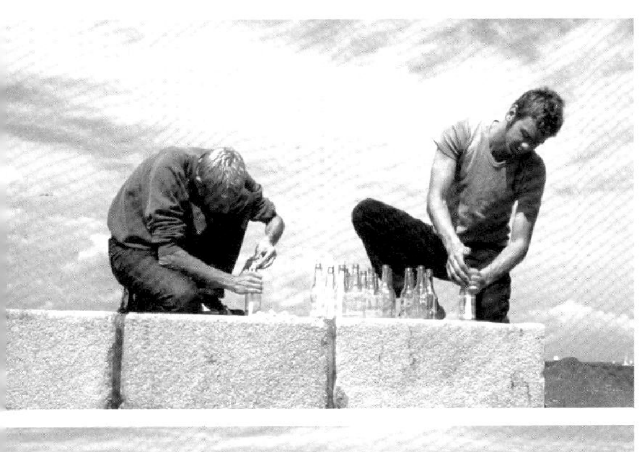
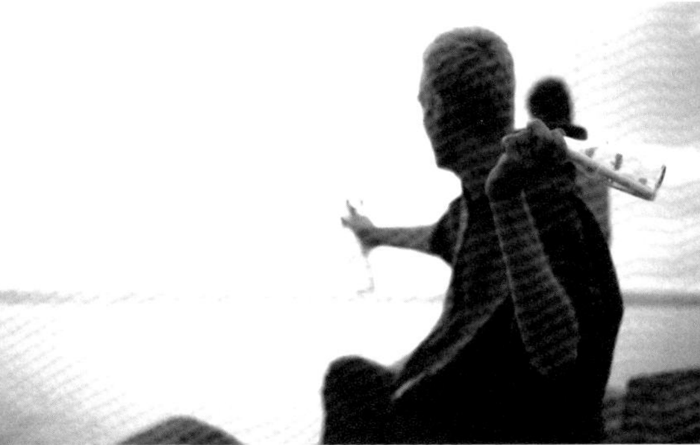
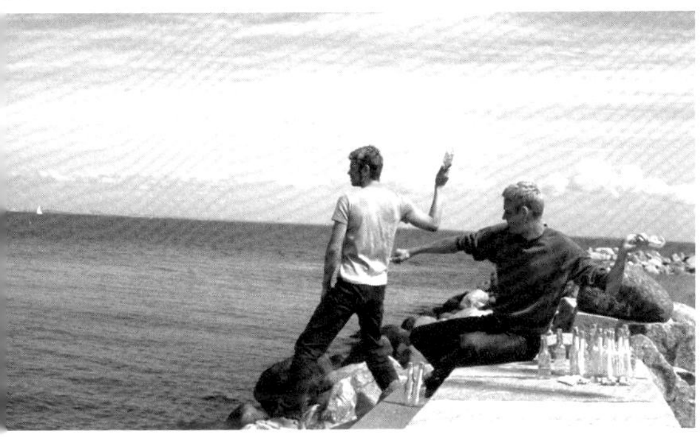
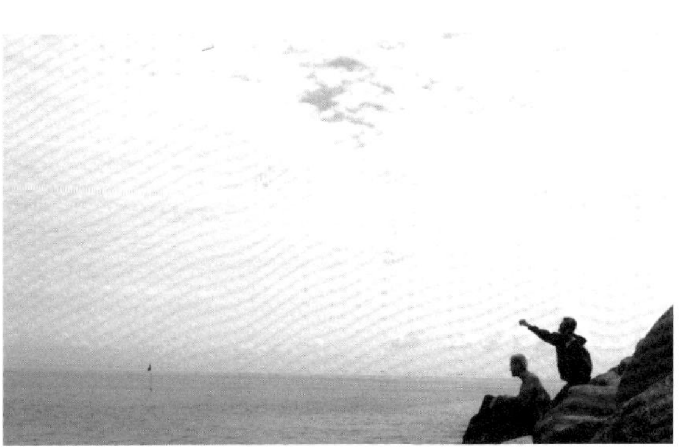

'OWERLESS STRUCTURES, FIG. 14
997

'urator Jacob Fabricius invited five artists to spend one week n a deserted island, a former military fortress between Den- ıark and Sweden. Elmgreen & Dragset spent the time creating oo drawings and sending them as messages in bottles.

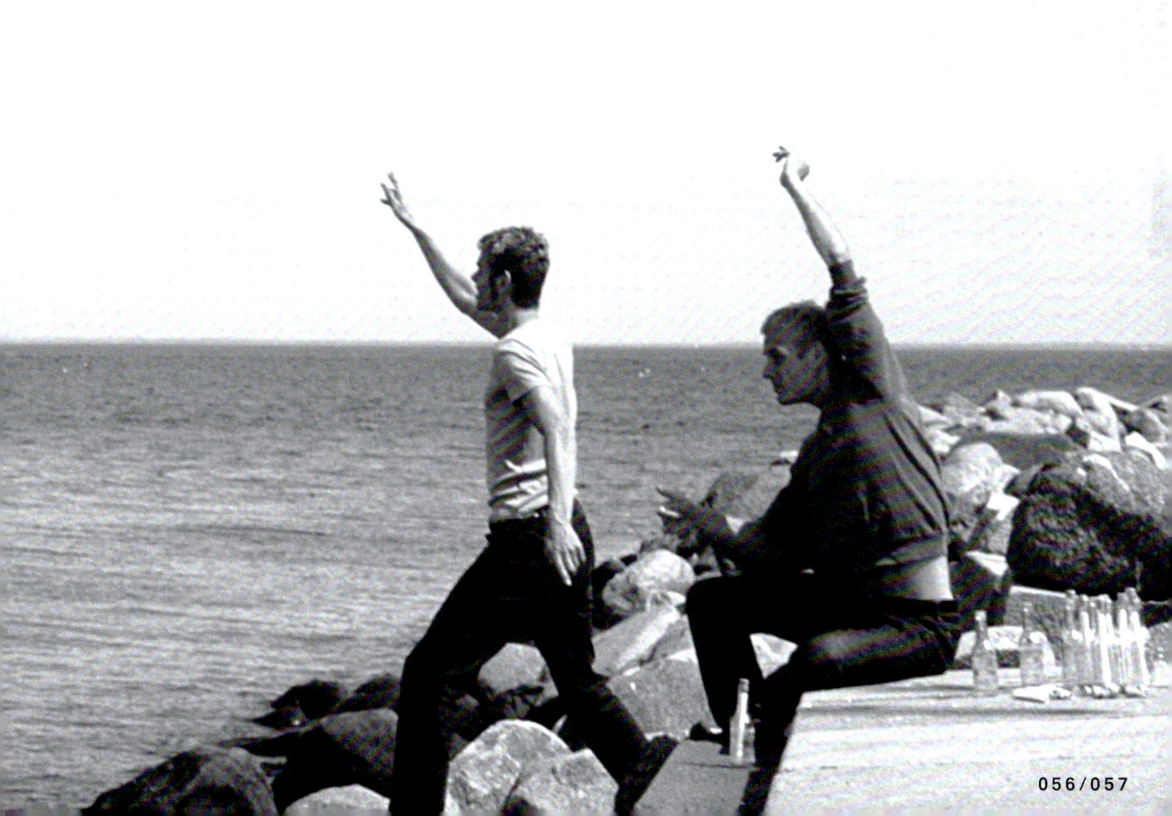

MATERIALS:	*mattress, beer, weights, microphone, small televisions, miscellaneous items*
PERFORMERS:	*the artists*
CLOTHING:	*sailor's uniforms*
DIMENSIONS:	*variable*
DURATION:	*four hours (throughout the opening reception for the exhibition)*
PERFORMED & EXHIBITED AT:	*"The Scream—Borealis 8," Arken Museum of Modern Art, Ishøj, 1996; A separate staging with the artists dressed as sailors is documented by photographs.*
COLLECTION:	*A customized burned and scratched selection of this series belongs to the collection of The National Gallery of Denmark, Copenhagen.*

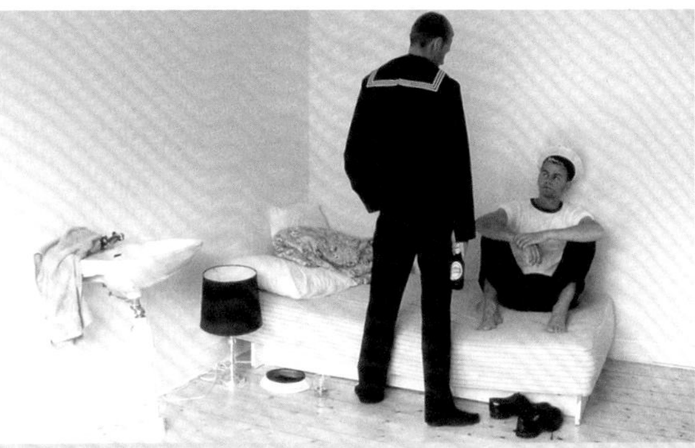

"I hate your love, I hate your sailor outfit, I hate your body, I hate your romantic notion to cry, I hate your busy life, I hate ...

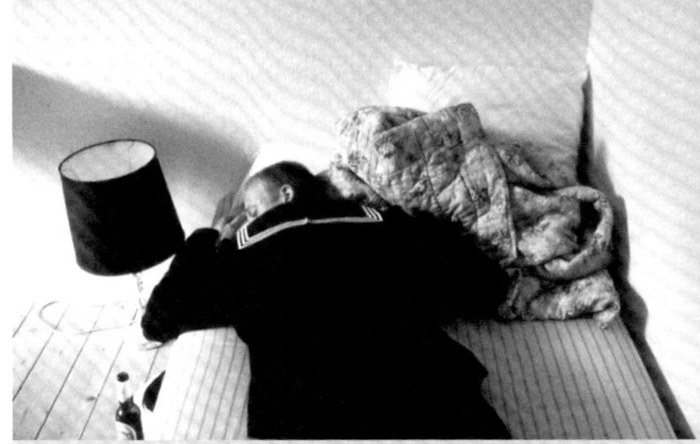

... your heart, I hate your ass, I hate your home, I hate your dreams, I hate your mom, I hate your car, I hate your suntan oil, I hate ...

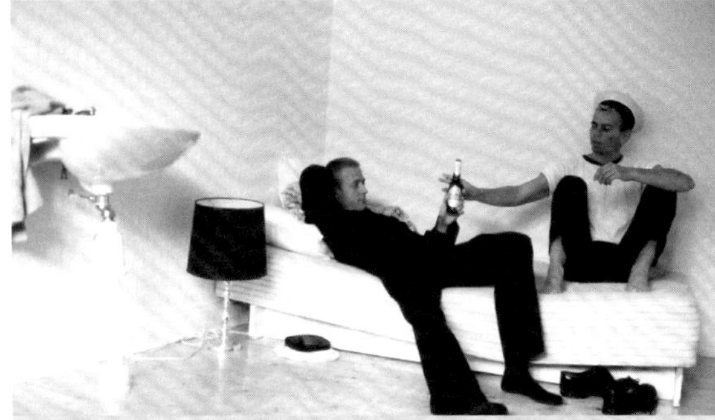

... your dependency, I hate your habits, I hate your lack of dignity, I hate your arms, I hate your cigarettes, I hate ...

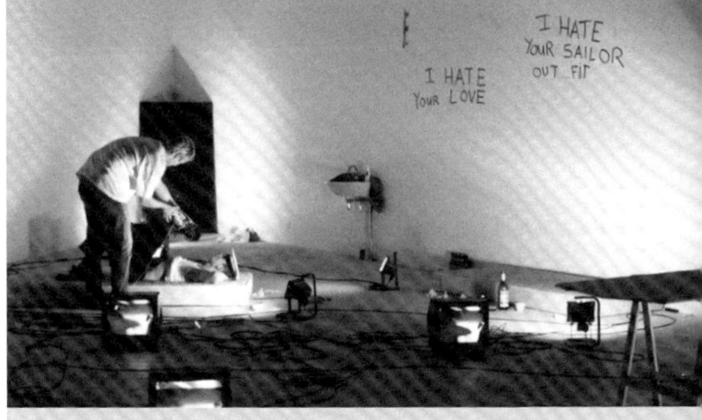

... your skin, I hate your coat, I hate your jokes, I hate your trying to be a party animal, I hate your cock, I hate your thoughts ..."

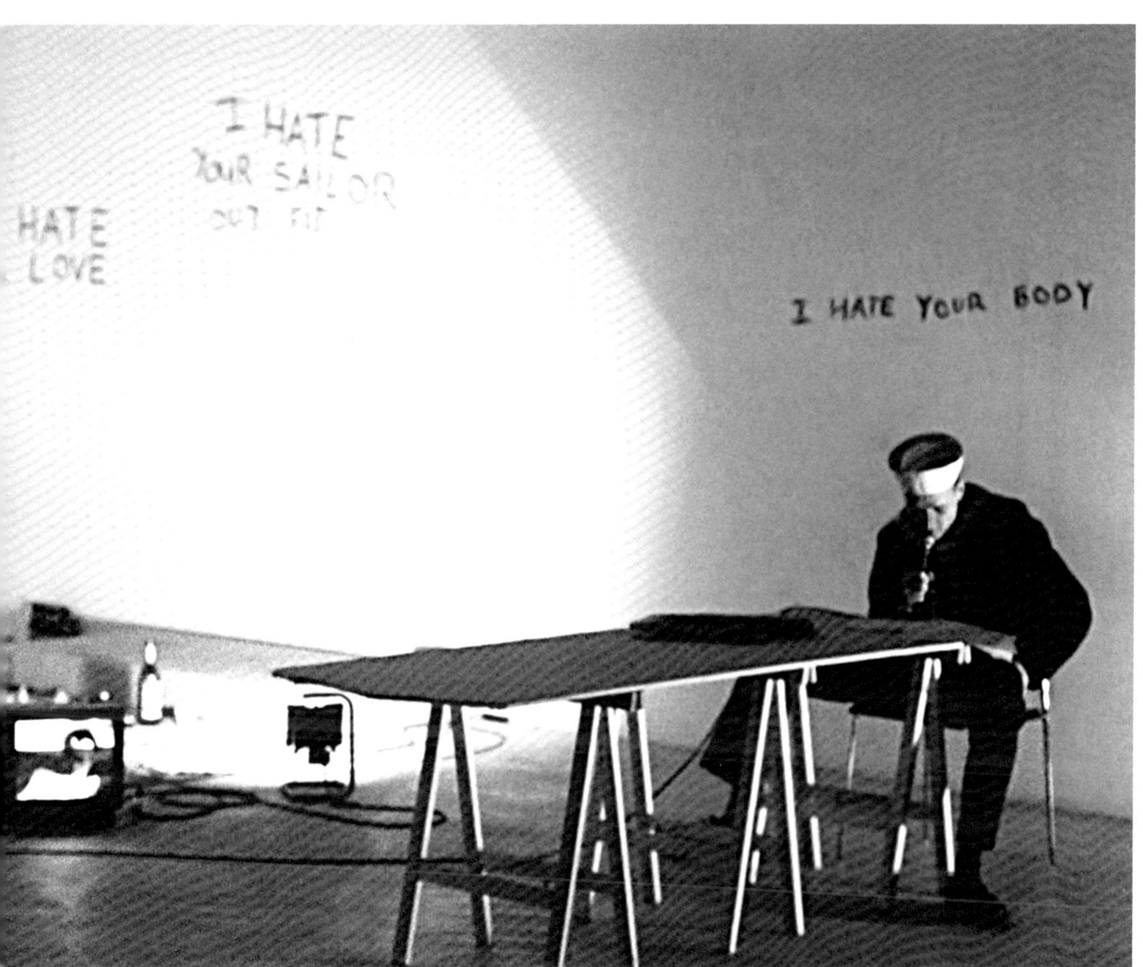

HE END OF NATURAL BEHAVIOR
996

---

erformance: Elmgreen & Dragset dress up in sailor's uni-
rms in a stylized take on the iconic image of the "gay sailor."
ctivities include sleeping, working out, drinking beer and
ooting fake heroin, with Elmgreen occasionally speaking
to a microphone, listing various things about Dragset: "I
ate your..." The performance is simultaneously filmed from
fferent angles and shown on multiple small televisions set
on the floor. The performance took place at the Arken
The Ark") Museum of Modern Art in Denmark, a postmod-
n building shaped like a stranded ship.

MATERIALS:	*white paint (160 l), aluminum paint cans, painting equipment, water hose with high-pressure gun*
PERFORMERS:	*the artists*
CLOTHING:	*white T-shirts, black overalls*
DIMENSIONS:	*variable*
DURATION:	*twelve hours*
PERFORMED AT:	*Galleri Tommy Lund, Odense, 1997; Muestra de Performance Internacional, Mexico City, 1997*
COLLECTION:	*(photo documentation) Museet for Samtidskunst, Roskilde*

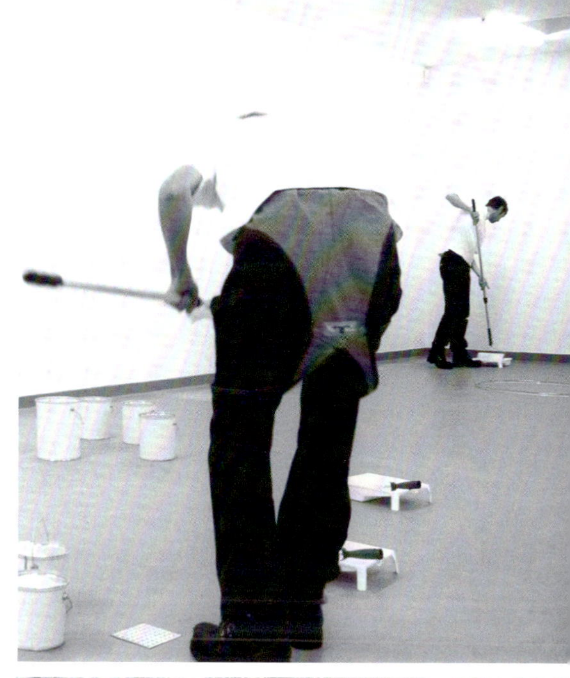

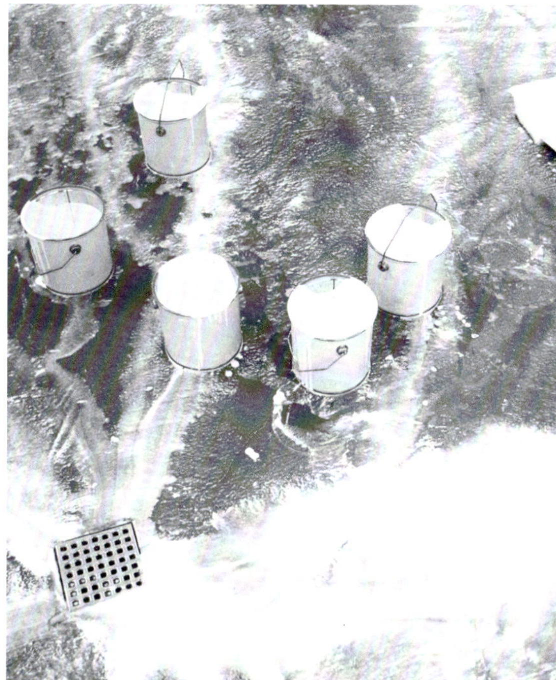

TWELVE HOURS OF WHITE PAINT / POWERLESS STRUCTURES, FIG. 15
1997

A typical white cube exhibition space is repeatedly painted white and hosed down by the artists in the course of twelve hours. Photo documentation exists as a separate work, in an edition of 5 + 2.

2.

WORKS

TEXTS

2.

INSTITUTION AND SPACE

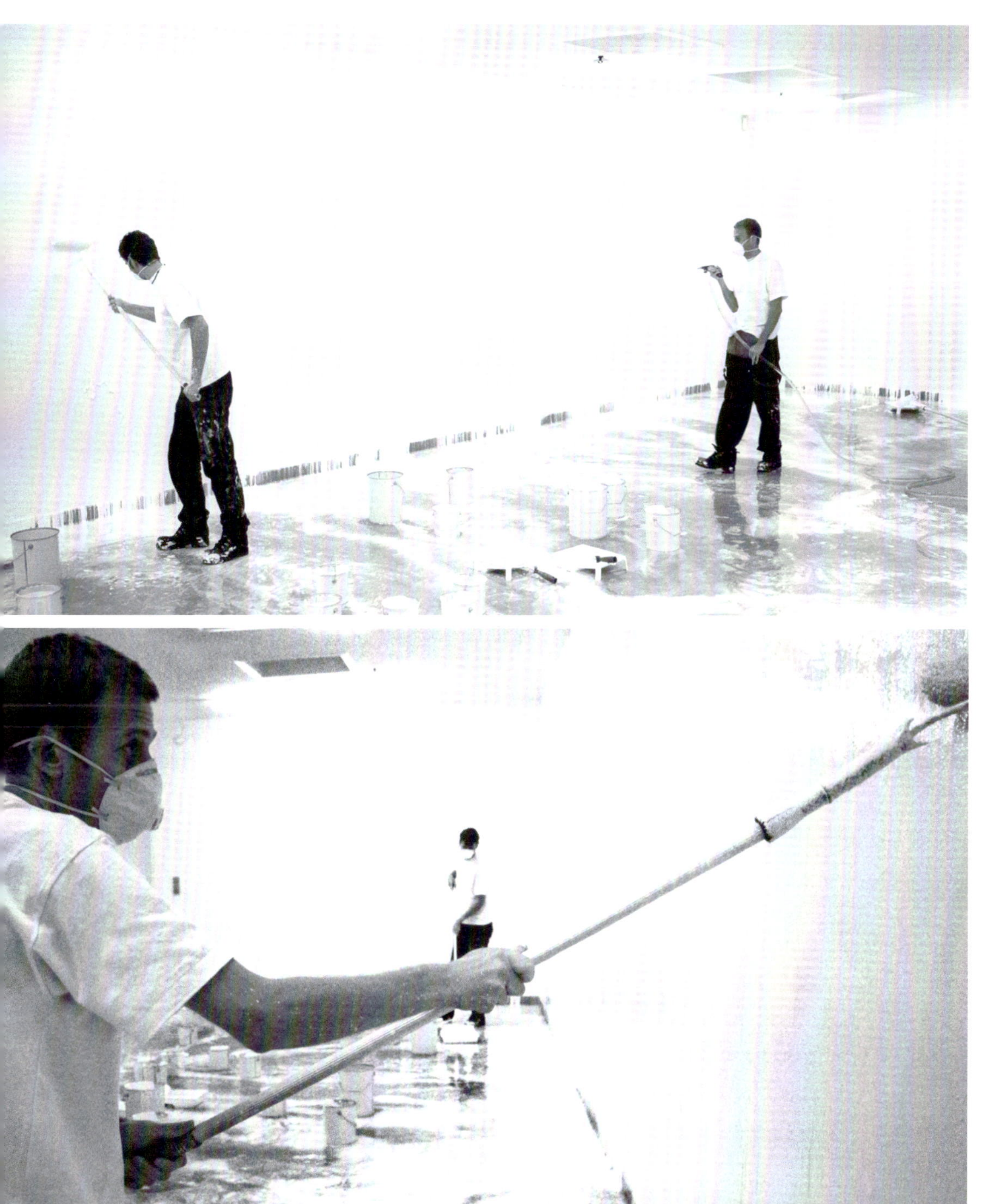

MATERIALS: *steel, glass, white paint, aluminum paint cans, painting equipment, water hose with high-pressure gun*
PERFORMERS: *the artists*
CLOTHING: *white T-shirts, black pants*
DIMENSIONS: *glass box: 230 x 600 x 600 cm*
DURATION: *throughout the opening reception for the exhibition; remains on view the entire exhibition period (three to six weeks)*
PERFORMED & EXHIBITED AT: *"Junge Szene," Secession, Vienna, 1998; "Carnegie Art Award," Kunstnernes Hus, Oslo, 1999*

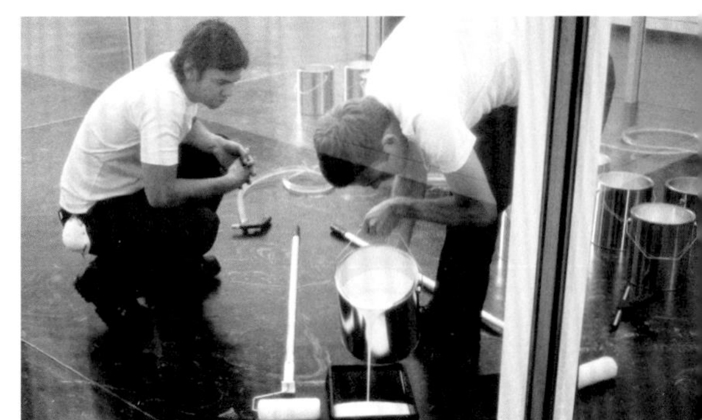

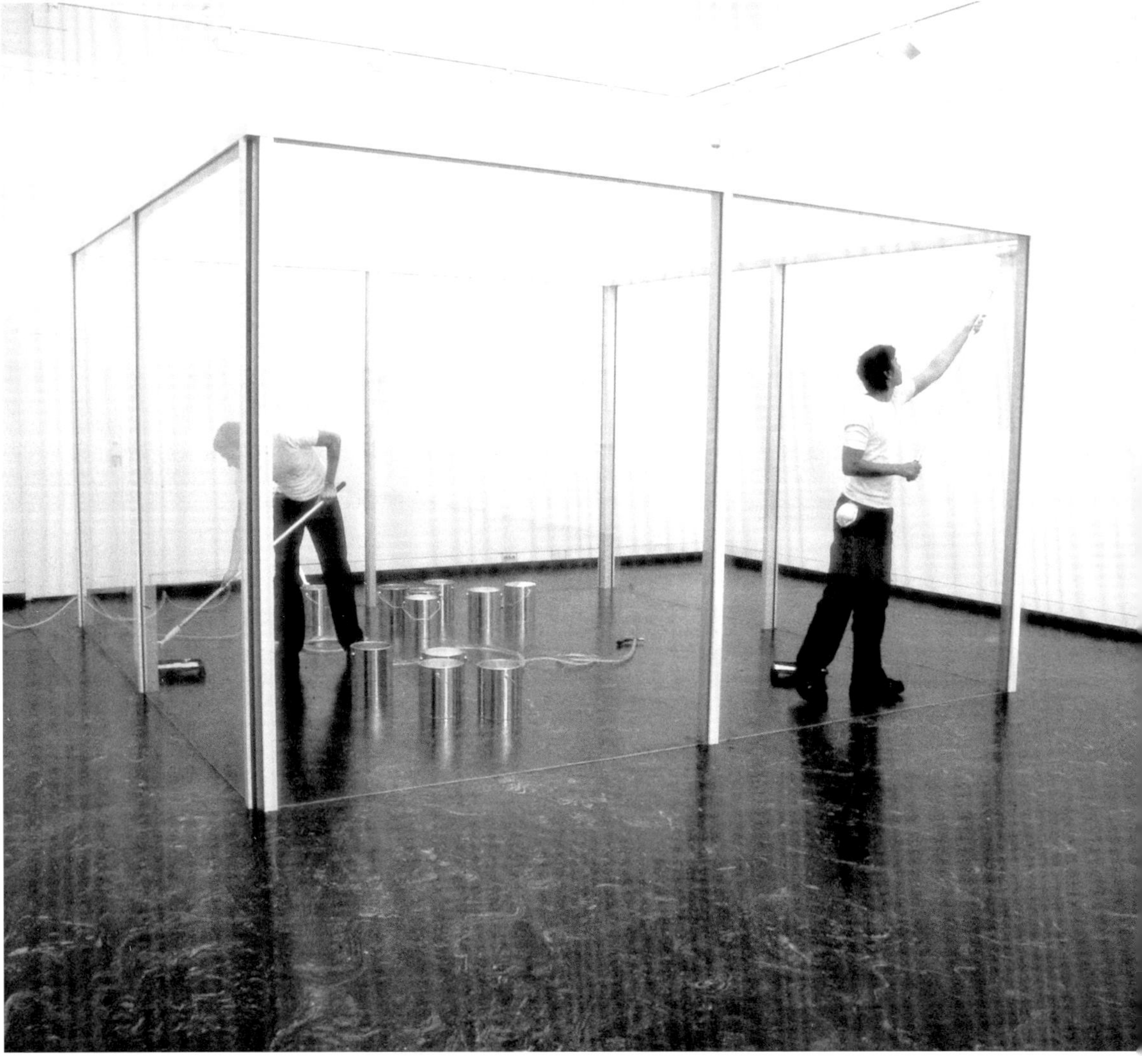

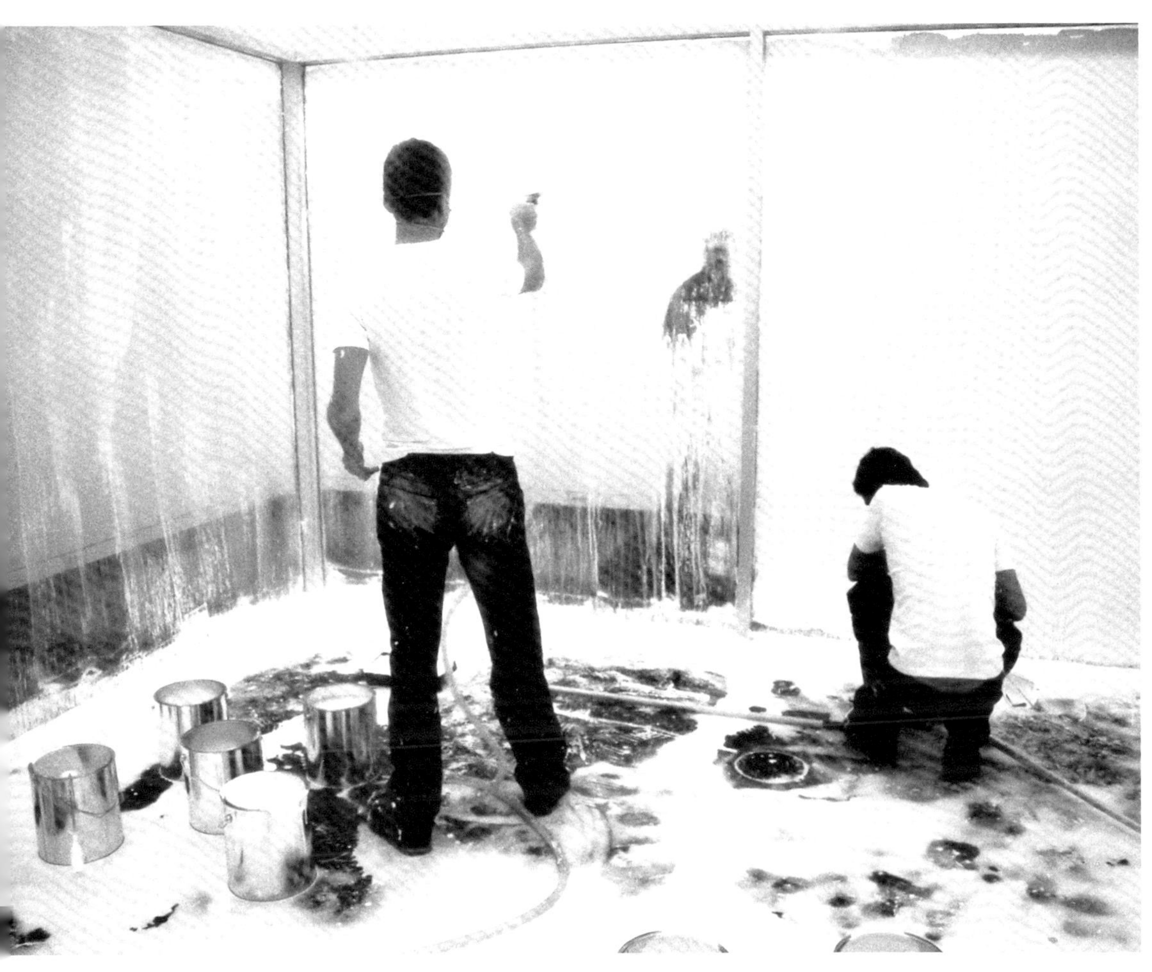

'OWERLESS STRUCTURES, FIG. 44
'998

ılass cube, inside which the artists repeatedly paint and hose .own the walls during the opening reception for the exhibition. hoto documentation of the two performances exists as sepa- ıte works, each in an edition of 5 + 2. *Powerless Structures, Fig. 44* (2000), shown at "Century of Innocence—The History of ıe White Monochrome," Rooseum, Malmö, 2000, is a related erformance installation with a glass wall dividing the exhibi- ion space into two parts, behind which the artists apply and ash away layers of white paint repeatedly.

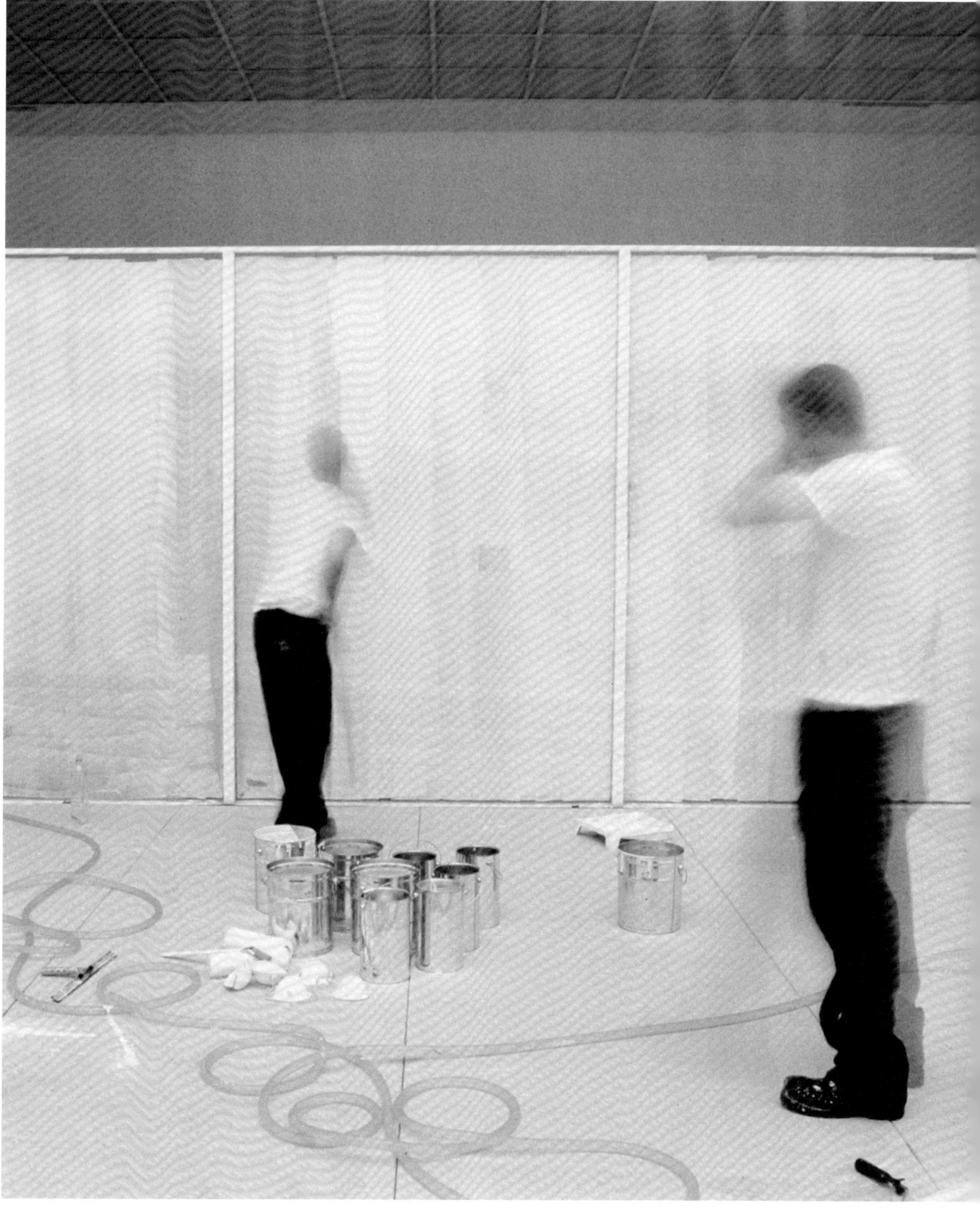

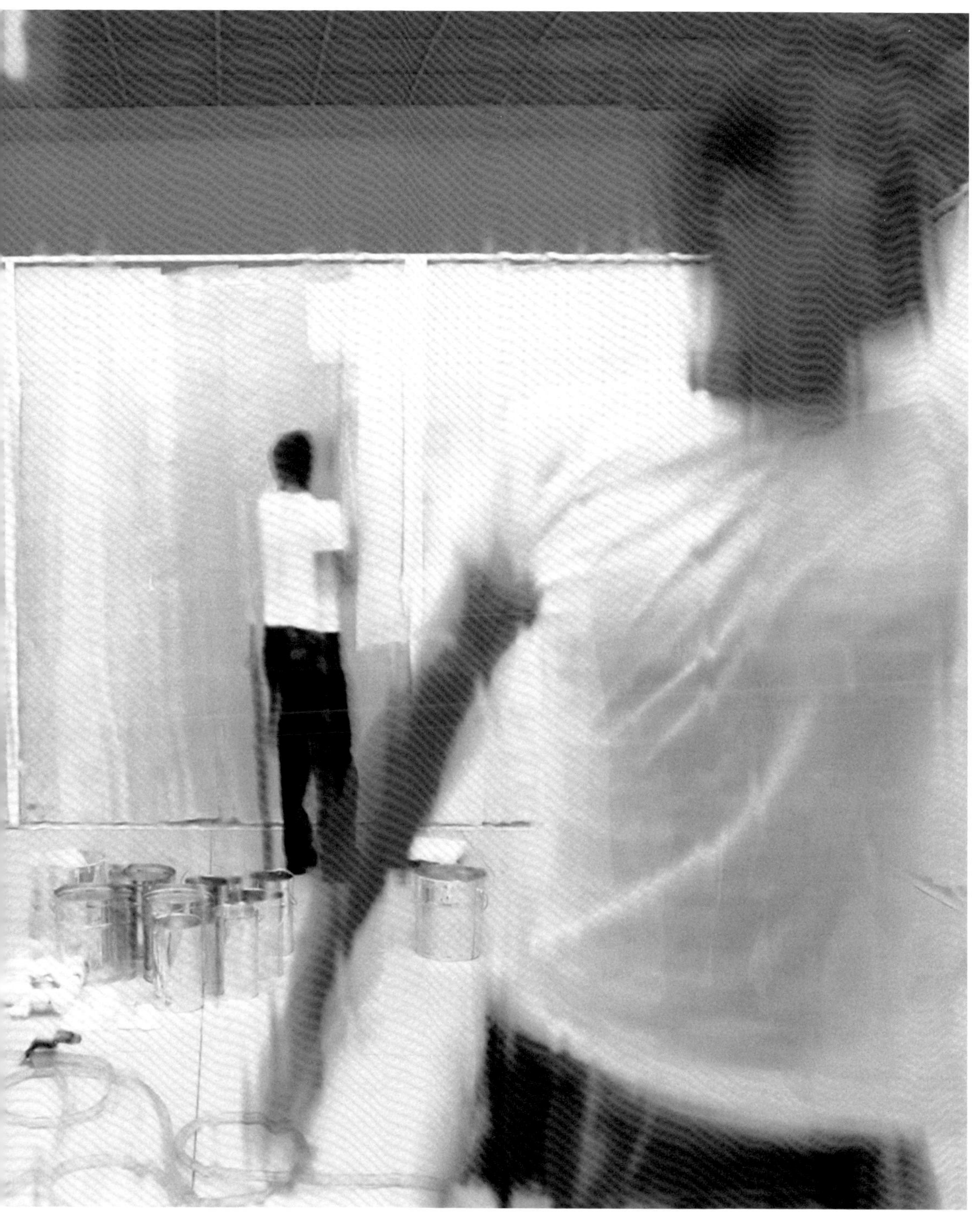

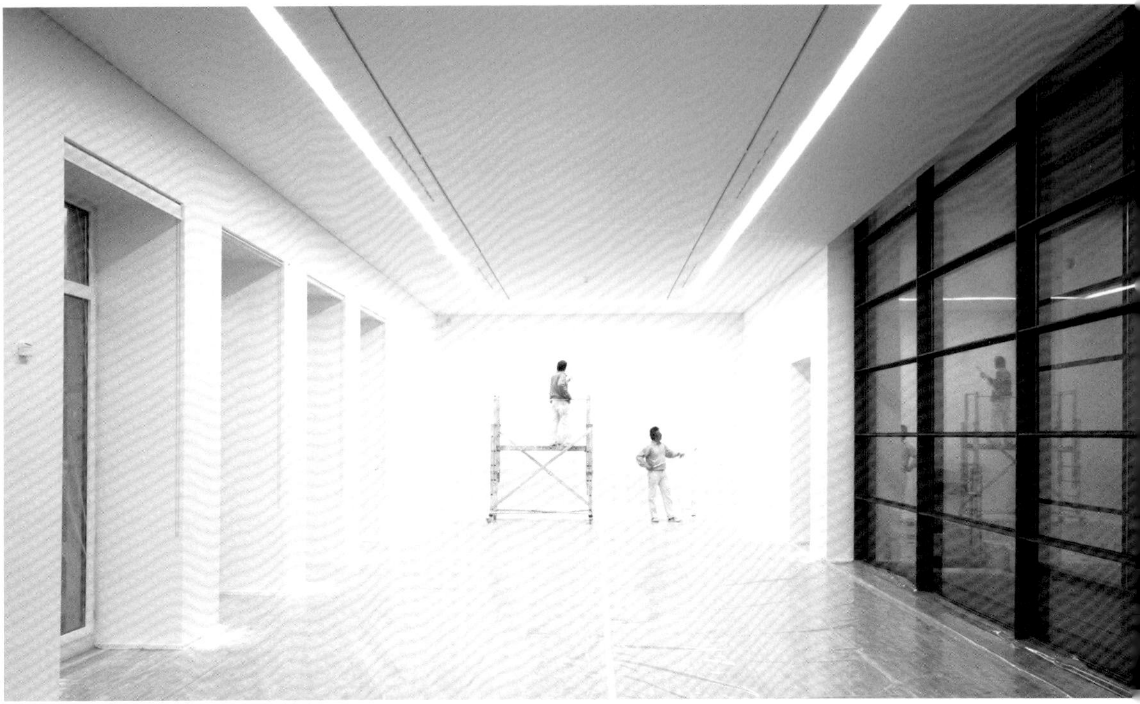

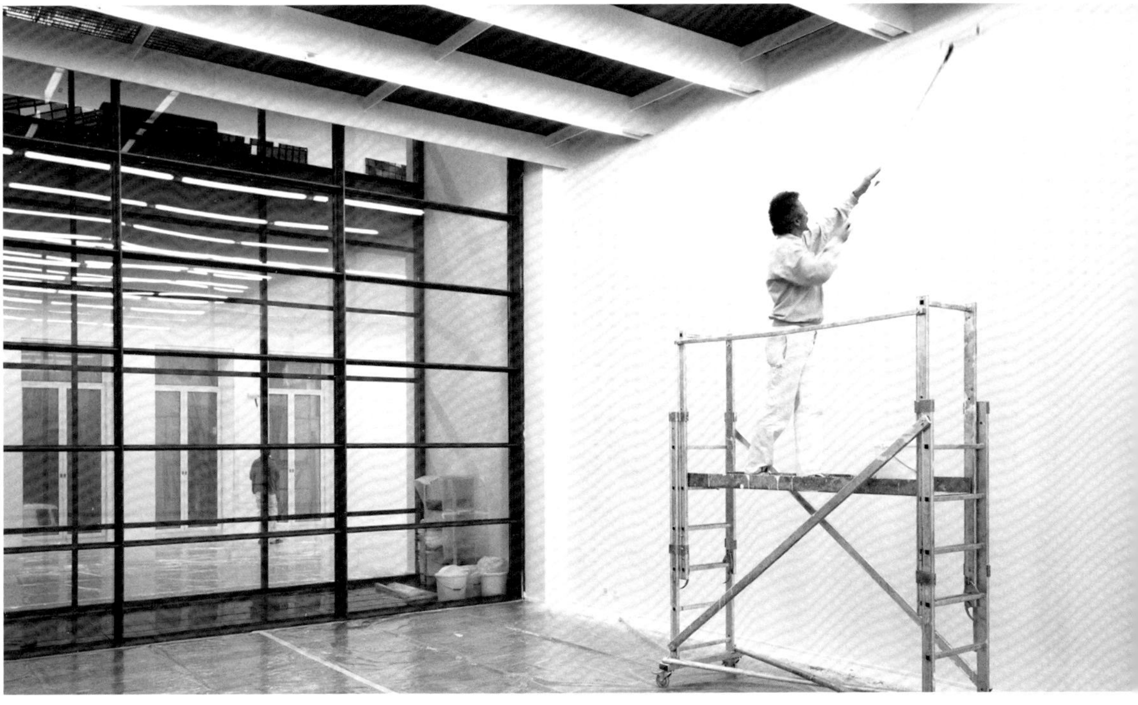

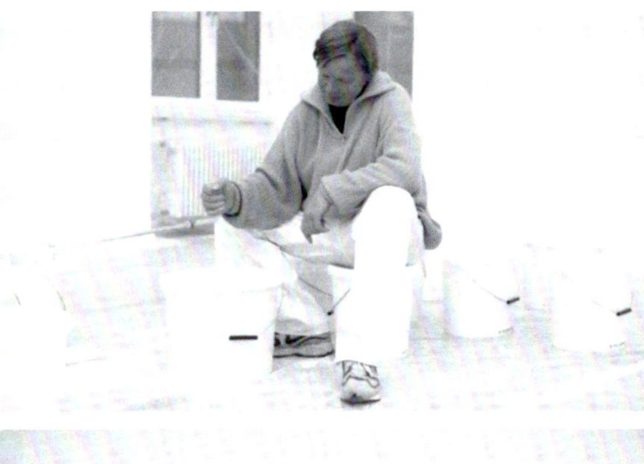

MATERIALS:	*white paint, painting utensils, cellophane floor-covering, mobile scaffolding*
PERFORMERS:	*two house painters*
CLOTHING:	*their own work outfits*
DIMENSIONS:	*site-specific project (the ground floor of the Galerie für Zeitgenössische Kunst is approximately 525 m²)*
DURATION:	*the entire exhibition period (seven weeks)*
EXHIBITED AT:	*Galerie für Zeitgenössische Kunst, Leipzig, 2000*

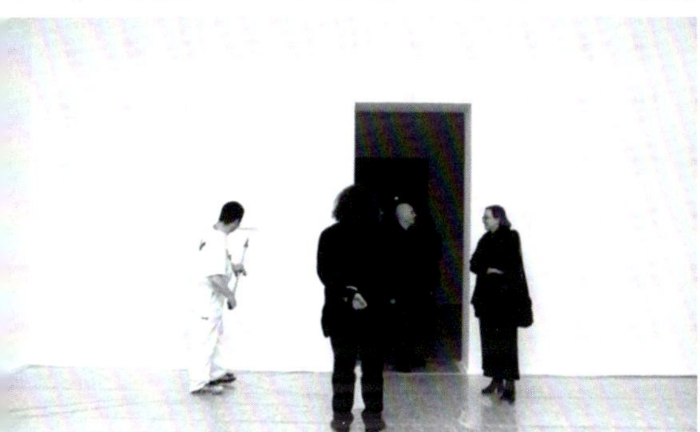

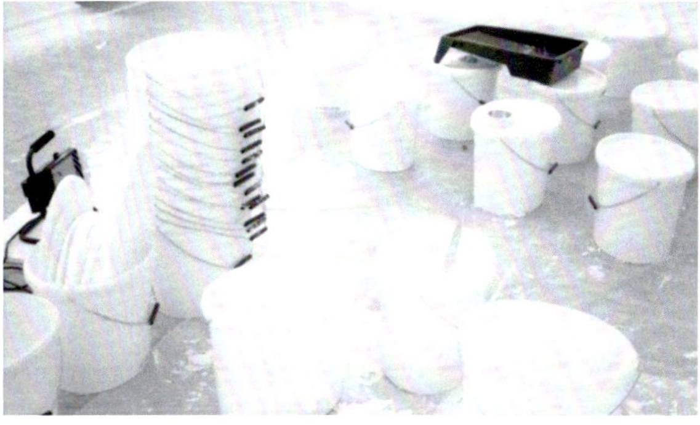

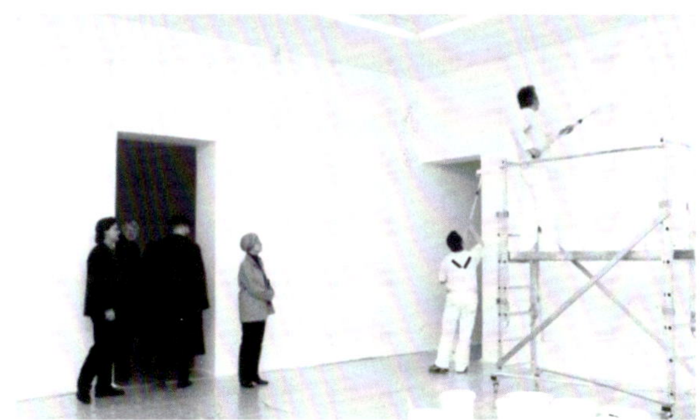

WISCHEN ANDEREN EREIGNISSEN (BETWEEN OTHER EVENTS) 000

urational performance with two unemployed housepaint-rs painting the already white walls of the gallery space ith 35 layers of white paint throughout the duration of the 1ow. A renovation of the exhibition space was necessary af-rwards (the seven weeks of painting added 1 centimeter of epth to the walls).

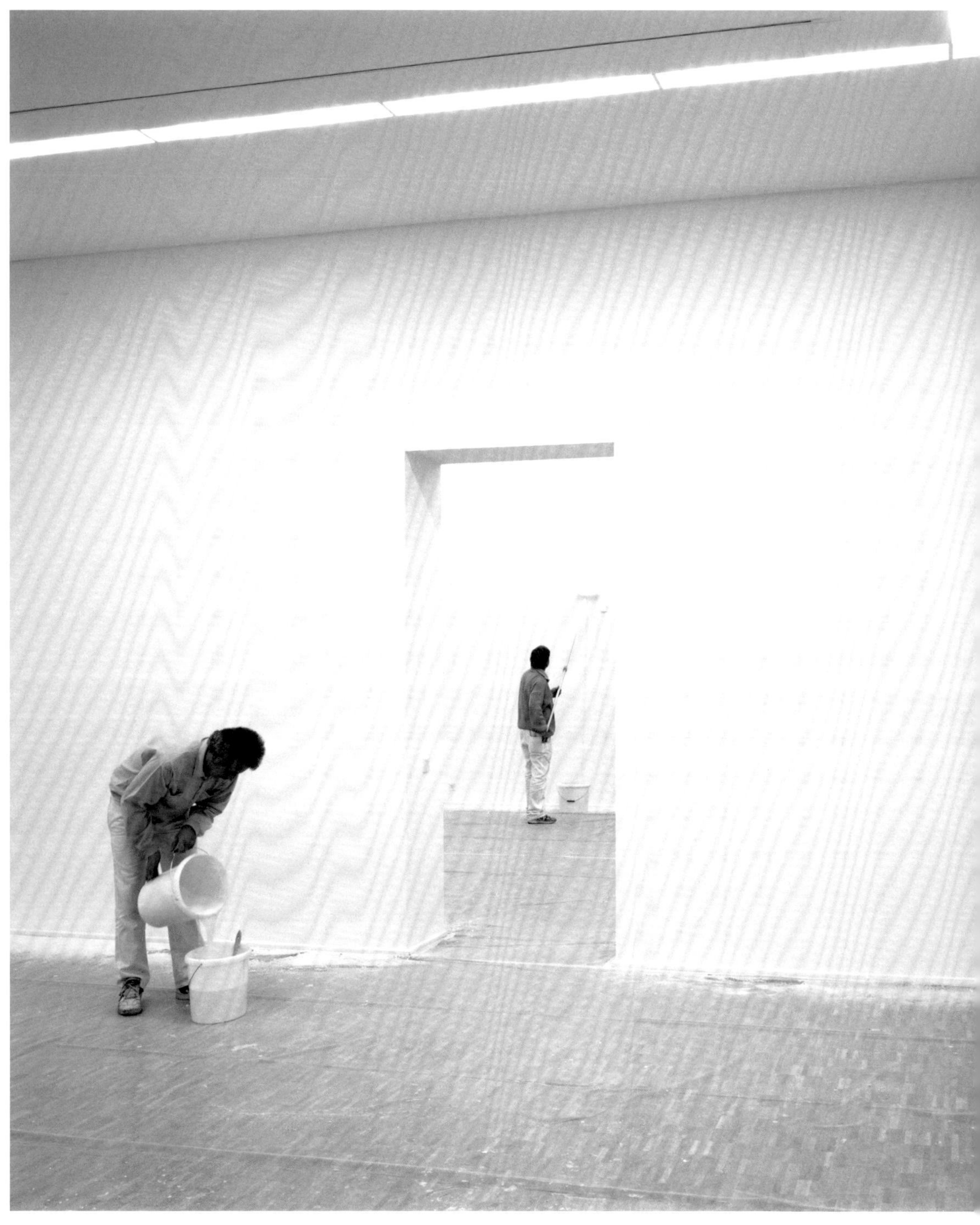

The Cure of the Cube

BY LARS BANG LARSEN

With reference to established co-ordinates, in-betweenness is to be conceived as a continual reorganization (which has its own built-in distances). As the Brazilian artist Lygia Clark wrote:

> I often wake up at my bedroom window seeking the outside space as if it were the "inside." I am afraid of space—but I rebuild myself from it... I am the before and the after, I am the future in the present. I am the inside and the outside, the face and the reverse.

—

Just as there is social and spatial alienation in trying to locate authenticity in space, there are innumerable intimate alienations in the protracted search for an affirmation of the individual body.

—

Henri Michaux wrote in *Passages* (1963) that the arts resign themselves too much to their being constrained by the nature of objects and their belief in final stages. Ironically, now that the arts don't exclusively resign themselves to their material constraints and unfold in processes and temporal developments, ephemeral organizations are being called up by the market, and by other final stages just as conventional as the ones Michaux reacted against (rather than by complex notions of construction-destruction internal to the work, which are remembered and talked about, as in music).

—

The show *Zwischen anderen Ereignissen* was a white-out between exhibitions at the Galerie für Zeitgenössische Kunst Leipzig in February 2000. Two unemployed housepainters, Mr. Richter and Mr. Rothe, were commissioned to paint the white cube white, over and over again, for the duration of the show. ("How does it feel to be making art all day long?" a local reporter asked the two housepainters. "Good. It's a job like at any other construction site," said Richter.) It was an almost-exhibition, a precarious transition that asserted itself simultaneously as a cool and unseasonable event. The white cube calls for its own completion, it is a standing invitation: you can't see it empty.

—

Here it was turned into an "unsafe" frame, where the space between phenomenon and interpretation was predominantly social. *Zwischen anderen Ereignissen* was the blue hour of gallery routine—literally so, because the empty exhibition halls were exceptionally sensitive to changes in natural light. The walls may have been white, but they weren't toneless. In the first hall, the atmosphere was bluish from the light that fell from above through the galvanized network of a metal floor; in the three other halls, the early spring sun shone low and sharp on the plastic on the floor, reflecting flickering petroleum shades onto the walls.

—

The visual paucity of the "show" also established a certain reality loss on the flawed horizon of expectation, as if the retinal and the real were substitutions for each other: like in some absurd Chinese play, the photographer squatted before her gear on the plastic covering, while Richter painted away on the scaffolding, supported by Rothe. Or the event itself was an annoyingly deadpan answer to the demands of conventionally productive organizations: "What on Earth are you doing?" "We are painting." "But is that supposed to be art?" "Oh yes, we paint." The white cube was painted white, and performance art became phlegmatic.

—

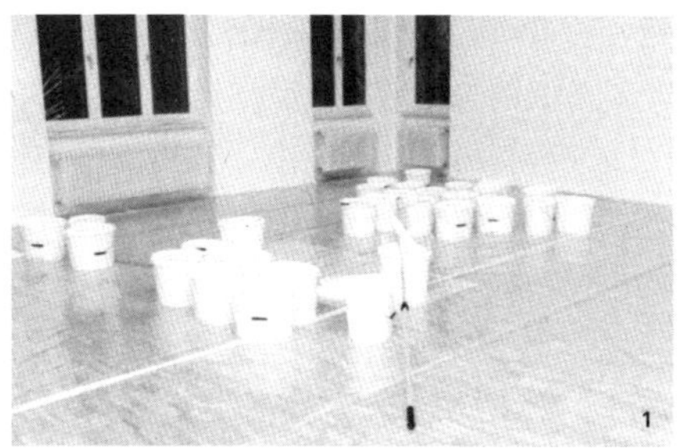

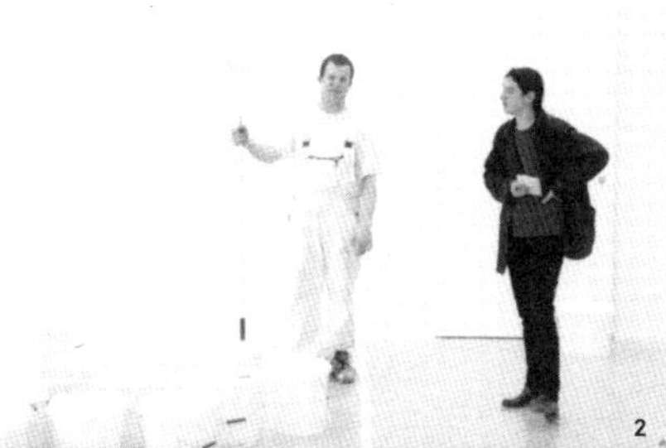

In a sense the intermission merely stated, with the neutrality of an eight-hour working day: it paints. The inadmissible "absence" in the gallery also colored the professional but disturbing, would-be invisible activity of Richter and Rothe, and the artists' behind-the-scenes ghostliness.

—

Still, the show naturally wasn't non-productive (although it raised an un-produced territory, a zombie-space). What does it mean to produce an intermission? It is to give the finger to those who believe if not in meaning proper, then in the rapid turnover of its concrete abstractions, such as money. With regard to art's narrower economy and ecology, producing an intermission is to not create a visual spectacle. It is to set up a blank screen for a backwards projection of all the stuff weighing on our retinas; because looking at art otherwise tends to be a packed scenario (of doubles and little inner movements) with adamant use-by dates. In this sense, this level of producing-by-not-creating is meant for us to identify who are in on the art flow—we who have seen the spectacles. But more than that, displacing activity and inactivity, production-disguised-as-cancellation, or coupling the concrete and the metaphorical acts as production, asks what is required for identification. No job, no money: all right, here are jobs and money for seven weeks. As real as they come, for as long as they last.

—

Fig. 1 _ Exhibition view, *Zwischen anderen Ereignissen*, 2000, Galerie für Zeitgenössische Kunst, Leipzig.
Fig. 2 _ A visitor with one of the painters.

Zwischen anderen Ereignissen was told via repetition and uneventful differences: if you visited the gallery twice, the same activity would be taking place, only Richter and Rothe and their scaffolding would find themselves somewhere else in the gallery. Their elusive trail prepared an invocation of the extremes of the white cube's architectural affiliations—white as a saint and dark as a predator, for one thing—and channelled them into new mundane processes, resonating between other events (and not only those of the Galerie für Zeitgenössische Kunst).

—

All of Leipzig has been renovated, polished. The fashion boutiques offer last year's collections to a population with soaring unemployment rates. The logic, rationality and hygiene of the East's homecoming to the West, and its dolled up completion are reflected in Elmgreen & Dragset's interregnum, where each new stroke of whitewash became doubly significant: one for the white cube, one for the city...

—

In fact, during the course of the exhibition the white cube became so white that it acquired physical bulk: seven weeks of paint applications added a depth to each wall that subsequently had to be ground down. Which goes to show that not only are there limits to how many times you can paint a wall; but also the repeated inscription of the white cube's message on its own walls demanded a counterstroke, a direct reduction, determined as an equivalent response. Paint it up; grind it down. Too much fondling and maintenance isn't expected in a place tradition has primed for resistance and transgression.

—

The period of rest between shows was thus briefly signified by the imperceptible growth of the gallery's thin supports, by the contraction of space, as if time had become viscous and deposited its monumentality on the walls. If affirmation of surfaces is what you want, then here you are. In this way, at the same time as it shrunk, the gallery space *Zwischen anderen Ereignissen* produced an unsheathing of the white cube vis-à-vis the surrounding city and its local specificity.

—

The white cube as an inverted emblem of Modernist (over-)determination, and the new relationship to the real and to the thermal body that this inversion pointed to, reminded me of an apocryphal anecdote about a polar explorer who, during a fierce snow storm, was forced to erect an impromptu igloo, barely any larger than his own frame. Lying on the floor, the air he exhaled with each breath formed another thin layer of ice on the igloo's inner walls, gradually threatening to immobilize him. His sad predicament was that if he didn't breathe, he wouldn't live; if he breathed, he couldn't move. In *Zwischen anderen Ereignissen*, suspicion of the claustrophobia of high culture was confirmed, while the wobbly qualities of the real pressed down through accumulated layers of white paint. This is the paradox of contemporary art, and of our desire for it: without the white cube as a real or metaphorical frame, you have no space; with it, you have an institutional affiliation that, for better or worse, is restrictive. In fact, all the whiteness may not have been something added from the outside, but the secretion of the white cube's formal properties, like a bleeding saint. As always, miraculous presences like that confirm the limits of human agency. Who produces whom? Was *Zwischen anderen Ereignissen* ultimately all of us getting white cubed?

—

The obsessive paint job was an abstract proxy for anonymity and boredom, acknowledging that violence is sometimes a symptom of the need to create sites of enunciation for yourself in places that don't acknowledge you. Its blank surfaces were the perfect backdrop for activity, just about any kind of activity. We can speculate that the effort of renovation pre-emptively takes place against malicious damage, vandalism—the negative imprints of self-sufficient spatial hegemonies, a slow process of entropy that echoes the conformity that follows social welfare and signifies the brutalizing of all its good

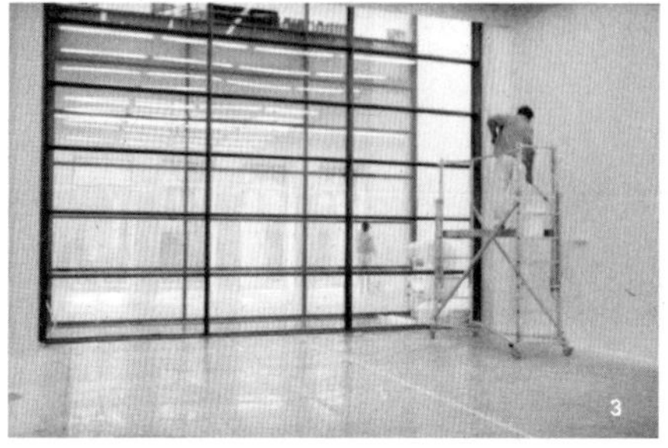

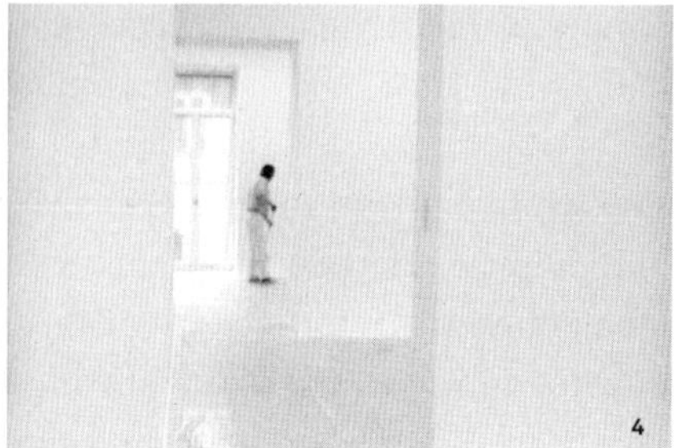

intentions. Violence is the extreme transformation of an object, a stab at the wish for liberation. Space in Elmgreen & Dragset's work doesn't announce itself, it has to be brought out, challenged by the mundane presence of the activities that frame it; it asks you to perform. Rather: it makes you perform, because it analogizes several types of behavior. Violence is inherent in walking the wrong way down a one-way street, and in spasms of libidinal activity; just as violence was an integral part of Modernist architecture's effective and ideological denigration of negative space. Henri Lefebvre wrote about this in *The Production of Space* (1999):

> There is a violence intrinsic to abstraction, and to abstraction's practical (social) use. Abstraction passes for an "absence"—as distinct from the concrete "presence" of objects, of things. Nothing could be more false. For abstraction's modus operandi is devastation, destruction (even if such destruction may sometimes herald creation).

—

By establishing social space as the active and fickle inner logic of abstraction, the Modernist rationale is turned back on itself in a deconstruction of abstraction that points towards the reassembling of social forces.

—

Fig. 3 _ Painter in action.

Fig. 4 _ White on white: a view through a doorway in the Galerie für Zeitgenössische Kunst.

In other works, Elmgreen & Dragset have launched critiques of statistically dominant sexual ideologies. These critiques have been performed in what you might term interactive works, environments and performances, where everyday, concrete activity is solicited or commented on; as well as in deconstructions of recent art history from a gay point of view.

—

Gay culture has traditionally been forced to convert settings reserved for other purposes—toilets, parks—into intimate spaces; and Elmgreen & Dragset go with and against this grain of gay culture. While some of their architectures—between social functions—solicit "illegitimate" types of behavior, others perform allegorical crackdowns on the functionality of queer coding. Queer space is being queered; the codes and routines that hold it together as a cultural arrangement are being worn thin. This is in keeping with a process that implicitly questions what can be particularly "gay" about any representation, when gay culture has gained relative access to the mainstream. Finding yourself in these displaced ambiences is to feel the pull of your identity, irrespective of your, in this sense, being "inside" or "outside," of whether you are the face or the reverse. Again, *Zwischen anderen Ereignissen* didn't produce transgression as such: seen from the perspective of Elmgreen & Dragset's sexually-oriented work, it was an intermission that ideally tried to hollow out the iceberg of any convention.

—

Space is fucked up because function is fucked up. "What are you about?" the works seem to ask. "What are you hung up on?" On the one hand, there is the suggestion of a fading "we" that refers to the loneliness of violently separated identities; on the other hand, the sense of a failure to condense things into any kind of productive logic that can speak for the coherence and relevance of group identity. The banal and disruptive process of "maintenance" in *Zwischen anderen Ereignissen* de-exalted conventional flows of production and relied instead on an in-betweenness, a down-spacing, a counter-coding of human activities. You could say that this took place with the aim of prefiguring a more individual subjectivity (the stepping stone to, or pre-figuration of a new group identity?). As Félix Guattari wrote in *Soft Subversions*:

> Even though its enunciation is individuated, there is nothing less individual than capitalist subjectivity. The over-coding by Capital of human activities, thoughts, and feelings makes all particularized modes of subjectivation equivalent and resonant with each other.

—

Elmgreen & Dragset work with and belabor space in its multiple meanings—as architectural space, mental space, private space, sexual space, art space, public space—simultaneously domesticated and alienated in their displacements, repetitions and overlaps. Identities and intensities flicker and are gone, to appear elsewhere. As soon as you acknowledge that something is fundamentally wrong in the social body you are born into and the history you have grown up with, and your ability to interpret this wrong has no fixed locus, the conclusion of a stance that includes not just elaborated positions, but also new places for the subject, is that everything is connected to everything else like a cycle, with no beginning or end and no fixed insides or outsides. This, then, offers the possibility of intervening on the level of every plateau, every given surface in the world; however, it does not guarantee any master narratives for unifying flows with the purpose of conversion or radical alternation, but you may be able to split parts of the dominant flows by squeezing in.

—

While knowing that the double bound activity does not necessarily step outside any established order, *Zwischen anderen Ereignissen* argues that doing less is more, when staging the disjunctions between artistic process and mental and social space and the invisible relations of production that are harbored here, in-between. ———

This text was previously published in
Zwischen anderen Ereignissen, exh. cat. (Leipzig: Galerie für Zeitgenössische Kunst, 2000).

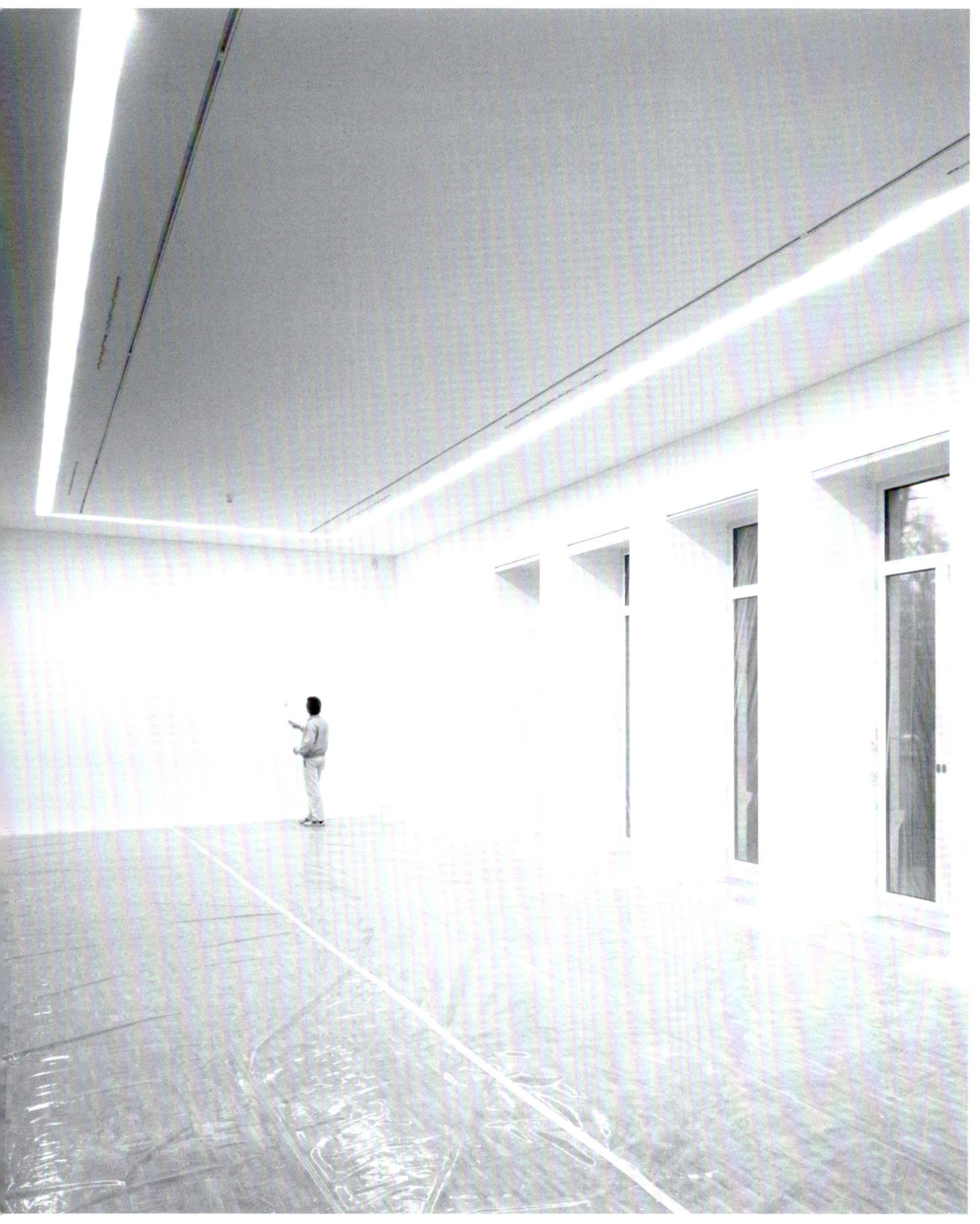

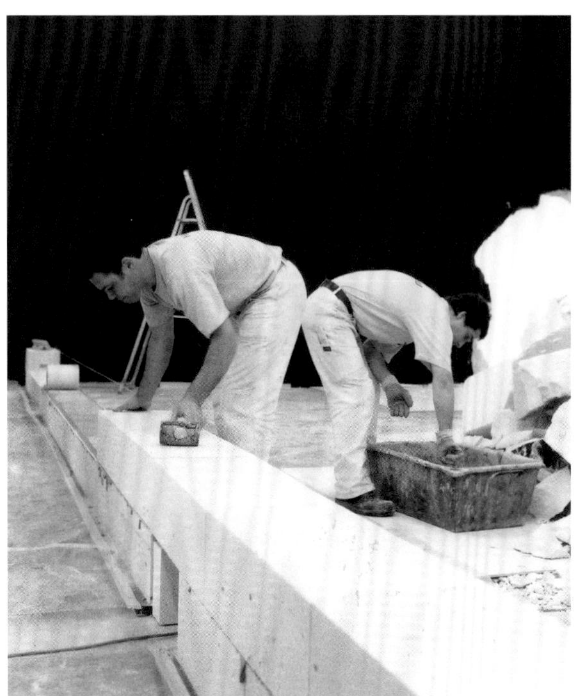

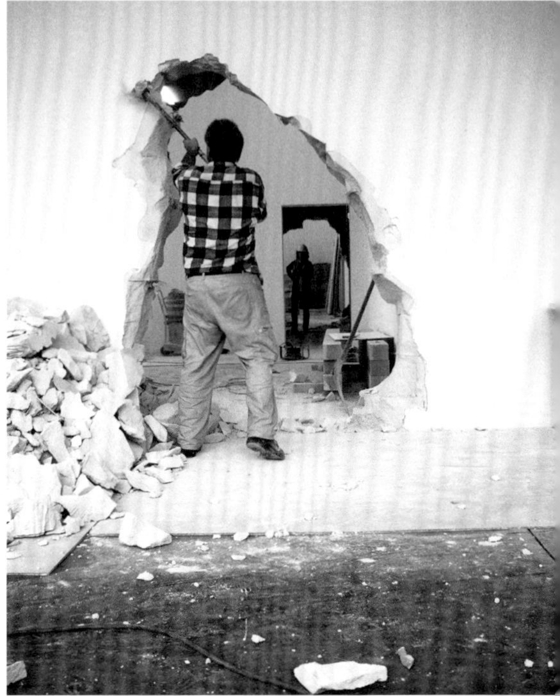

TAKING PLACE
2001 - 2002

The forthcoming renovation of the Kunsthalle Zürich was appropriated by the artists, publicly exposing the demolition and rebuilding process of both the exhibition spaces and non-public offices throughout the duration of the show. In dialogue with the director of the Kunsthalle and the initial architects of the space, a new configuration of the spaces was planned. This new plan included a social gathering point at the entrance, a library accessible to the public, moving offices to the front, and changing the general movement of the audience throughout the institution. The reconstruction took place only when the museum was open and was completed on the last day of the ten-week exhibition, when the electrician put the last bulb in its socket. By nature (of renovation), this performative exhibition became increasingly minimal with each passing week. Photo documentation exists as a separate work, in an edition of 5 + 2.

MATERIALS:	*demolition and construction materials*
PERFORMERS:	*construction crew*
CLOTHING:	*their own work outfits*
DIMENSIONS:	*site-specific project (the Kunsthalle Zürich is approximately 1000 m²)*
DURATION:	*the entire exhibition period (ten weeks)*
EXHIBITED AT:	*Kunsthalle Zürich, 2001-2002*

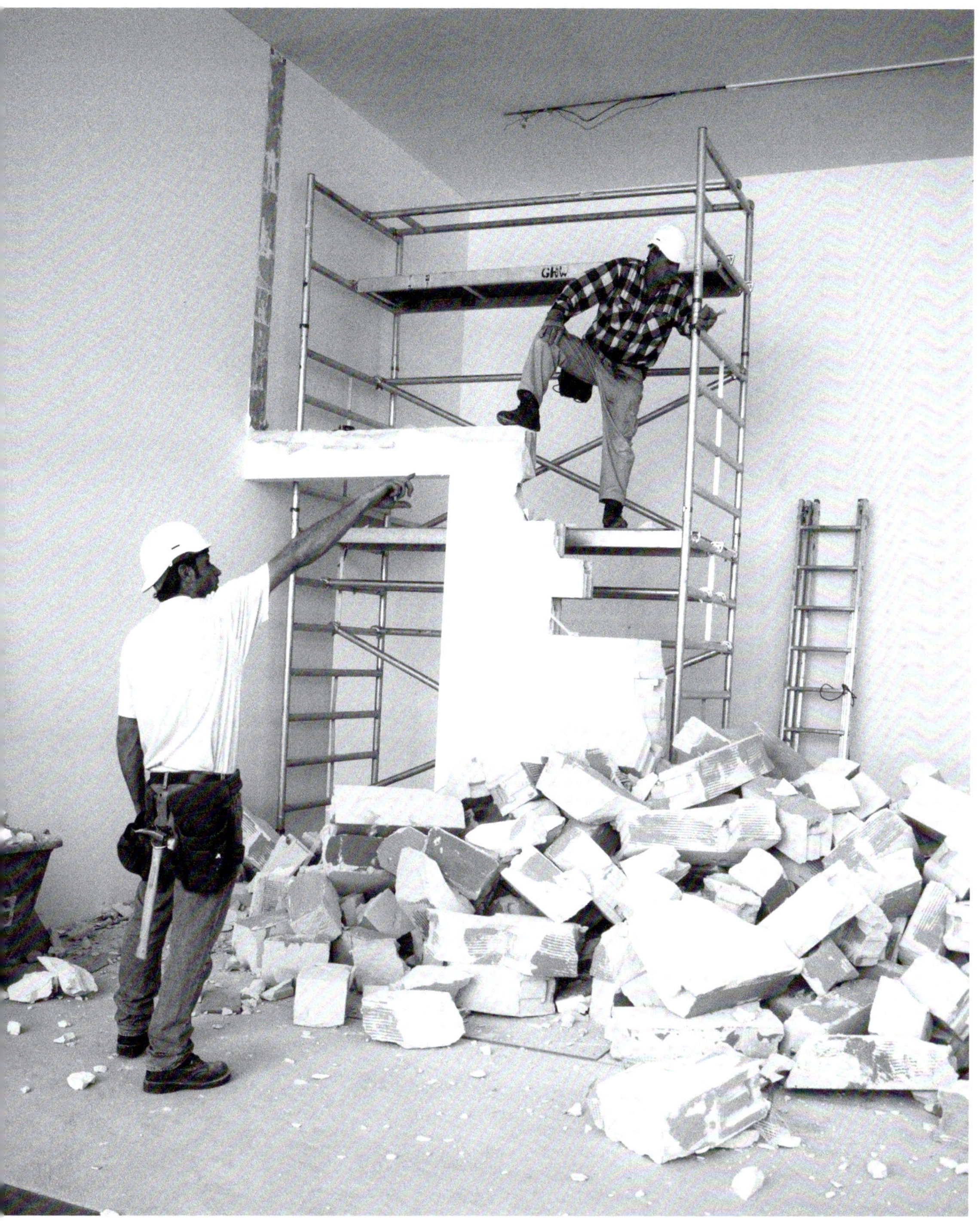

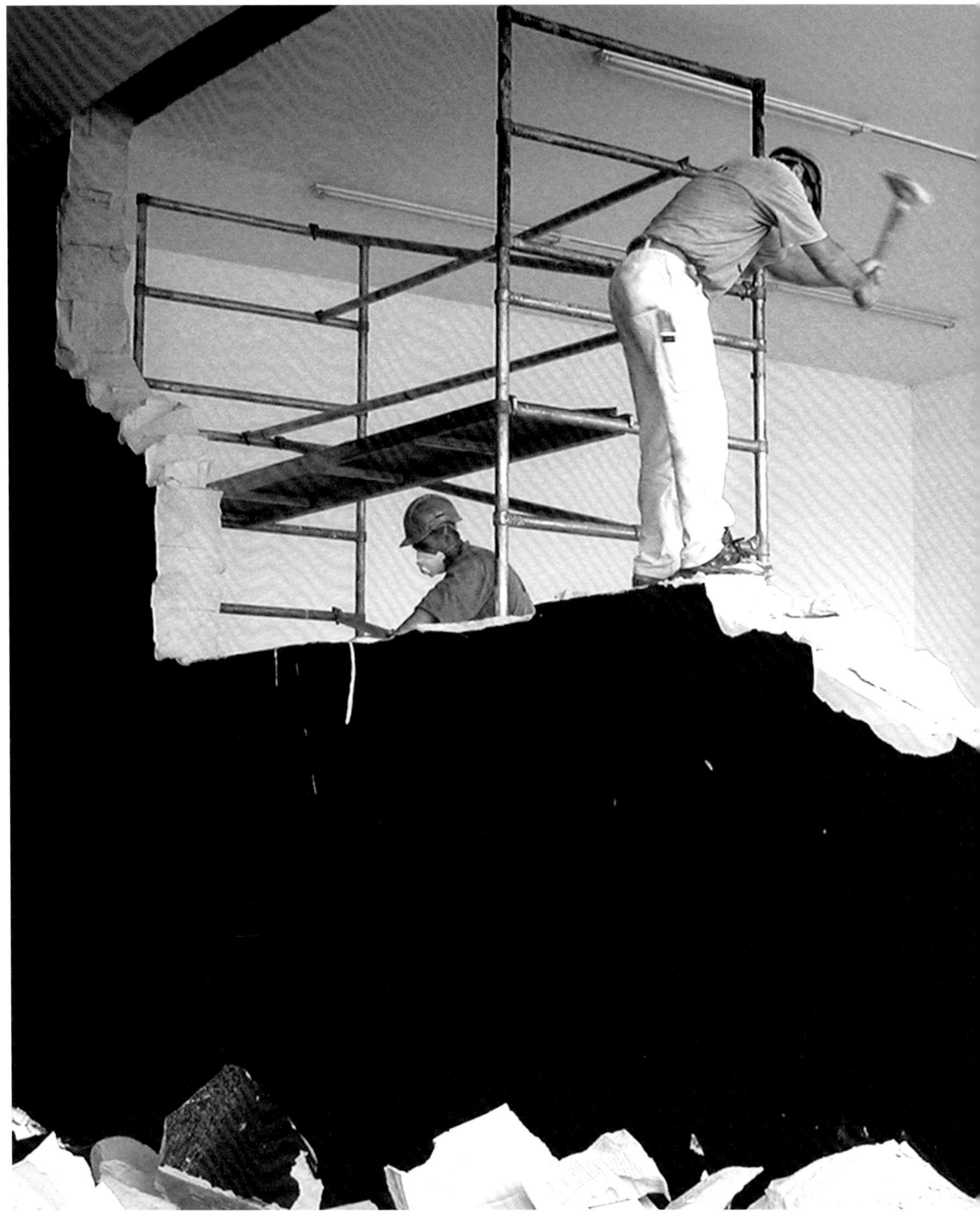

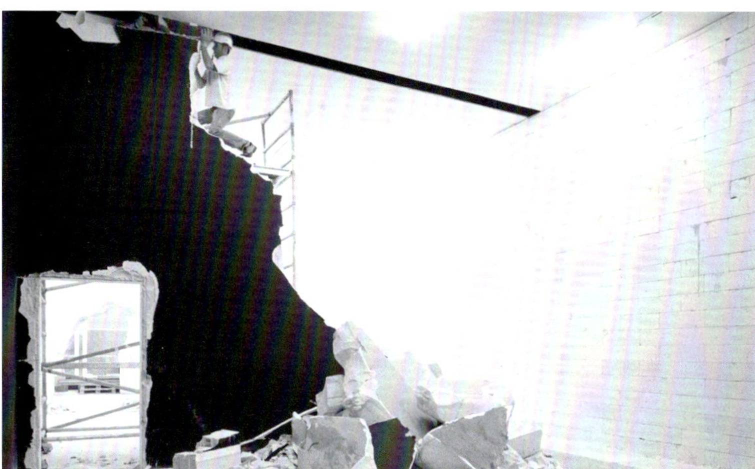

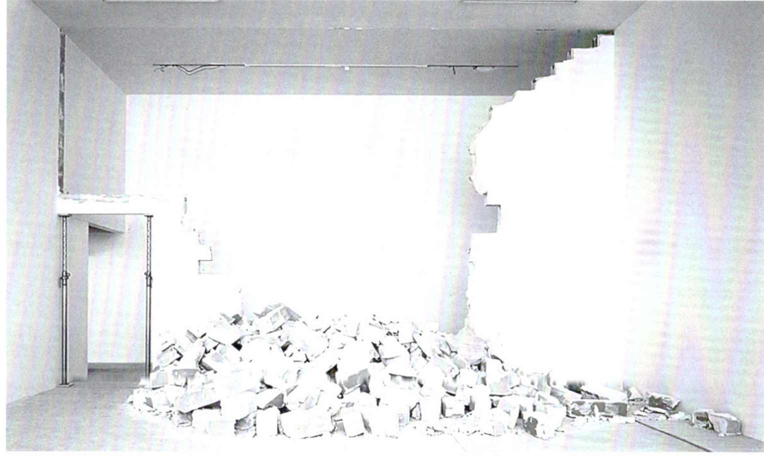

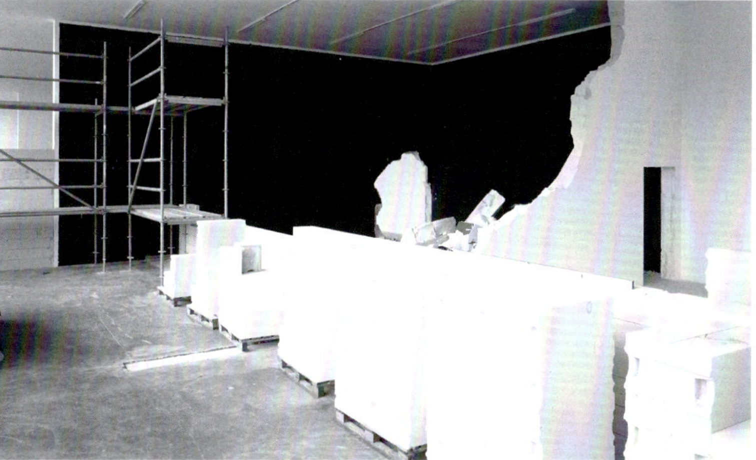

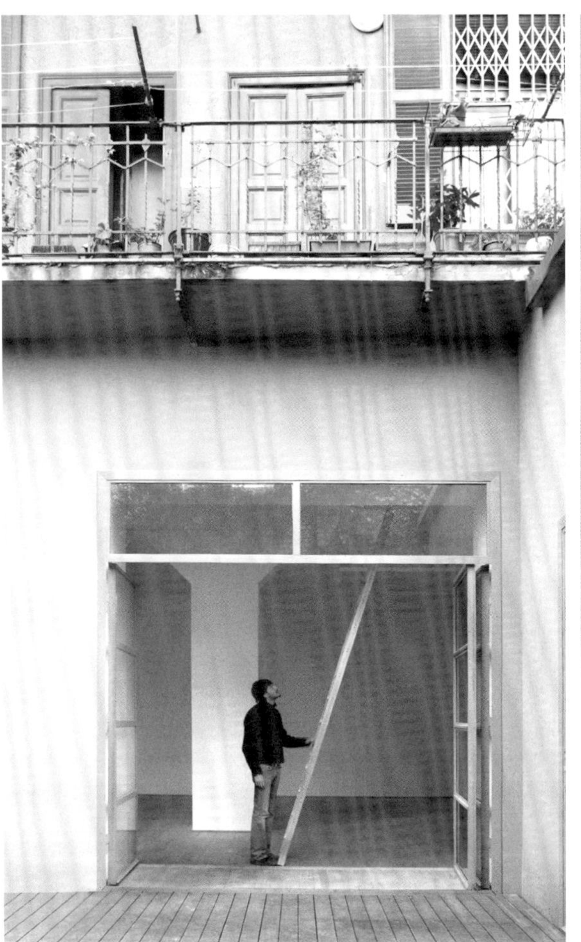

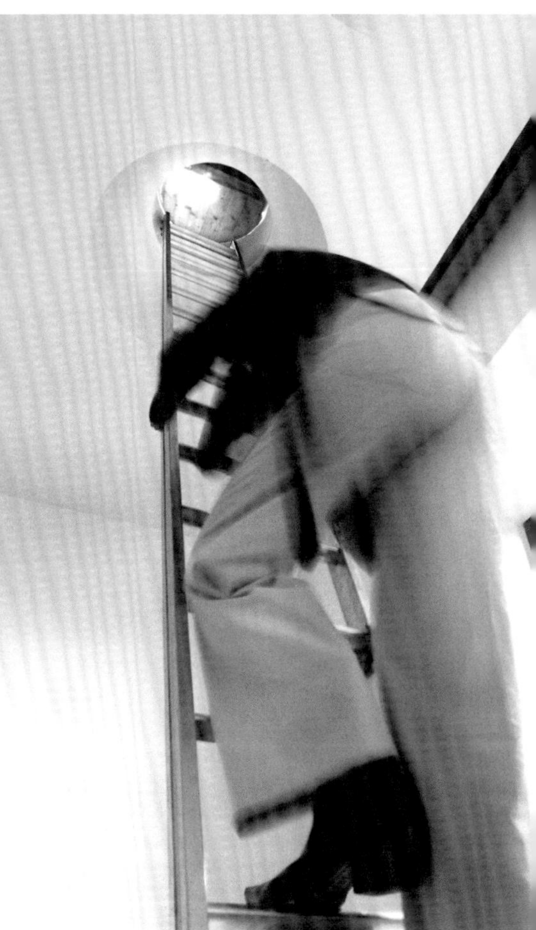

MATERIALS:	*aluminum ladder, plaster, wood, perspex dome*
PERFORMERS:	*can be debated: Mrs. Moxedano living above the gallery or the audience climbing the ladder peering into her apartment*
DIMENSIONS:	*variable*
DURATION:	*the entire exhibition period (five weeks)*
EXHIBITED AT:	*Galleria Massimo De Carlo, Milan, 2002*

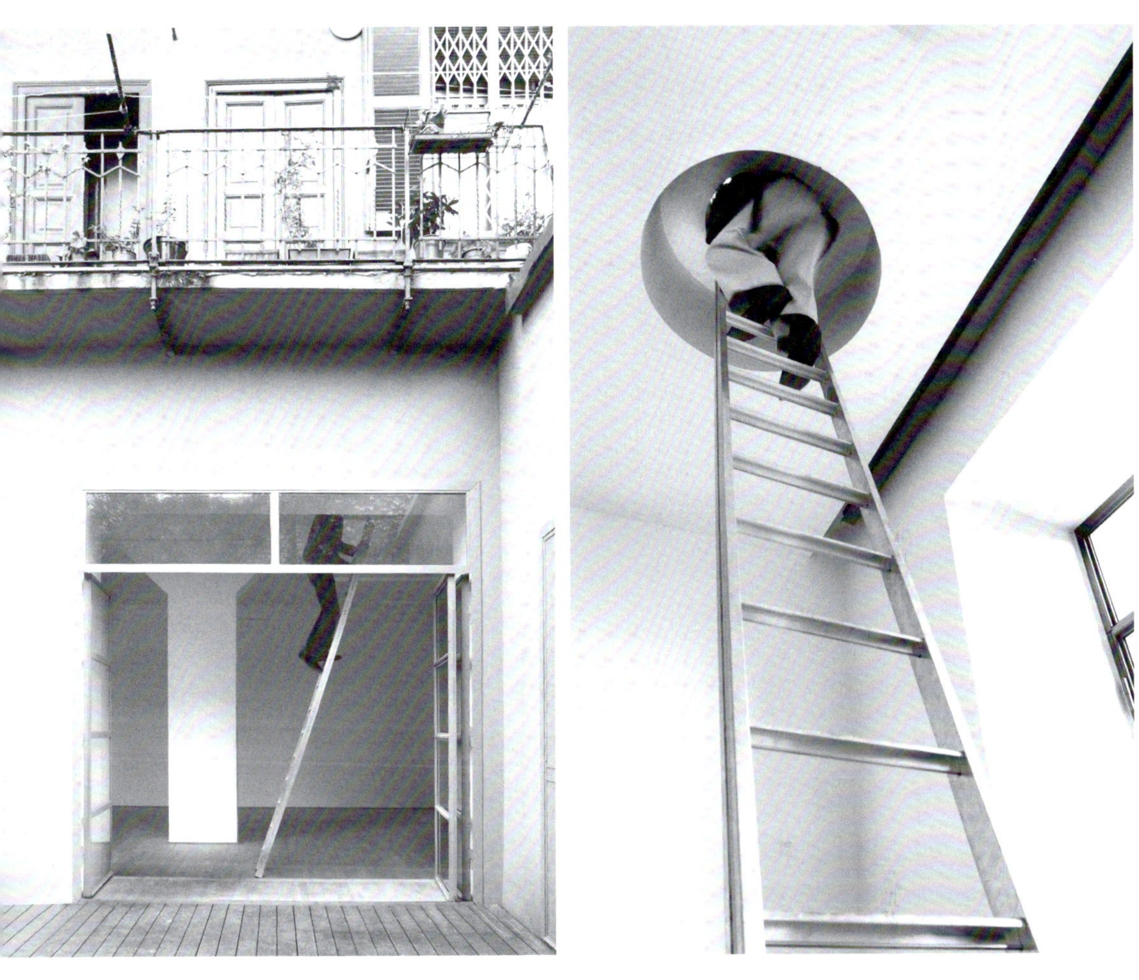

IOW ARE YOU TODAY?
'002

. hole drilled in the ceiling of the gallery opens it up into he existing apartment situated above. By climbing a ladler, visitors can watch the daily routines going on inside he private space through a transparent cupola. Prior to the xhibition, the woman living in the apartment had never isited the gallery.

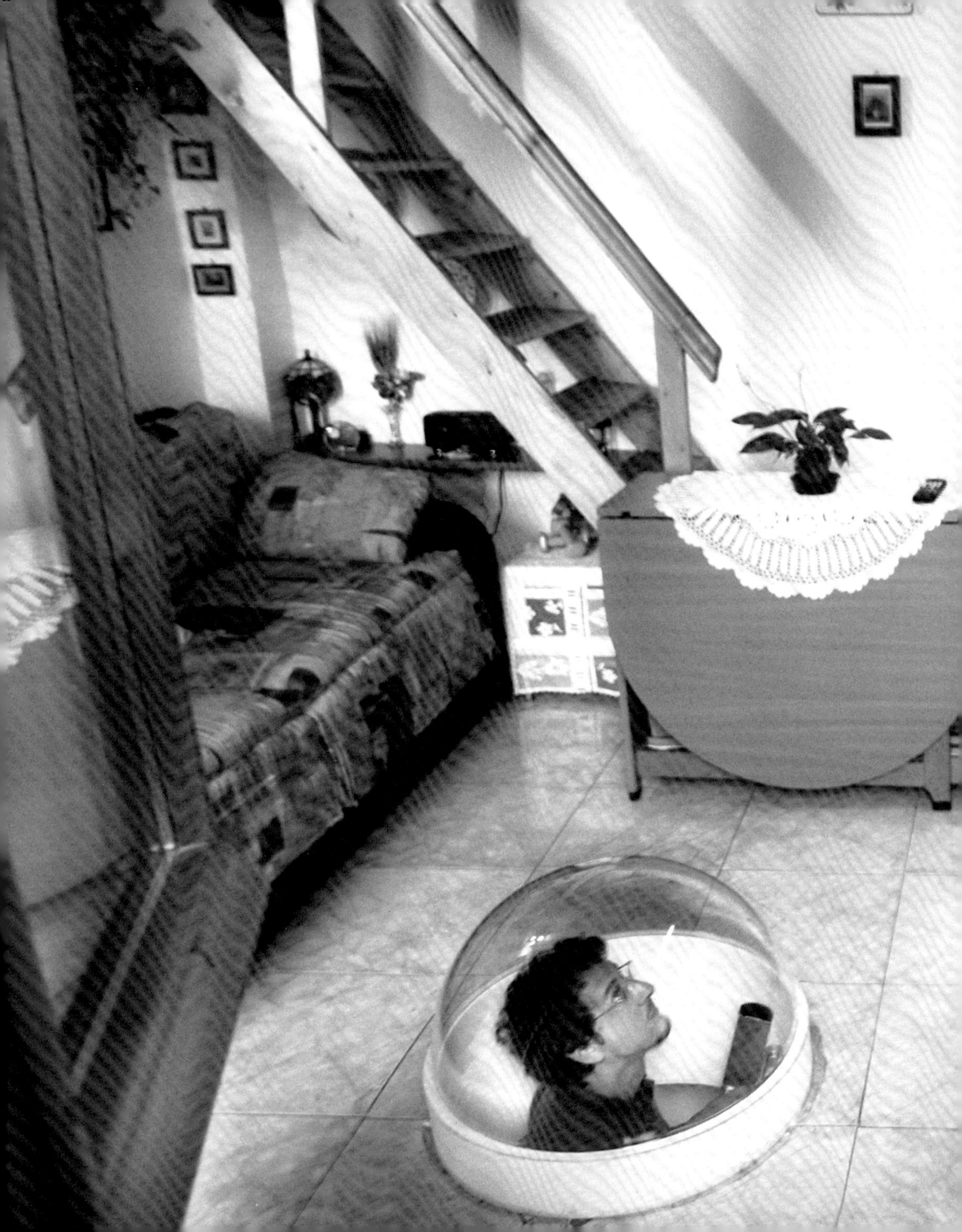

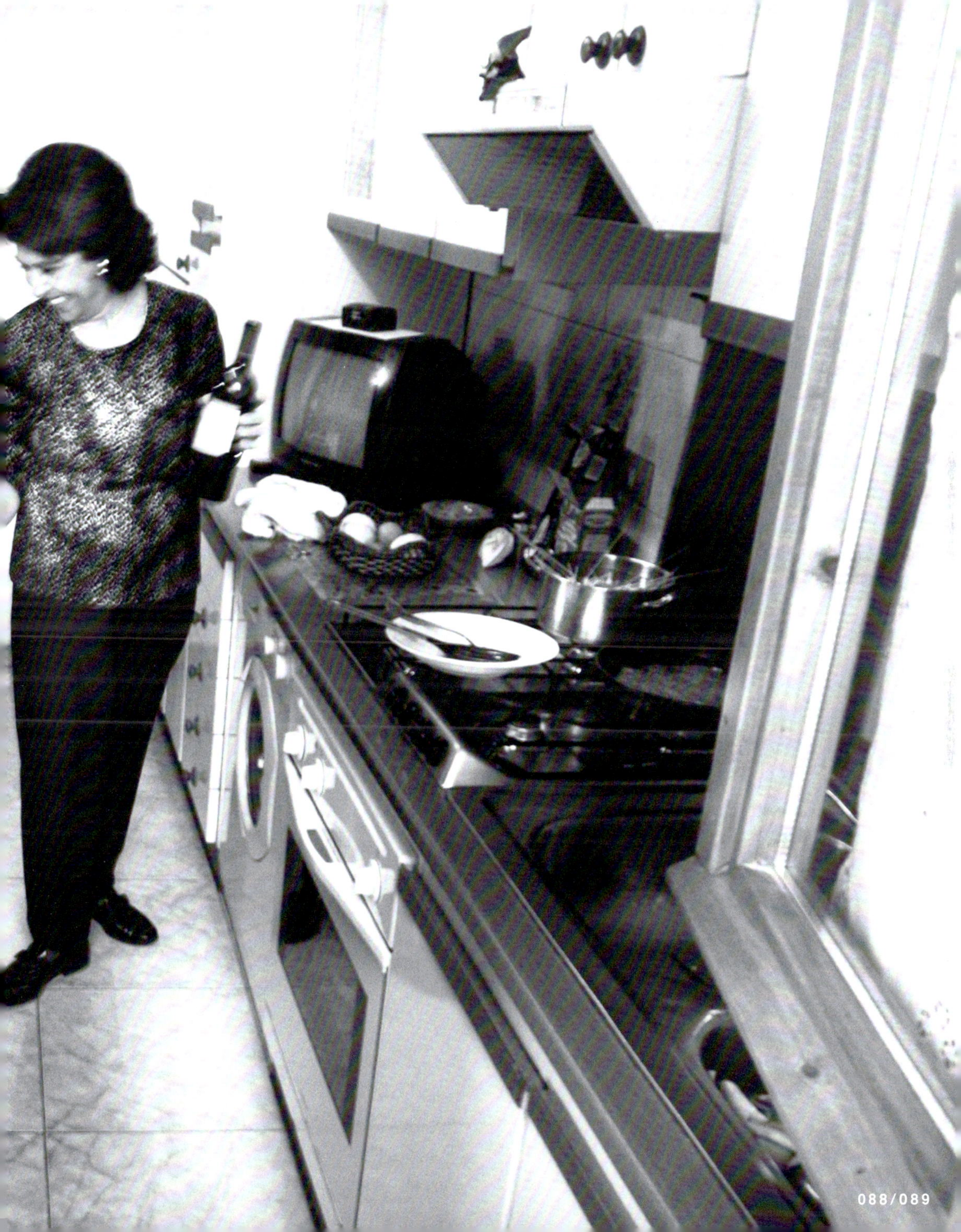

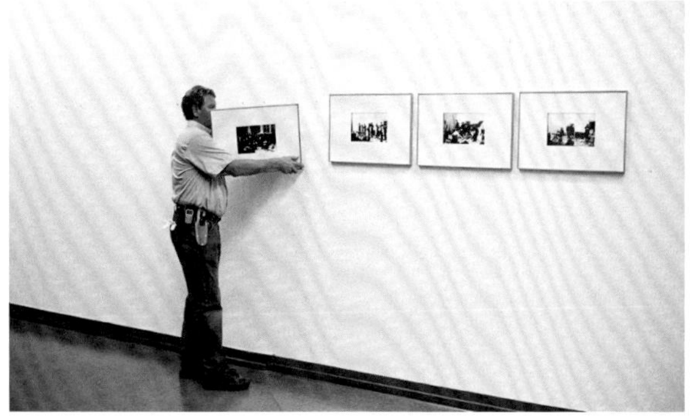

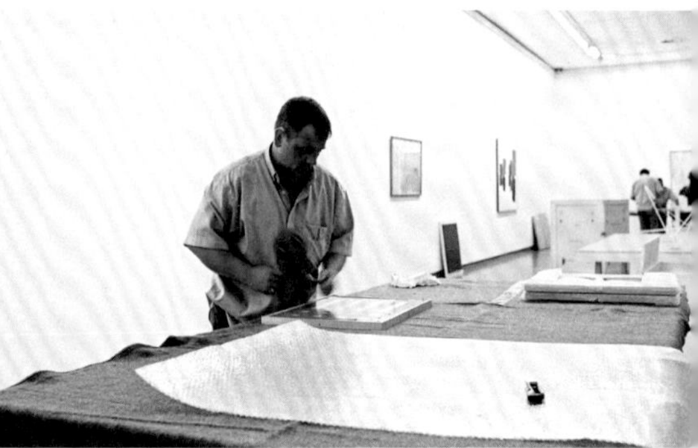

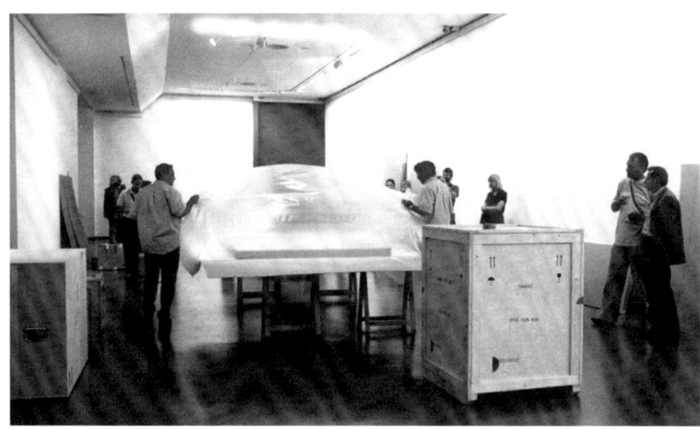

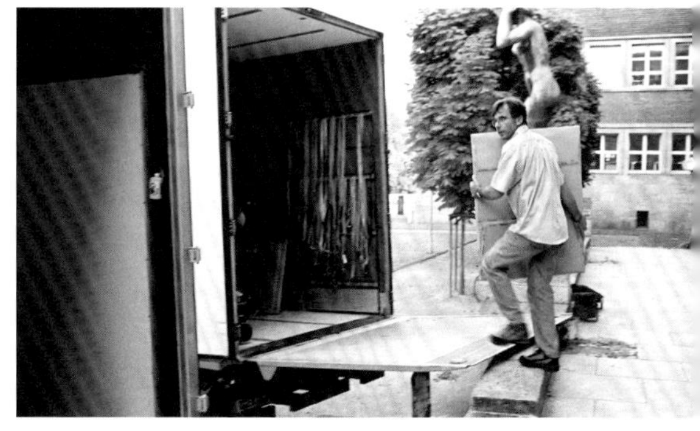

MATERIALS:	*Museum Kunstpalast collection, art crating supplies, trucks, installation tools*
PERFORMERS:	*professional art handlers*
CLOTHING:	*Knab Art Handling Company uniforms*
DIMENSIONS:	*site-specific*
DURATION:	*one day*
PERFORMED AT:	*"Spectacular: The Art of Action," Museum Kunstpalast, Düsseldorf, 2003*

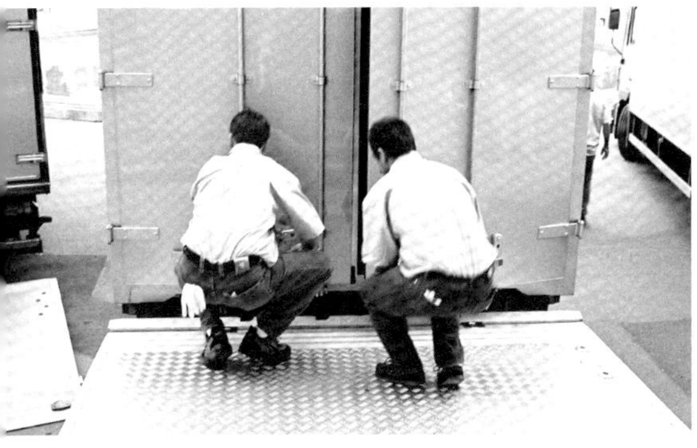

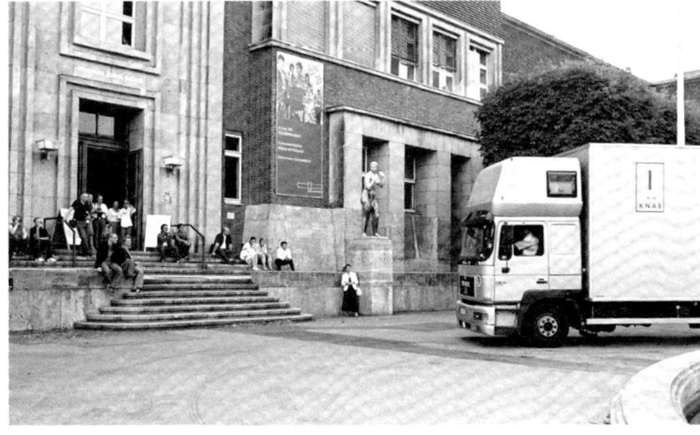

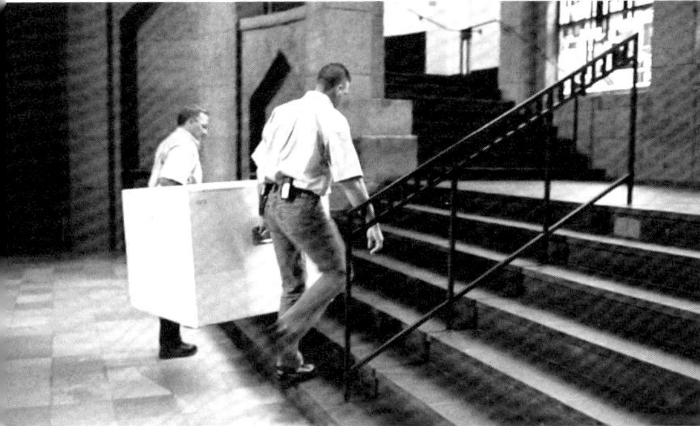

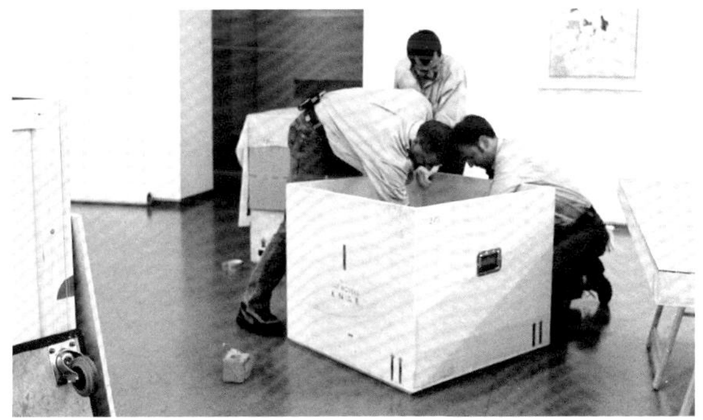

HE GREAT ESCAPE
003

—

erformance involving Knab Art Handling Company and art-orks on display at Düsseldorf's Museum Kunstpalast. The useum's collection was taken down, crated and loaded onto ucks by professional art handlers, driven around the block nd then re-installed later the same day. The audience could llow the process up close, and some chose to tail the trucks s they slowly drove around the block.

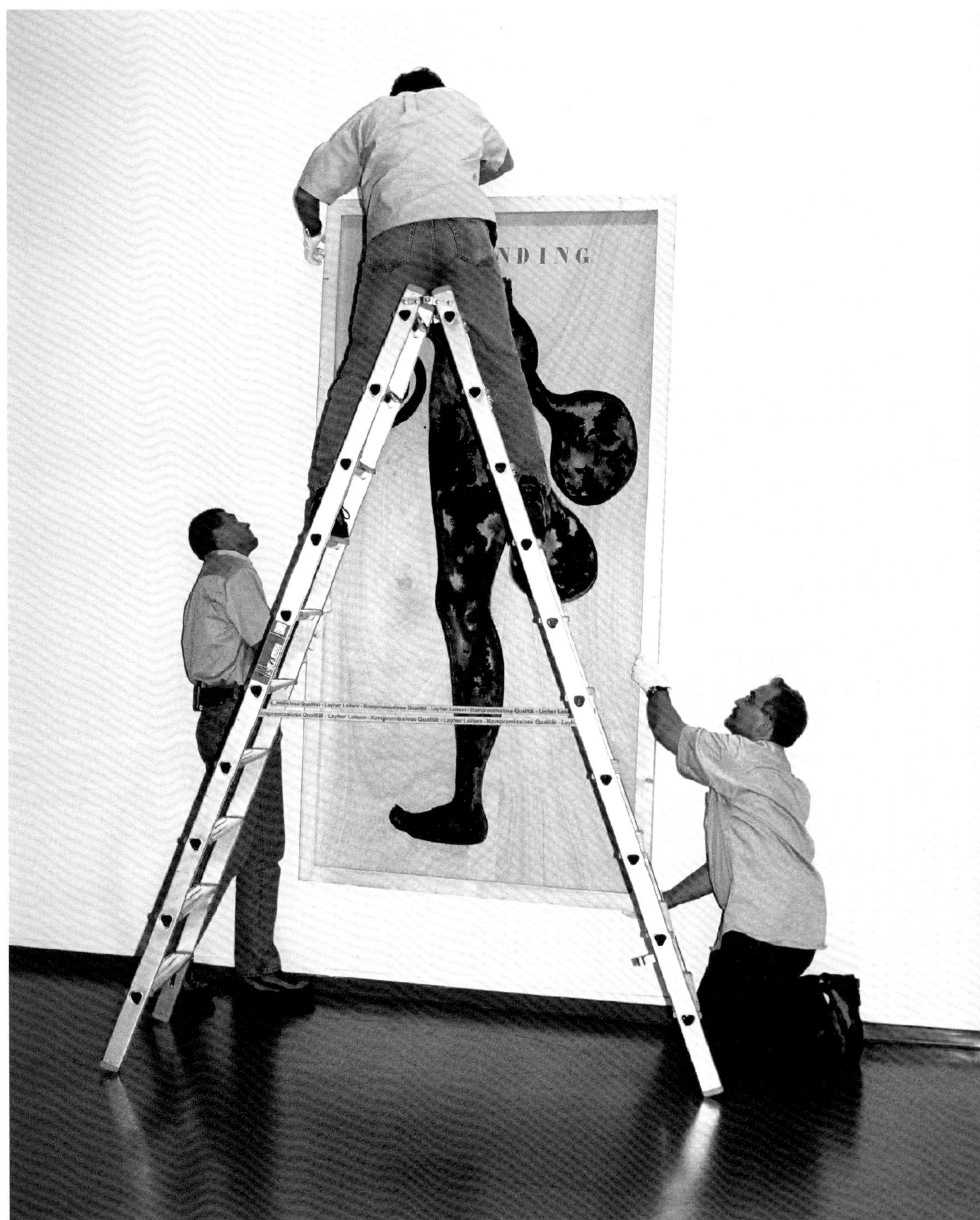
NDING
Layher Leitern - Kompromisslose Qualität - Layher Leitern - Kompromisslose Qualität

Escape Artists

BY JENS HOFFMANN

Escape artists, also known as escapologists, are performers who, in front of an audience, manage to escape from restraints or contraptions: everything from handcuffs, straightjackets, wooden boxes, or metal cages to oversize fish tanks, burning buildings, being buried alive, or any imaginative combination of these. The most famous of all escape artists was Harry Houdini, who at the turn of the 20th century turned escapology into both an art form and spectacular entertainment.

—

In 2003, Michael Elmgreen and Ingar Dragset were invited to participate in a program at the Museum Kunstpalast in Düsseldorf titled "Spectacular: The Art of Action," which set out to investigate the relationship between performance art and the art institution. The program, running over the course of a year, consisted of five parts, including a large number of live performances; a series of screenings of classic performance works from the late 1960s and early 1970s, selected by Joan Jonas and John Baldessari; and a series of lectures that helped to frame the program historically and theoretically.

—

"Spectacular" aspired to demonstrate that performance art has evolved over time to include a wide range of artistic strategies and forms related to or inspired by theater, dance and choreography, film, installation, relational aesthetics, social practice, community art, and pedagogy. Since all of these are also central elements in the work of Elmgreen & Dragset, the artists seemed a perfect fit for this particular program. To have their work included in "Spectacular" also offered the chance to examine the influence of a range of artistic practices that are often grouped under the label Institutional Critique. Markus Brüderlin's text "Working on the White Cube"[1] outlines in great detail the connections between the duo's work and that of other artists associated with Institutional Critique, but also makes clear how Elmgreen & Dragset in fact have pushed the discussion decidedly further. For many years the deconstruction of the white cube through various non-theatrical performative interventions has been a central aim of the duo's practice.

—

Their work for "Spectacular," entitled *The Great Escape*, is perhaps one of their lesser-known works but certainly one of their more radical ideas. The performance took place over a period of 24 hours and involved the larger part of the collection of the Museum Kunstpalast, which includes more than 100,000 pieces, ranging from modern and contemporary art back to the Gothic, Renaissance, and Baroque eras, and even classical antiquity. The piece involved removing the collection from the galleries by a team of professional art handlers, placing it into a number of trucks, driving the trucks (literally) around the museum, and then reinstalling the works. While the drive was going on, the museum's janitors cleaned the galleries.

—

It is important to note that the "escape" of the artworks was prepared long in advance, in dialogue with the museum's administration, and that a few of the most precious and fragile works in the collection had been replaced with artworks of lesser importance or value before the performance took place. Given

---

1 _ Markus Brüderlin, "Working on the White Cube" in *Taking Place*, ed. Beatrix Ruf, exh. cat. Kunsthalle Zürich (Ostfildern: Hatje Cantz, 2002).

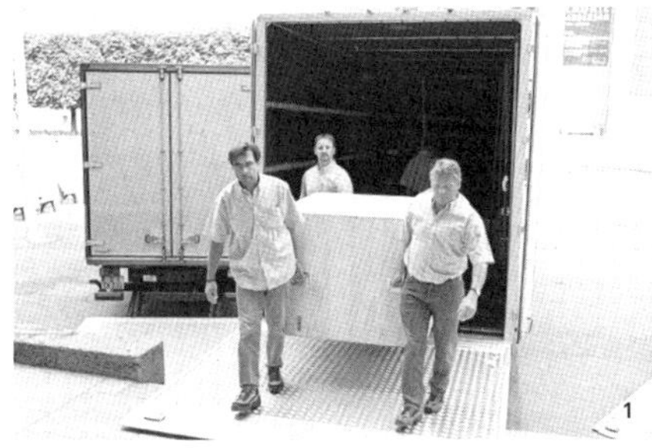
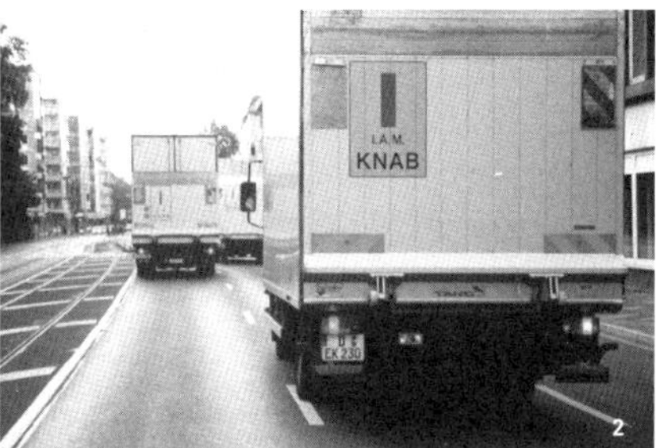

the large number of art handlers who were on site (the whole work was sponsored by a prominent Düsseldorf-based art handling company), the actual act of taking down the works and filling up the trucks took only a few hours. The drive around the museum was a 30-minute ride at most. The piece started during the regular open hours of the museum, so that the audience—who had been invited to come and see a performance by Elmgreen & Dragset, but had not been given any specifics—was able to witness closely the activities of packing, crating, and handling.

—

The beginning and end of the performance disclosed to a general audience how a museum installation takes place, and unveiled the physical activity of taking down and putting up a large number of artworks, something that the public usually does not get to see. Looking at *The Great Escape* from this perspective, the work becomes one of several by the artists devoted to uncovering the labor that goes on behind closed doors in galleries and museums. Such work is usually rather unspectacular and non-dramatic. In this context, actions which are usually "neutral" and hidden—packing, crating, carrying, driving, drilling, lifting—are rendered substantive and performative.

—

Fig. 1 _ Art handlers moving works from the collection of the Museum Kunstpalast in Düsseldorf for *The Great Escape*, 2003, for the exhibition "Spectacular: The Art of Action."

Fig. 2 _ Driving the trucks around the Museum Kunstpalast.

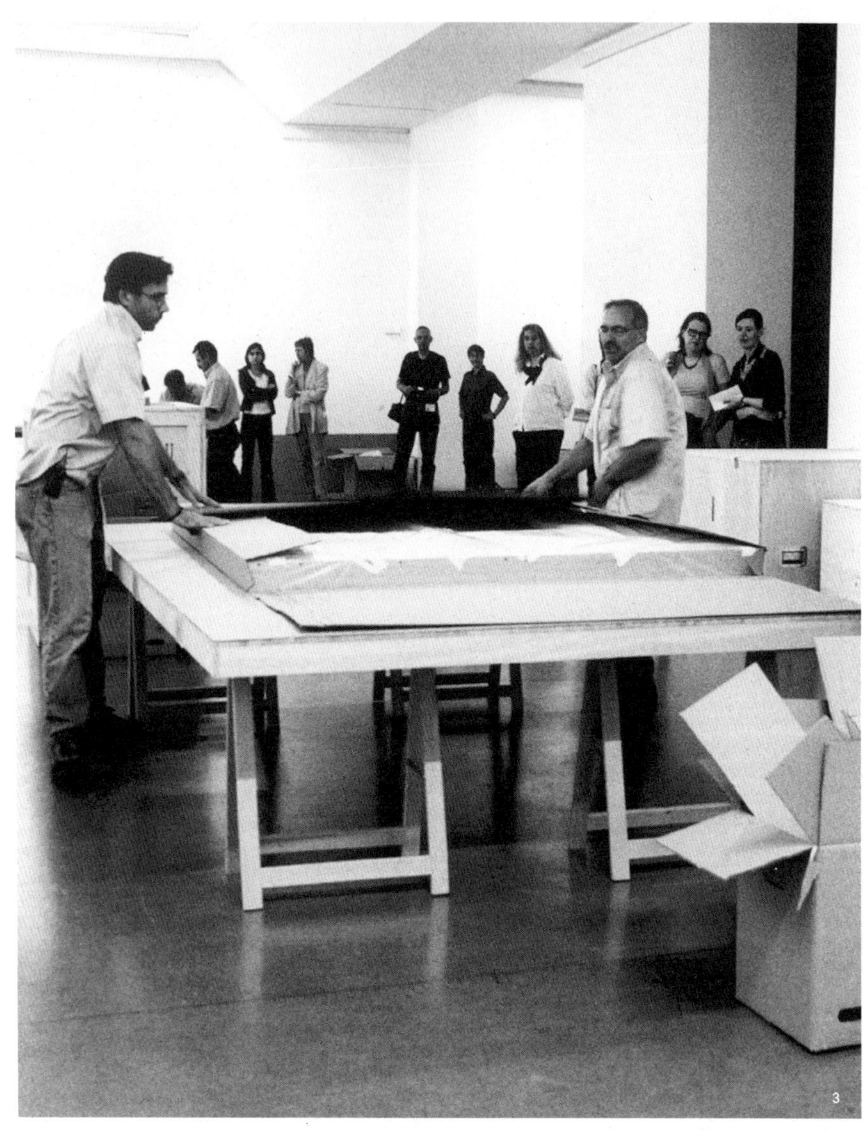

Fig. 3 _ Art handlers packing and crating works from the Museum Kunstpalast collection.

Two of their best-known works in this category are *Zwischen anderen Ereignissen* (Between Other Events, 2000), presented at the Galerie für Zeitgenössische Kunst in Leipzig, Germany, and *Taking Place* (2001-2002) at Kunsthalle Zürich in Switzerland. *Zwischen anderen Ereignissen* featured two ordinary house painters who painted the gallery walls white over and over again for the duration of the show. Once they finished at one end of the building, they went back to the beginning and started all over again. The entire budget was directed toward the fee of the painters, who got paid their standard hourly rate, and the paint. When the funds were used up, the exhibition ended. The work was also a comment on the high percentage of unemployed workers in East Germany, where the show was taking place. The artists had placed an advertisement in the local edition of Germany's most popular tabloid newspaper, the notorious Bild Zeitung, and together with the curator interviewed all the applicants, of which there where several dozen. *Taking Place* brought the idea of exposing labor to a whole new level when the artists decided, in collaboration with the curator and the architect, to present the renovation of the Kunsthalle Zürich as their piece. The entire process of demolishing the old structure and rebuilding it became, effectively, their work. During the exhibition, visitors witnessed the refurbishment of the gallery spaces and non-public office areas by a large group of professional construction workers. The completion of the new construction coincided with the end of the ten-week-long exhibition.

—

The title of Elmgreen & Dragset's project at the Museum Kunstpalast clearly references a well-known mass escape from a German prisoner-of-war camp during World War II, which was described in the 1950 book of the same name by Paul Brickhill and translated to the silver screen in 1963 by the legendary Hollywood director John Sturges. The movie featured an all-star cast, including Steve McQueen, James Garner, Richard Attenborough, Charles Bronson, Donald Pleasence, and James Coburn, among others. Interestingly, this mirrors the also predominantly male all-star cast of the museum collection: Pe-

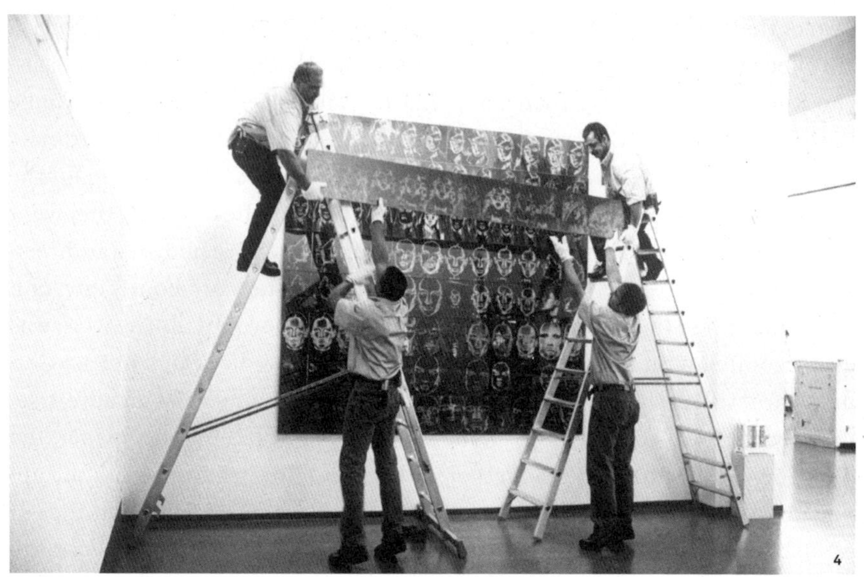

ter Paul Rubens, Adolph von Menzel, Caspar David Friedrich, Otto Dix, Max Ernst, Emil Nolde, Gerhard Richter, Sigmar Polke, Joseph Beuys. While it takes perhaps a moment or two to fully absorb the intended analogy, the idea of a museum as a Nazi prisoner-of-war camp seems extreme, if not outrightly ridiculous. Yet it is certainly a way of articulating the often-uneasy relationship artists have with art institutions, which involves power dynamics, hierarchies, and control on a number of levels, particularly in regard to the construction of an artistic canon and the interpretation, production, and display of artworks. Elmgreen & Dragset propose the idea of the artist as a figure in society who can never be fully caught or domesticated—a fugitive and renegade whom the powers that be want to put behind bars. To turn the figure of the artist into an outsider, a potentially marginalized character with unorthodox political and social viewpoints, reflects perhaps an outdated and nostalgic understanding

Fig. 4 _ During de-installation.

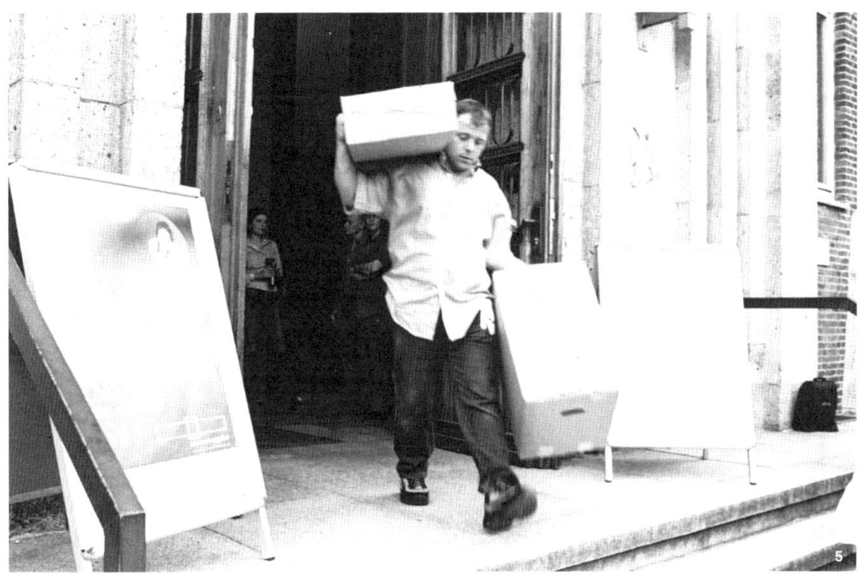

of what being an artist is. The real situation is far more complex than a simple binary, but it is still important to think about the potential conflict between artistic freedom and creativity on the one side and institutional authority and power on the other.

—

The fact that institutions are willing accomplices of apparent acts of Institutional Critique is not necessarily news, but it is an interesting condition, and worth exploring further. While the aim of "Spectacular" was to challenge the museum through performative interventions, it moved within a restricted territory that had been carefully negotiated with the museum's administration. In the case of *The Great Escape*, the director of the museum, Jean Hubert Martin, known for his interest in unorthodox artistic ideas, was quick to support the artists' proposal. The curators, however, had serious reservations and initially

Fig. 5 _ An art handler moving boxes.

refused to collaborate. The idea that their collection was in fact reconfigurable—could be made mobile, replaced in whole or in part, and even played with—was an alien concept to their somewhat dusty and certainly conservative minds, as they had not changed their collection displays in many years.

—

While this aspect of *The Great Escape* speaks most perhaps about the politics and power dynamics of museum administrations, it also points to the fact that even museum leadership has in various ways absorbed, and even appropriated and institutionalized, elements of Institutional Critique. It would probably not be an exaggeration to say that the term "Institutional Critique" is gradually being put on its head—shifting from being directed toward the institution to being authorized by the institution. If Elmgreen & Dragset had decided to dump the collection into the nearby river Rhine, or burn the museum down, the director would most likely not have responded so well. Of course these actions would have been probably just dumb ideas, but to think about them makes clear that no matter how critical art attempts to be, it still ultimately operates, for better or worse, within a sanctioned zone.

—

It is an idea worth pondering when thinking about questions of authority, control, power structures, and legitimization. Critical theory could probably give us profound analyses of the mechanisms at play, including an in-depth elucidation of the contradictions, complexities, and paradoxes of the museum system. For me, the most important thought that emerges from these ruminations around *The Great Escape* is a question of institutionalization. Is it simply inevitable, when one engages with the world, to sooner or later be absorbed by the object of one's criticism? How is it possible to create a critical practice that maintains its integrity without being corrupted by, and pacified by, institutions and their authorities? Is such a pursuit impossibly radical and utopian—meaning, extremist and ineffectively idealistic? Fewer and fewer artists seem to be asking these questions, let alone proposing possible answers. This is what makes Elmgreen & Dragset's practice so continually relevant. ____________

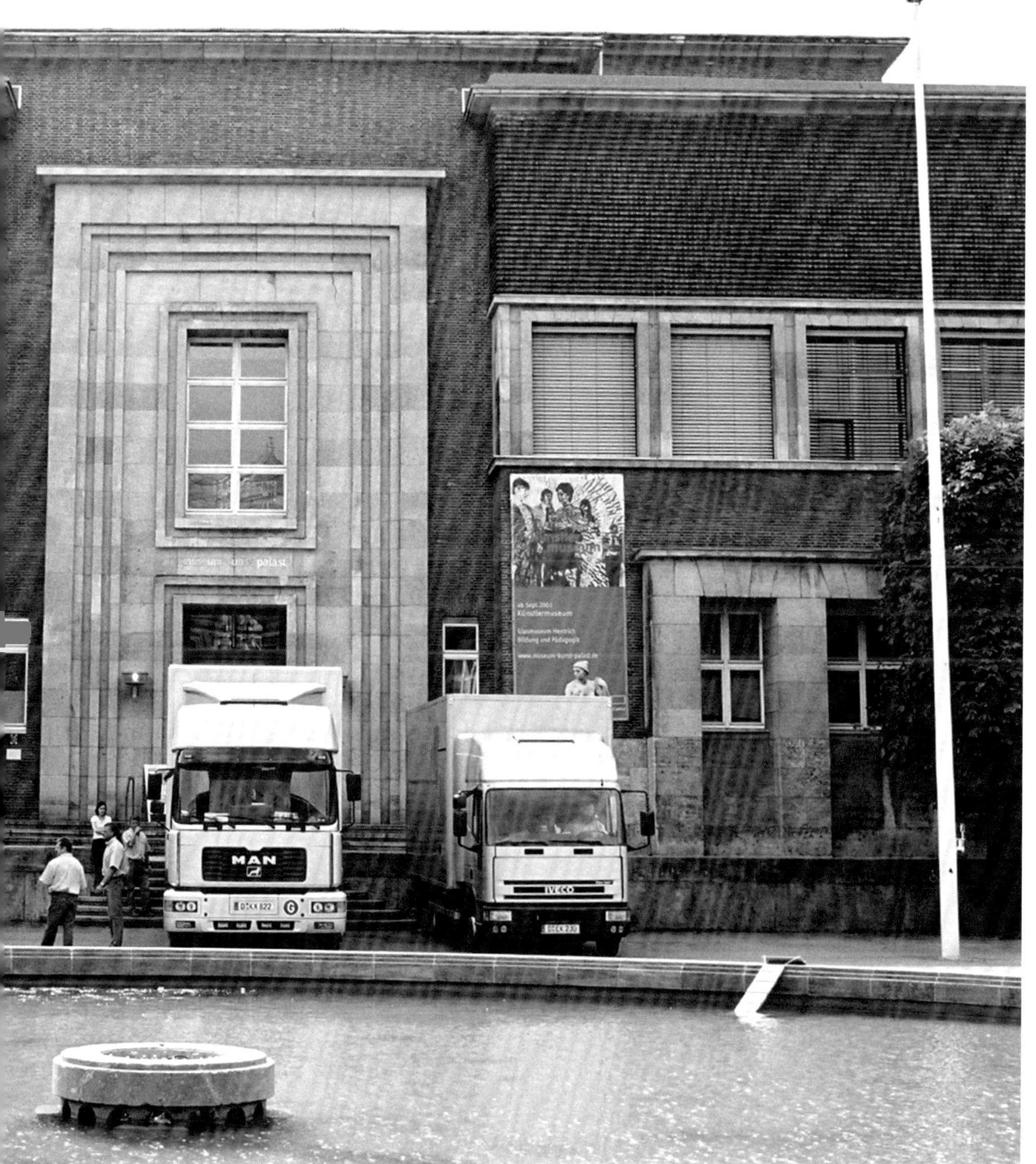
palast
ab Sept. 2001
Künstlermuseum
Glasmuseum Hentrich
Bildung und Pädagogik
MAN
IVECO

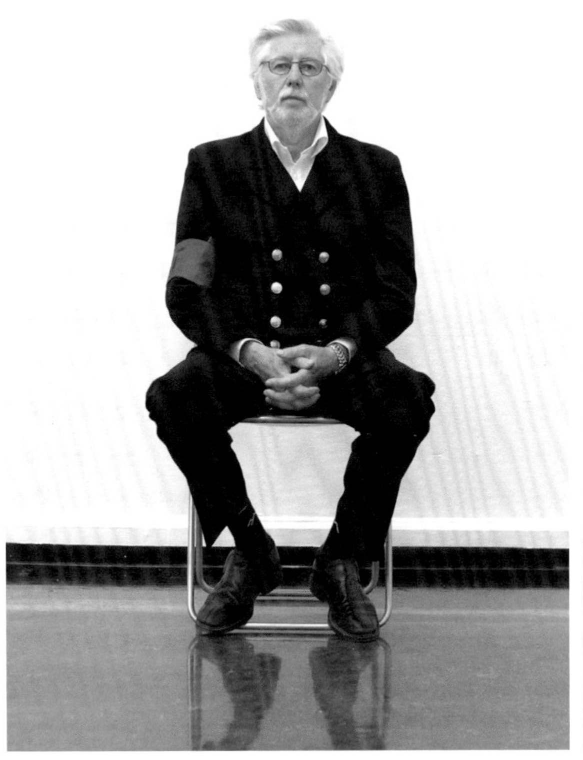

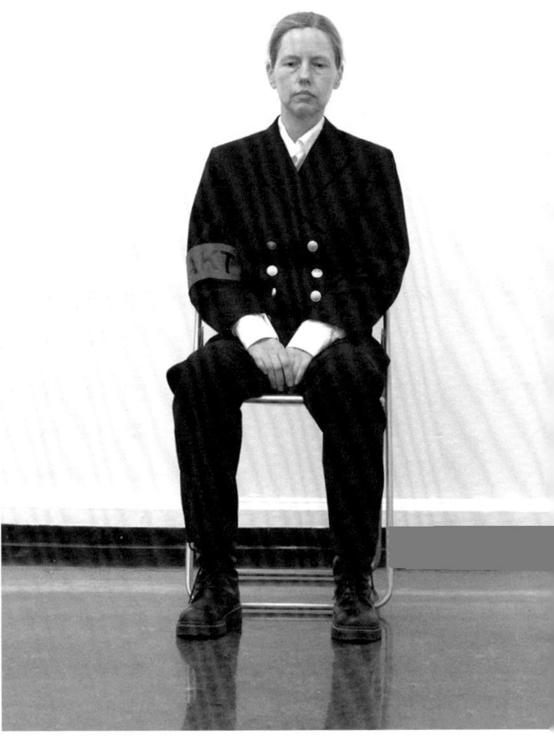

MATERIALS: *simple chairs*
PERFORMERS: *people of different ages, genders, and backgrounds*
CLOTHING: *matching museum guard uniforms*
DIMENSIONS: *space and number of performers variable*
DURATION: *the entire exhibition period (one to three months)*
PERFORMED AT: *"The Welfare Show," Bergen Kunsthall, Norway, 2005; "The Welfare Show," Serpentine Gallery, London, 2006*

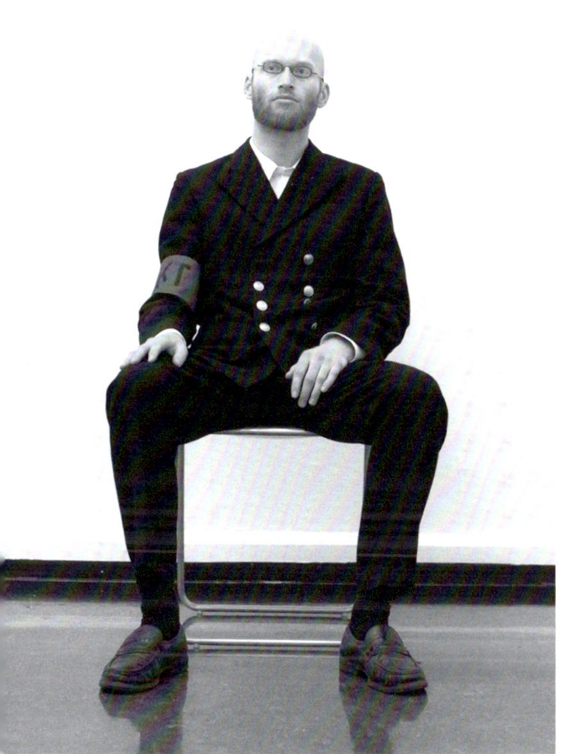

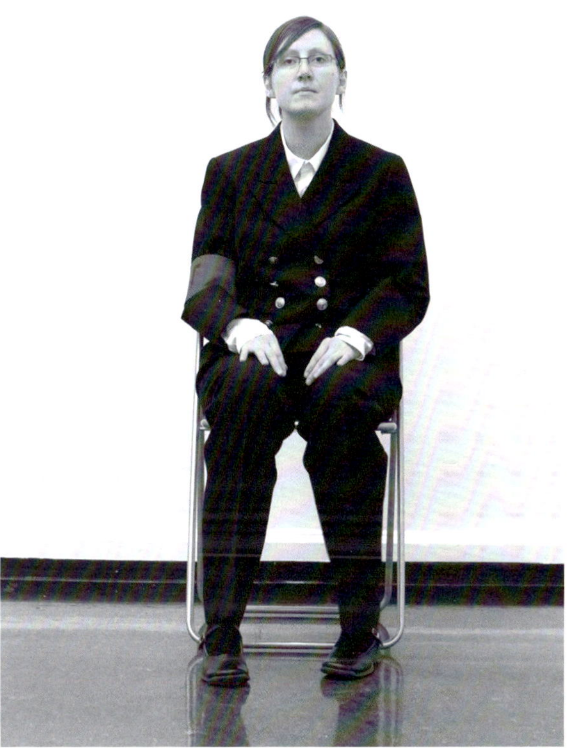

E-G(U)ARDING THE GUARDS
005

etween six and twelve uniformed museum guards sitting ong the walls of an otherwise empty room, watching the au-ience and each other. In the London version of "The Welfare how" the guards were recruited through the unemployment ffice.

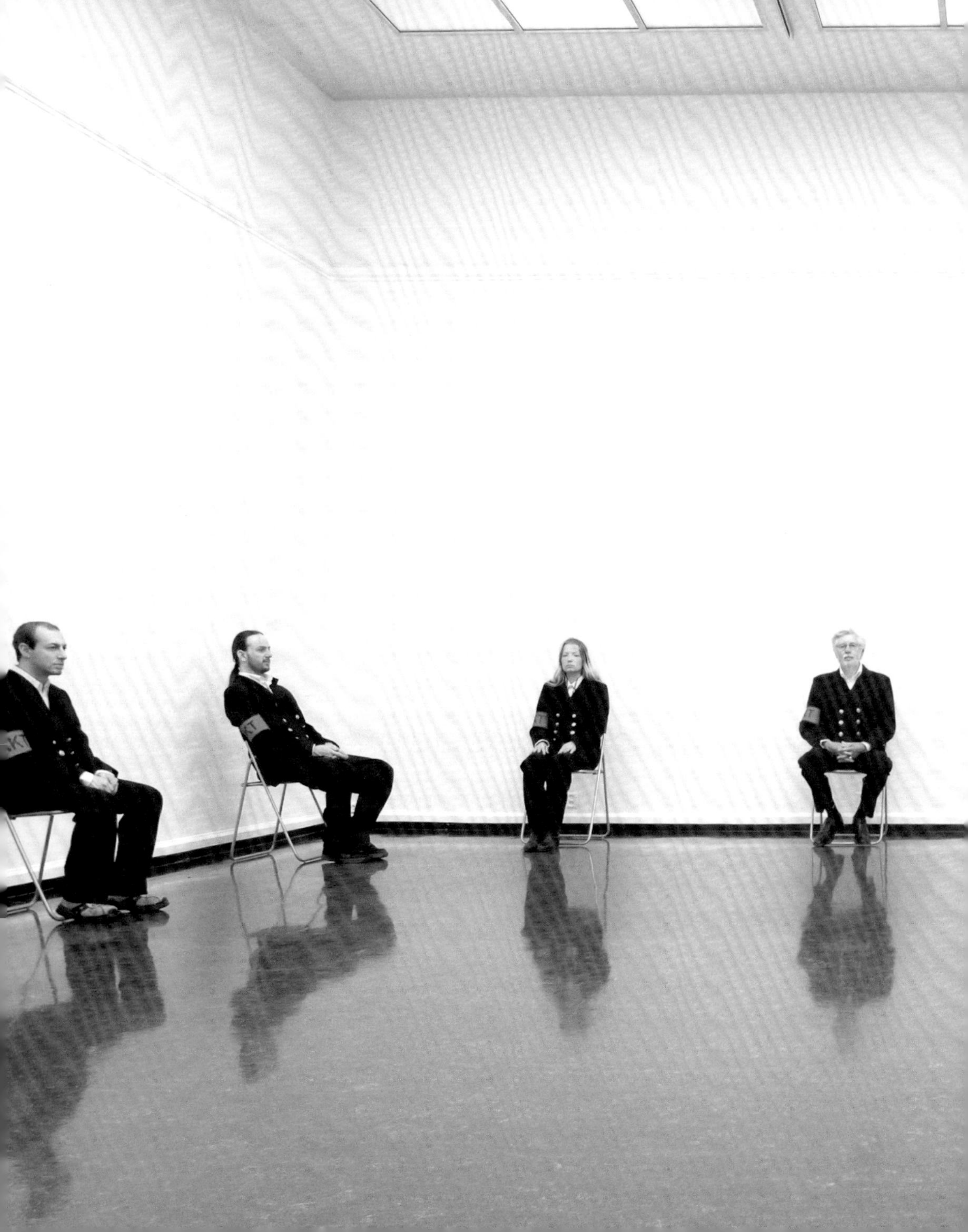

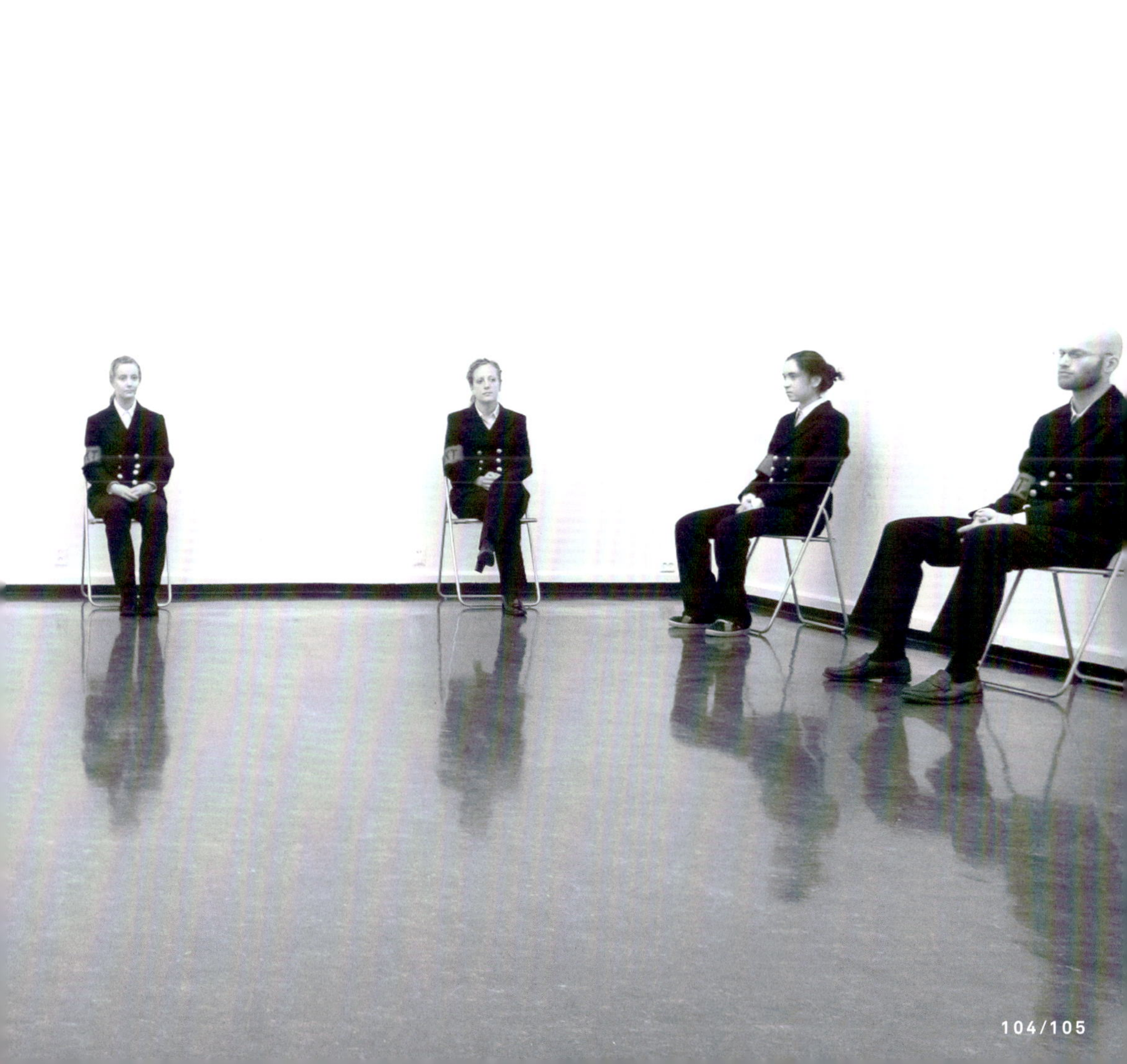

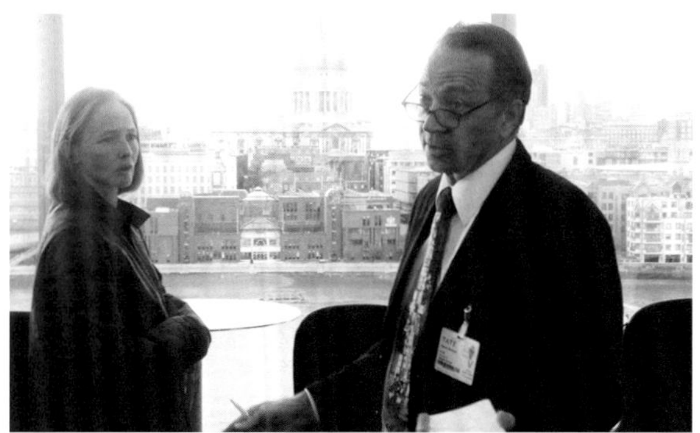

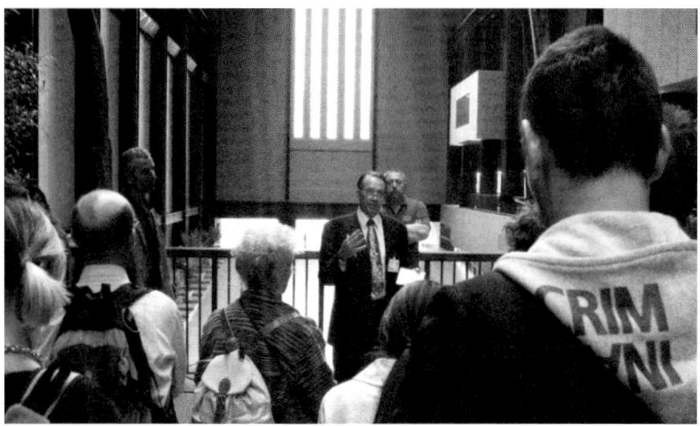

TATE MODERN WALKS—A POWER STATION REVISITED 2004

Mock historical tour through the Tate Modern building. The walk took the public beyond the white walls, prepared floors and high-tech lighting systems of the Tate, back into spaces of the former power station (built in 1947 and closed down in 1981)—"the smell of machine oil, armpits, lunch boxes, dirty jokes still hanging in the air." A vivid account of a not so distant history was presented by the character "Wilfred," a former lifelong power station employee. The script—written by Trevor Stuart based on instructions from the artists—included historical facts and descriptions as well as a fictional biography and anecdotes. At a cocktail reception following the performance, the actor stayed in character, due to the presence of a handful of widows of actual former power station employees, showing him their husbands' photo albums and keepsakes and jointly reminiscing with the baffled actor.

"Hello, Good Evening. I'm your designated guide. My name is Trevor Bedwell. I was named Trevor because I was born in 1948 just after my mother had seen 'Brief Encounter' and fallen in love with Trevor Howard. 1948 was the year work began on the Bankside power station."

"Just to bring you up to date. Dig under about 30 feet of water bearing ballast down to the foundations of this building and you'll come to the blue clay rich ground, which used to be the main street of the ancient town of Southwark. Bankside, was, in recent history, say 1613, a broken down mess of pubs, boarding houses and in the parlance, knocking shops also known very tastefully as stews which was the name for commercial fish ponds."

"And in 1824, the Phoenix Gas company began operation which became in 1891, The City of London Electric Light company coal fired power station. The chimneys pumped out smoke like black pea soup combining with the cold fog off the river to make some of the worst smogs since Krakatoa. Sensitive people kneeled over dead in these smogs."

"Originally, this building had two chimneys but they finally settled on one, I think personally, as a phallic symbol directly opposite that big feminine dome—like a sexual union across the river—the power meets the glory... By the way, there's Christopher Wren, the architect's house just over that wall. No. 49 Bankside and what's it called? The alley next to the house? Yes, Cardinal Cap Alley, Cardinal Cap. Check it out later."

"Essentially, oil as fuel is very dirty but coal is filthy. So they decided on oil, especially since the price was right at the time. Oil was burnt in massive boilers to make high pressure steam which drove turbine generators and then was cooled again in huge water condensers. The power was sent through feeders to the city but we had, still have, lines out to wherever necessary if the need be. It's just a matter of transforming the power up in steps to the sub stations."

"I was a C.E.G.B. trainer working first on maintenance then admin. and later, operations. I was in the control room above the switching house right above here. It's a 24 hour industry. Every day of the year. If told, we worked on Christmas day. The main shifts 7:00am to 3:00 then 3:00 'til 10:00 and 10:00 to 7:00am."

"See those two gantry cranes on rails. They take up to 150 tons. They were left here for functional purposes as well as historical. They've used them in every exhibition so far. Invaluable for the Anish Kapoor construction and to lift a Bourgeois spider. We used them to take the covers off the generators for cleaning about every two years."

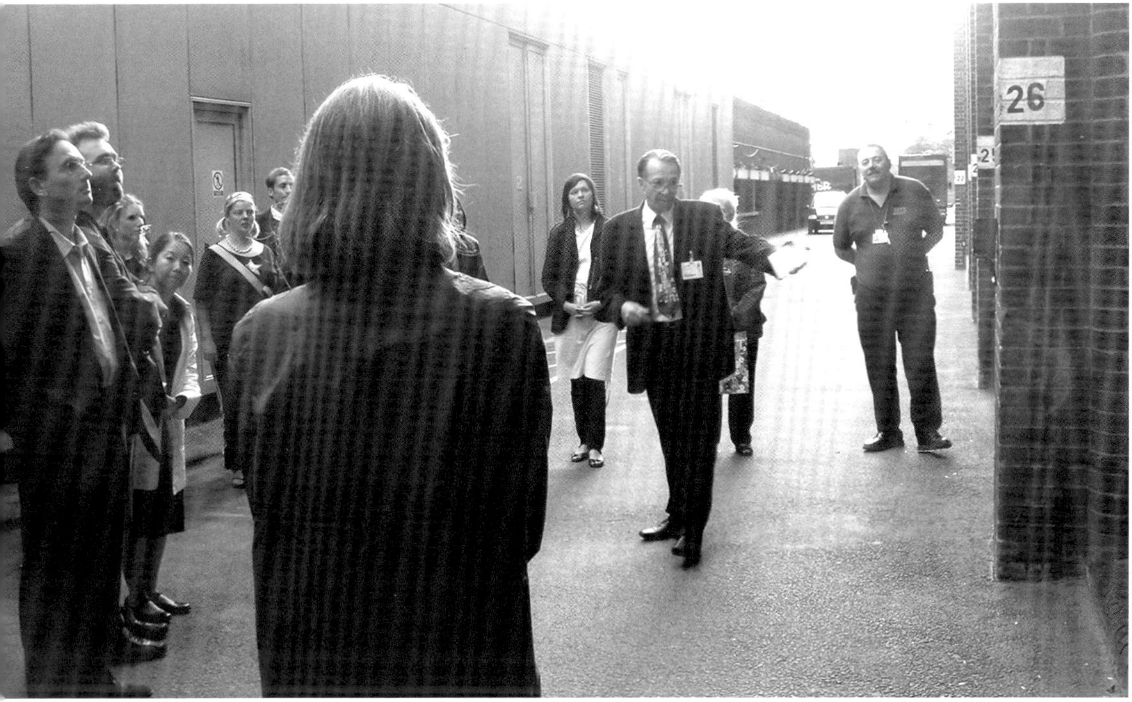

"The power station never received any accolades for design. It was refused a listing by English Heritage in 1993 and was going to be demolished. The new owners, Nuclear Electric, wanted to exploit the sight but thanks to the wisdom and acute vision of Nicholas Serota and the Tate gang, it was saved from oblivion. The Swiss architect firm, Herzog & de Meuron won the new contract. 10,000 tons of scrap metal was removed and the new Tate Modern was born from the shell of the old Bankside power station. It was opened in 2000 on the 11th of May—Salvador Dali's birthday."

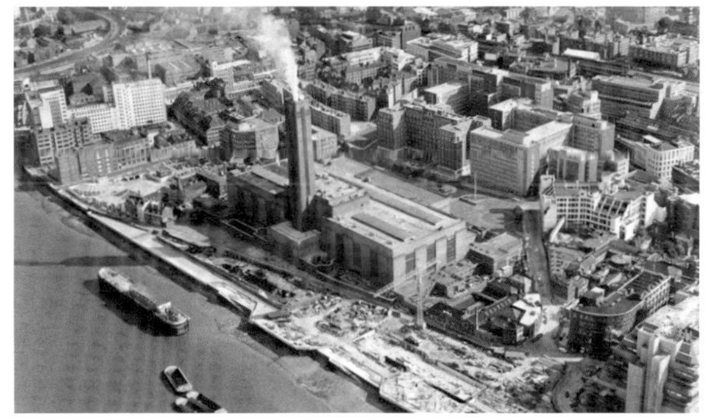

(selected excerpts from the script written by Trevor Stuart)

PERFORMER:	*professional actor (Trevor Stuart)*
CLOTHING:	*working-class suit and tie*
DIMENSIONS:	*site-specific*
DURATION:	*ninety minutes*
PERFORMED AT:	*Tate Modern, London, 2004*

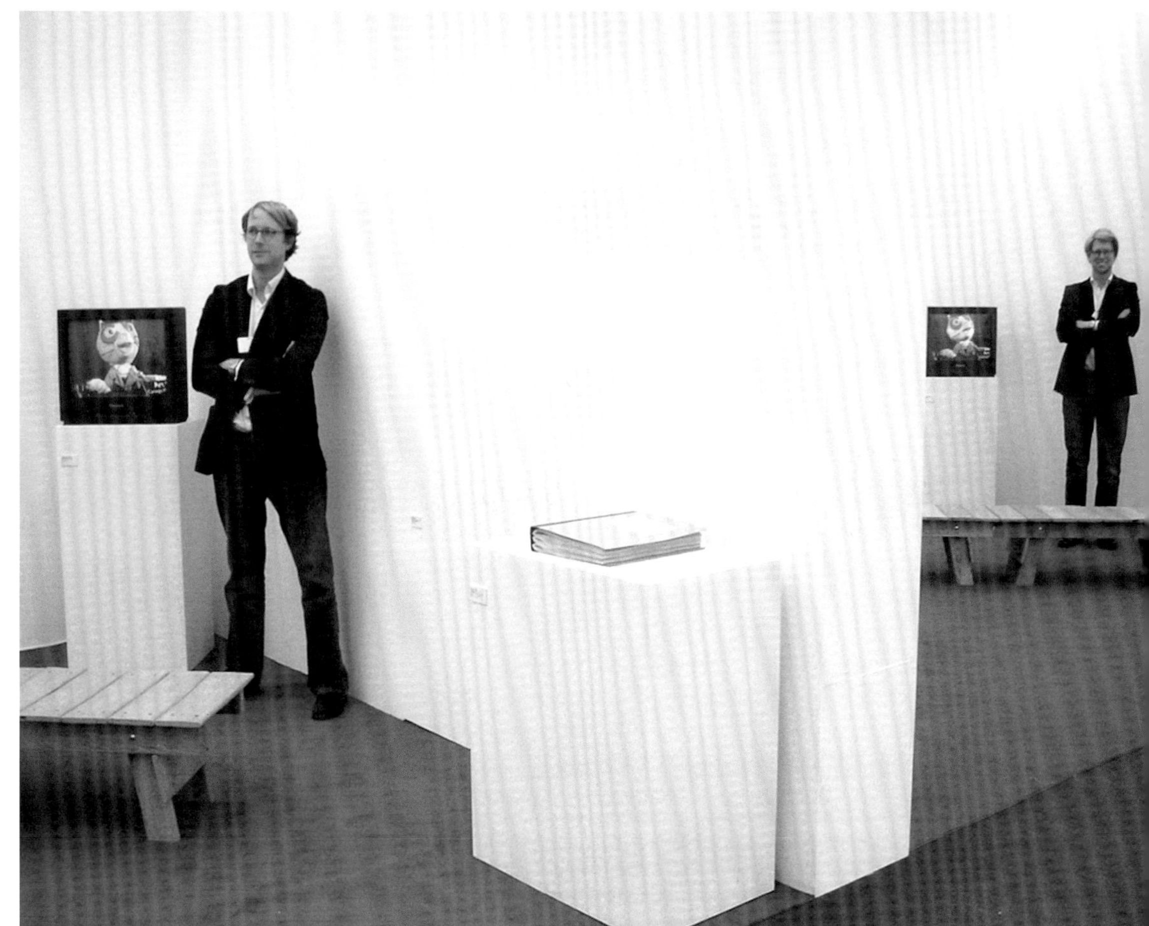

MATERIALS:	*mixed media*
PERFORMERS:	*professional "look-alike" actor; gallery owner Martin Klosterfelde*
CLOTHING:	*identical dapper black suits, white button-up shirts without ties, glasses*
DIMENSIONS:	*variable*
DURATION:	*the entire art fair period (four days)*
PERFORMED & EXHIBITED AT:	*Galerie Klosterfelde, Frieze Art Fair, London, 2005*

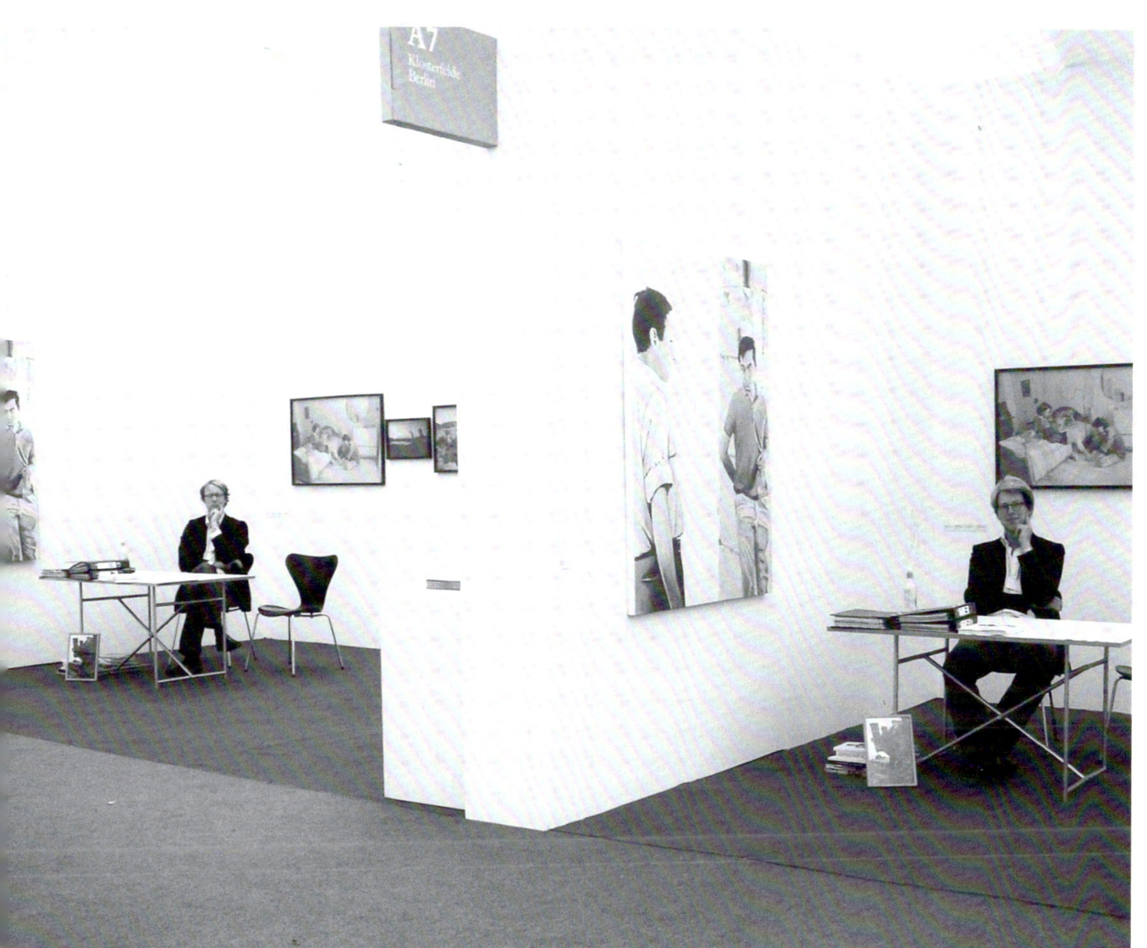

ᴧME SAME BUT DIFFERENT
ᵌ05

—

:act copy of the Klosterfelde art fair booth next to the origi-ıl—complete with a gallery owner/director Martin Kloster-ıde *Doppelgänger* wearing identical clothes, glasses and a g made from Mr. Klosterfelde's own hair. The two booths ıd the same configuration and furniture and displayed entical artworks including Matthew Antezzo paintings of ›bert Rauschenberg and Jasper Johns, and duplicate/edi-›ned works by Kirsten Pieroth, Dan Peterman, Christian nkowski and John Bock. Both gallerists—real and fake—ınded out identical business cards. The imposter gallerist perienced many people mistaking him for the actual Mr. osterfelde, including collectors and artists the gallery had ›rked with for many years.

3.

ROLES AND PROFESSIONS

ROLES AND PROFESSIONS

3.

WORKS

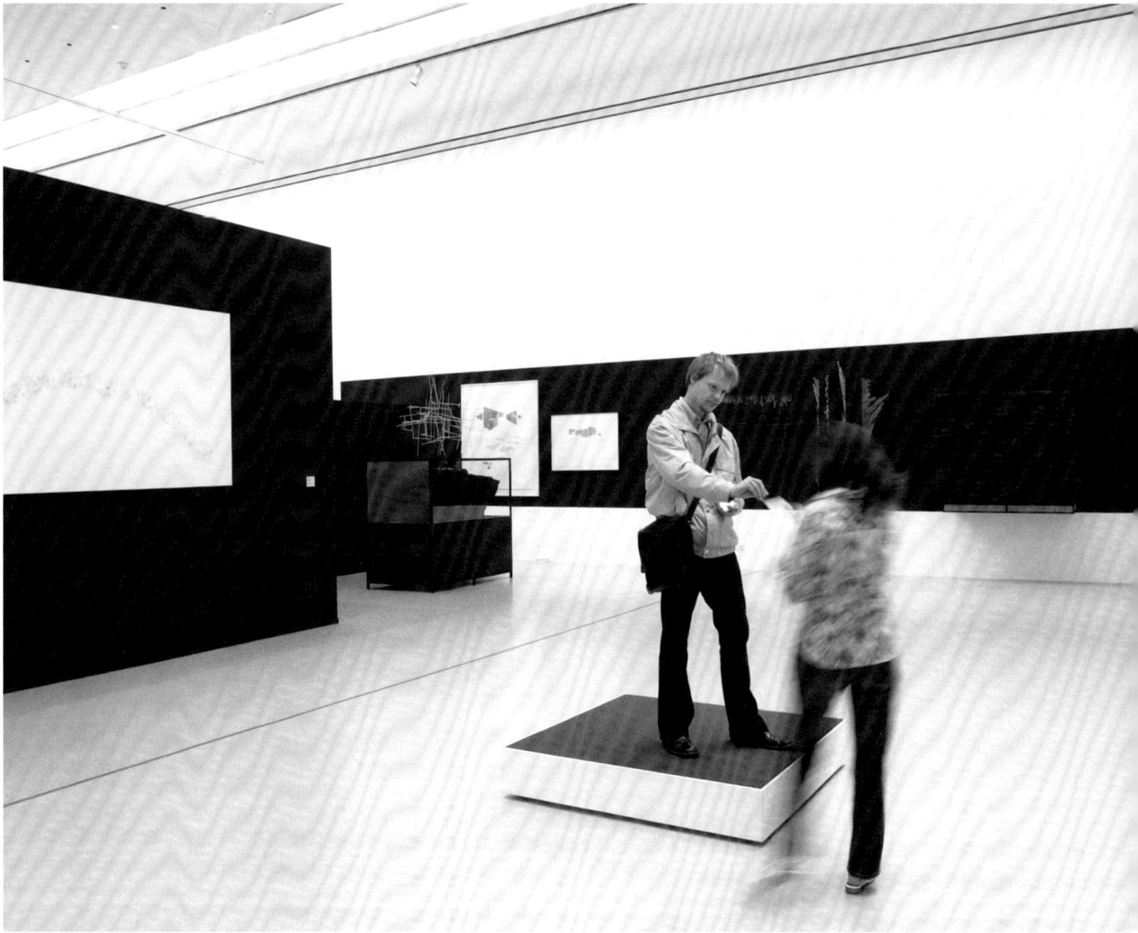

MATERIALS:	*plinth, visiting cards*
PERFORMER:	*young male, early 20s, fresh-faced*
CLOTHING:	*dressed as an office clerk or municipal offical*
DIMENSIONS:	*plinth: 30 x 120 x 120 cm; card: 90 x 60 mm*
DURATION:	*the entire exhibition period (three months)*
PERFORMED AT:	*"Made in Germany," Sprengel Museum, Hannover, 2007*

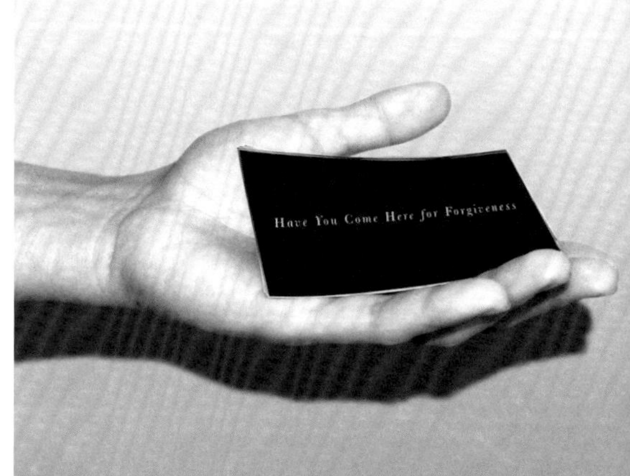

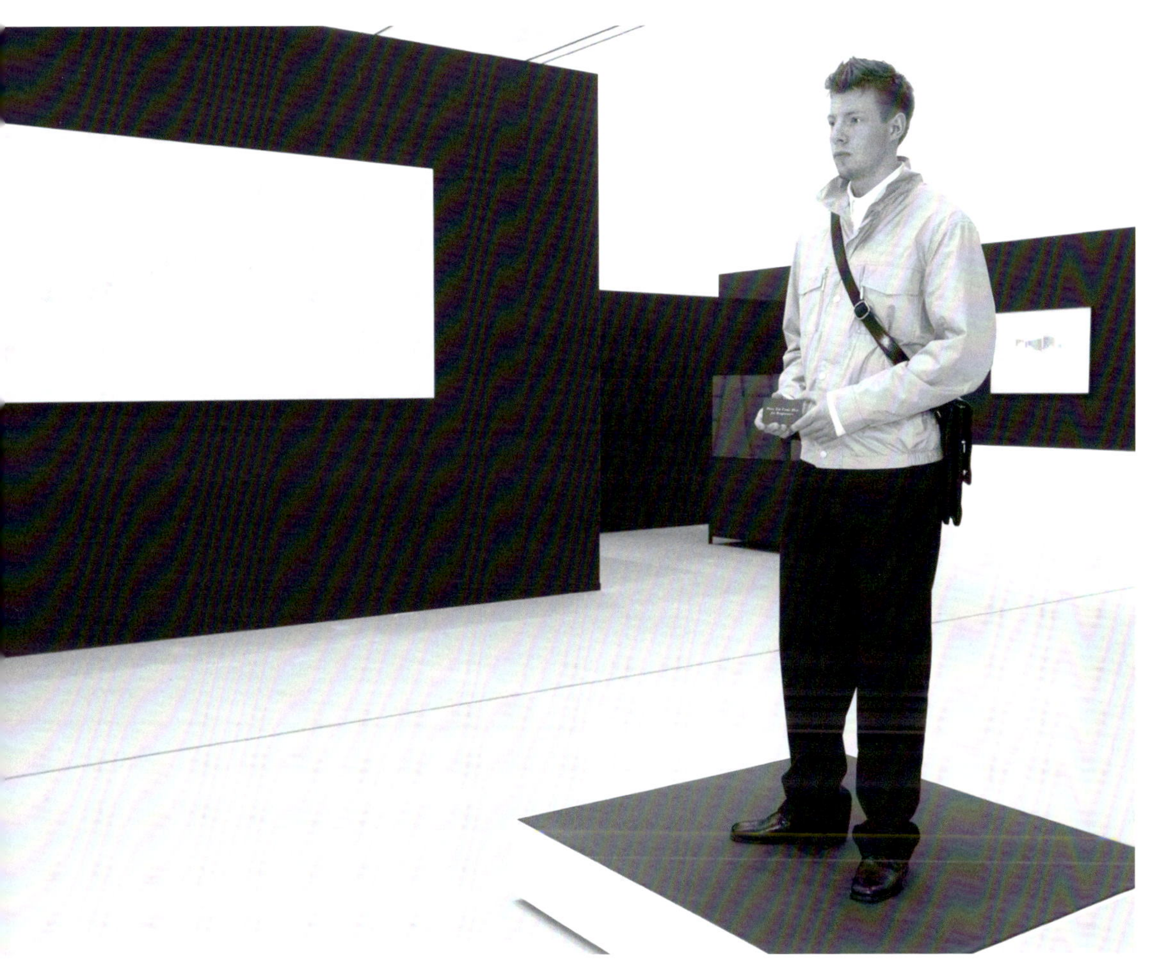

AVE YOU COME HERE FOR FORGIVENESS?
007

isiting cards with the text *Have You Come Here for Forgiveness* iven to exhibition visitors by a performer on a low plinth. Ref- rencing the title of the exhibition, "Made in Germany," this ork explores the idea that museum visitors (specifically in ermany) seek a different kind of redemption, with art having ubstituted the workings of religion for many citizens, but the neaning can also be applied to other cultures and peoples. he title is taken from the song "One" by the rock band U2.

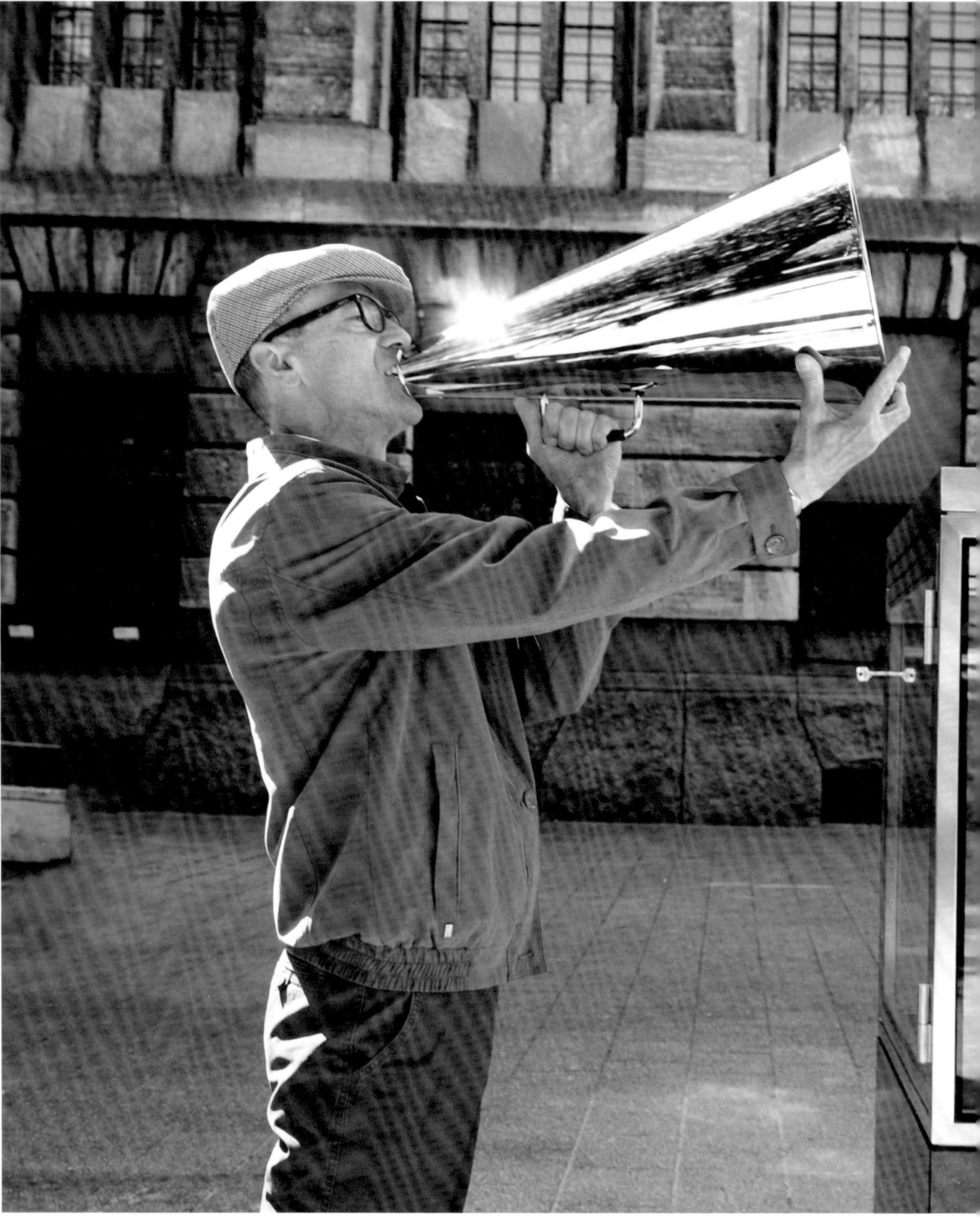

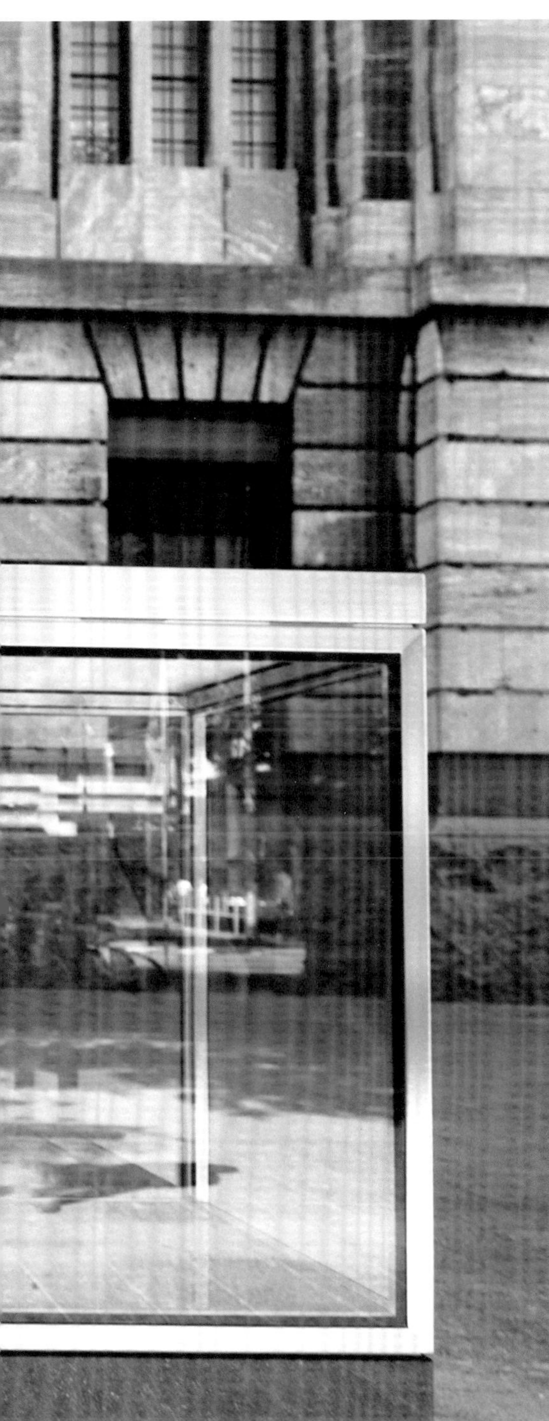

MATERIALS:	*plinth: granite; vitrine: steel and safety glass; megaphone: aluminum*
PERFORMER:	*Wim Konings*
CLOTHING:	*casual in khaki and gray tones, flat cap*
DIMENSIONS:	*160 x 70 x 70 cm*
DURATION:	*daily at noon for one year*
PERFORMED AT:	*the Coolsingel as part of Sculpture International Rotterdam's (SIR) public art program, Rotterdam, 2011 - 2012*

IT'S NEVER TOO LATE TO SAY SORRY
2011 - 2012

Daily performance in Rotterdam in which a performer shouts "It's never too late to say sorry" from a megaphone precisely at noon, for one year. The performance takes place next to the City Hall located on the Coolsingel, Rotterdam's central thoroughfare, a large shopping boulevard, and the location of the city's former post office.

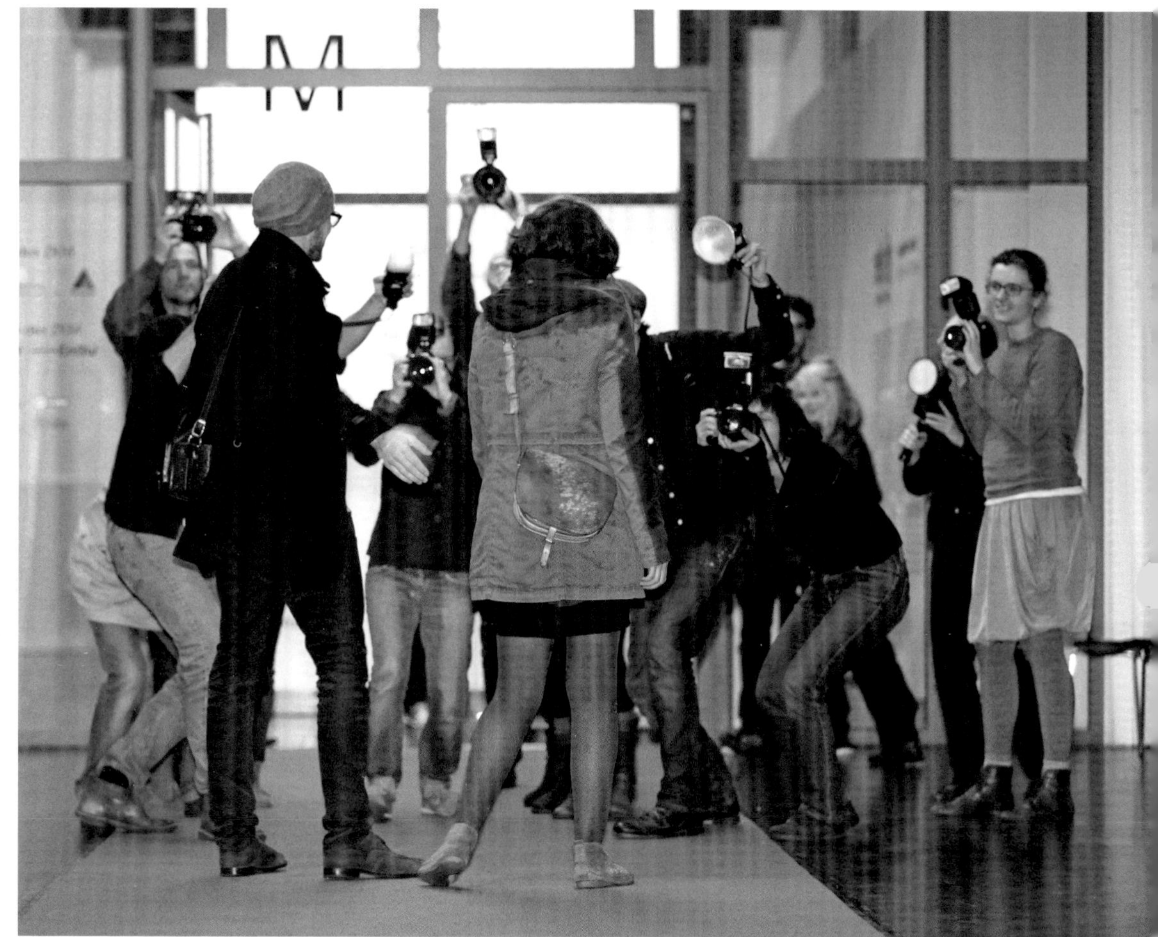

MATERIALS: *red carpet, professional cameras with large flash bulbs*
PERFORMERS: *professional and semi-professional photographers, male and female, different ages*
CLOTHING: *their own*
DIMENSIONS: *variable*
DURATION: *throughout the opening reception for the exhibition, then on select weekends (minimum two hours)*
PERFORMED AT: *"Celebrity—The One & The Many," ZKM | Center for Art and Media, Karlsruhe, 2010 - 2011*

PAPARAZZI
2010 - 2011

Four separate performances in which the "paparazzi" descen
upon the museum's entrance, with a red carpet, to photograp
visitors. There are approximately twenty photographers, all u
ing bright flashes and jostling each other to get closer to vis
tors. The images were later available for acquisition on the mu
seum's website.

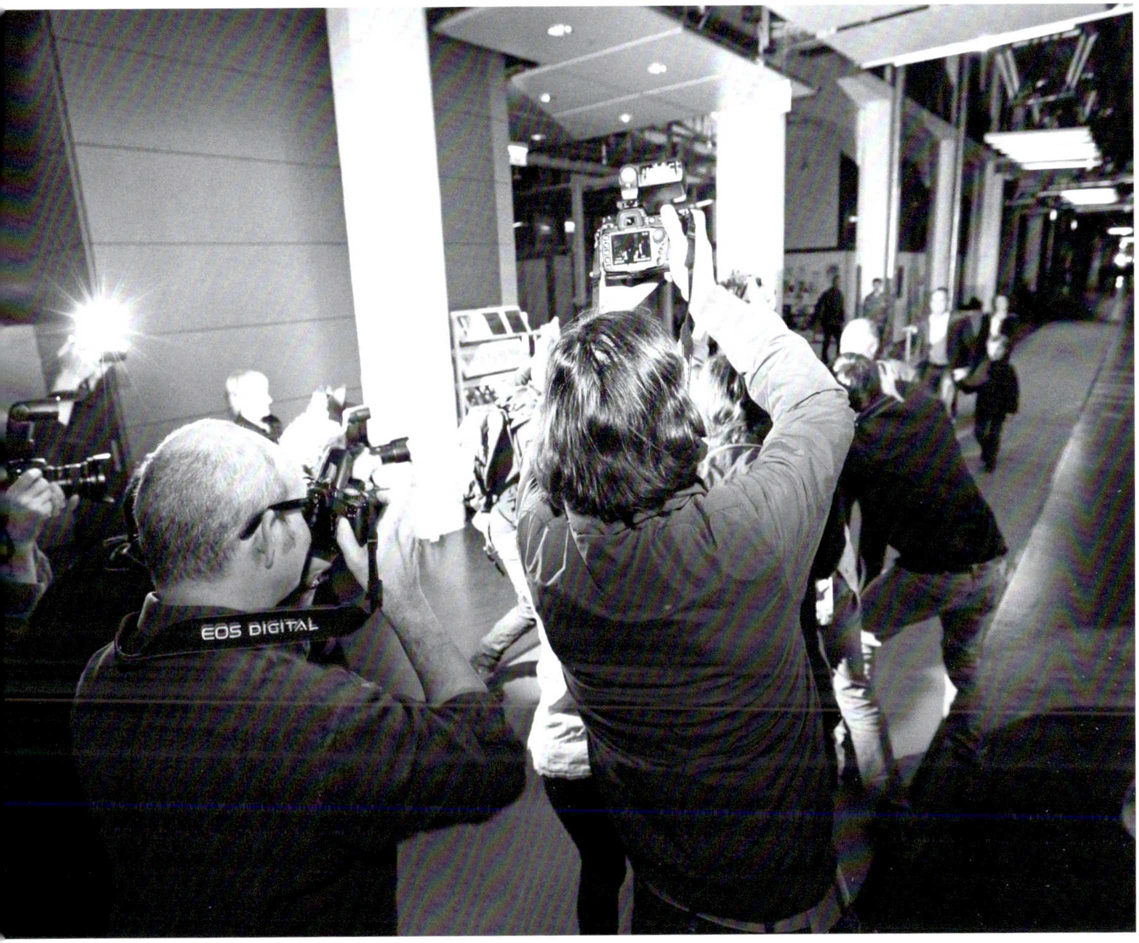

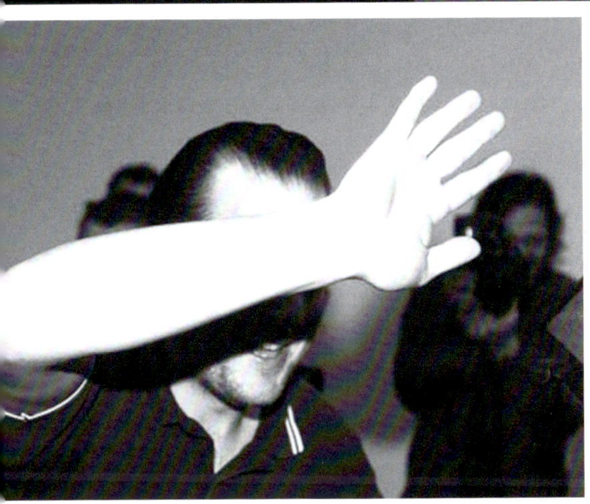

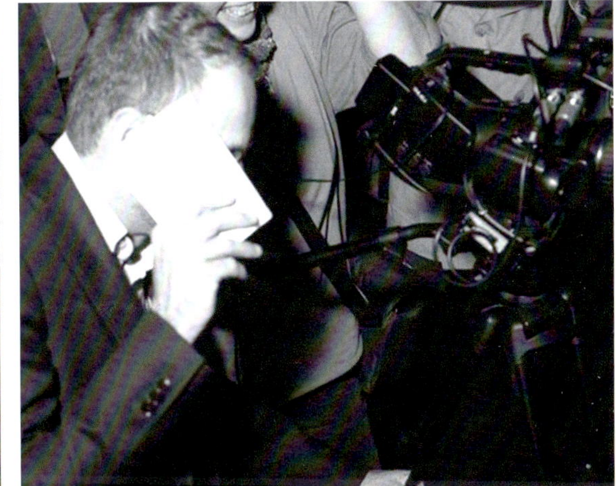

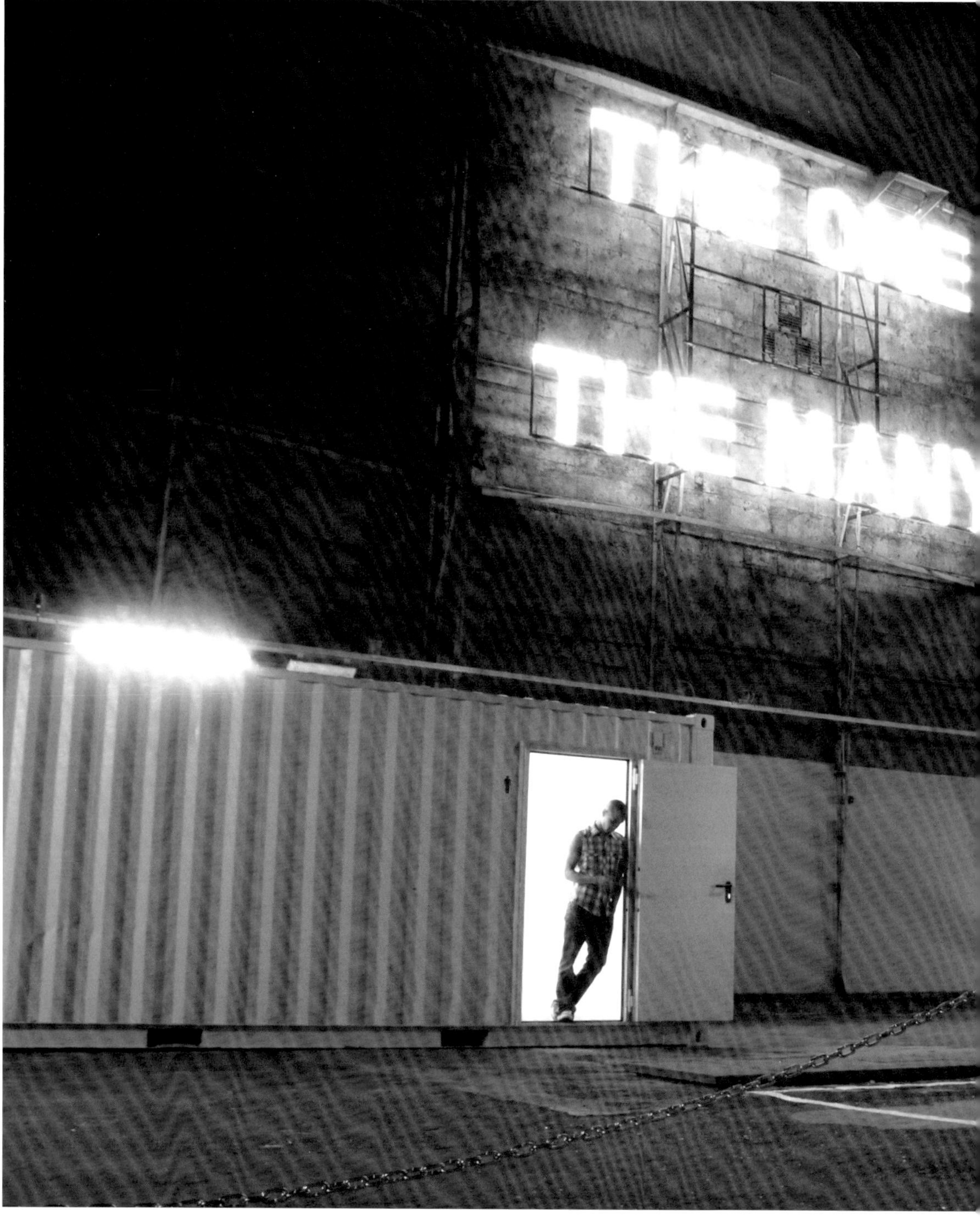

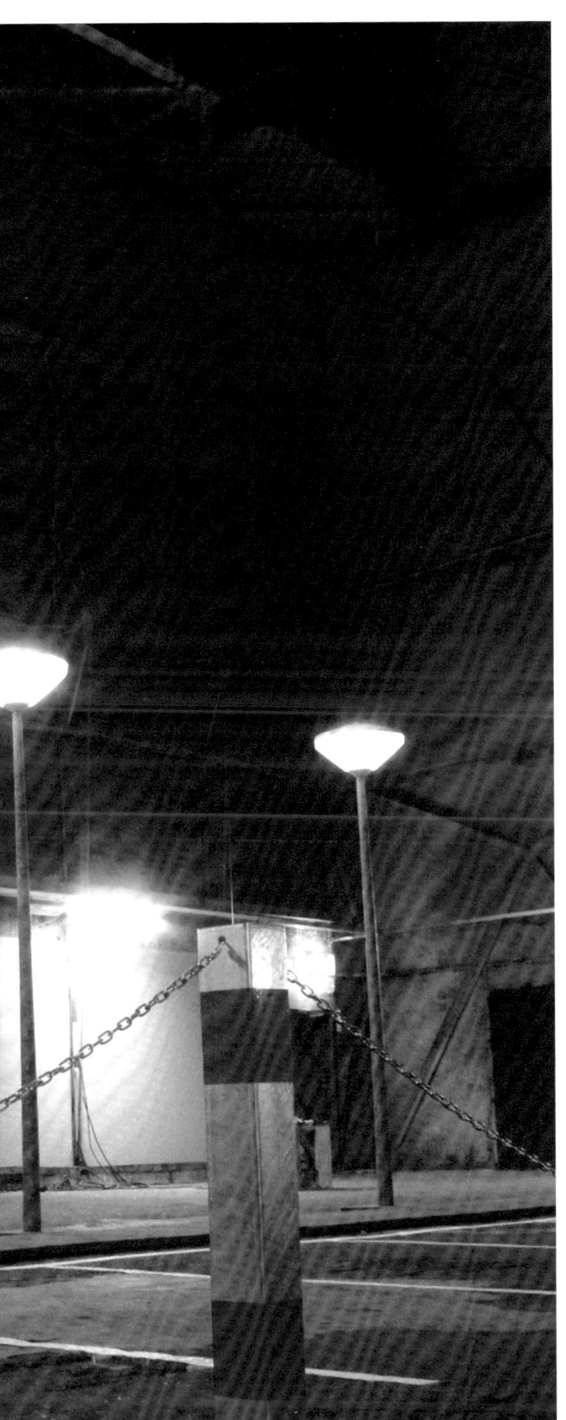

PERFORMERS:	*(two groups alternate throughout the exhibition period)* *Hustlers: two to four young males, around 20 years old, representing the suburban demographic of Rotterdam (mixture of European and North African descent)* *Teenage single mom: female, under 20, representing the suburban demographic of Rotterdam* *Street musician/busker: male, middle aged to older* *Car mechanics: two to three male and female, young, actual car mechanics/mechanic students* *Ferris wheel operators: father and son from an actual fairground equipment rental company*
CLOTHING:	*Hustlers: high street fashion singlets, T-shirts, bomber jackets, sweatpants, sneakers and sports sandals* *Teenage single mom: high street fashion tube dress, "bling" accessories, expensive (but empty) Stokke baby stroller* *Street musician/busker: his own attire, sunglasses (as if blind), white cane, accordion* *Car mechanics: overalls* *Ferris wheel operators: gray coats*
DIMENSIONS:	*variable*
DURATION:	*the entire exhibition period (four months)*
PERFORMED & EXHIBITED AT:	*"The One & The Many," Museum Boijmans van Beuningen, Submarine Wharf, Rotterdam, 2011*

THE ONE & THE MANY
2011

Large-scale installation depicting a bleak, run-down urban neighborhood, featuring an apartment building with furnished rooms, a full-size Ferris wheel, a public toilet area, street lamps, and park benches. Actors play the roles of the neighborhood's inhabitants, including a teenage mom, a street musician, young male hustlers, Ferris wheel operators, and auto mechanics. Visitors enter the exhibition through a long tunnel leading into the dimly lit Submarine Wharf situated on Rotterdam's harbor. Midway through the 50 meter long tunnel there is a realistic looking baby in a carrying case abandoned in front of a cash machine.

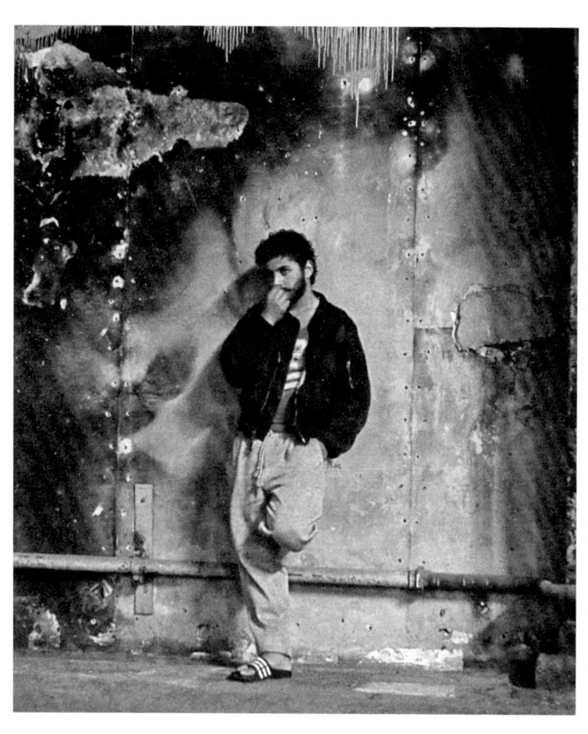

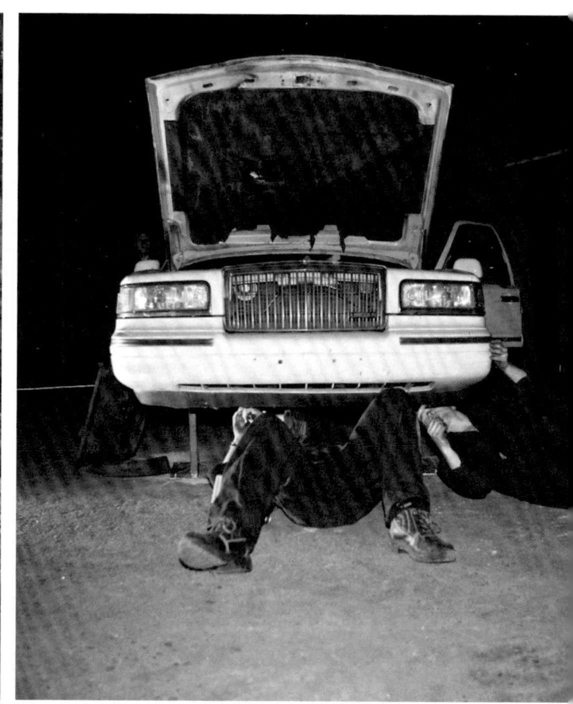

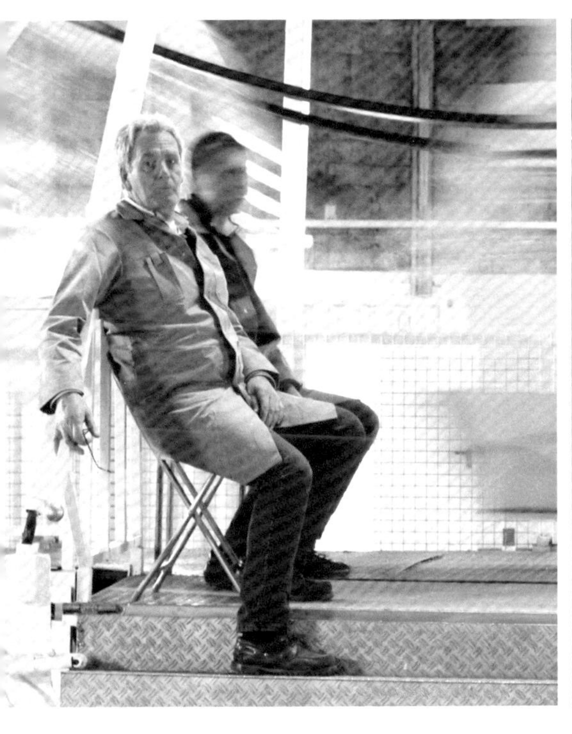

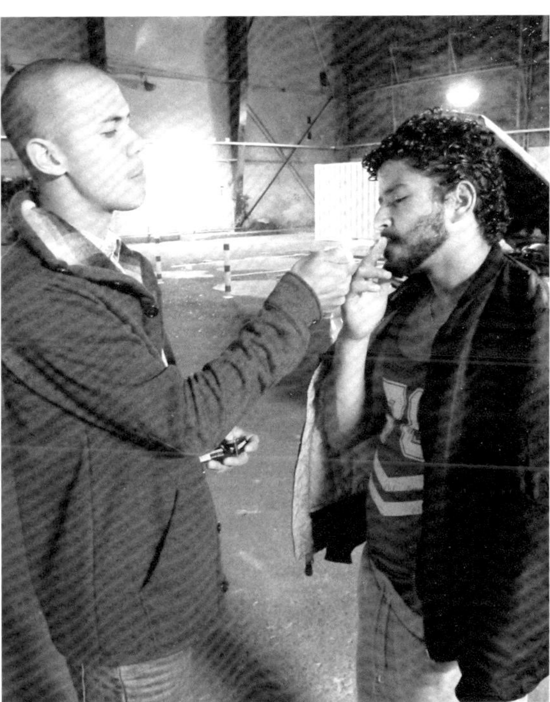

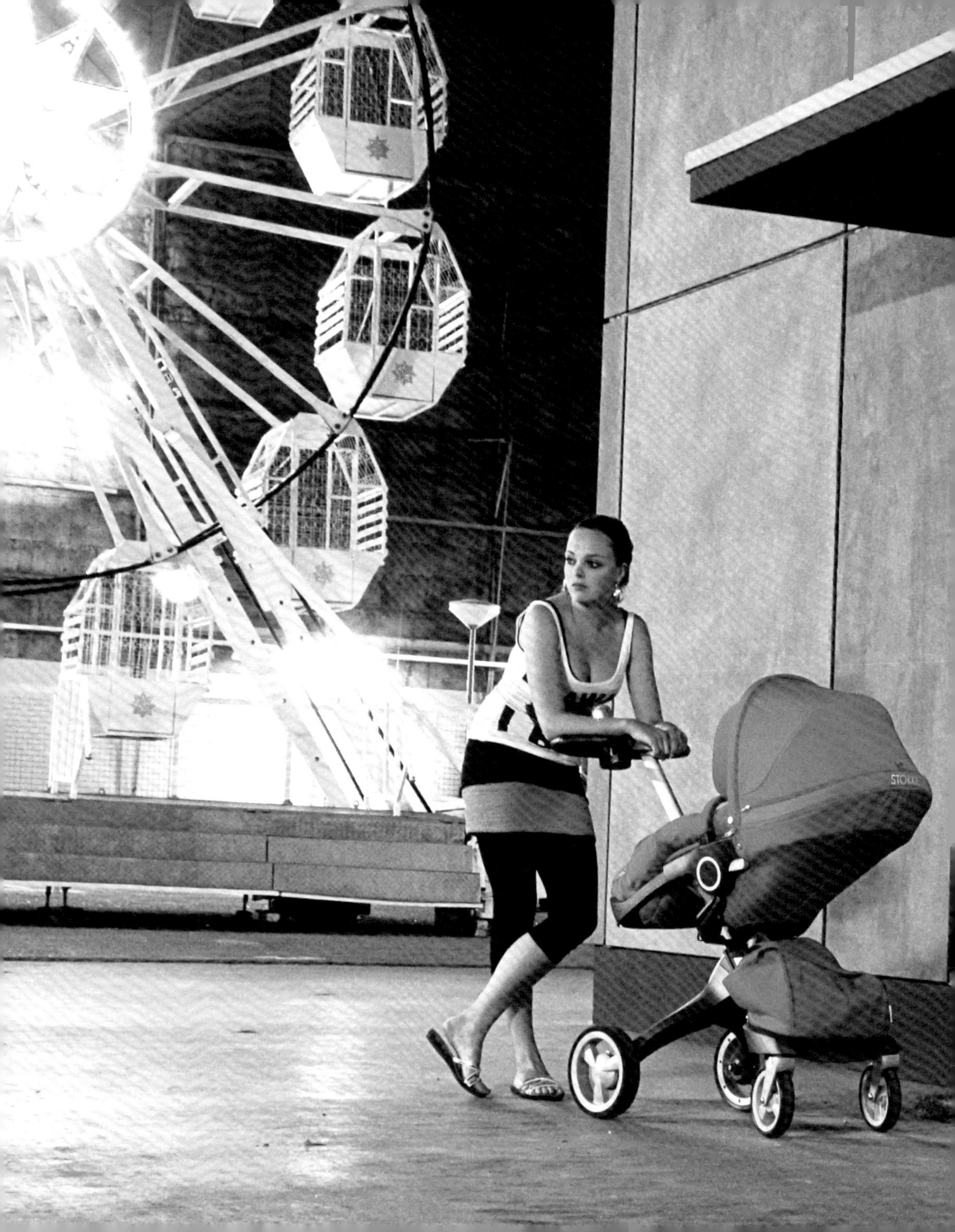
STOKKE

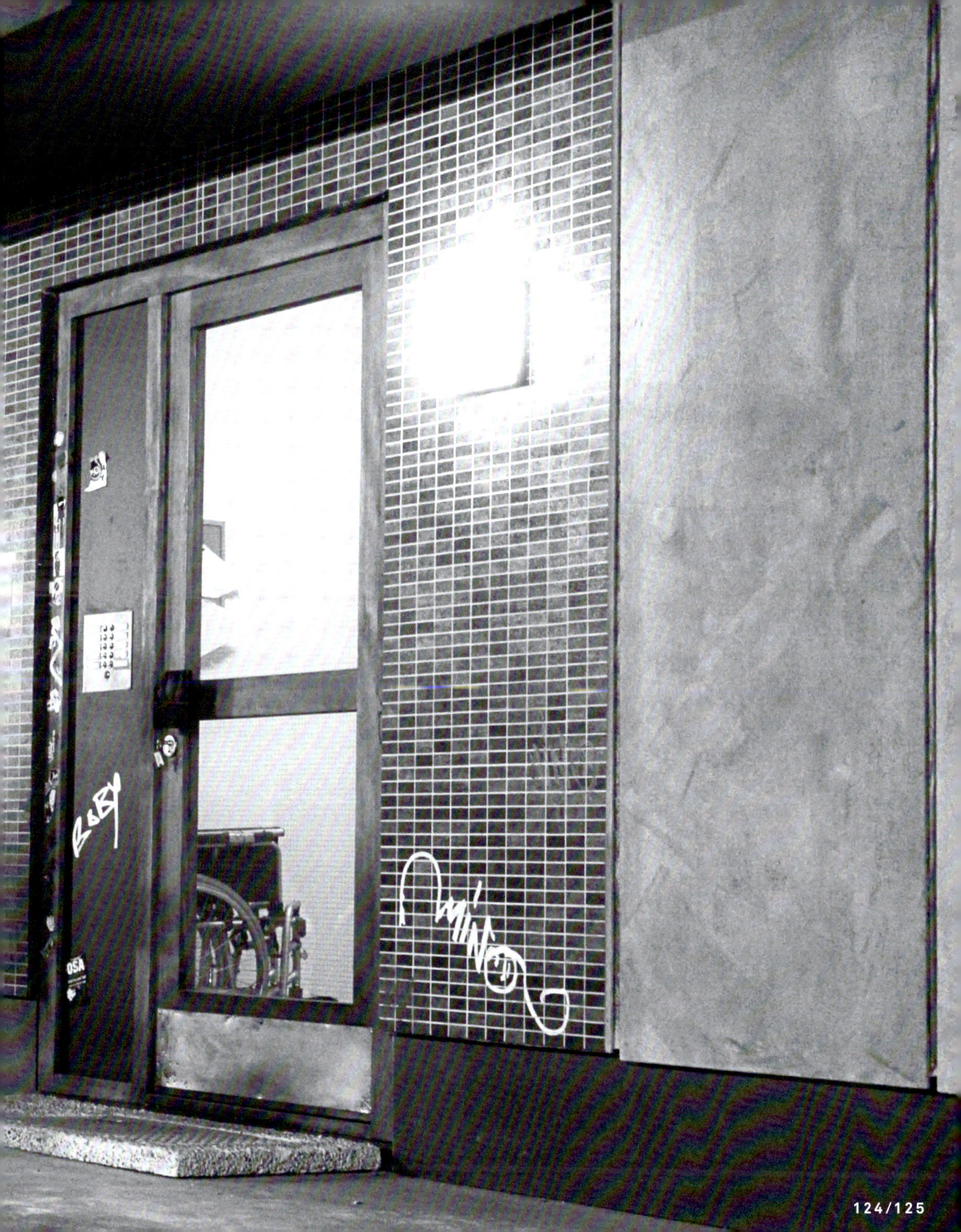

REAL ESTATE AGENTS
2009

Guided tour led by two performers acting as real estate agents through the "For Sale" Danish Pavilion at the 53rd Venice Biennale. The tour includes a brief history of the building and tells the story of the Bergman-esque family dramas that previously haunted the house.

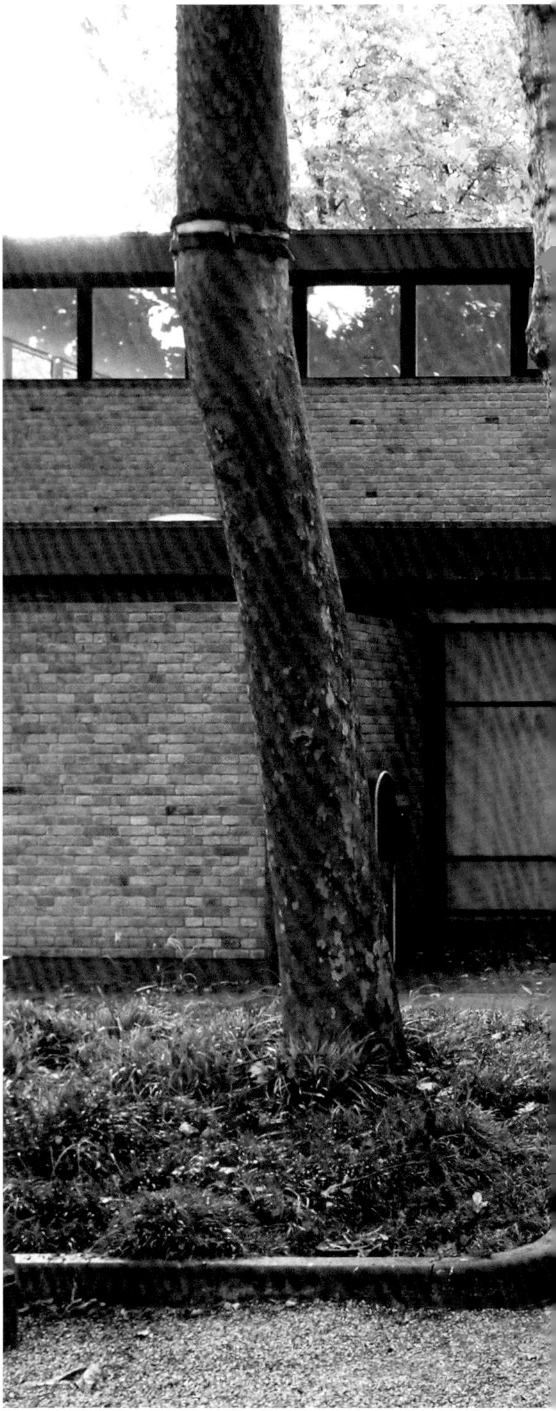

MATERIALS:	*sales brochures and business cards*
PERFORMERS:	*professional actors/comedians (Trevor Stuart and Helen Statman)*
CLOTHING:	*aspirational formal, not quite successful; suit and tie for him, summer dress for her*
DURATION:	*multiple fifteen-minute tours*
PERFORMED AT:	*"The Collectors," Danish Pavilion, 53rd Venice Biennale, 2009*

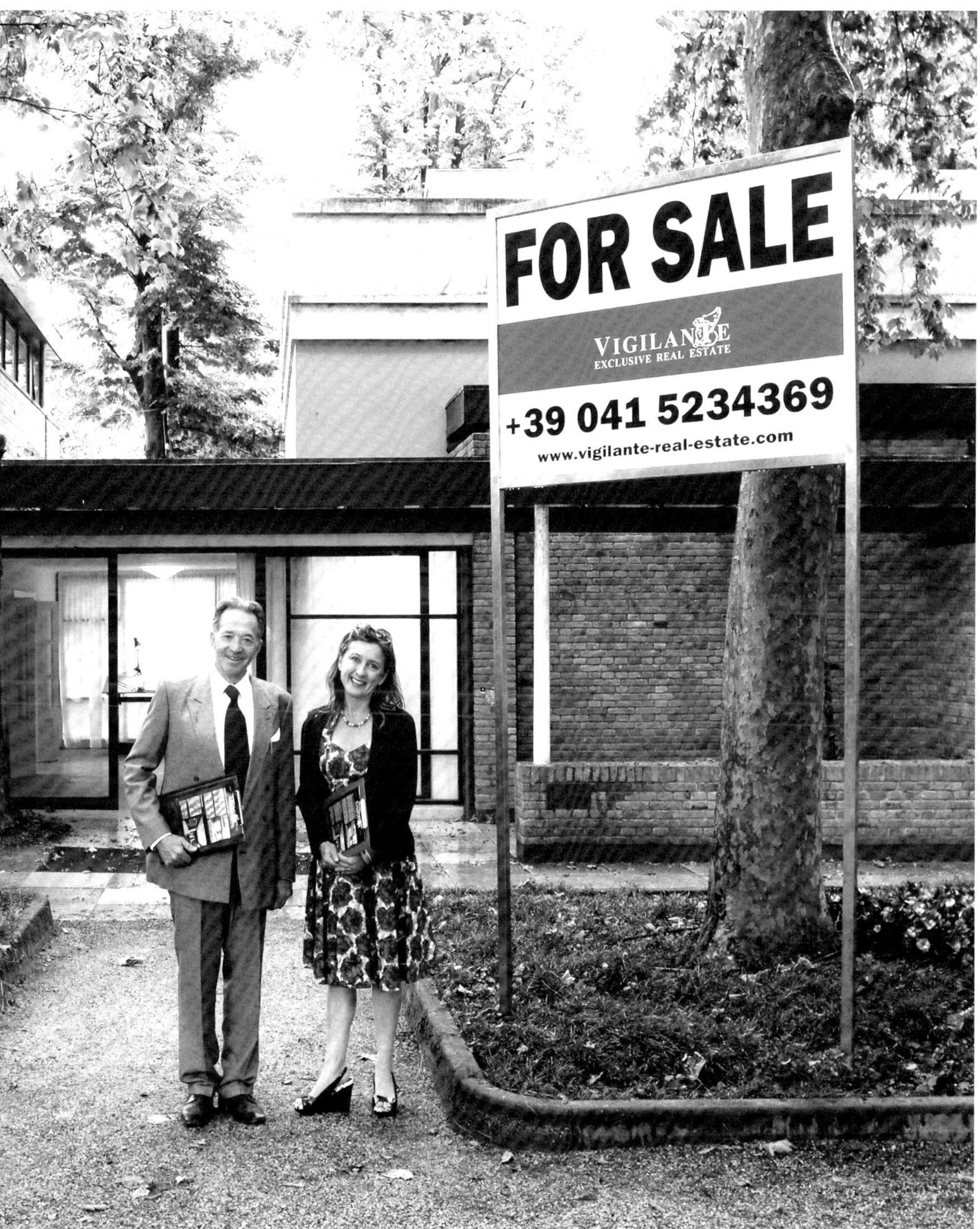
FOR SALE
VIGILANTE
EXCLUSIVE REAL ESTATE
+39 041 5234369
www.vigilante-real-estate.com

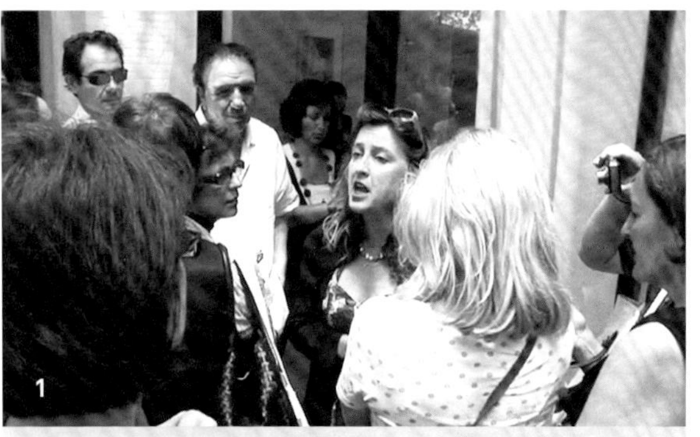

"We have a busy agenda and I'm asking you all to please keep up with the group on our brief tour of the property, another fine example in our current series of opulent offerings. And I'm afraid we don't have time for questions. I'd like to stress that the family is interested in a prompt sale, and we at Vigilante will take that into account should you opt for an early commitment towards ownership."

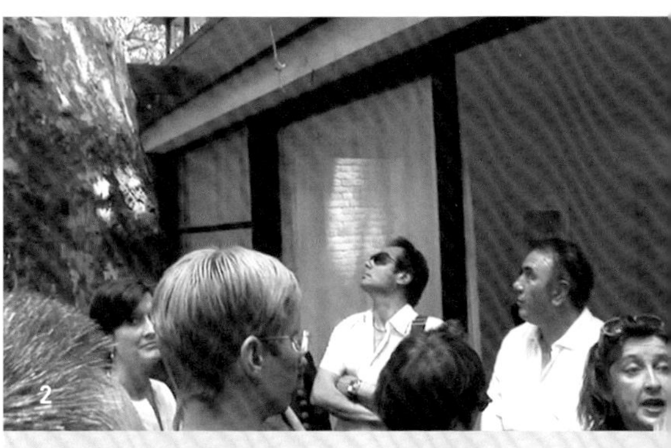

"This building was designed in 1930 by Carl Brummer in the neoclassical style at the rear. Here, we have the modern 1960s late extensions, by another Danish architect, Peter Koch. It has a neoclassical breezy sixties feel to it, with some gorgeous interiors. Do come in..."

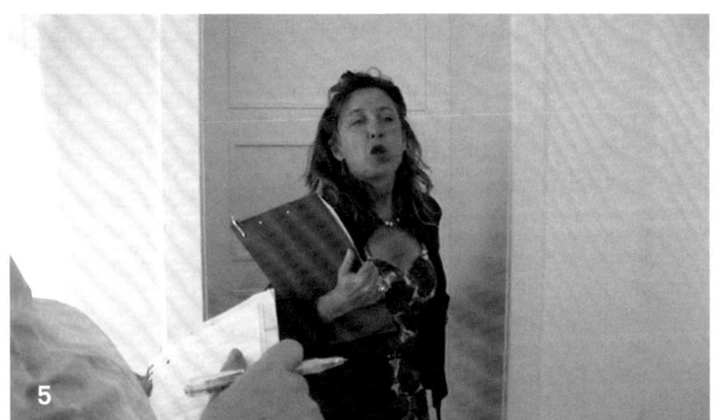

"Ah, the teenage girl who lived here was rather crazy as teenagers do tend to be, so please excuse the, ah, gothic nature of the room... As I said, the family did leave rather hastily, but this room could easily be converted into a classic Danish sauna, and down here we have the escape hatch, which was used by the teenage girl. I think that would easily make an excellent large cat flap."

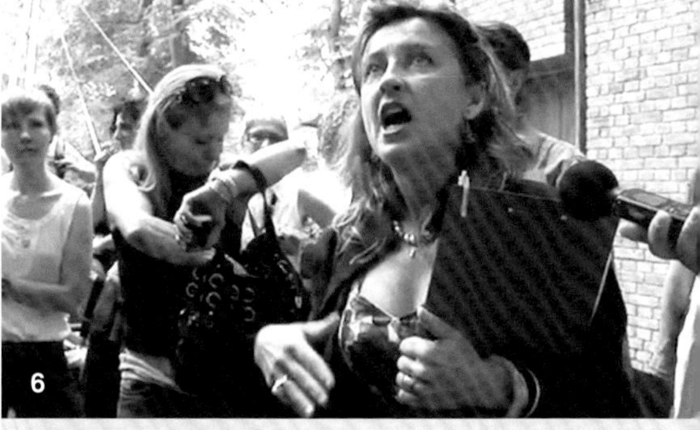

"Now, the current owner is an architect, and, being aware of the building's artistic and historical background, is very desirous for passing it on to somebody of similar taste and values. However, I'm sure that anyone would fall in love with the place, it has excellent transportation facilities and it does share with the rest of the city some charming seasonal water features. So we'll go through to the dining room now..."

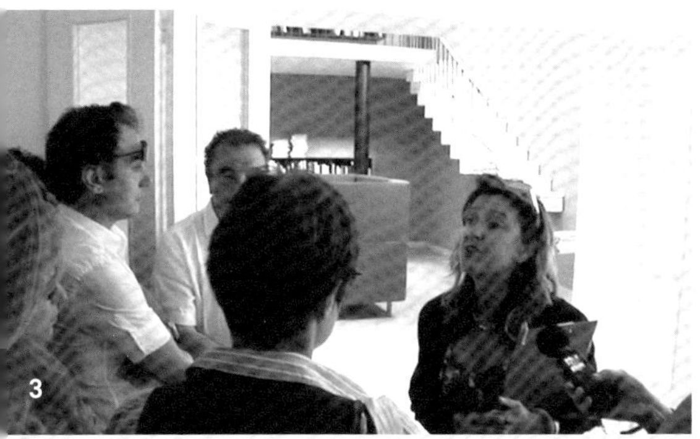

3

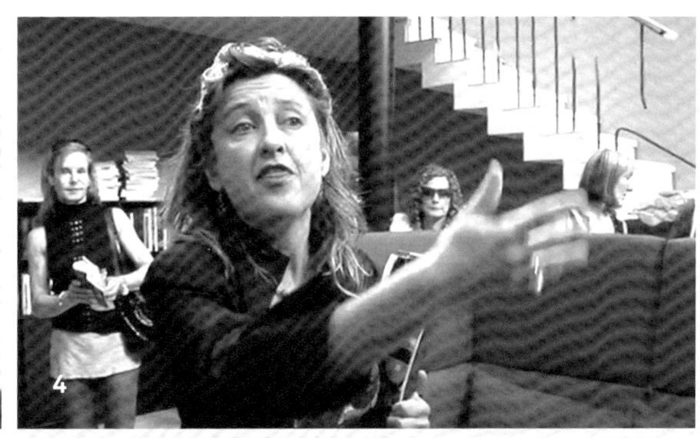

4

"Some of the family's decorations and furniture, personal belongings, have been left here, but I assure you they will all be removed very soon. The family wishes to remain anonymous and all commerce will be dealt solely through the Vigilante Group. You can trust us, we won't disappoint you. 'D.I.E.—discretion, integrity, efficiency' is our mantra."

"I needn't point out that the family has a penchant for collecting all sorts of things. Anything from insects to furnishings to various eclectic accoutrements. It's all very stylish and chic, if you like that sort of thing. Most of the artwork, I'm told, is authentic and made by some quite well known names in the art world, so please do enjoy it whilst it's briefly here."

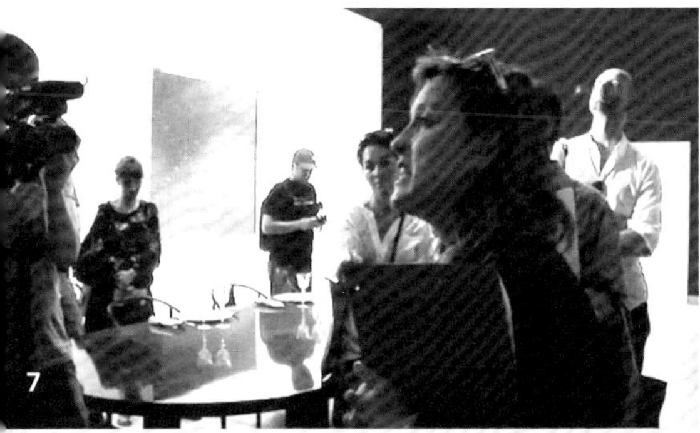

7

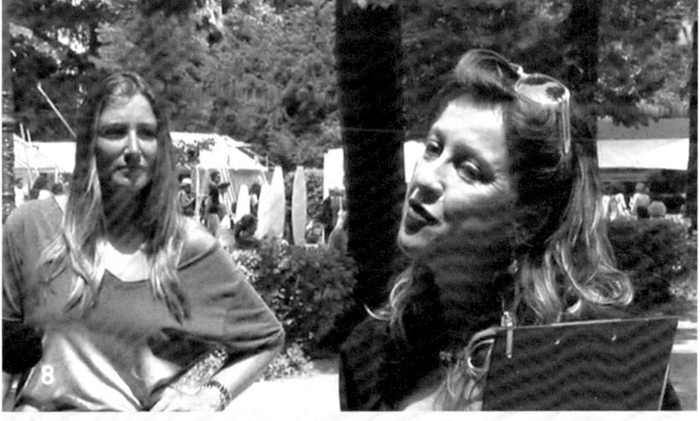

8

"It's really a little piece of country in the city. Now if we take into account the current economic situation in the world, coupled with the location and the time of year, I believe this is a very, very good investment."

"If you would like to have a second viewing, or if you would like to make an offer, please don't hesitate to contact me. In the meantime, I suggest you go over to your neighbor, his house has not been yet put on the market, but he's a very friendly fellow. Ah, of Nordic descent, very special, very modern tastes. I'm sure he will open his arms and welcome you. Ah, it's very, very important for you to know who your neighbors are, so don't be shy, do go next door. Thank you for viewing. Goodbye!"

(selected excerpts from the script by Trevor Stuart)

MATERIALS: *mixed media*
PERFORMER: *male, age 20 - 30*
CLOTHING: *his own*
DIMENSIONS: *site-specific*
DURATION: *the entire exhibition period (ten weeks)*
PERFORMED AT: *"The Welfare Show," Bawag Foundation, Vienna, 2005*

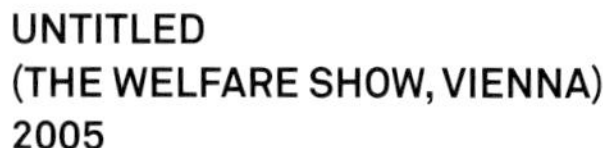

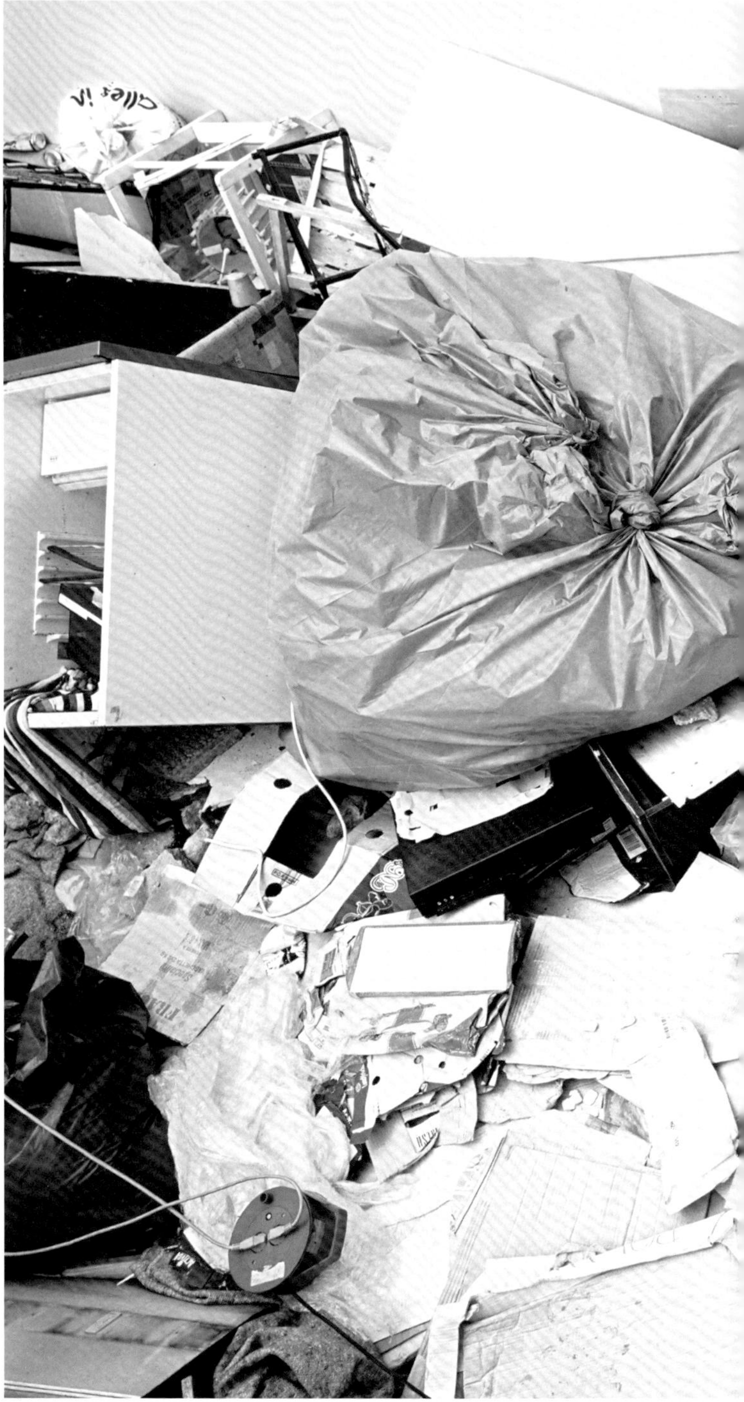

UNTITLED (THE WELFARE SHOW, VIENNA) 2005

Two viewing points with coin operated telescopes. One was located at the entrance, from which spectators could observe the guests in a fancy restaurant across the street, which was frequently visited by prominent bankers and politicians. (One week after the exhibition's opening, the restaurant hung curtains on the windows.) The other viewing point was installed in the foundation director's office with a view into an exhibition space filled with rubbish, with a person rummaging through it looking for anything still useful.

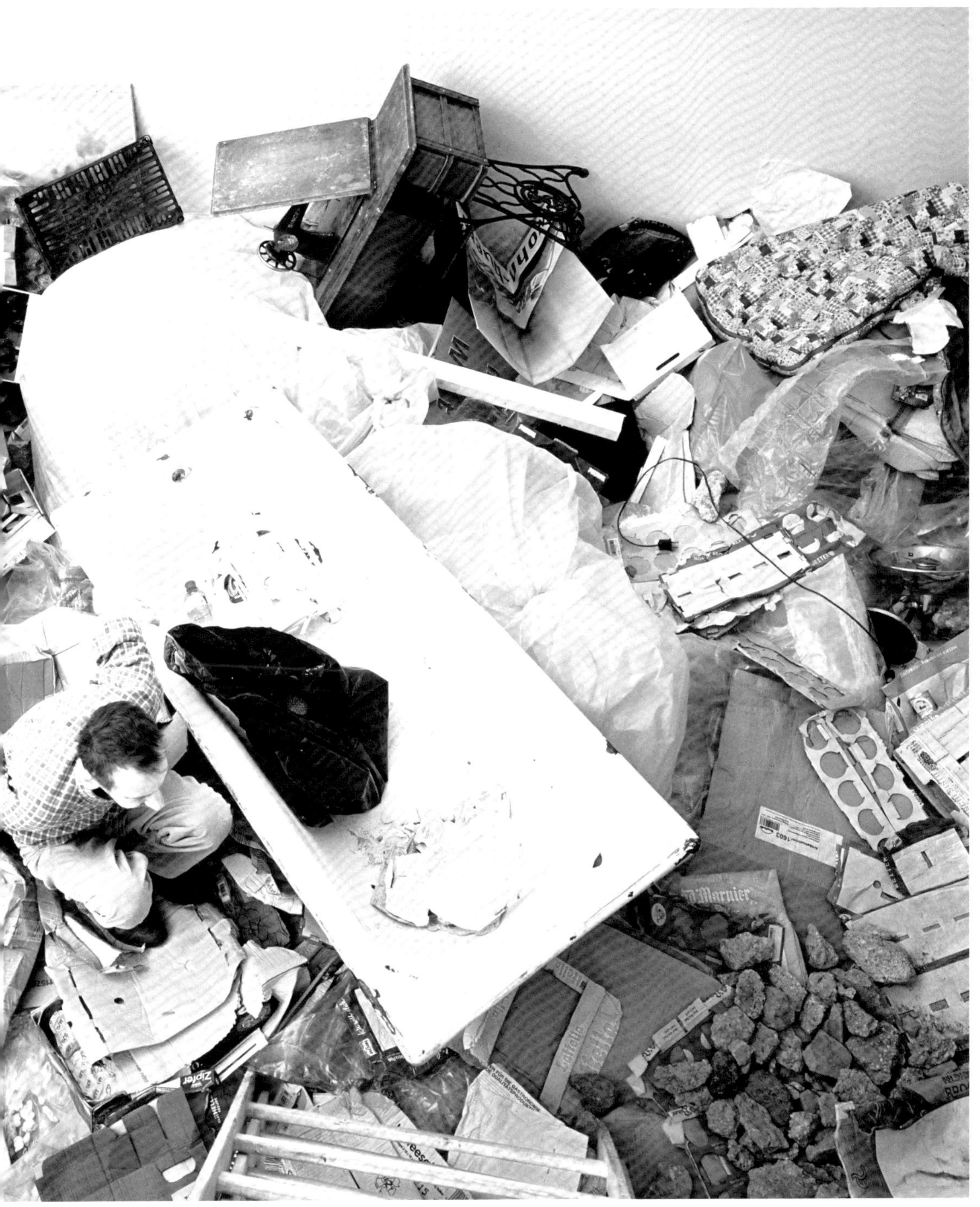
Zipfer

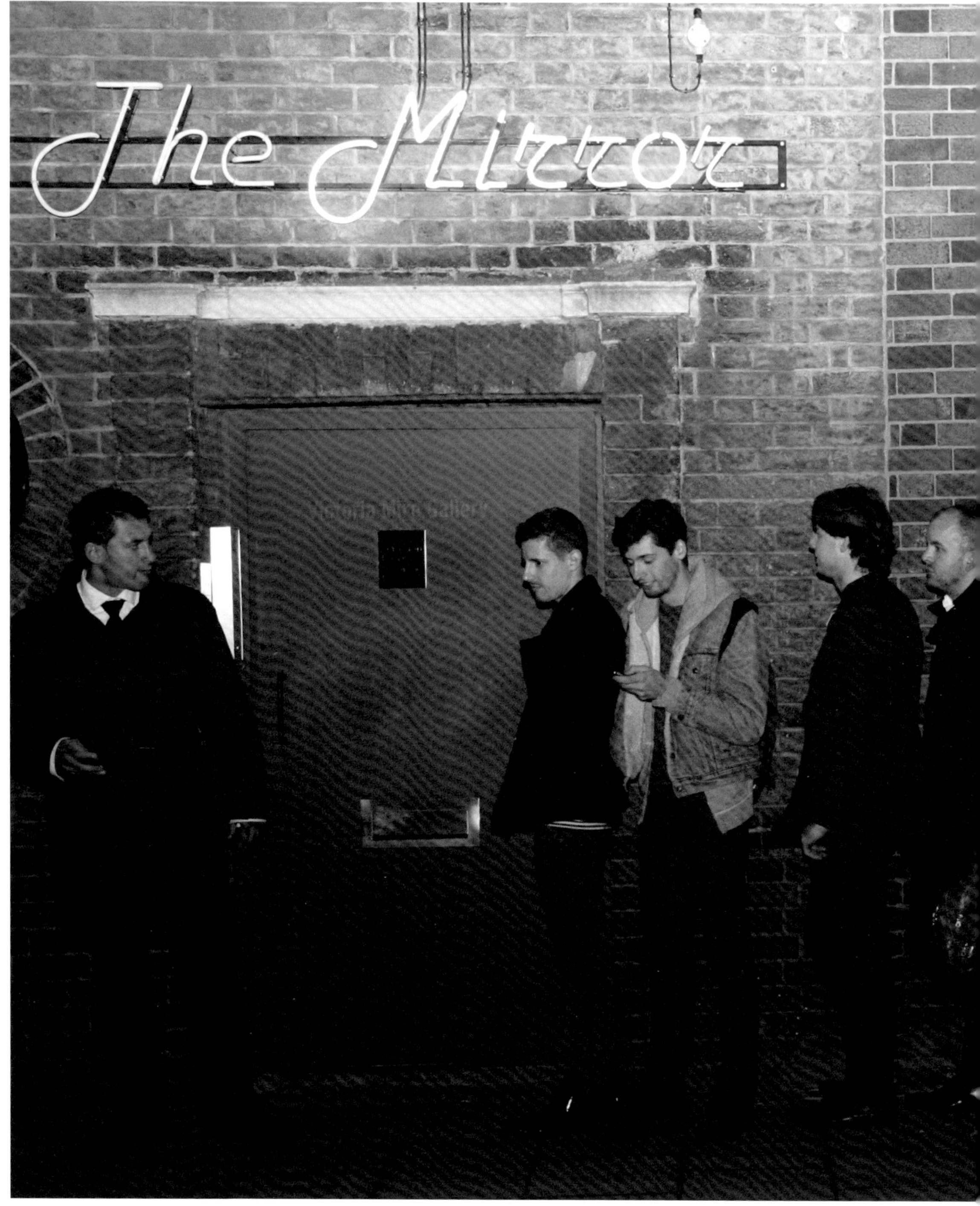
The Mirror

MATERIALS:	*mixed media*
PERFORMERS:	*the party participants*
CLOTHING:	*their own*
DIMENSIONS:	*site-specific*
DURATION:	*party: one night; exhibition: one month*
PERFORMED & EXHIBITED AT:	*Victoria Miro Gallery, London, 2008*

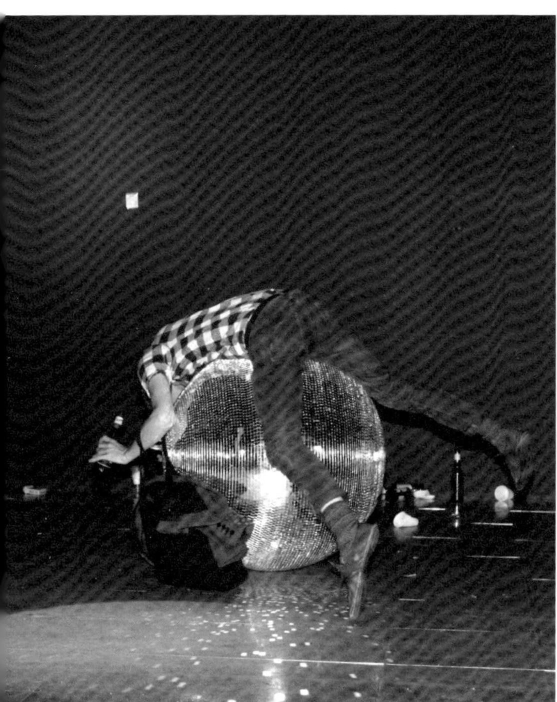

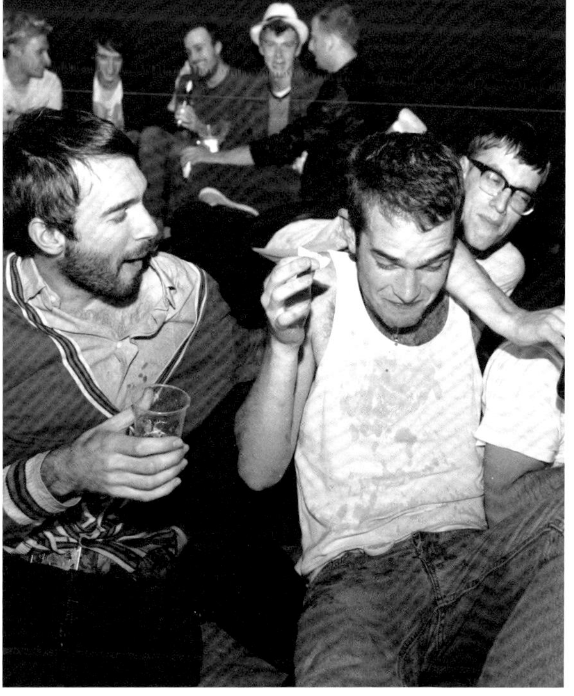

ͻO LATE
ͻ08

ɪmgreen & Dragset transformed the spaces of Victoria ɪiro Gallery in London into a gay club environment dubbed ʻhe Mirror," complete with a coat check, dance floor, disco ghting, seating, bar counter, DJ booth, wall decorations, ilet cubicles, and a visible but inaccessible upstairs VIP ʻea. The exhibition contained the remains of a one-night en-only party held prior to the opening. The guests, DJs ıd guards at the party all knew they were part of a documented, staged event with the purpose of conserving the par-'s remains as sculptural material for the exhibition, which ɔened a couple of days later.

News Front Page

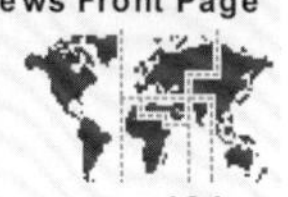

Africa
Americas
Asia-Pacific
Europe
Middle East
South Asia
UK
Business
Health
Science & Environment
Technology
Entertainment
Arts & Culture
Also in the news

Video and Audio

Programmes
Have Your Say
In Pictures
Country Profiles
Special Reports

RELATED BBC SITES
SPORT
WEATHER
ON THIS DAY
EDITORS' BLOG

Last Updated: Monday, 16 June, 2003, 11:31 GMT 12:31 UK

E-mail this to a friend   Printable version

Chimp display is Biennale 'hit'

An art display which features a chimpanzee trying to spell "utopia" using giant lettered blocks has become a huge hit at Venice's Biennale exhibition, according to reports.

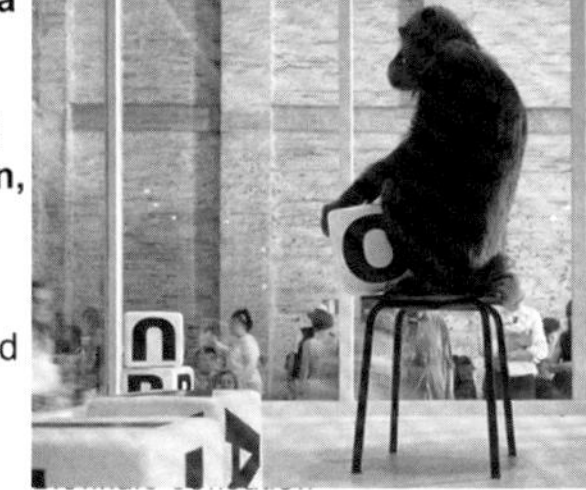

The display, which features an Italian-resident chimpanzee called Lala, was created by the Berlin-based Scandinavian artists Ingar Dragset and Michael Elmgreen.

The show, Spelling U-T-O-P-I-A, features the 20-year-old chimp - who is a star of Italian films including Bongo Bongo - has not yet managed to spell the word, it was reported in The Guardian on Monday.

The installation has been a hit despite the fact Lala has made only two brief appearances in the festival's first two days.

'True diva'

In her first attempt, she nearly spelled the word. In her second, she formed the words T-I-P, T-I-T and then O-U-T before throwing a tantrum, the paper reported.

"You cannot mess with her. She is a true diva," Mr Elmgreen said. "Chimpanzees are very, very strong animals. If they are really provoked, they could kill a human being."

After her two days on show Lala has now returned to her home in Rome.

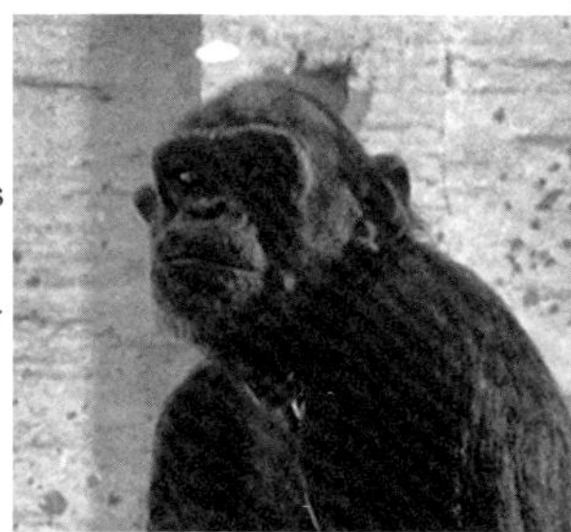

Mr Elmgreen denied claims the chimpanzee had been mistreated by being forced to perform.

"Lala is an old professional. She is the star of many Italian films... we didn't want her to get distressed, so we were very careful to limit her appearances."

While she was staying in Venice, Lala stayed at a secluded garden away from the city's tourist hordes.

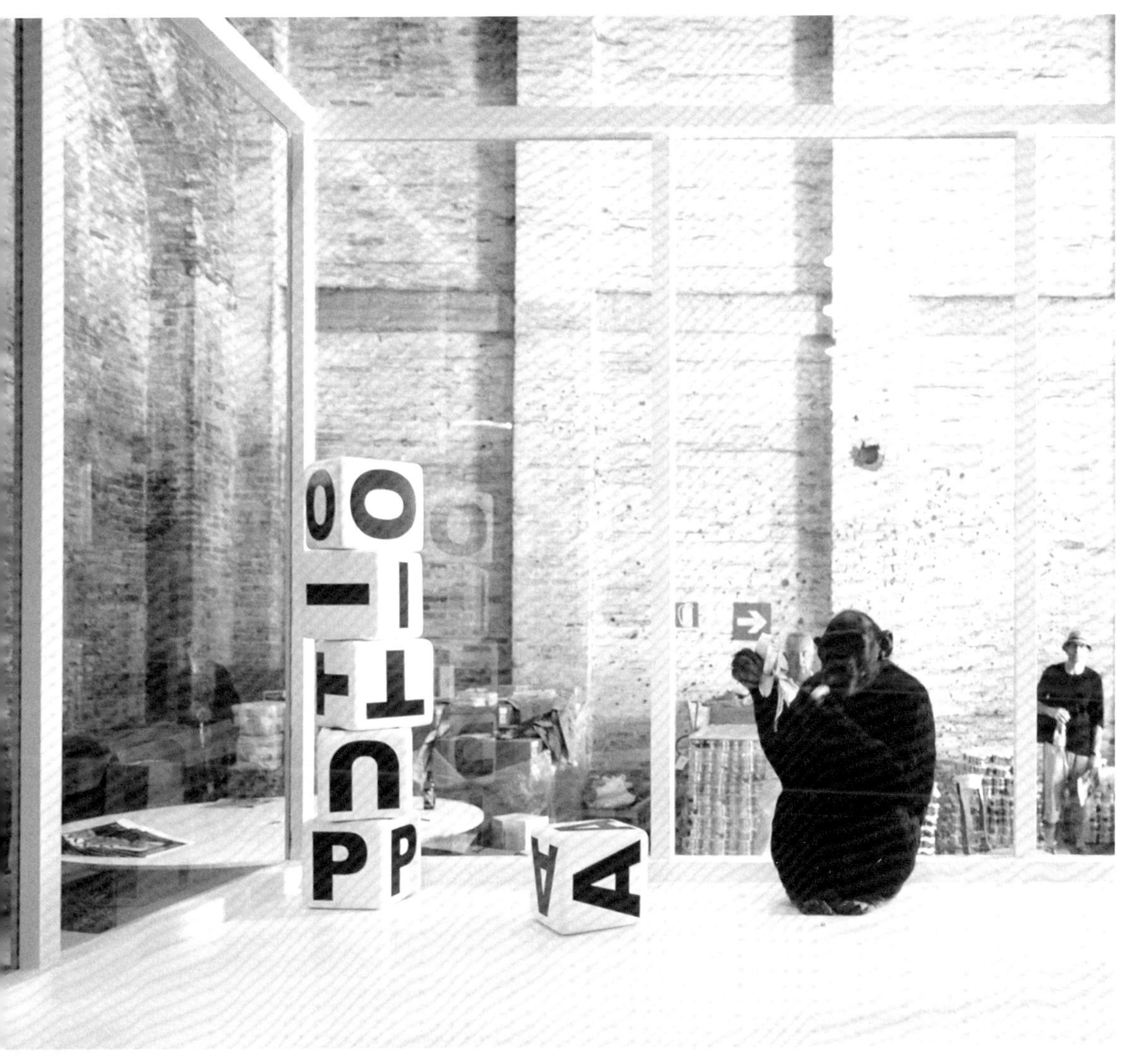

ATERIALS:	*glass, wood, alphabet building blocks*
RFORMER:	*Lala the chimpanzee, aided by her trainer*
MENSIONS:	*glass box: 240 x 400 x 400 cm*
RATION:	*two hours*
RFORMED & HIBITED AT:	*"Utopia Station," 50th Venice Biennale, 2003*

SPELLING U-T-O-P-I-A
2003

Performance installation: glass pavilion with a chimpanzee learning to spell the word "utopia," with the aid of six alphabet building blocks.

4.

THE MALE BODY

4.

WORKS

TEXTS

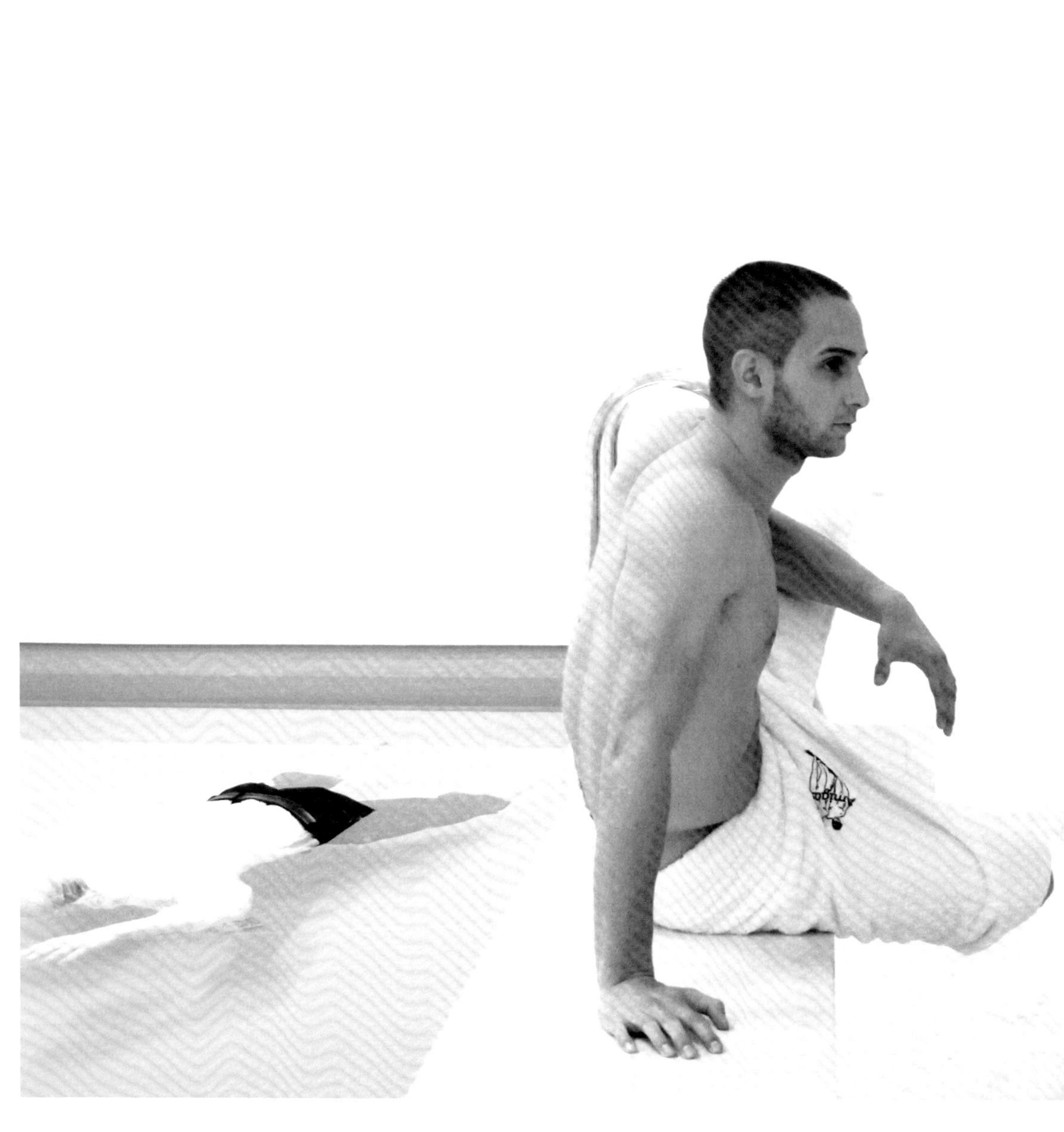

Scenario Planning: Elmgreen & Dragset Queer Agitprop

BY AARON BETSKY

What used to be sublime is now a scenario. We set ourselves up to have extraordinary experiences, whether by taking drugs or setting the stage for great sex, by going to locations far beyond our daily experience, or by going to see art we know will amaze us. We can, to a certain extent, predict our reactions. For almost two centuries, art and architecture had as their core business the presentation of such a sublime in its most compact manner. In the last decade, though artists as varied as Matthew Barney and Anish Kapoor still vend the sublime, more and more makers eschew the minimalism in which the frame disappears and the "oh wow" moment miraculously appears. Instead, they present the scenario itself as the work of art. The masters of such scenario planning and presentation are Elmgreen & Dragset.

—

The roots for such an approach lie in the performances staged during the spring of the Russian Revolution. Big set pieces such as Soyuz Molodyozhi's and Vsevolod Meyerhold's *Victory Over the Sun*, with its Kazimir Malevich sets, and the "agitprop" performances staged all over Russia out of special trains, combined visual art, performance and politics to not just show, but to enact a new society. In a manner that critics such as Walter Benjamin and Berthold Brecht[1] later codified, these performative appearances sought to counter the assimilation of the audience by art's fiction, preferring instead to make them aware of the very mechanisms by which a new world could be created, and inviting them to participate in that activity.

—

The problem with much of the work was that it—by design—made the audience uncomfortable. It was—and is—therefore difficult to make it popular. When forms of agitprop or "total theater" reappeared in the 1960s and 1970s, they did so either by jettisoning the messaging and enforced awareness of the artificial nature of what was going on in favor of hallucinatory performances such as those staged by La Mama in New York, or by breaking the performance down in time and space, integrating it into daily life while maintaining a more enclosed form of fiction. From the performances of Joseph Beuys and his many imitators, to those of Marina Abramović or Bruce Nauman, artists saved the romantic grandeur of gesture and the sublimation of the self in the act of viewing by making it fragmentary, violent, and sexy. By approaching pornography or the ritual reenactment of war that dominates so much of our popular culture, such an art turned the ecstatic experiences you could find in those arenas into moments of self-awareness. The body and its alienation from self and society came back into play, as did the manner in which power structures attempt to control and mediate that alienation, but now in a manner that was fleetingly both pleasurable and painful.[2]

—

Architects and designers picked up on such proposals in staging—or, more often than not, proposing to stage—other worlds that were neither utopian nor dystopian, but were palimpsests of existing conditions. The designers grouped around the Institute for Architecture and Urban Studies (IAUS) in New York and the Architectural Association (AA) in London imagined parallel

1 _ Walter Benjamin, "The Work of Art in the Age of Mechanical Reproduction," in *Illuminations*, trans. Harry Zohn (New York: Schocken Books, 1969), 217-52; Bertold Brecht, *Brecht on Theatre: The Development of an Aesthetic*, trans. John Willett (New York: Hill and Wang, 1977).

2 _ The classic compendium of this work remains RoseLee Goldberg, *Performance: Live Art 1909 to the Present* (London: Thames & Hudson, 1979).

histories for our cities, possible futures, and ways of breaking open existing conditions. Allied with the punk movement in London, the group around Nigel Coates (NATO) spun out ripped and torn urban scenarios, while Bernard Tschumi and Rem Koolhaas, first in London and then in New York, and John Hejduk, produced what the latter came to call "masques:" proposed participatory reorganizations and reenactments of urban environments. Looking back consciously at Russian Constructivism and other foundational moments of modern art as politically engaged collage and reenactment, architects and designers sought to capture the construction of a new world, but in a reflexive, and at times ironic manner.[3]

—

What all this work shared was a reveling in and revealing of decline and mediocrity. "To create great architecture, you might even have to commit a murder," Tschumi claimed,[4] but proceeded to create only visual assassinations of buildings or urban forms, tearing away at existing structures in a manner that later came to be sold by The Museum of Modern Art as "deconstructivism."[5] In this work, at least at its purest as practiced by the IAUS's erstwhile founder Peter Eisenman, and others, architecture was not the making of new forms, but a kind of "archaeology of the real"[6] that sought to unearth the internal contradictions latent in the imposed normalcy of form and norms. Another approach was that favored by Frank Gehry during these days: he sought to assemble structures by reassembling the non-valued aspects of the physical environment, from chain-link fence to exposed wood studs and plywood.

—

A similar impulse opened up in color photography, which during the 1970s and 1980s moved from either documentary criticism or stylized poses towards reveling in the ordinary not as a gritty critique of high art and money, but as having an haunting quality. Just as the architecture critic Mark Wigley had claimed that the clean white forms of modernism were haunted by the real, the repressed, decay, and sex,[7] so photographers such as William Eggleston

---

3 _ For a good review of this period, see K. Michael Hays, *Architecture's Desire: Reading the Late Avant-Garde* (Cambridge, MA: The MIT Press, 2009).

4 _ Bernard Tschumi, *Manhattan Transcripts* (New York: John Wiley & Sons, 1992).

5 _ Philip Johnson and Mark Wigley, *Deconstructivist Architecture* (New York: The Museum of Modern Art, 1998).

6 _ Peter Eisenman, "The Representation of Doubt: At the Sign of the Sign," in *Eisenman Inside Out: Selected Writings, 1963-1988* (New Haven: Yale University Press, 2004), 143-151.

7 _ Mark Wigley, *White Walls, Designer Dresses: The Fashioning of Modern Architecture* (Cambridge, MA: The MIT Press, 2001).

and Joel Sternfeld found within the real an eerie beauty.[8] It was only a step from these meticulously crafted scenes of the almost-everyday to the large-scale enactments of Gregory Crewdson, the computer-manipulated quasi-sublime of Andreas Gursky, and the completely artificial environments of Thomas Demand.

—

A kind of consensus then developed, I believe, in the art of the turn of the 21st century. Furthered, as art always is, by technology, which in this case made it possible to make anything look and even feel real, art and design from many different avenues became interested in the documenting of the other. That subject was not some violent ogre hiding behind the ego, nor was it the disenfranchised millions those of us with means try to ignore. It was not material reality hiding behind consumer fantasy. Rather, this other was the mirror of the social self and thus that which provides the engine for both social and personal transformation. It was what Henri Lefebvre called "representational space,"[9] as opposed to the "spaces of representation" that control our reality. It was our dreams and nightmares hovering at the edges of visibility or enactment. It was any attempt to destroy imposed orders that slither away from class or gender consciousness. It was a sense of self enacted, acted out, only for a moment, before that realization was appropriated and consumed, becoming a representation. Art tried to extend that moment through ambivalence, and that ambivalence through verisimilitude, and the verisimilitude through the capture of the sublime, which is to say some sense of an out-of-body experience that guaranteed the real through experience—but without a set scene that made you aware of its otherness.

—

The theoretical positions surrounding such an art were no longer those of post-structuralism, but rather the peculiar combinations of mimicking and enabling existing social structures and their critique that became evident in the work of Ulrich Beck, with his theories of risk,[10] Peter Sloterdijk and his

---

8 _ Kevin Moore and James Crump, *Starburst: Color Photography in America 1970-1980* (Cologne: Hatje Kantz, 2010).

9 _ Henri Lefebvre, *The Production of Space*, trans. D. Nicholson-Smith (Cambridge: Blackwell Publishers, 1974), 33ff.

10 _ Ulrich Beck, *Risk Society: Towards a New Modernity*, trans. Mark Ritter (London: Sage Publications, 1992).

theories of "spheres" or cocoons,[11] and Anthony Giddens, who proposed that we all seek to act out the roles we would like to appropriate on the stage into which we would like to transform our world.[12] It is the latter's work especially that seems appropriate to read in relation to Elmgreen & Dragset, who came onto the scene right before the turn of the century:

> The self is seen as a reflexive project, for which the individual is responsible… We are, not what we are, but what we make of ourselves… The self forms a trajectory of development from the past to the anticipated future. The individual appropriates this past by sifting through it in light of what is anticipated for an (organized) future.[13]

—

Giddens goes on to explain that, by attempting to control, at least momentarily, time and space, as well as one's body, the self seeks self-actualization, including of his or her own body, but can only do so in a social setting—by "playing" or acting out in a scenario of "opportunity and risk" that lets the self create a kind of sphere of socialized self.[14]

—

It is this kind of acting and acting out that Elmgreen & Dragset have turned into art. They have done so in a manner that carves out a palimpsest of our normal lives, but restages it at the edge of the absurd, risking the return of the repressed in various ways and guises, while tearing away at the art museum's stage to allow a participatory scenario to unfold. They do so while setting their art up as an art experience, which has a distinct place and role in our society.

—

The strategy itself mirrors the manner in which late capitalism does business. Instead of free-flowing profit maximization and entrepreneurship, both the corporate and the state world is dominated by scenario planning, which was first developed by the U.S. military in the 1960s and then adapted by companies such as Shell Oil. It calls for the incorporation of risk and the planning

---

11 _ Peter Sloterdijk, *Sphaeren* (Frankfurt: Suhrkamp Verlag, 1998).

12 _ Anthony Giddens, *Modernity and Self-Identity: Self and Society in the Late Modern Age* (Palo Alto: Stanford University Press, 1991).

13 _ Ibid., 75.

14 _ Ibid., 76, 79.

for an environment that will allow goals to be maximized in terms of human, physical, and financial resources.[15] A good organization sets the stage for its own success, plans its actions, and sells itself in the context it has set up. At the same time, it also imagines alternative outcomes, and plans its behavior for such parallel worlds. It is the multiple and potentially simultaneous staging of such outcomes that distinguishes Elmgreen & Dragset's art from the prioritizing mode of business or government.[16]

—

Two aspects of their character result in many of the particularities and strengths of their work. The first is the rather obvious one that they are, or have chosen to work (as they had no formal training in the field) as installation artists. This is more significant for what they have chosen not to do than anything else. Elmgreen & Dragset are not actors or directors, though they have acted in both capacities. They do not express themselves with painting or what might be recognizable as sculpture. They instead assemble the bits and pieces of a Brechtian theater, Beuysian performance, architectural assemblies perhaps familiar from the work of hybrid artist/designers such as Elizabeth Diller and Ricardo Scofidio, and the particular making or remaking of gallery spaces we today call installation art into stages for the enactment of their and the audience's selves.

—

It is the fact that they are both queer that gives the tone to many of these pieces, while also providing the narrative along which many of their works unfold. The two aspects of their lives are intertwined, both consciously and unconsciously. Elmgreen & Dragset have dedicated much of their work to articulating not just gay identities, but power as well, most famously in the Berlin *Memorial for the Homosexual Victims of the Nazi Regime* (2008). Beyond such a militant stance, there is a sense that the very issues of staging an identity is central to their work not just for ideological reasons, but because that is what queer men and women have tried to do. As I argued in my 1997 book *Queer*

---

15 _ Kees van der Heijden, *Scenarios: The Art of the Strategic Conversation* (New York: John Wiley & Sons, 1996).

16 _ See also Manuel Castells, *The Rise of the Networked Society* (Oxford: Malden Press, 1996), and Reinhold Martin, *The Organizational Complex: Architecture, Media, and Corporate Space* (Cambridge, MA: The MIT Press, 2003).

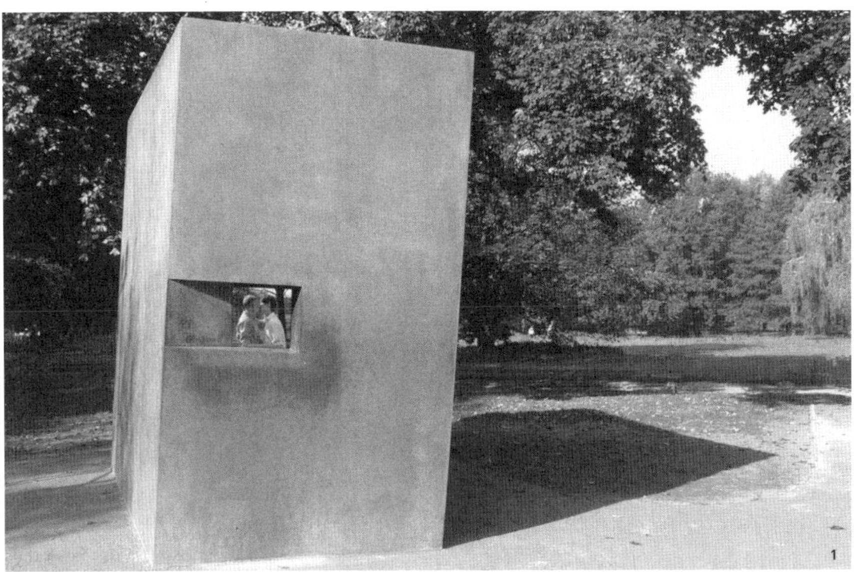

Space,[17] queers have had to create a world for themselves, as they have generally not been able to rely on the structures provided by family, class, or even profession. This "acting out" is evident on many levels, from the manner in which many queer men and women carefully construct the way they appear, to the role playing and fantasy games that attends much queer sex, to the construction of neighborhoods (the West Village, Castro, Mitte) that can act as substitutes for the community environments from which many of them had been ejected, to the choosing of occupations such as hairdressing, flower arranging, decoration and set decoration, and fashion, all of which concentrate on setting the scene.

—

In addition, there is a queer sensibility, one that concentrates on the frustration of power and discipline, either through its denial or through its reenactment. The proliferation of decorative patterns and forms of organization

17 _ Aaron Betsky, *Queer Space: Architecture and Same Sex Desire* (New York: William Morrow, 1997).

Fig. 1 _ *Memorial for the Homosexual Victims of the Nazi Regime*, 2008, Berlin.

that deny perspective or hierarchy are certainly part of this, but so is the fascination with a purely notional scene of discipline, the kind of reenactment of Genetian prison in minimalist modern architecture. Without speculating about the psychological roots for this sensibility, it is clear that it is related, in a social sense, to an attempt to act out the dominant role men are supposed to play in sex as well as in public life, while also appropriating the power structures from which so many queers have been excluded for so long.

—

Finally, there is the interest in voyeurism and public sex. Again, the reason for this phenomenon is, without a doubt, the necessity of having to find a place to meet others and then engage in sexual activity when you can't do it at home. From the first appearance of public space as such (as opposed to unused space, commons, market space, parade places, or other such environments, but specifically places for a newly constituted public to appear and act), queers have appropriated the stock markets of Amsterdam, the alleyways and squares of most cities, the edge where urban forms peter out, the public beach, and especially public lavatory facilities for sex. In so doing, they have found that these spaces have a particular character. They are utilitarian first of all, giving them the hard sense of order. They are expressions of rationality and technology. They are spaces to see and been seen. They are also often liminal, and thus provide vistas of where order breaks down and nature appears or reappears. In all these ways, these sets deny, but also heighten an awareness of the reality of the body, allowing queers to bring the feeling and smell of corporeality back into what is meant to be the most abstract of spaces.

—

There is, without any doubt, a queerness to Elmgreen & Dragset's work, from their frequent references to "tea rooms," or bathrooms used as places of assignations, to the interest in voyeurism in public (the straight version relies more on domestic settings), to the acting out of scenarios of restraint, to the use of attractive young men, sometimes naked, as props in their work. To a certain extent, this is because the scenarios they construct are ones that extend their own lives, as all artists must. Beyond that autobiographical content, however, these scenarios place queer sensibilities at the heart of the art world, in major institutions, public spaces, and trend-setting art festivals.[18]

—

These are also profoundly middle class spaces. They are, in fact, the space where the bourgeoisie, that group of people who do not belong to a place because they either own it or are owned by the people who own it, appear. It is the place of freedom where they can make a world for themselves. They do so by creating stage sets on which they can appear, whether public ones such as the public square, the theater, or the arenas of democracy, and later of course the department store and mall, semi-private ones such as places of work, or domestic ones, where they create, around the religion of education and moral rectitude, a logical and believable universe to carry on.

—

Queers (as opposed to men and women with same-sex desires) are made possible by the emergence of the middle class, and extend their need to make a world for themselves, with its own order and aesthetic. They also take the artifice of their social relations, which are continually invented, reinvented, and calculated, to an extreme. At the same time, they bring back what the middle class must repress in order to create its rational world, and that is the messiness of the body and all the attempts to control it.

—

Thus queerness is in itself a palimpsest of the middle class attempt to create a stage on which to appear, while the middle class is the group of people who need to act out Giddens' scenario. Elmgreen & Dragset work exactly at the point where this becomes clear, covering the range of roles in which the middle class individual makes her- or himself in the arenas, from the office to the supermarket, where this occurs. In more recent work, in particular the set pieces associated with "The Welfare Show" (2005-2006) in its various itera-

---

18 _ For other uses of sexuality in art, see Lesley Hall Higgins, *The Modernist Cult of Ugliness: Aesthetic and Gender Politics* (New York: Palgrave Macmillan, 2002).

tions and with the similarly morphing series they call “The One & The Many” (2010-2011), these concerns have become particularly explicit.

—

What makes these pieces come alive is the fact that they work at the fringes of middle class life, reenacting the place where it falls apart. In general, this is the place where bourgeois norms shade off into state supported poverty, on the one hand, and the ostentatious pretensions of aristocracy on the other hand. It is also where the middle class must assimilate diverse populations in order to keep its economic logic. Thus, while some versions of “The Welfare Show” treat us to what appears to be a dole office or uses people on the dole (acting as guards), “The One & The Many” offers tableaux of the mass produced, cellular containers for middle class life filled with a variety of ethnicities, tribal associations, and “lifestyle” interests.

—

In themselves, these more and more elaborate sets repeat themes that occurred earlier in the work. What are missing, however, are the activities and objects that were overtly critical in early work. There is not the critique of both work and art in the repetitive acts such as the continual repainting of galleries with which they launched their career, nor are there the objects, such as the camper crashing into the ground (*Short Cut*, 2003) or the Prada store (*Prada Marfa*, 2005), that used metaphor and fetishism to refer to the internal contradictions and imminent failures of the bourgeois system. Now there is just reenactment, kept at the level of ambivalence in terms of its meaning. If many of the previous pieces were part of what Elmgreen & Dragset called *Powerless Structures*, which made their anger at or cynicism about, but above all else their desire to deliciously pervert, the artifices by which middle class norms are enforced overt, the current shows are interactive efforts of great complexity, in which all you can do is wander and wonder.

—

The series that make up both "The Welfare Show" and "The One & The Many" are quite literally scenarios. They are also queer fantasies brought to life (and, in the case of "The Collectors," their contribution to the 2009 Venice Biennale, perhaps queer nightmares). They are also enactments of the hidden lives of the middle class.

—

In the first sense, Elmgreen & Dragset's pieces are without precedent in the world of installation art in terms of the elaborateness of both their sets and their stories. While other artists have acted out plays, and others have and are creating *trompe l'oeil* environments (think of Mike Nelson), none have created this kind of combination of the two. The effect is close to a Wangerian *gesamtskunstwerk*—all that is missing is the music to make it all meld together. It is, however, the fact that there is no music, as well as no barrier between actors and audience, that makes these pieces live out Wagner's dream (though not in a way he would have imagined) by creating a complete, immersive environment.

—

Elmgreen & Dragset queer that situation not only in those situations where sex or its promise is an essential part of the "action," but in the way that they depend on posing for dramatic effect. Their actors spend most of their time striking the pose, which is to say taking a standard body posture into the realm where it invites desire. When they are not posing, they are collecting or decorating, thus creating a substitute world in which they can act, or they are acting in poses of control (as guards) or submission (as naked models). This is not just any scenario, but one that is permeated with the modes of same-sex desire.

—

What makes that perversion possible is the manner in which it creeps into the scenes of an everyday middle class life: going to the supermarket or, in these difficult times, the dole office; sitting at home around the television or the computer; using the ATM machine or attending a cocktail party. The underclass seeps in, working on your limousine or threatening you as you walk down a long

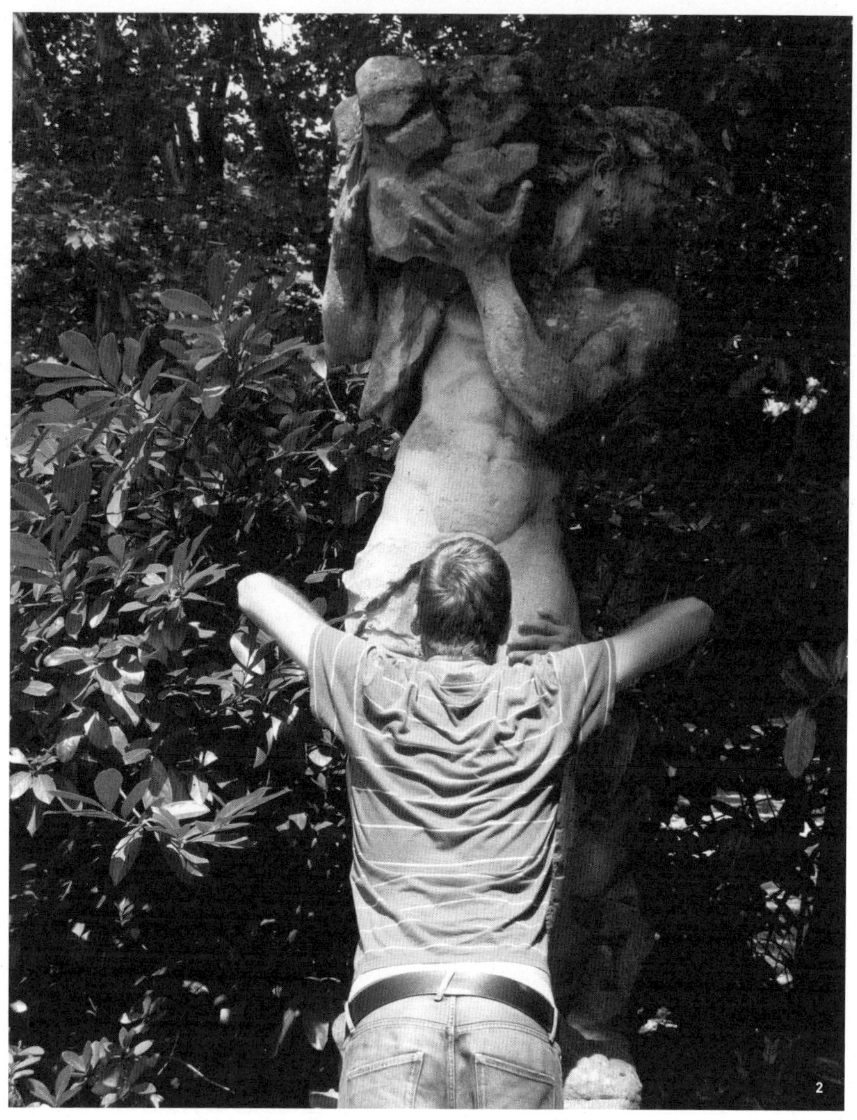

Fig. 2 _ A photograph from *The Incidental Self*, 2006-2007.

tube, but that danger only makes you realize the achievements of bourgeois life. Childhood memories come back as a child curled up by a fireplace. Elmgreen & Dragset reveal middle class life, and show that there are bodies, desires, dangers, and perversions built into it. What there is not is any hope. These are claustrophobic scenes. Luckily, they are just scenes.

—

Except, of course, they are more than that. In these pieces, you might be an actor, and you run the danger of being accosted or made a participant in these tableaux. The actors make you uncomfortable first because you don't know whether they are them or you, whether they are playing a role for play or playing out their role in society. They also work at questioning your norms, confronting you with threats of violence, outrageous interpersonal behavior, or offers of sex.

—

What Elmgreen & Dragset achieve in this latest series of works is an outing. Not only are hidden desires made explicit, but also the hypocrisy of those who would repress those desires becomes evident. It is not just latent sex or violence that is at issue. Those without work or home are outed, placed in uniforms as objects for us to view or talk to. The fact that so many of us are, as the Dutch put it so politely, *allochtoon*, or from other places—a reality that we too often forget when we enter into the precincts of art—not only becomes evident, but becomes real in such a way that you realize your own prejudices about the other among us.

—

For these artists, it is all personal. In commenting on their own work, they often have spoken about feeling like voyeurs.[19] That is not only because of their queerness, but also because they chose not to take the academic route through the art world, being trained and then acting on their education in the making of beautiful objects, images, and spaces. Perhaps it is even their position as foreigners operating in Berlin that contributes to that sensibility. One of the telling motifs that plays through *The Incidental Self*, their 2006-2007 display of hundreds of highly personal snapshots and photographs propped up in a manner that was

19 _ "Michael Elmgreen and Ingar Dragset: Celebrity—The One & The Many. ZKM Museum of Contemporary Art," Vernissage TV video, 4:13, November 9, 2010. Online at http://vernissage.tv/blog/2010/11/09/michael-elmgreen-and-ingar-dragset-celebrity-the-one-the-many-zkm-museum-of-contemporary-art/.

ambivalently between the display in a store and in a gallery, was the recurring images of great and not so great classical sculptures photographed so as to bring out their homoerotic quality. We can queer all art, and catch you watching, they seemed to be saying.

—

Thus Elmgreen & Dragset have turned the agitprop theater into drag, which is to say, a self-consciously theatrical acting out of the forms in such a manner that norms break and desire seeps out. They have created art that is not metaphorical, allegorical, or representational, but queering and acting out. In their hands, neither public space nor the white walls of the gallery are neutral, but rather are there to heighten perversion. It's all an act, and you are acting in it, if you like it or not.

—

Ultimately, this art is about power. There is the power to appropriate all structures, from the monumental to the mundane, which is proper to the artifices of art, but not used nearly enough. There is the power of performance itself, which heightens and opens up personas. There is the revolutionary power in these theatrical appropriations and enactments, which take these structures away from the functions, both socially and in terms of use they were designed to have. There is the power of queering, which uses the quasi-outsider status based on the most human of our attributes, sexual desire, to pervert middle class norms and re-enact them in a parallel scenario.

—

There is also the power to make you look. This is art that can be pornographic, or titillating, and thus subjects you to its will by making you, despite your training or even inclinations, regard it, and then be absorbed by it. The moment you are reassured that this giving over of your power is acceptable, because, after all, it is art you are regarding, and art wants to take us out of ourselves, this art takes you back to the grittiness, the mundaneness, and the hypocrisy of everyday life. The sublime never transports you, and you come crashing down to yourself and your society.

—

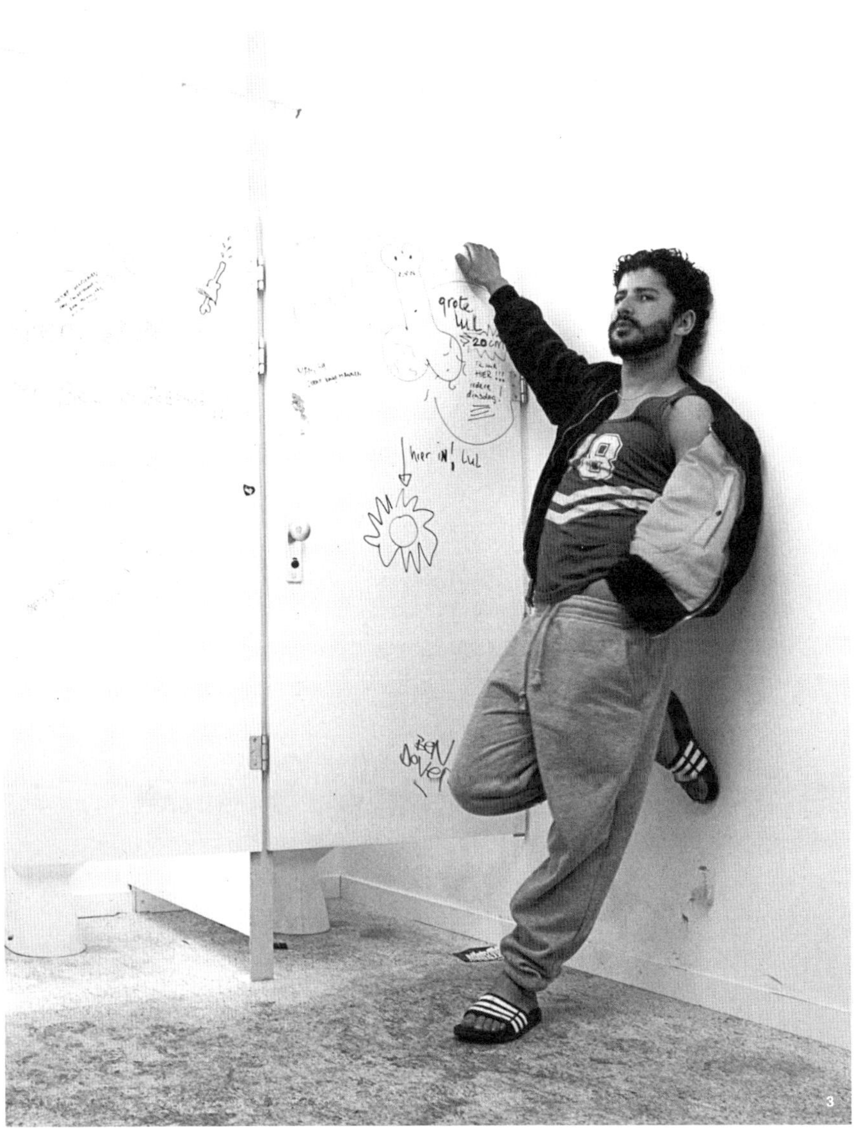

Fig. 3 _ An actor portraying a young gay hustler in *The One & The Many*, 2011, Museum Boijmans Van Beuningen, Submarine Wharf, Rotterdam.

But, you know what you are doing. You know this is art. There now, don't worry, your power is restored. As a connoisseur, you can arrange what you experienced as you see possible and appropriate. You can, as I am doing now, categorize it, analyze it, and make it work for you. Until, that is, that guy in the hoodie scares you enough to make you sidle away at calmly regarding the poor gay kid asleep in his room, with Gay Romeo on his computer connecting him to countless others who don't know he's not real, making you wonder about what you are seeing on the Internet, and then another guy turns out the light in the bathroom and makes a move on you.

—

In the end, you emerge. It is, thank heavens, just art. There are limits, both to the actors' behavior and to the place in which this all takes place. We still live in a functioning society in which art, queerness, and anything else weird or wonderful has its place. The power of this place is to weird you out, to make you wonder at its beauty, and question what makes it possible. There, you have a role to play. ———

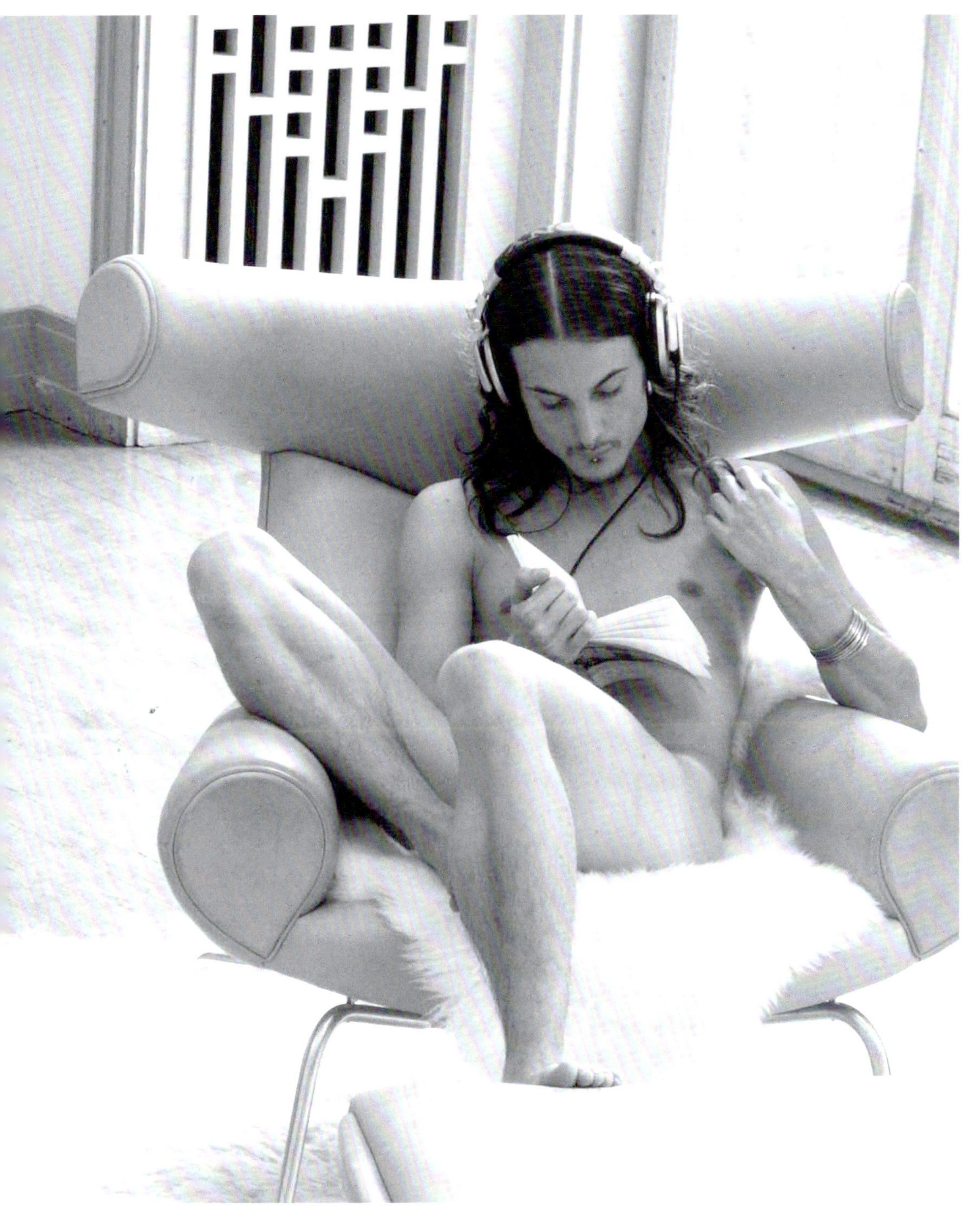

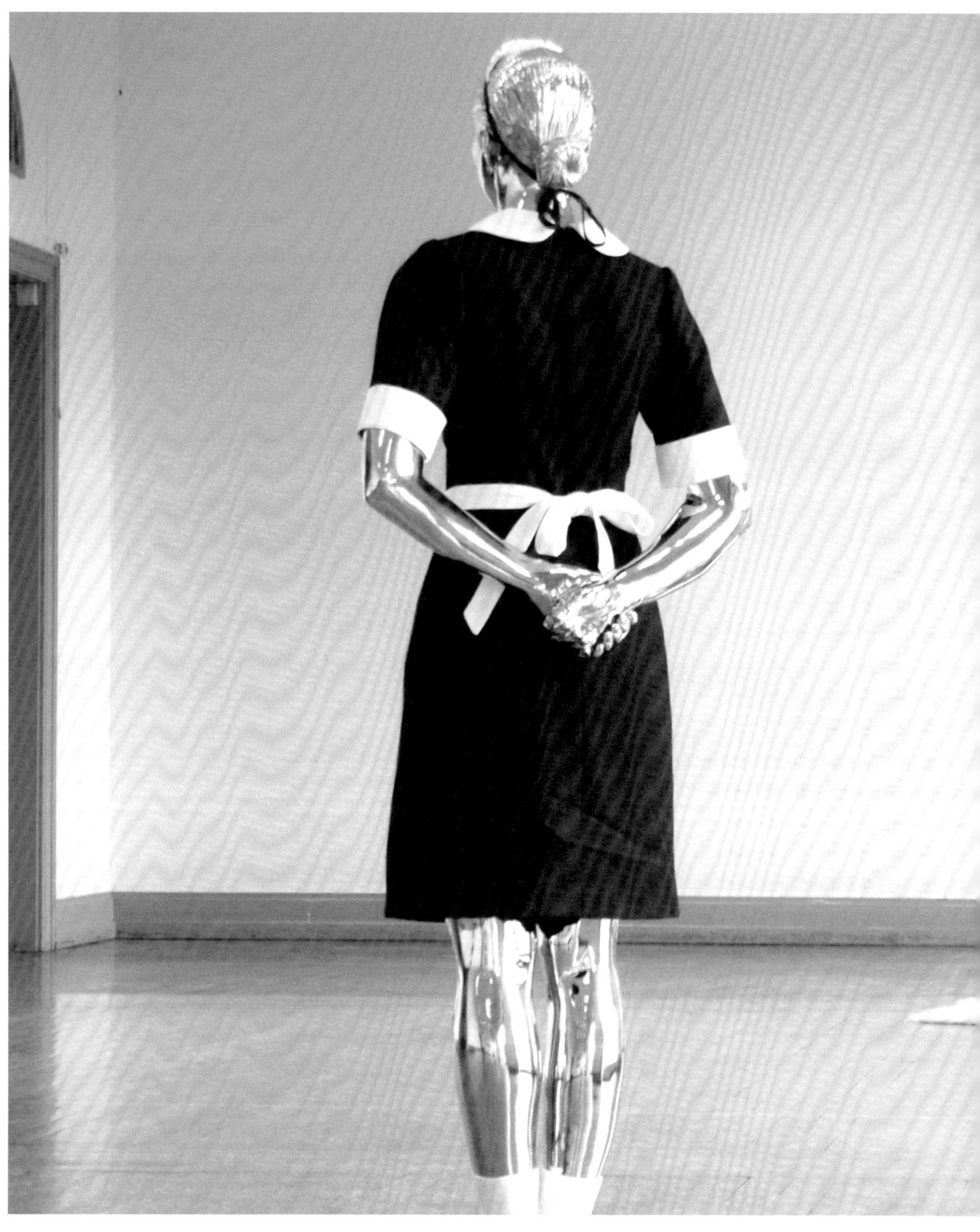

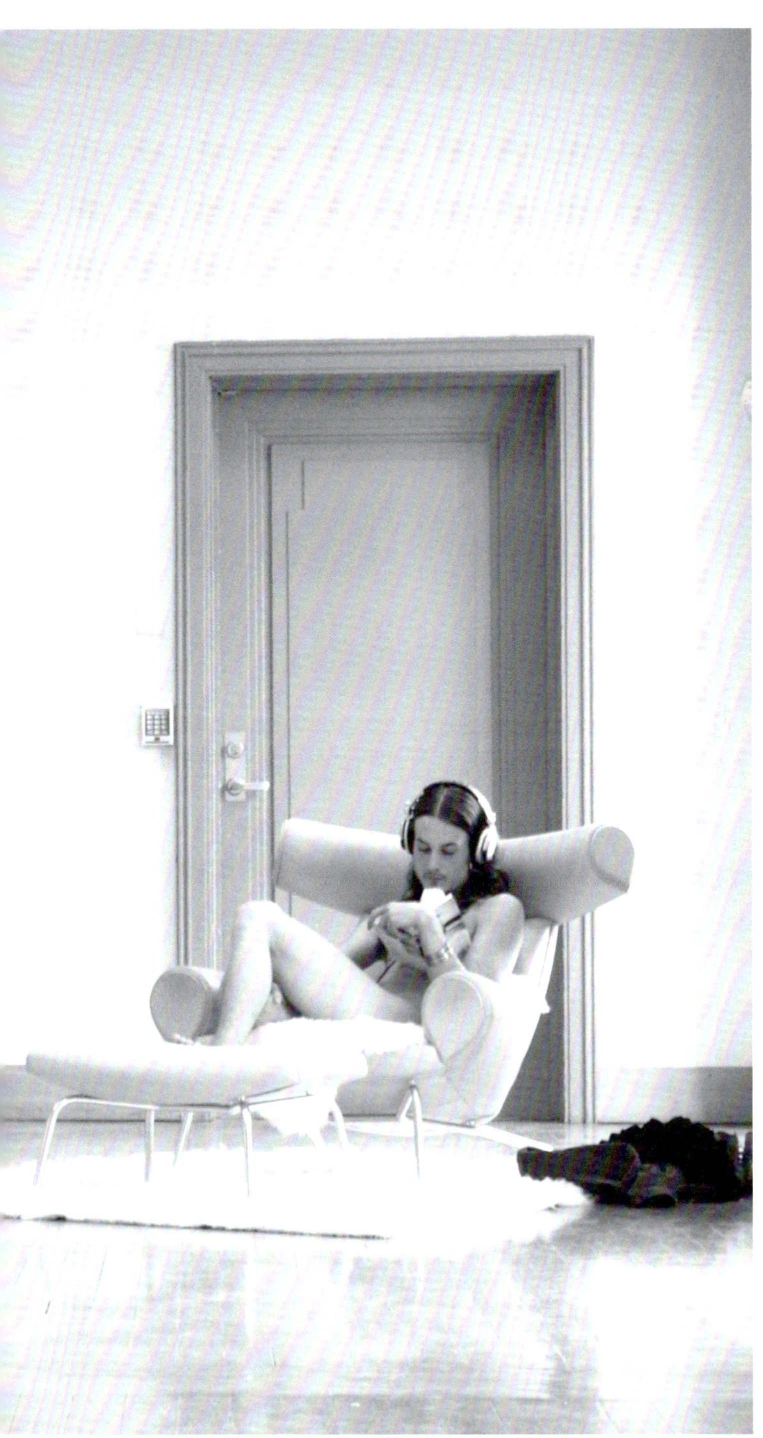

MATERIALS:	*Wegner Ox chair (black or beige), shag rug, headphones, iPod, book*
PERFORMER:	*young male, age 18 - 25*
CLOTHING:	*naked*
DURATION:	*throughout the opening reception for the exhibition (minimum two hours)*
PERFORMED AT:	*"Home is the Place You Left," Trondheim Kunstmuseum, 2008; "The Collectors," Nordic Pavilion, 53rd Venice Biennale, 2009*

UNTITLED (HOME IS THE PLACE YOU LEFT) 2008

A naked young man sitting in a chair, listening to music on an iPod/headphones (chosen by the young man) and reading a book (chosen by the artists). For the first performance at the Trondheim Kunstmuseum, the performer was reading the stories in the publication that accompanied the exhibition "Home is the Place You Left." For the second performance at "The Collectors" at the Venice Biennale in 2009, he was reading a collection of William Blake's poems.

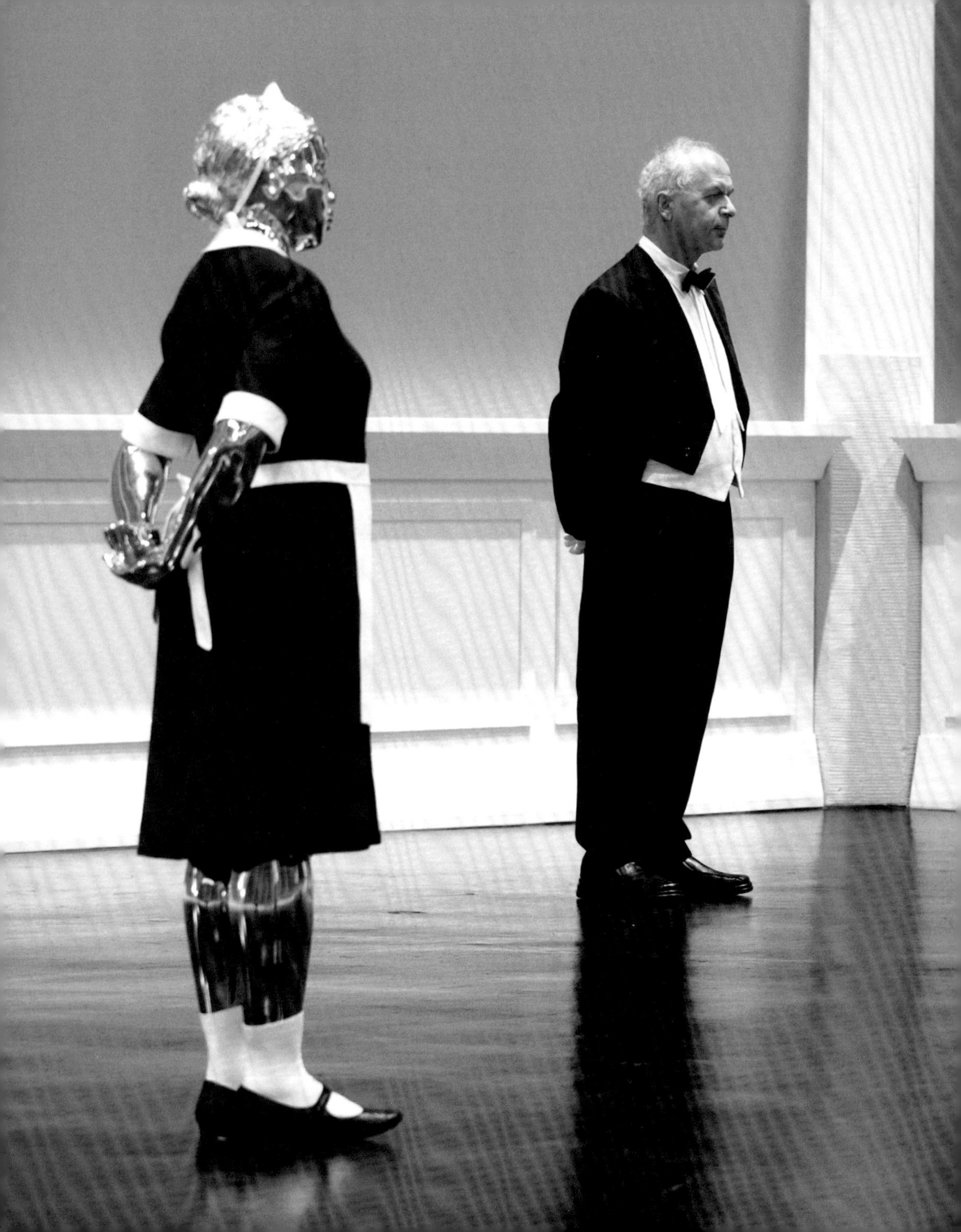

BUTLER
2010 - 2011

A silent, immobile museum guard dressed in a traditional butler's uniform in the ballroom installation at the ZKM | Center for Art and Media, Karlsruhe, 2010 - 2011, Karlsruhe. The installation also includes two gilded maid sculptures standing upright and a realistic looking boy figure crouching inside a large fireplace, creating a surprise effect with the audience whenever the live butler blinks or makes small movements.

ERFORMER: *male, middle aged to older*
LOTHING: *traditional butler's uniform*
URATION: *the entire exhibition period (four months)*
ERFORMED AT: *"Celebrity —The One & The Many," ZKM | Center for Art and Media, Karlsruhe, 2010 - 2011*

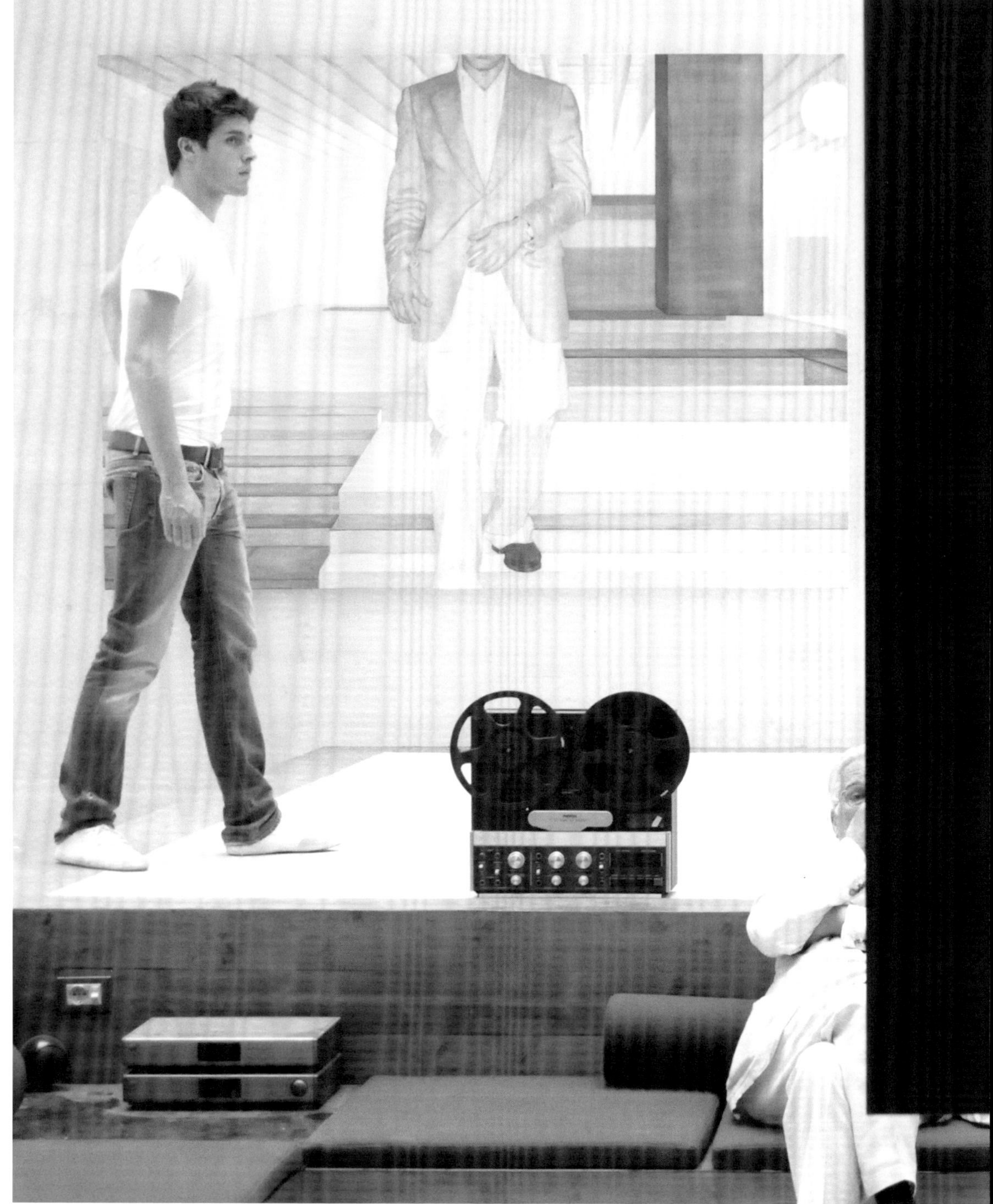

PERFORMERS:	*young males, in their 20s*
CLOTHING:	*jeans and T-shirts*
DIMENSIONS:	*variable*
DURATION:	*the entire exhibition period (five weeks)*
PERFORMED AT:	*"The Collectors," Nordic Pavilion, 53rd Venice Biennale, 2009*

GUARDIANS
2009

At the 53rd Venice Biennale, a group of young male "hustlers" hang out inside the Nordic Pavilion, a flamboyant bachelor pad filled with the domestic remnants of the mysterious Mister B. The young men also act as actual guards of the exhibition.

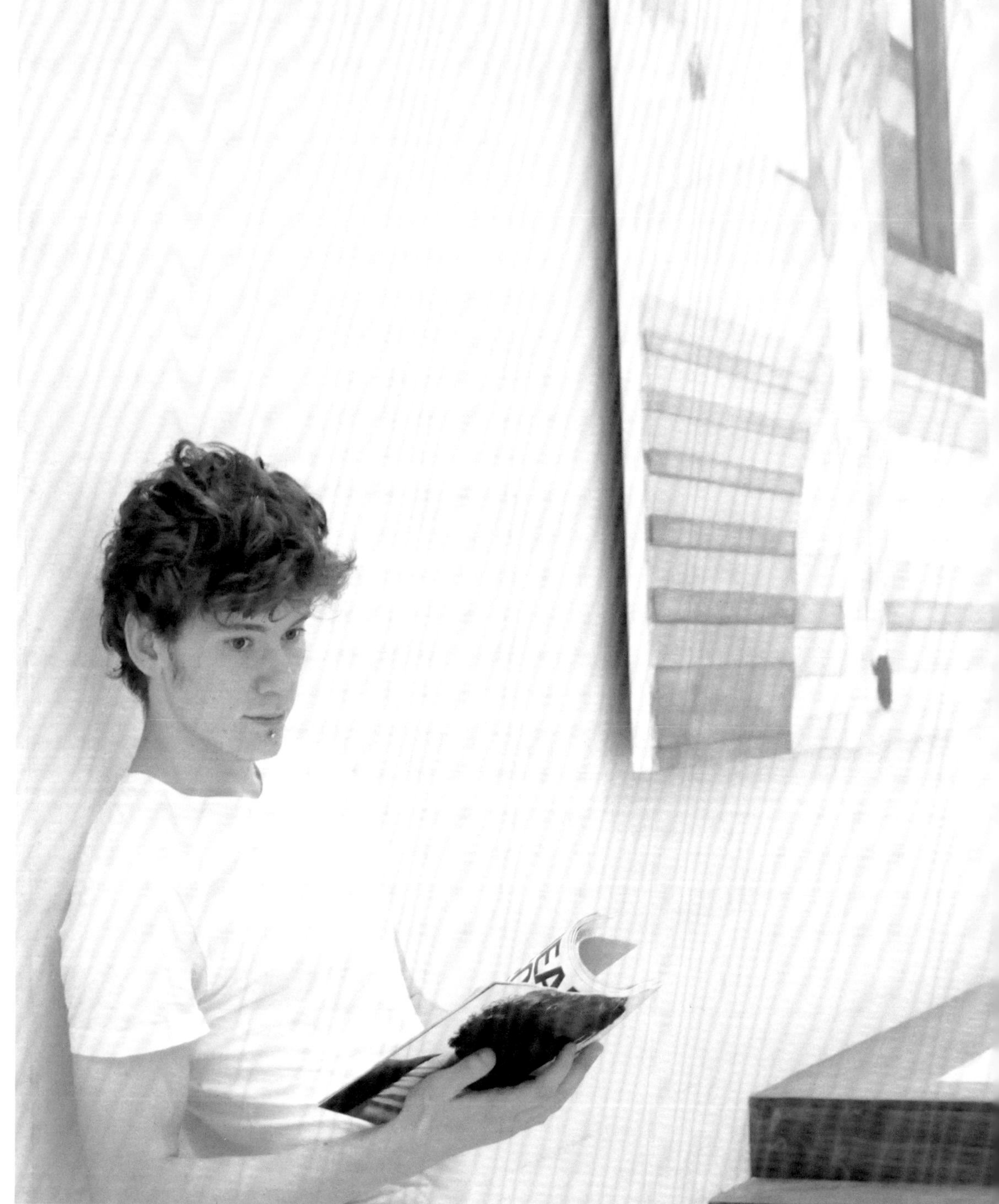

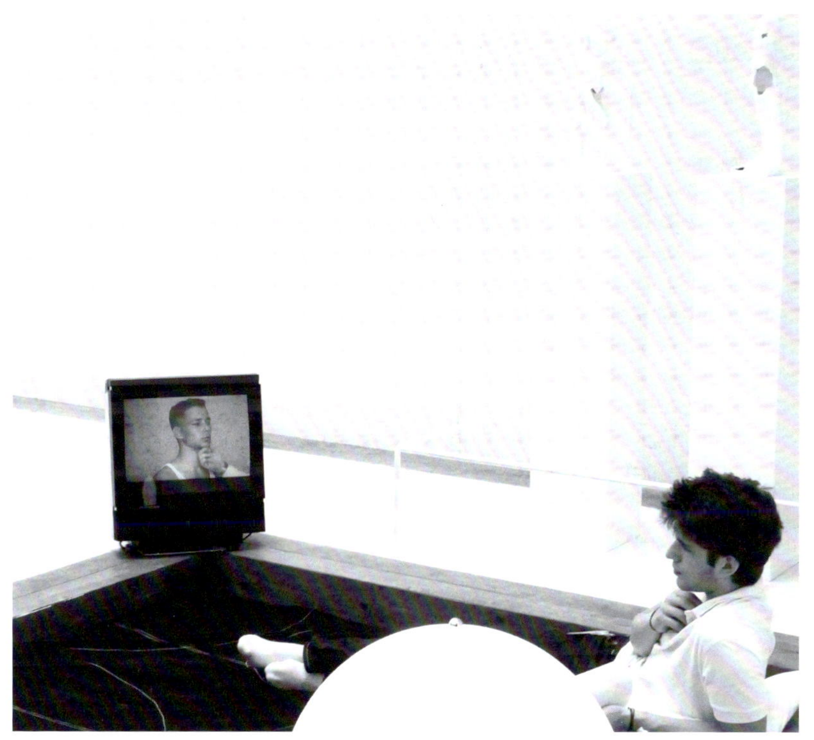

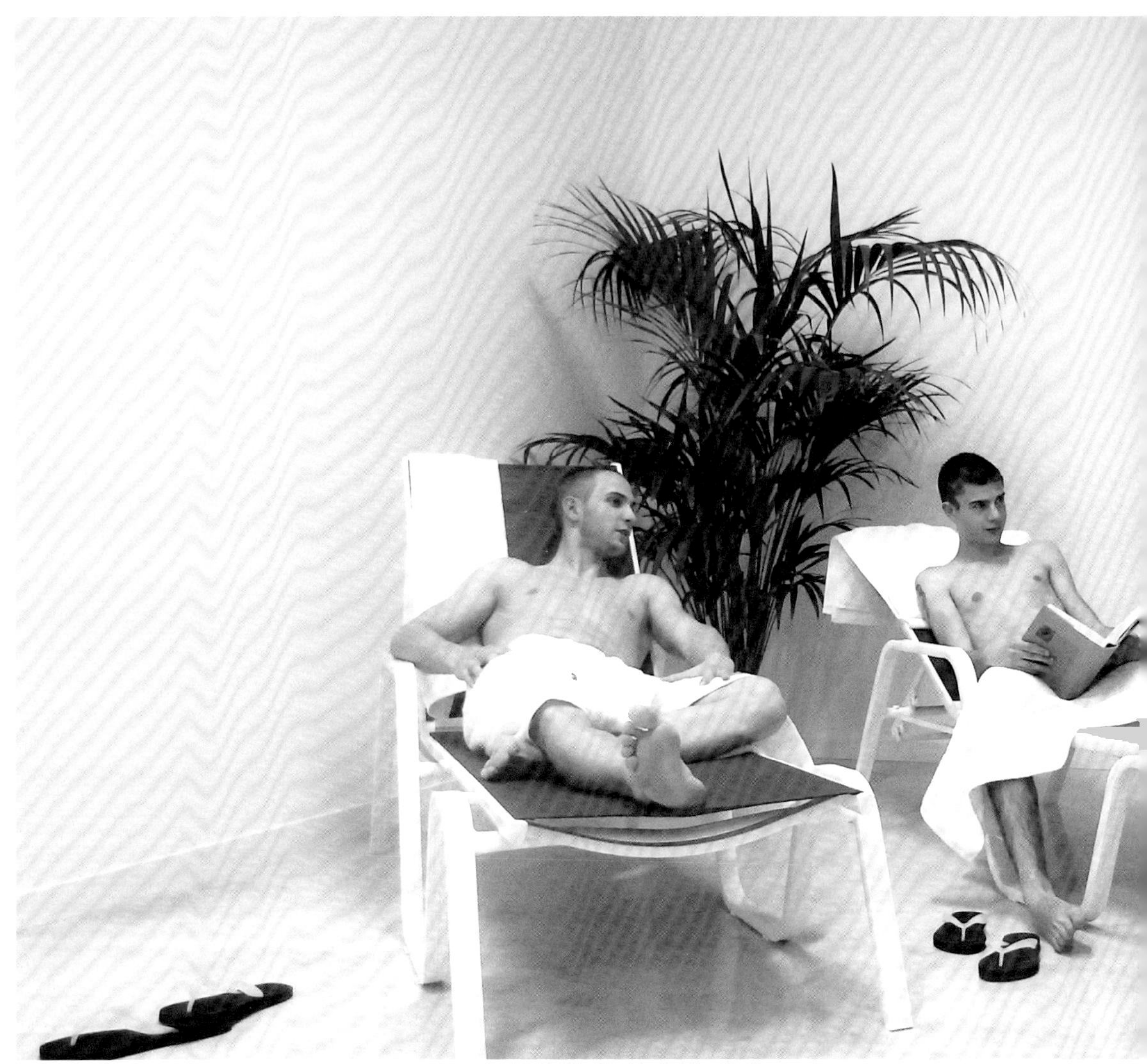

AMIGOS
2011

Young male performers act like sauna guests, lounging in white towels emblazoned with the "Amigos" logo. Their scant clothing highly contrasts that of the audience coming in from the January winter cold.

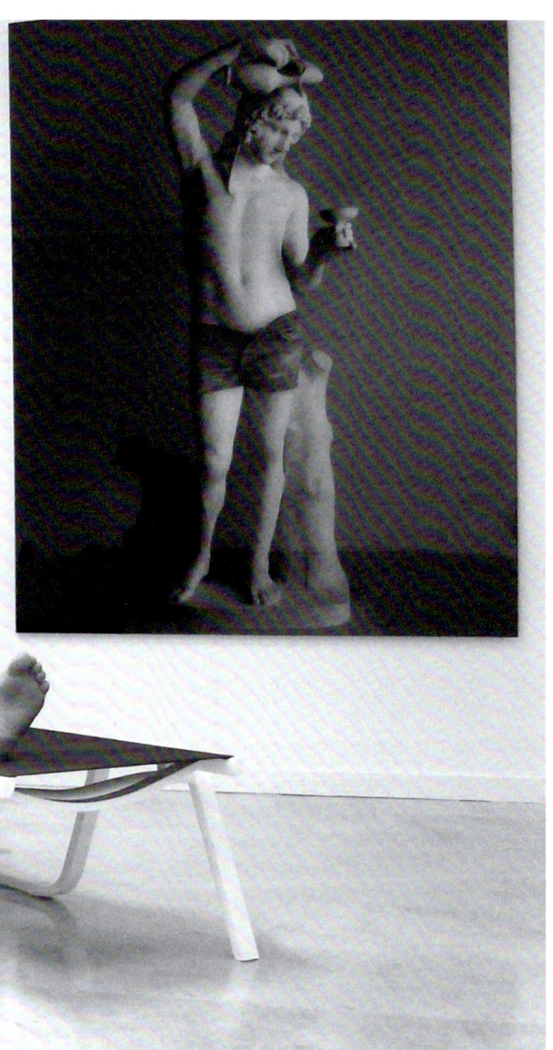

PERFORMERS:	*six males, in their 20s and 30s*
CLOTHING:	*white towels with "Amigos" logo*
DIMENSIONS:	*variable*
DURATION:	*four hours*
PERFORMED & EXHIBITED AT:	*"Amigos," Galería Helga de Alvear, Madrid, 2011*

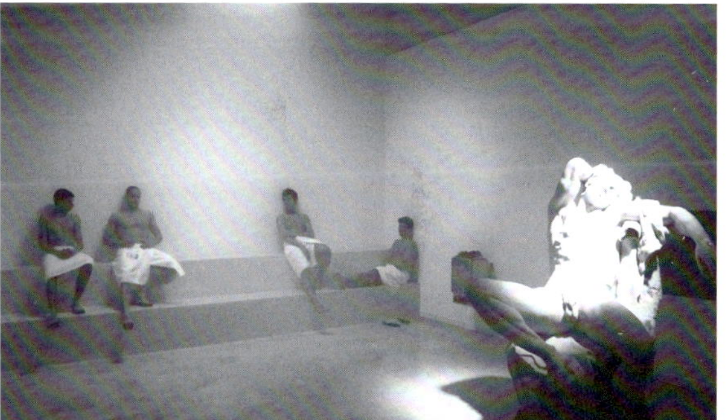

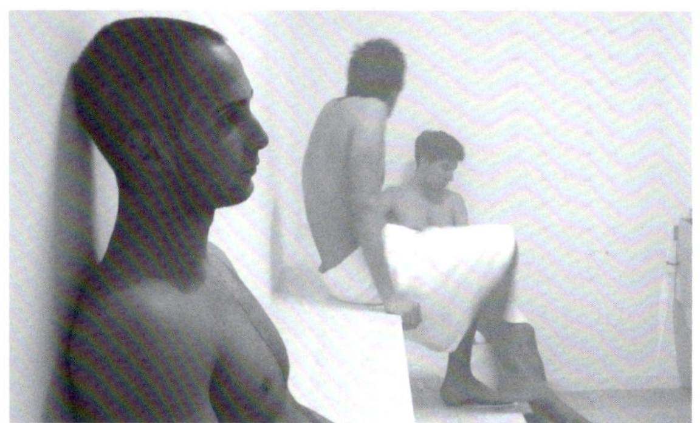

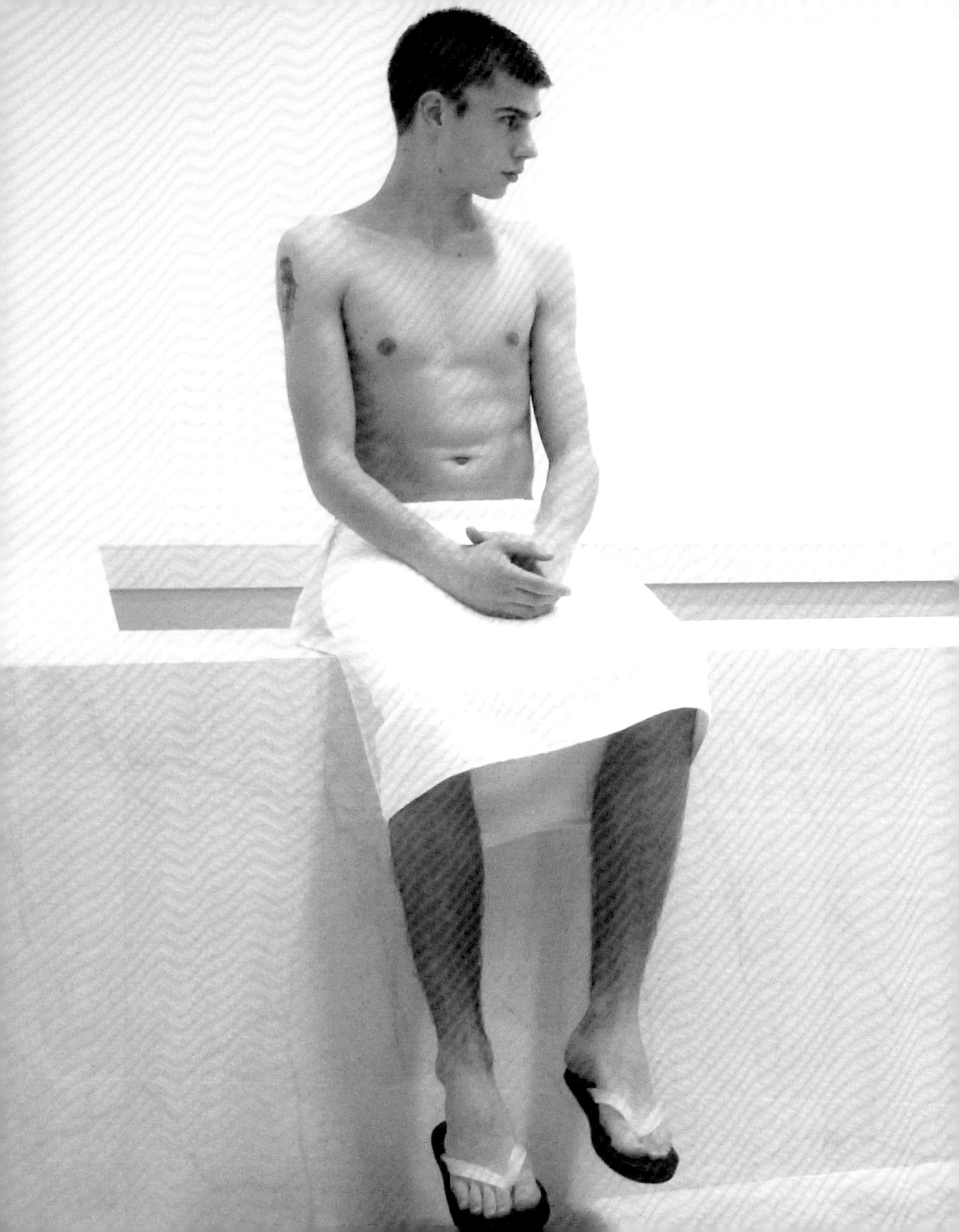

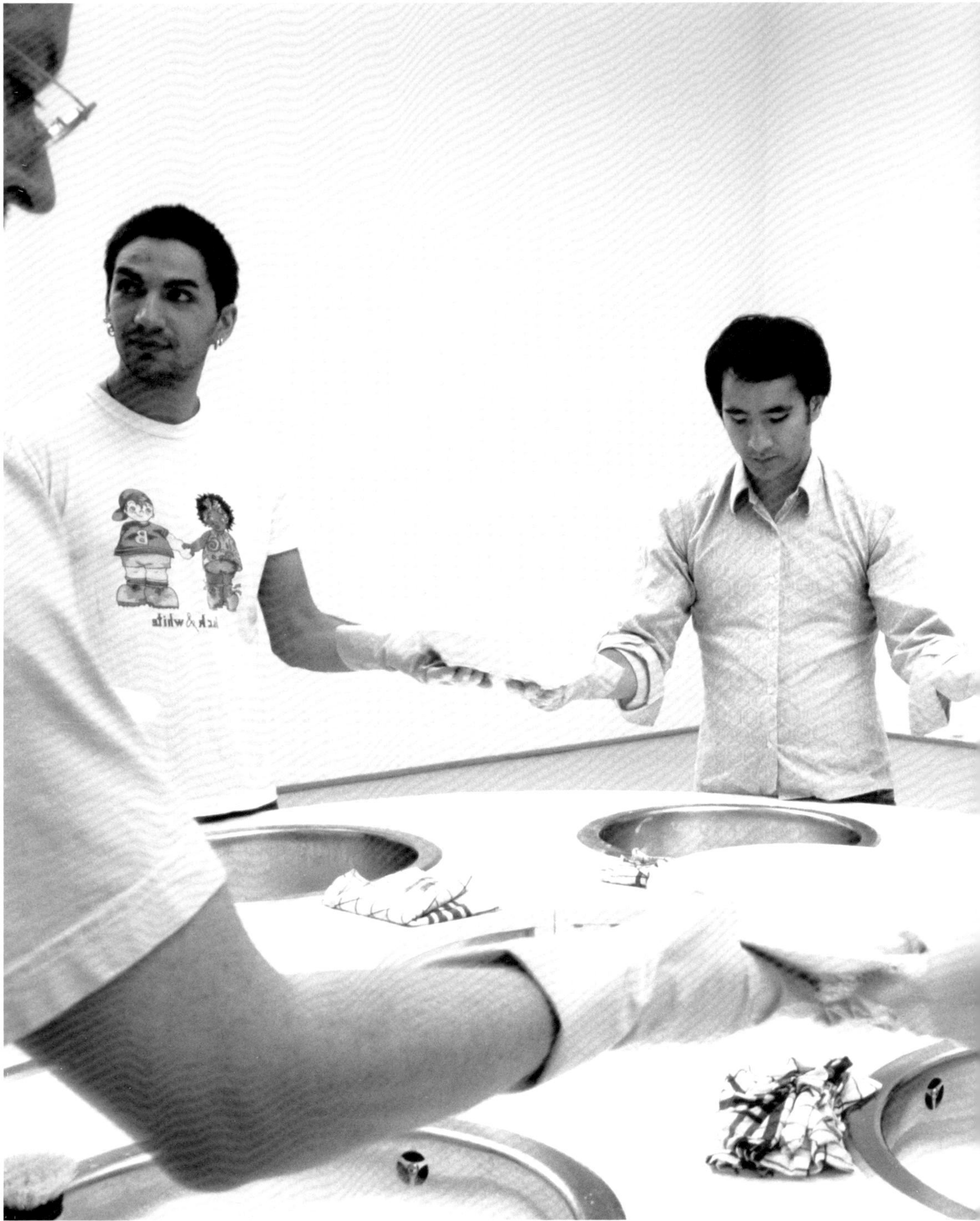

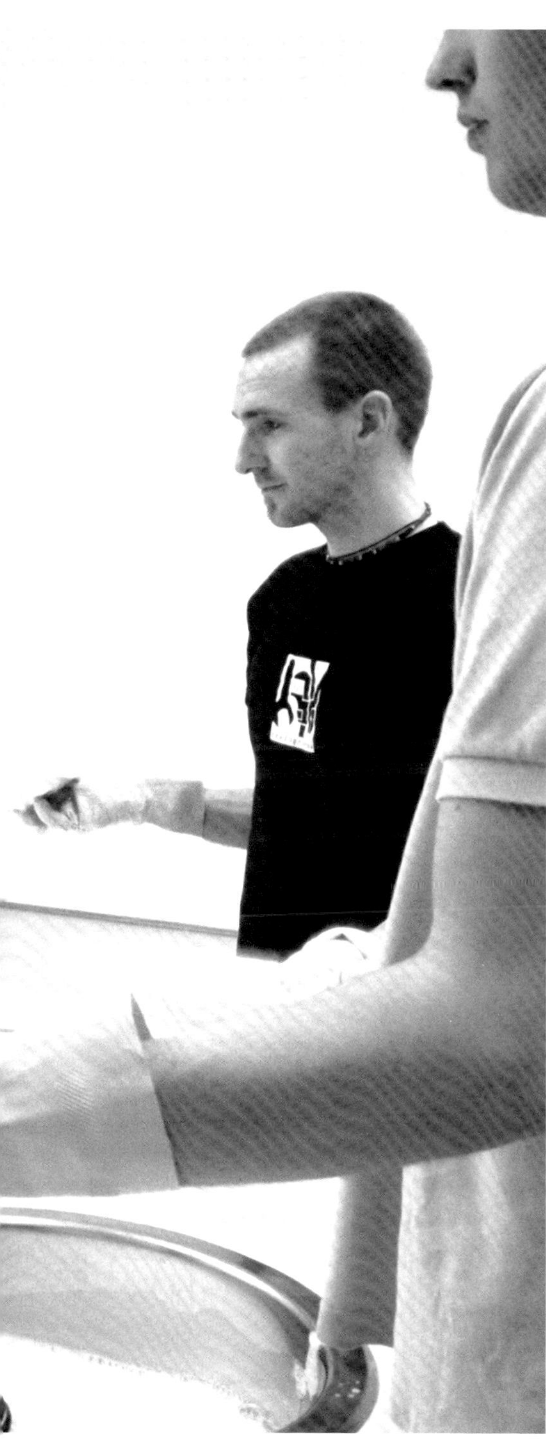

MATERIALS:	*round counter with six kitchen sinks, water, six plates, dishwashing supplies*
PERFORMERS:	*six males, ages 20 - 30*
CLOTHING:	*their own*
DIMENSIONS:	*diameter: 202 cm; height: 88 cm*
DURATION:	*minimum two hours*
PERFORMED & EXHIBITED AT:	*Galleri Nicolai Wallner at Artforum Berlin, 2002; "The Living Museum," Museum für Moderne Kunst, Frankfurt, 2003; Nasjonalmuseet for Kunst, Arkitektur og Design, Oslo, 2006*
COLLECTION:	*Nasjonalmuseet for Kunst, Arkitektur og Design, Oslo*

ONGOING
2003

Installation performance: round counter with six kitchen sinks, six plates, and six men doing the dishes, rhythmically passing around the plates. Each man scrubs diligently with meditative, circular movements before passing the plate to his neighbor, continuing for a minimum of two hours.

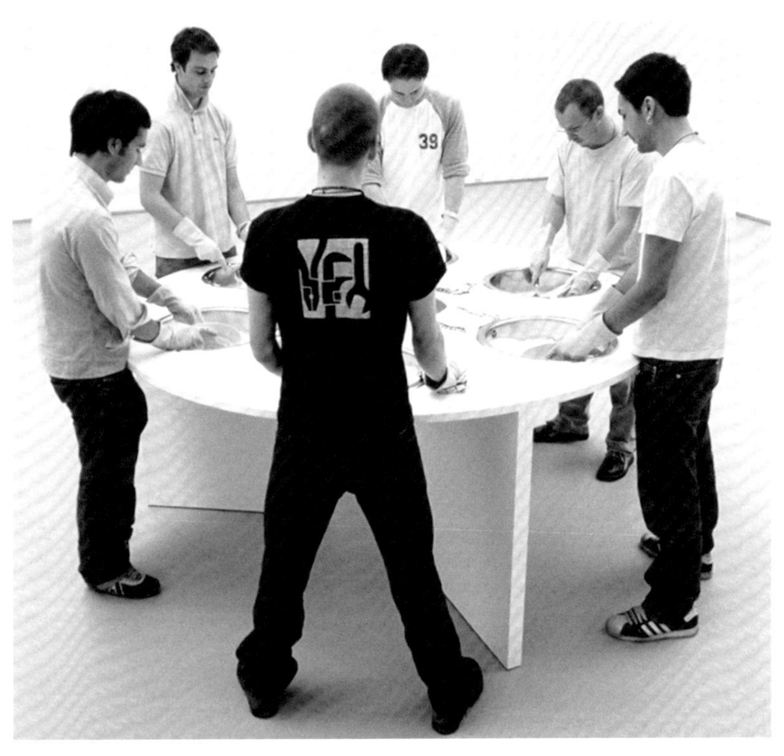
39

Ongoing: Reflections on Performativity and the Art Object

BY ANDREA KROKSNES

Six young men are washing dishes. They are each in front of a round sink, which is placed next to another sink on a minimalist looking, round, white kitchen counter. Every plate that has been cleaned has to be handed on to the neighbor, who now has to clean it again. The act of dishwashing is ongoing, repetitive and without any perspective of the task ever being completed. The physicality of the young men in this collaboration resembles the choreography of a contemporary dance performance. This slow and almost sensual "group dance" might trigger (homo)erotic desires, but the scene also simultaneously poses a latent threat. The viewer is ambiguously caught between desire and the fear of getting wet and messed up—or worse, of being caught up in their unclear perpetual interactions.

—

Since artists increasingly began engaging in identity politics in the early 1990s, the male body has become more and more the focus of artistic investigations. Elmgreen & Dragset are concerned with issues of gay politics as well as multiplying concepts of maleness. In many of their works, masculinity is performed as contingent and hysterical. The artists question the patriarchal idea of a transcendent male body. They negate the macho masquerade of impenetrability that is meant to secure male domination. They perform psychosis, abjection, and deviance. They pervert and threaten the boundaries of normative masculinity. *Ongoing* enacts a narrative of the terrifying loss of control. It displays a masculine body that performs a lowly and feminine domestic task, a body that is domesticated and almost hysterical in its ongoing and repetitive washing of the dishes. This is the very horror that Western culture labors to repress: the castrated and unmanly male body. The fear of impotence and homophobia are its symptomatic manifestations. In *Ongoing*, Elmgreen & Dragset de-sublimate masculinity, performing it as vulnerable and pathetic. And—as in many of their works—they queer purist notions of minimalist sculpture.

—

While *Ongoing* cites minimalist sculpture on the one hand, it simultaneously deconstructs minimalist sculpture on the other. Elmgreen & Dragset show that in the act of citing, the conventions of authority must not always be followed; moreover therein also lies the possibility of a different interpretation. According to the queer theory philosopher Judith Butler, citation is never an exact repetition of the absent original and always the place for critical reformulations of hegemonic conditions. Elmgreen & Dragset's installations follow in the tradition of the ideas of Minimalism. In their case, however, the long-consecrated high-culture position of Minimalism is penetrated, distorted, and perverted by citations of various everyday and subcultural practices.

—

The artists already make their interest in such a type of "queering" of structures explicit in their often-used title: *Powerless Structures.* The French poststructuralist philosopher Michel Foucault impressively described how architectural structures tend to produce subjects and institutionalize identities. Why, asks the French architecture theorist Denis Hollier, can they not also be used the other way around and lead us to a space before the constitution of the subject?[1] Not as a structure that regiments and interpellates subjects or calls us to take a position, but rather allows for an upending of such structures. This would then be a performative architecture that is a performance of spacing, and in the end allows the subject itself to move. The architectonic installation *Ongoing* is such an inverted space charged with a queer subculture. The round structure seduces our bodies to move, to walk around it, and to measure ourselves against it. Such a type of physical contact and docking maneuver might be dismissed as a surface effect: relationships between the surface of the body and the objects of the world. They are, nonetheless, not merely superficial or external but instead generate deeper effects such as desire and subjectivity.

—

The theatricality that we experience as observers in such situations no longer has very much in common with the theatrical aura of minimalist objects à la Michael

---

1 _ Denis Hollier, *Against Architecture* (Cambridge/London: The MIT Press, 1992), xi-xii.

Fried, but is rather something amplified. Current trends toward expanding Minimal Art to include a socio-cultural context are necessary. From the vantage point of the present, the minimalist gesture can no longer be understood only as a reference to the inclusion of the observer's body—as a pure summons to participation. The erstwhile aesthetics of refusal in the minimalist neo-avant-garde has long since advanced to become the dominant product design for the polished surface of our late-capitalist system. Passive consumption replaces participation. In the minimal hype of the last decade, we have often forgotten to reflect on this new context. Elmgreen & Dragset abandon the smooth forms of the minimalist object in order to concentrate more intensively on questions that were already posed in Minimalism but today must be formulated in another way: their works deal with dialectic processes between interior and exterior, subject and object, high and sub-culture, aesthetics and politics.

—

The attempt to interpret *Ongoing* leads to a dissolving of polarized models of thinking. Neither the semiotic contextualism of the theoretical analyses of the 1990s nor a more traditional aesthetic or phenomenological approach does justice to the work. One instead has to consider the installation from a dialectical starting point. This interpretive project can be seen as a continuation of a context-oriented reading, only that in the process, the concept of context is extended. We find context in the margins and framings that refer to things that are absent from the actual work yet stand in for them at the same time. Context is, however, also the immediate material surroundings of the work that observers can experience physically. In the current theoretical discourse, such a dialectic model continues to seem infeasible, or a paradox. With its socio-cultural and political claim, the endless tracing of tortuous meanings within the conditions that frame the work of the deconstructivist model seems to stand in an irreconcilable contradiction to an aesthetic model, in which what is concerned is the direct sensual experience of the spatial situatedness of the work. Elmgreen & Dragset's project carries forward the strategies of feminist and queer theory deconstruction in that it sounds out traditional binary concepts.

—

Reading *Ongoing* poses another interpretive dilemma: it is both a sculpture and a performance. For the artists, both facets of the works seem to be of equal importance; the live performance of the dishwashing young men only happens at certain times and the round kitchen counter remains in the gallery as a sculptural installation. This dialectic between the authentic moment of the performance and the objects involved or the documentation that remains (which respectively reiterate or provide a record of the performance) is actually quite typical of many performances. Performance artists of the 1970s made representations of their live performance as an integral part of the artwork. The documentations of their performances are famous today although few people ever saw those performances. The sculptural remainder of *Ongoing* is not a documentation of the performance, but it functions as a stand-in for the "whole" piece when the performance is not taking place. In this respect, the stand-in is not something inferior but rather something that helps to transcend performance to become something bigger than just the singular and ephemeral live moment. There is an interesting shift between the "live" that is valid in the current moment and something that one can access later. And, of course, in this shifting process the meaning of the work changes.

—

There has been a controversy about this dialectic in recent theory production in the field of performance studies. Some argue ontologically for the live moment in performance art and against any kind of mediatisation, while others understand the live moment and its mediated forms as already intertwined and constituting each other. This latter approach could figure interestingly within a reading of *Ongoing*. If there were merely the singular act of performing it would be an entirely abstract moment. Yet it is only by recalling that moment that we can make connections and understand it in a broader context. Only when the performance is remembered, performed again and again, does it become articulated in terms of a political agenda or manifesto. ____

Translated from the German by Amy J. Klement.

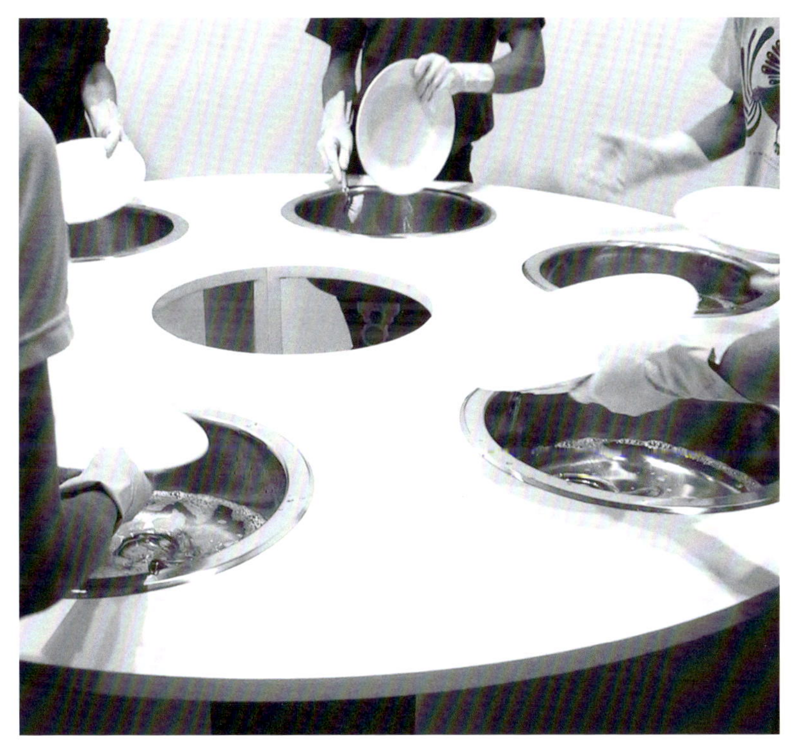

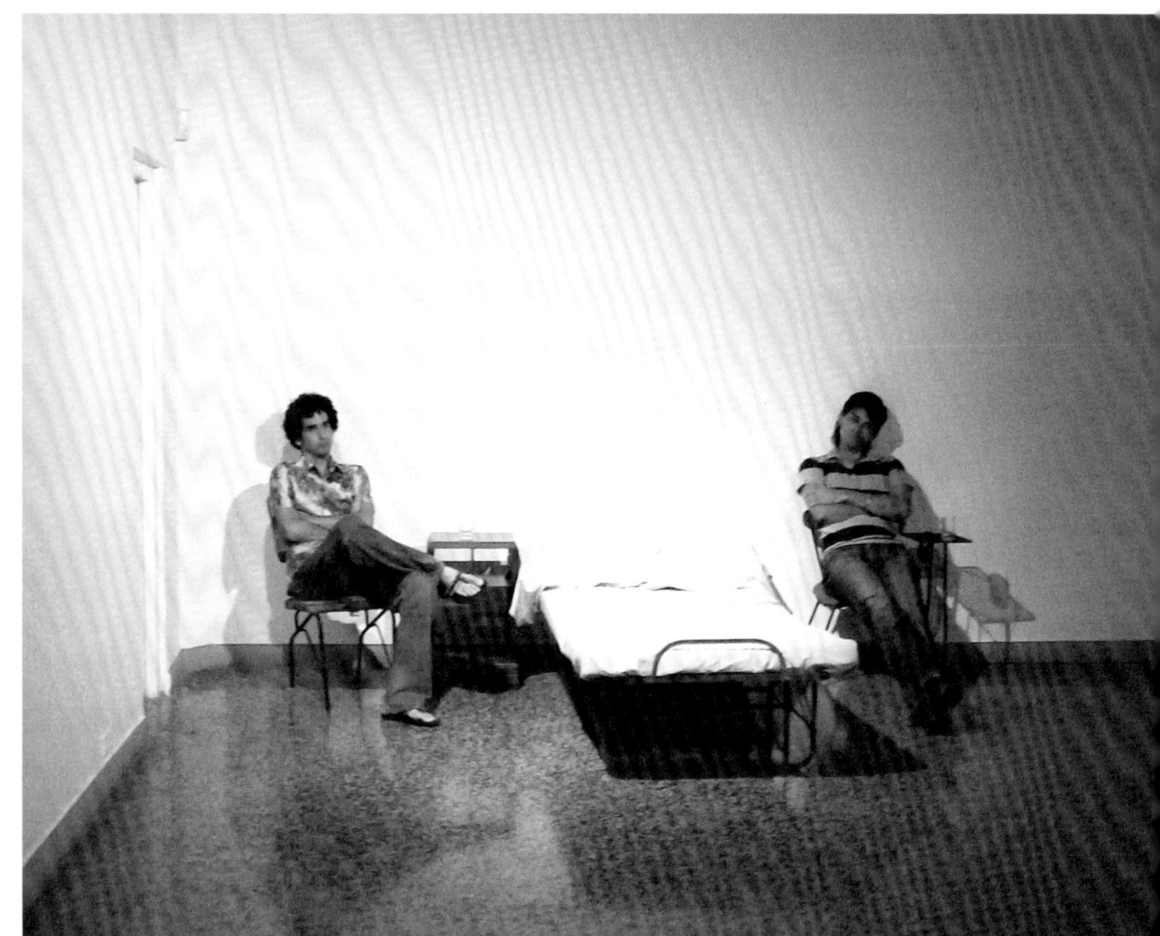

MATERIALS:	*two chairs, two bedside tables, one bed*
PERFORMERS:	*two young males, early 20s*
CLOTHING:	*their own: shoes, socks, pants, underwear, T-shirts*
DIMENSIONS:	*variable*
DURATION:	*four hours (minimum two hours)*
PERFORMED AT:	*10th Havana Biennial, Cuba, 2009*

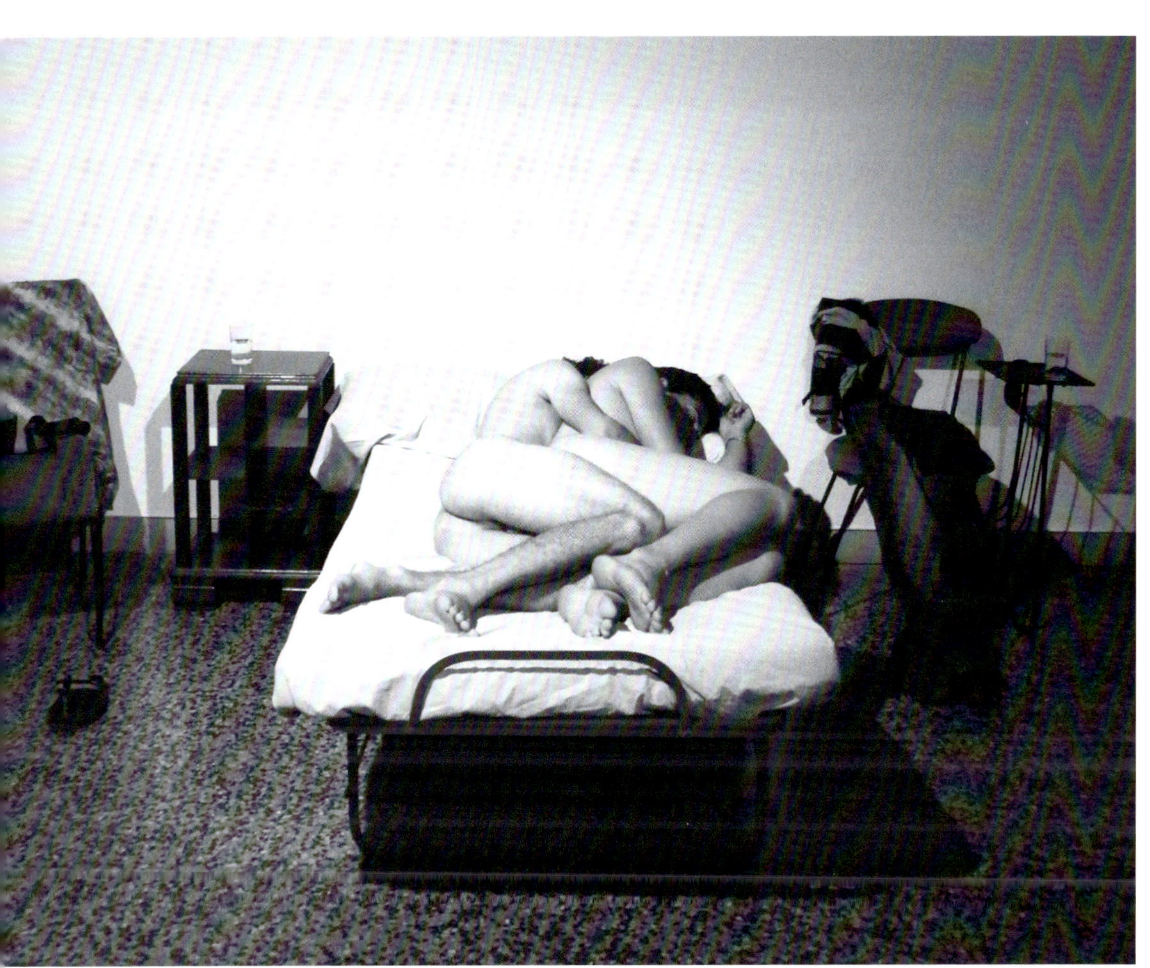

4/7/365
009

wo young men sit on chairs on either side of a bed, then tand up, undress, and spoon on the bed, before dressing and itting again, repeating these actions for four hours.

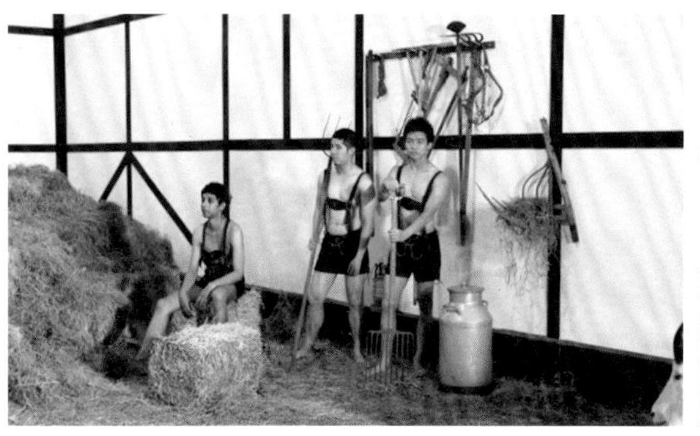

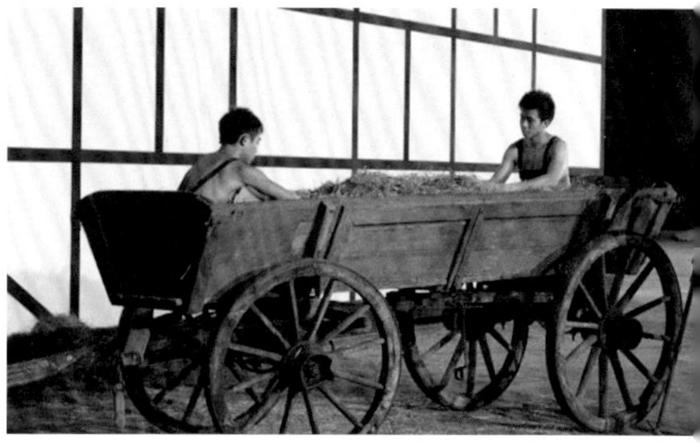

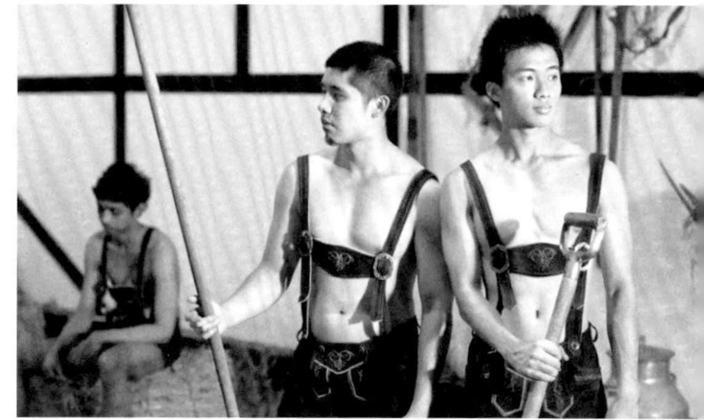

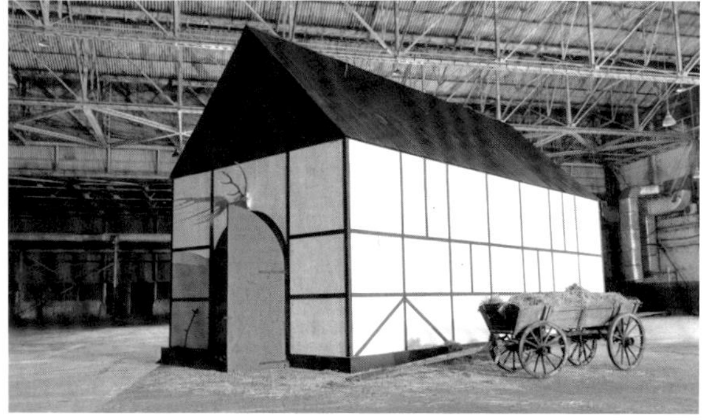

DEUTSCHE SCHEUNE (GERMAN BARN)
2011

MATERIALS:	*steel, plywood, concrete, paint, hay, taxidermy goat, tire, horse carriage, tools, farming tools, antlers, miscellaneous items*
PERFORMERS:	*teams of four to six young men, local Singaporeans*
CLOTHING:	*traditional German "Lederhosen"*
DIMENSIONS:	*variable*
DURATION:	*the entire exhibition period (two months)*
PERFORMED & EXHIBITED AT:	*"Open House," 3rd Singapore Biennial, 2011*

Full-scale mock-up of a traditional German barn shown in Si gapore (an almost completely urbanized city) inside an unuse hangar on the grounds of the modernist Kallang Airport. Th barn is filled with imported hay and includes a taxidermy goa referencing Robert Rauschenberg's *Monogram,* with local pe formers dressed in "Lederhosen"—traditional-style Germa farmer costumes. The performers are alternately sleeping reading books on rural Bavaria or writing poetry in notebooks or lounging and playing in the hay. The smell of hay in the ho and humid climate is, in itself, an experience to the typical cit dweller visitor.

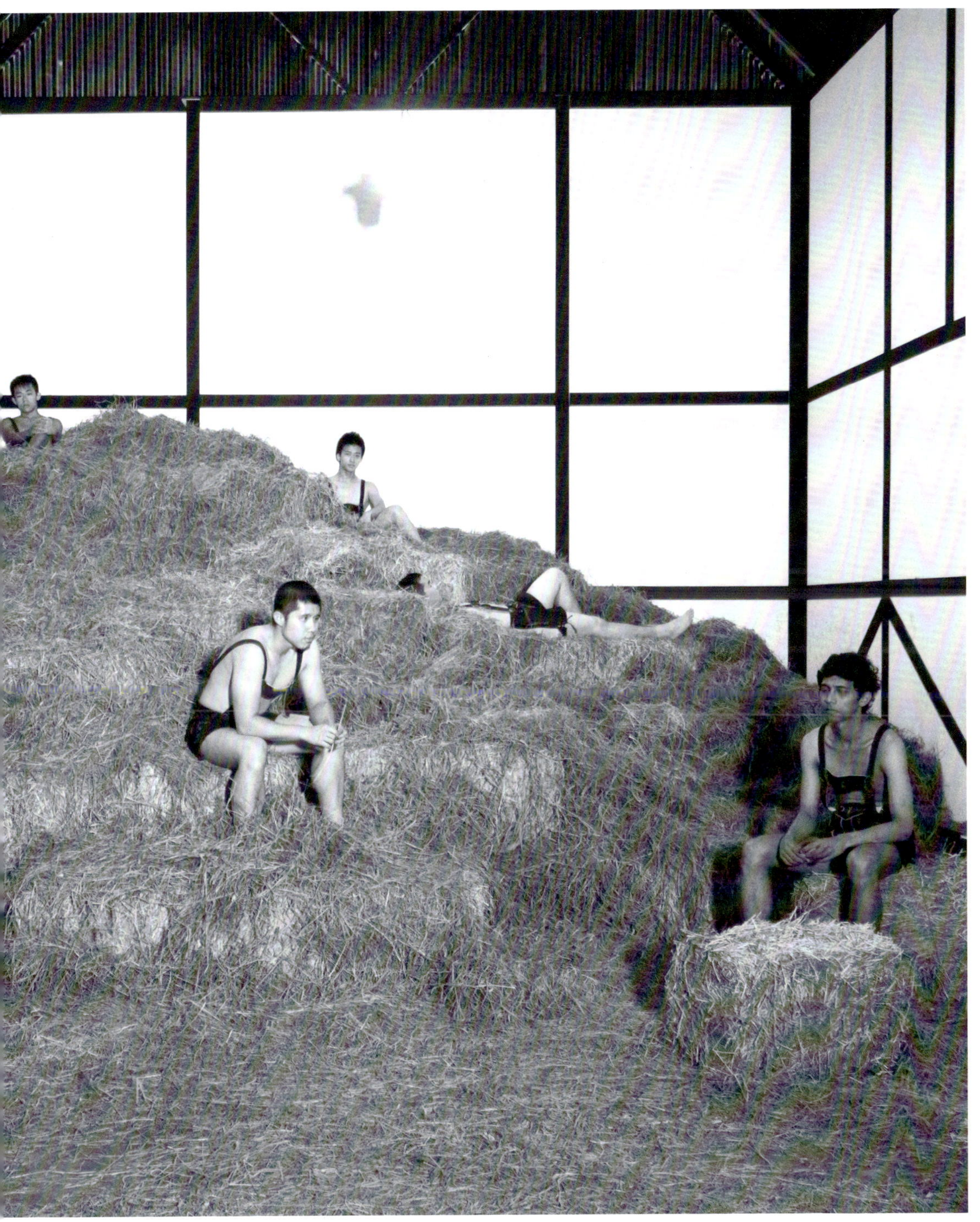

15h : Sorti de la galerie, je suis rentré chez moi à pied, par un nouvel itinéraire que j'ai découvert le matin même et dont la ruse consiste à traverser l'hôpital plutôt qu'à le contourner. Eh bien c'est 15 min de sommeil supplémentaire, 15 gouttes d'eau dans mon verre que les autres ne pourront pas boire et d'après notre brève réflexion sur le temps, ce sont 15 gouttes d'eau bien précieuses.
Vous me direz oui, certes, alors autant ne pas les perdre à dormir. Et vous aurez raison.
15h20 : De retour chez moi, les automatismes prennent le dessus sur ma conscience. J'enlève bonnet, écharpe et blouson, habituellement dans cet ordre, puis clés, porte-feuille et téléphone de mes poches. Lorsque je me déchausse, je me sent enfin à l'aise chez moi. Vous savez à quoi je fait allusion... Pour les plus scientifiques d'entre vous, vous remarquerez que ce trajet se fait en 20 min.
15h21 : Consultation de mes mails, rien. L'ordinateur déjà allumé lorsque je suis parti le matin.
Je discute avec Sylvain connecté en ce moment même sur internet.
15h22 : Fin de la conversation qui n'avait pas pour finalité celle de changer le monde.
15h23 : Je me laisse guider par les notes si talentueusement choisies par Pat Metheny pendant l'heure de sieste dont je dispose (les amateurs comprendront).
Si un jour je pouvais avoir le centième de son talent...
17h : Après un sommeil saccadé, je me prépare (c.f 15h20 mais à l'envers...)
Trajet en métro rien à signaler.
17h30 : Arrivé chez Myrène à qui je donne des cours de soutien scolaire. Au programme la multiplication décimale, la différence entre la, là et l'a et préparation au contrôle de lecture. Concentrée le cours s'est déroulé sans incident, les leçons ont bien été comprises et apprises...

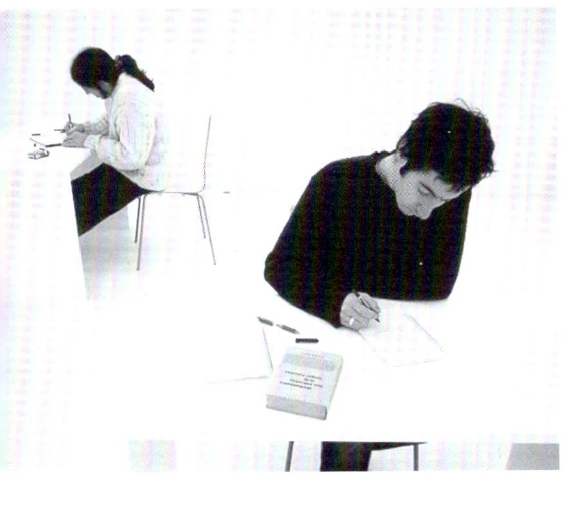

MATERIALS:	*tables, chairs, notebooks, writing tools, personal items*
PERFORMERS:	*five young men, ages 20 – 30, from different backgrounds/with diverse identities*
CLOTHING:	*their own*
DIMENSIONS:	*variable*
DURATION:	*the entire exhibition period (five weeks)*
PERFORMED & EXHIBITED AT:	*Galerie Emmanuel Perrotin, Paris, 2003*

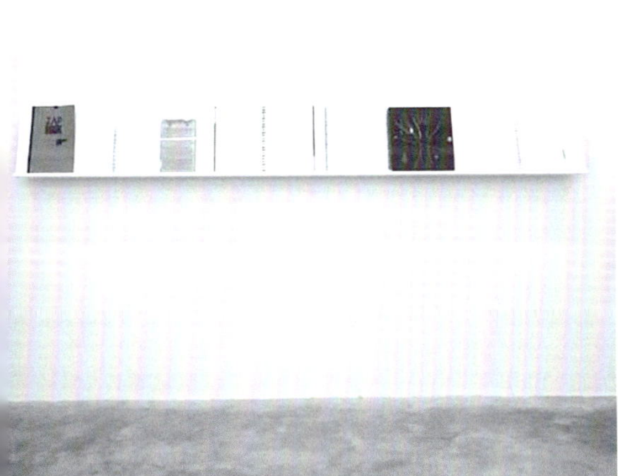

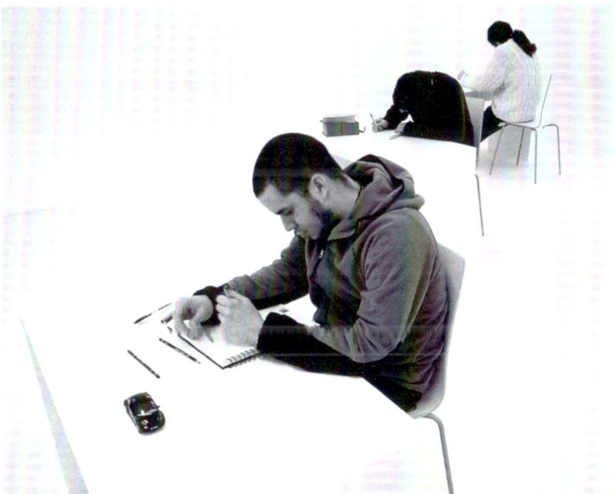

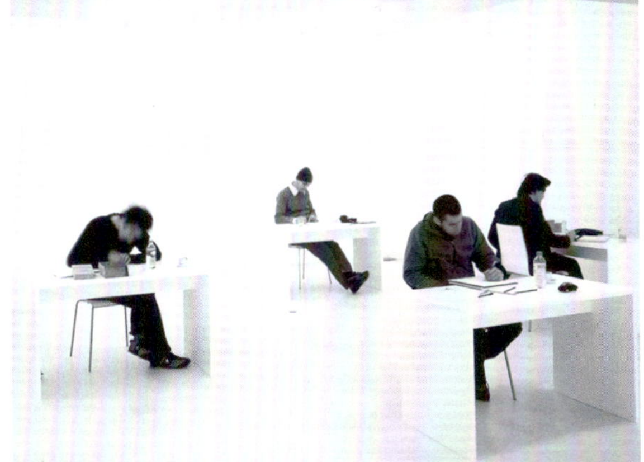

ARIS DIARIES
003

erformance installation with five young men keeping their iaries in the gallery on a day-to-day basis throughout the five-eek exhibition, each seated at his own desk. The audience is ee to walk around, read over the diarist's shoulder and flip rough the diaries when the performer is on a break. The dia-es exist as an individual work.

VOX CLAMANTIS IN DESERTO, c'est ce qui est écrit sur l'autocollant qui orne le casque sous lequel Esope conduit une planche à roulettes sur la piste cyclable. C'est le frère, c'est le fils, il a quinze ans et assiste médusé à l'année 2003, lato sensu.

	1987	1991	1999	2002	2003 01/01 → 10/01
amour, en %	27	12	14	14	7
Kebabs	0	2	210	315	20
cancer	0	0	0	0	0

Il s'amuse à illustrer ces données sous formes de camemberts, de graphiques à bâtons. Il est con, ce con, c'est pas drôle et en plus ça me prend un temps fou à expliquer. Si seulement les gamins ne grimpaient pas aux arbres, on en serait pas là, à décrire des existences débiles d'une famille de dégénérés.

Oh Manika, Manika, la mémé folle morte d'on sait pas trop quoi, mais certainement trop tôt, tu leur manques tu sais avec tes yeux de vieille lapine, quand au coin du feu tu racontais n'importe quoi, mais c'était jamais n'importe quoi, mémé Manika, non tu as ouvert les yeux avant de les fermer tu étais raide comme un robot, molle comme une vieille carne mais quand tu souriais c'était toute la vieille Espagne à la con, on comprenais rien mais j'étais pas là de toute manière. [Ahhaw, je baille ici] Je te connais pas mémé Manika, mais si ces gens existaient vraiment, ils foutraient ta vie en carte postale, le feu à la Garonne en ton honneur. Bon ça suffit maintenant je ne parlerai plus jamais de toi c'est trop crevant.

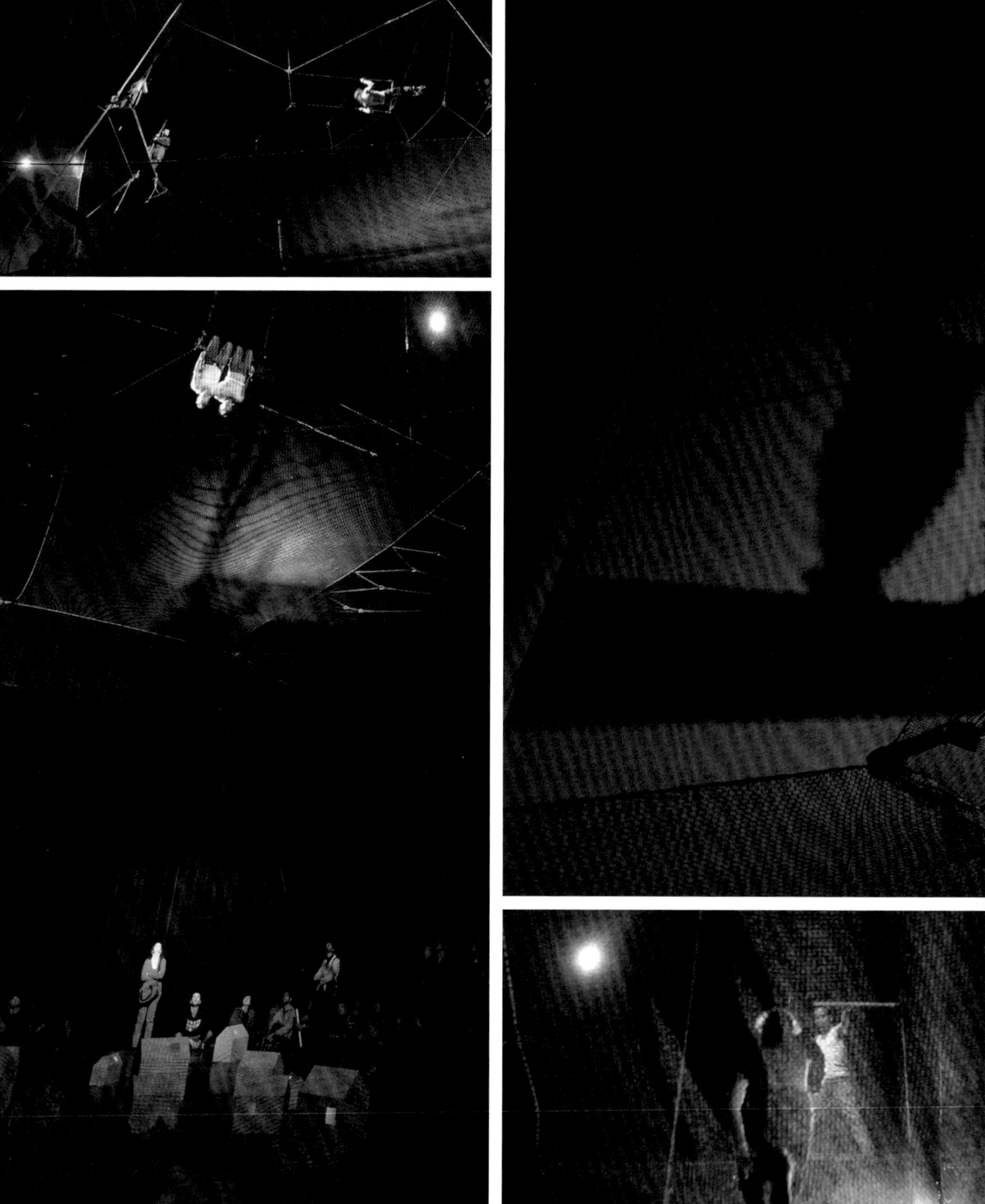

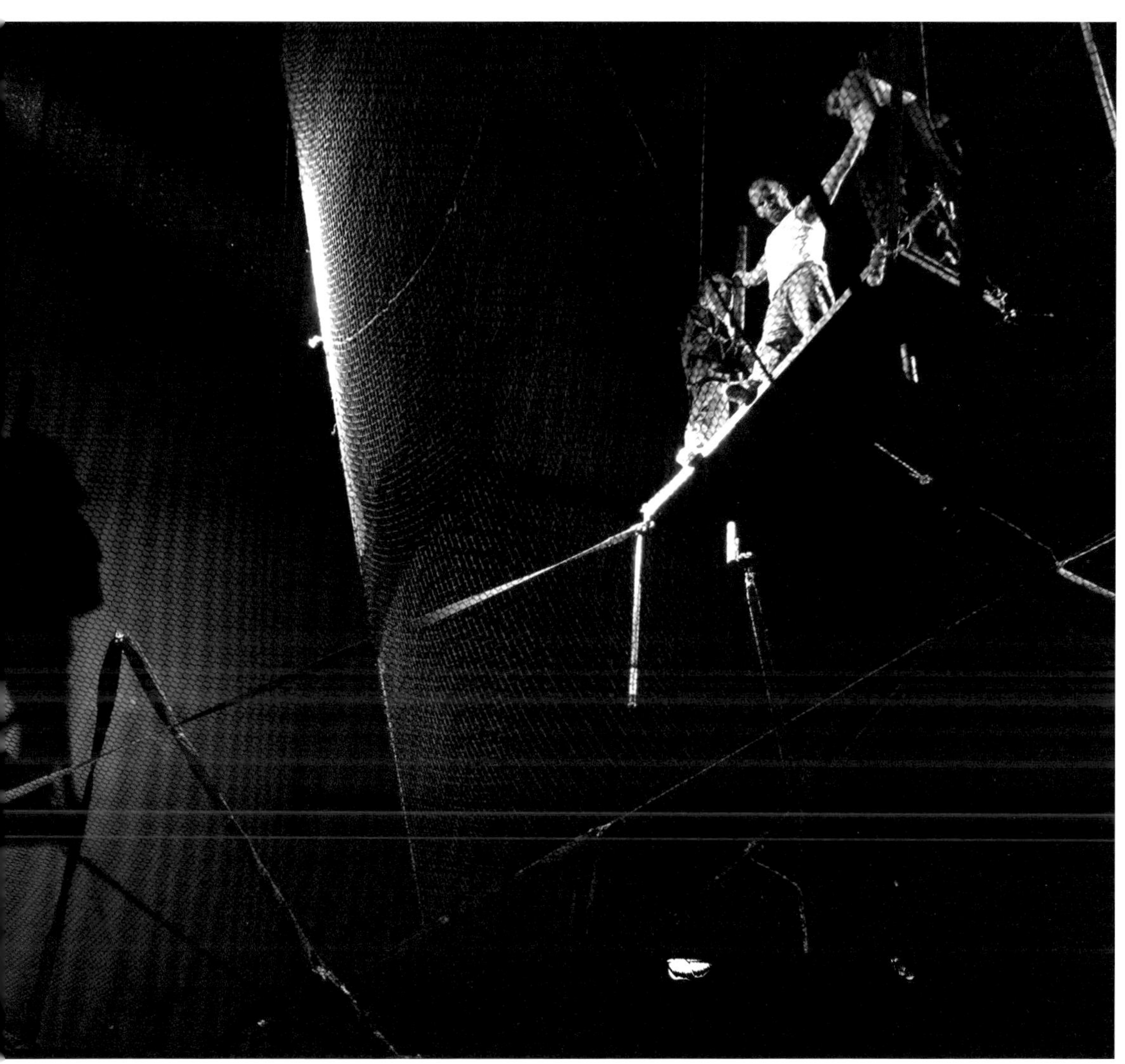

TERIALS: *trapeze, safety net, dim lighting*
RFORMERS: *professional male trapeze artists*
OTHING: *blue jeans, white T-shirts or singlets or topless, sneakers or barefoot*
MENSIONS: *variable*
RATION: *occasional one hour sets*
RFORMED &
HIBITED AT: *"Trying to Remember What We Once Wanted to Forget," Museo de Arte Contemporáneo de Castilla y León (MUSAC), León, 2009*

THE GROUND WILL MAKE YOU STUMBLE
2009

Performance conceived by the artists featuring the trapeze company *Kambahiota*. On weekends throughout the exhibition period of "Trying to Remember What We Once Wanted to Forget" the three male trapeze artists performed their stunts above the heads of museum visitors. The title of the performance is taken from a piece that Jean Genet wrote to his lover, the tightrope walker Abdallah Bentaga, after his death.

A SCULPTURE SPEAKS NO EVIL
2010

Performance in which four men (including both of the artists) are bondaged and immobile inside the White Cubicle Toilet Gallery for two hours. The White Cubicle Toilet Gallery is located inside the women's restroom of the Hackney Road pub "The George and Dragon" and measures only 1.4 x 1.4 meters.

PERFORMERS: *four men, various ages*
CLOTHING: *bondage tape, bondage masks with mouth zippers*
DIMENSIONS: *site-specific*
DURATION: *two hours*
PERFORMED AT: *White Cubicle Toilet Gallery, London, 2010*

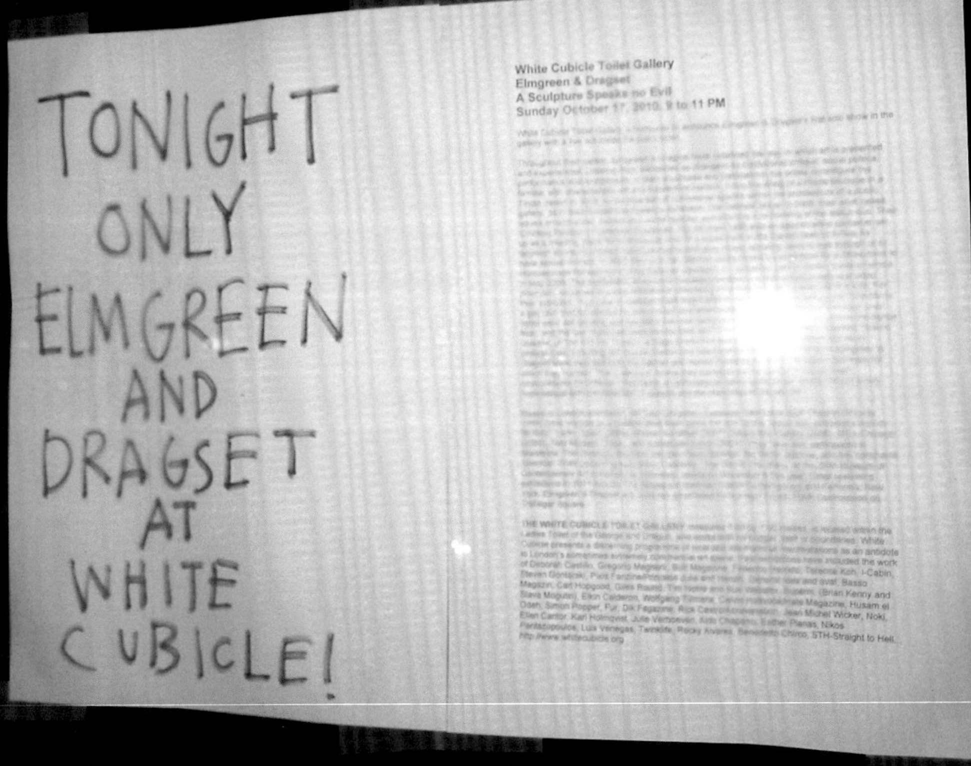

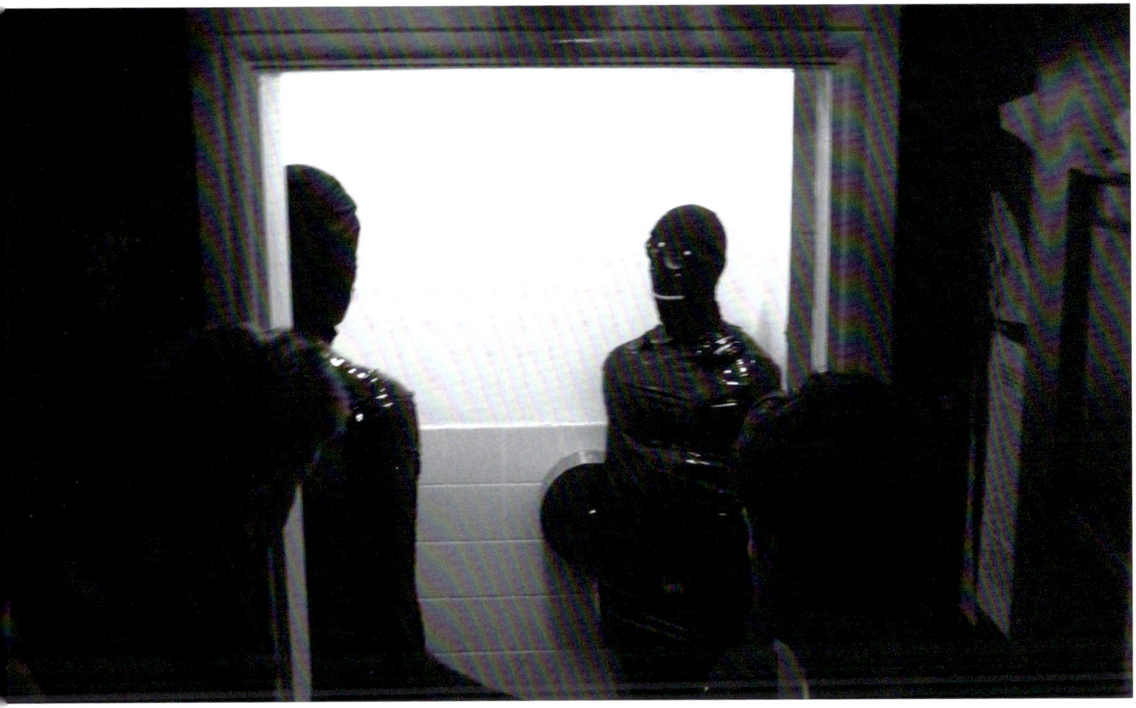

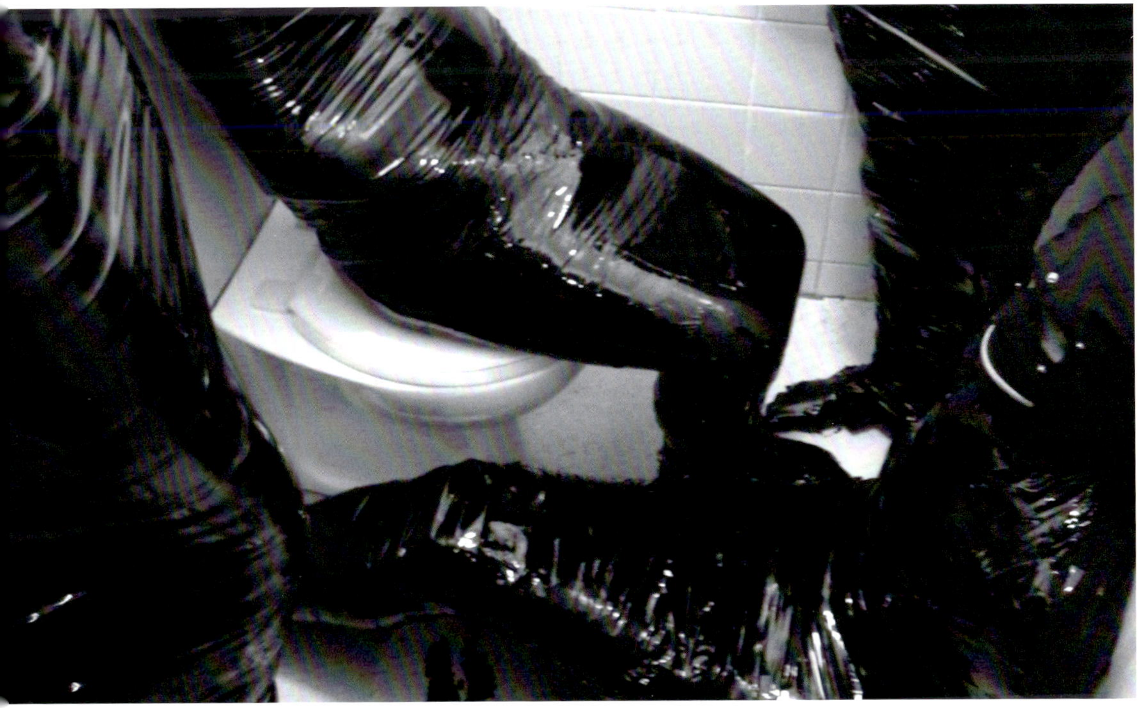

5.

THEATER AND STAGE

5.

WORKS

TEXTS

MATERIALS:	*vinyl print on theater safety curtain*
DIMENSIONS:	*variable, according to the size of the stage*
DURATION:	*the 2002 - 2003 opera season*
EXHIBITED AT:	*Komische Oper, Berlin, 2002 - 2003 co-produced with Museum in Progress, Vienna*

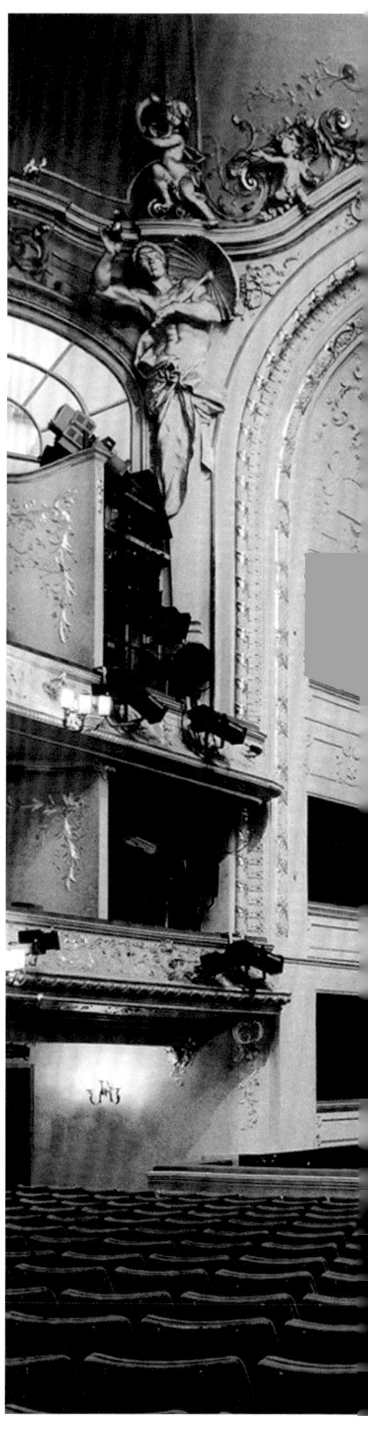

SAFETY CURTAIN
2002 - 2003

Theater safety curtain with a vinyl print of an eye peering through a hole, looking out from the stage towards the seats.

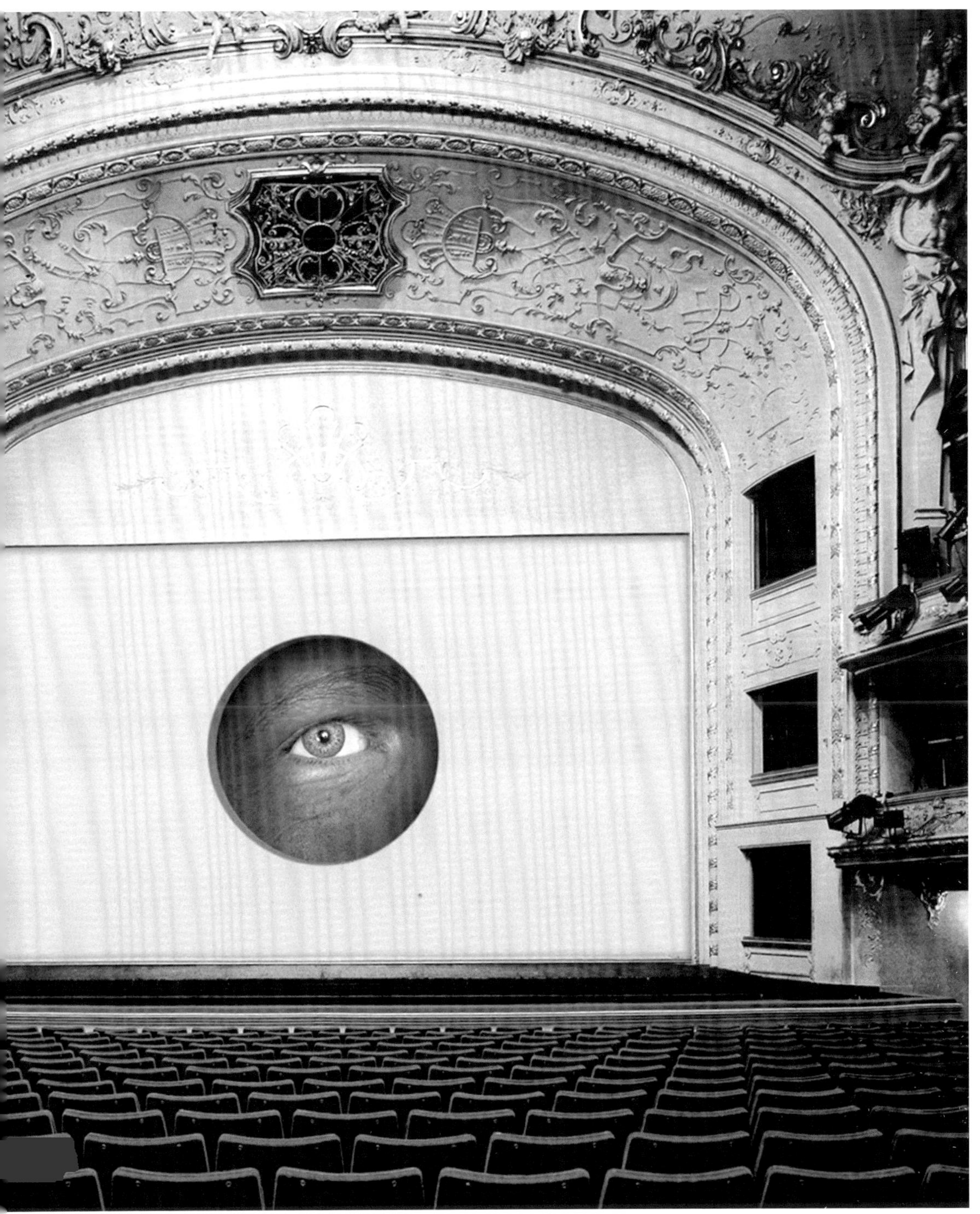

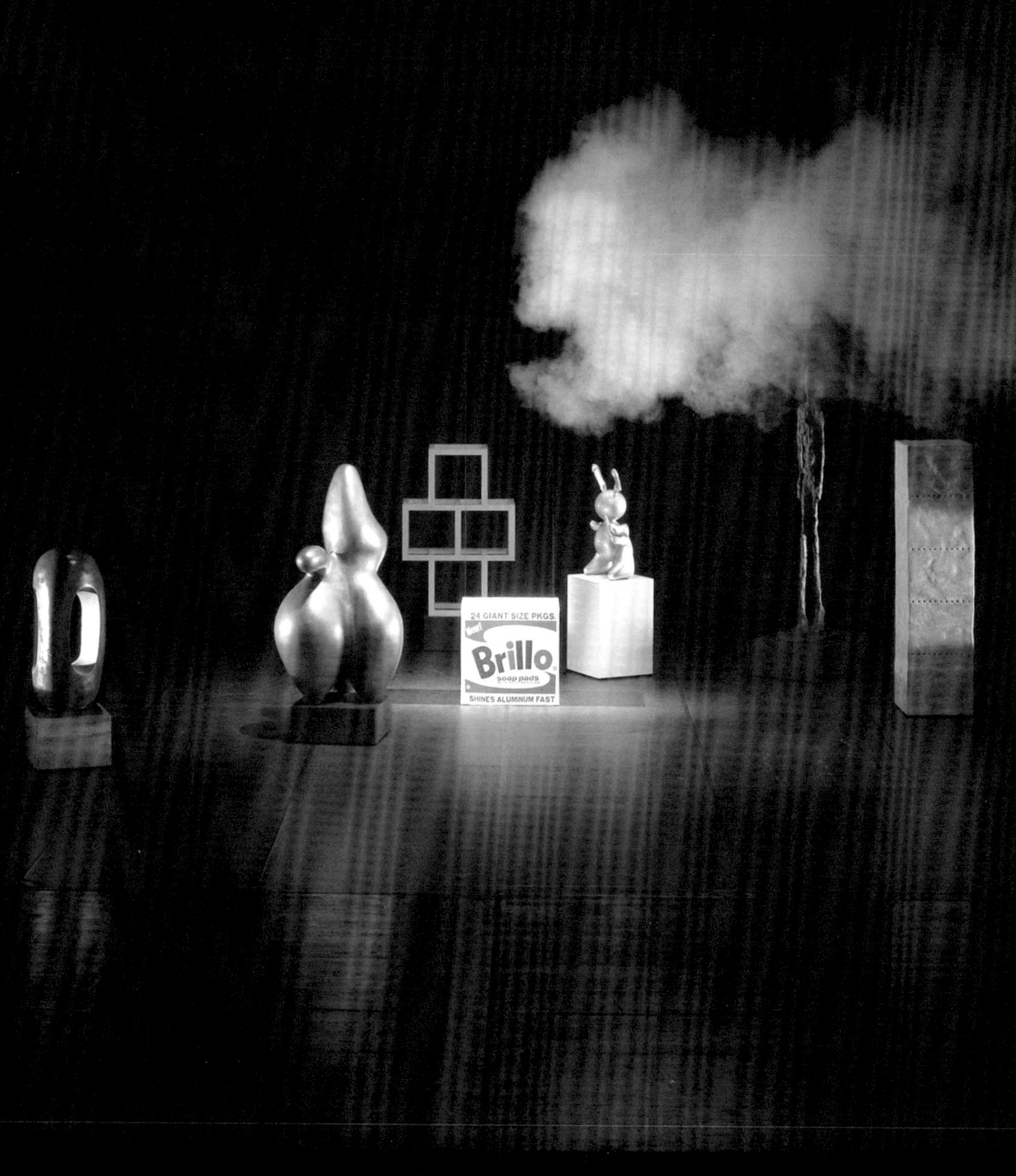

24 GIANT SIZE PKGS.
New!
Brillo
soap pads
SHINES ALUMINUM FAST

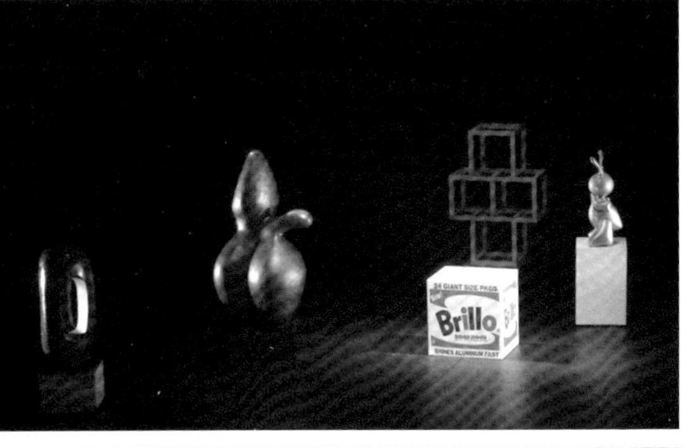

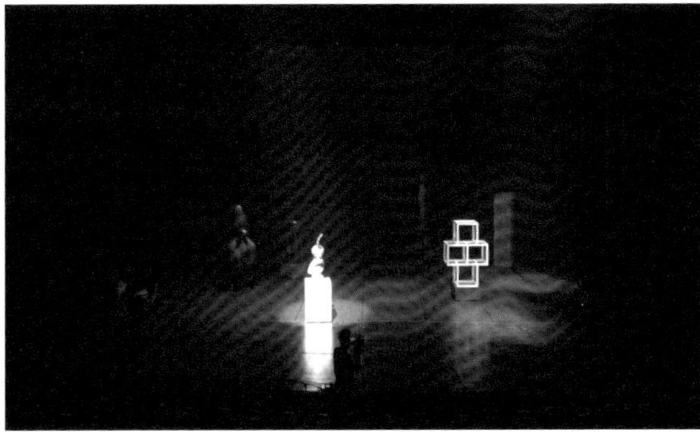

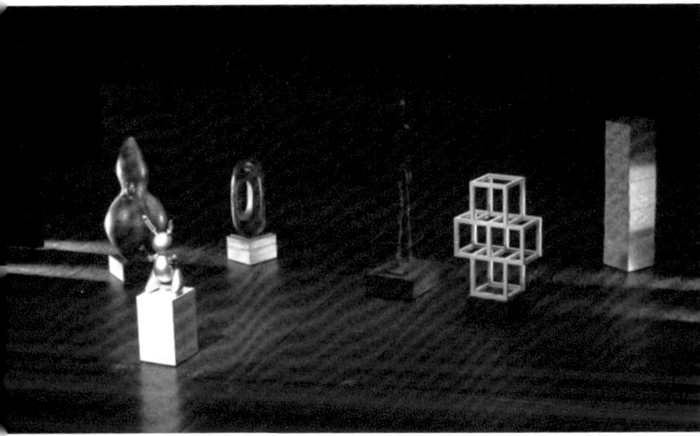

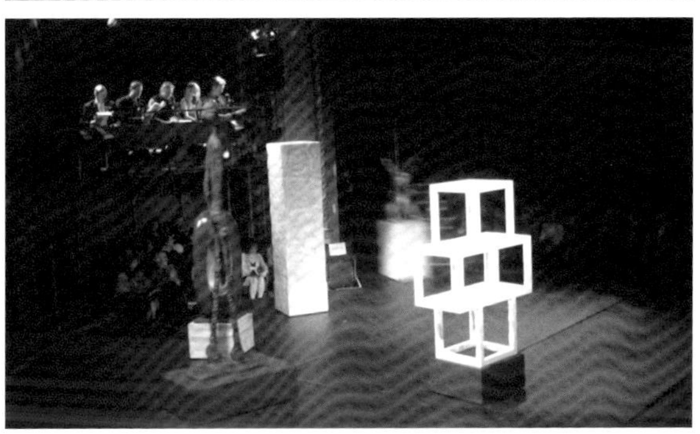

DRAMA QUEENS
2007

A play conceived for and produced in collaboration with Skulptur Projekte Münster 07. Seven remote controlled life-size sculptures from the 20th century meet on stage and talk about life and art. Sculptures inspired by Hans Arp's *Cloud Shepherd* (1953), Alberto Giacometti's *Walking Man* (1947), Barbara Hepworth's *Elegy III* (1966), Jeff Koons's *Rabbit* (1986), Sol Lewitt's *Four Cubes* (1971), an untitled granite sculpture by Ulrich Rückriem (1984), and Andy Warhol's *Brillo Box* (1964). Text written by Tim Etchells based on characters invented by Elmgreen & Dragset. Seven lightweight sculptures on pedestals with hidden motors and wheels, receiving signals from seven remote controls operated by staff offstage. The sculptures' movements are choreographed to correspond with the recorded dialogue voiced by professional actors. Two later versions of the play with only six sculptures on stage were developed for The Old Vic Theatre in London and for Centre Pompidou in Paris. At The Old Vic Theatre, the voices were done live, with actors and remote controllers sitting in opposite loges on each side above the stage. The cast included Kevin Spacey, Jeremy Irons, Joseph Fiennes, Lesley Manville and Alex Jennings. The original version is documented on film and exists as a separate work in an edition of 5 + 2.

ATERIALS: *mixed media*

MENSIONS: *seven life-size sculptures, the tallest of which (Walking Man) is approximately 260 cm including pedestal*

RATION: *fifty minutes*

HIBITED AT: *Skulptur Projekte Münster 07, Städtische Bühnen Münster, 2007 (play); Theater Basel, Art Basel, 2008 (play); The Old Vic Theatre, London, 2008 (play); CPH: DOX International Documentary Film Festival, Copenhagen, 2008 (video); "Nouveau Festival," Centre Pompidou, Paris, 2009 (play); "Coup de Ville / A Chambres d'amis for the 21st century," Art Platform WARP, Sint-Niklaas, Belgium, 2010 (video); Garage Center for Contemporary Culture, Moscow, 2010 (video); Look, Budapest, 2010 (video); Musées de la Ville de Strasbourg, 2010 (video); Salon Populaire, Berlin, 2010 (video); "Produced by Migros," Kunsthalle Fridericianum, Kassel, 2011 (video); "Puppets & Sculptures," Opernpavillion München, 2011 (video)*

LLECTIONS: *Chazen Museum of Art at the University of Wisconsin, Madison; Migros Museum für Gegenwartskunst, Zürich; Nasjonalmuseet for kunst, arkitektur og design, Oslo; National Gallery of Canada, Ottawa; Staatliche Kunstsammlung/Skulpturensammlung, Dresden*

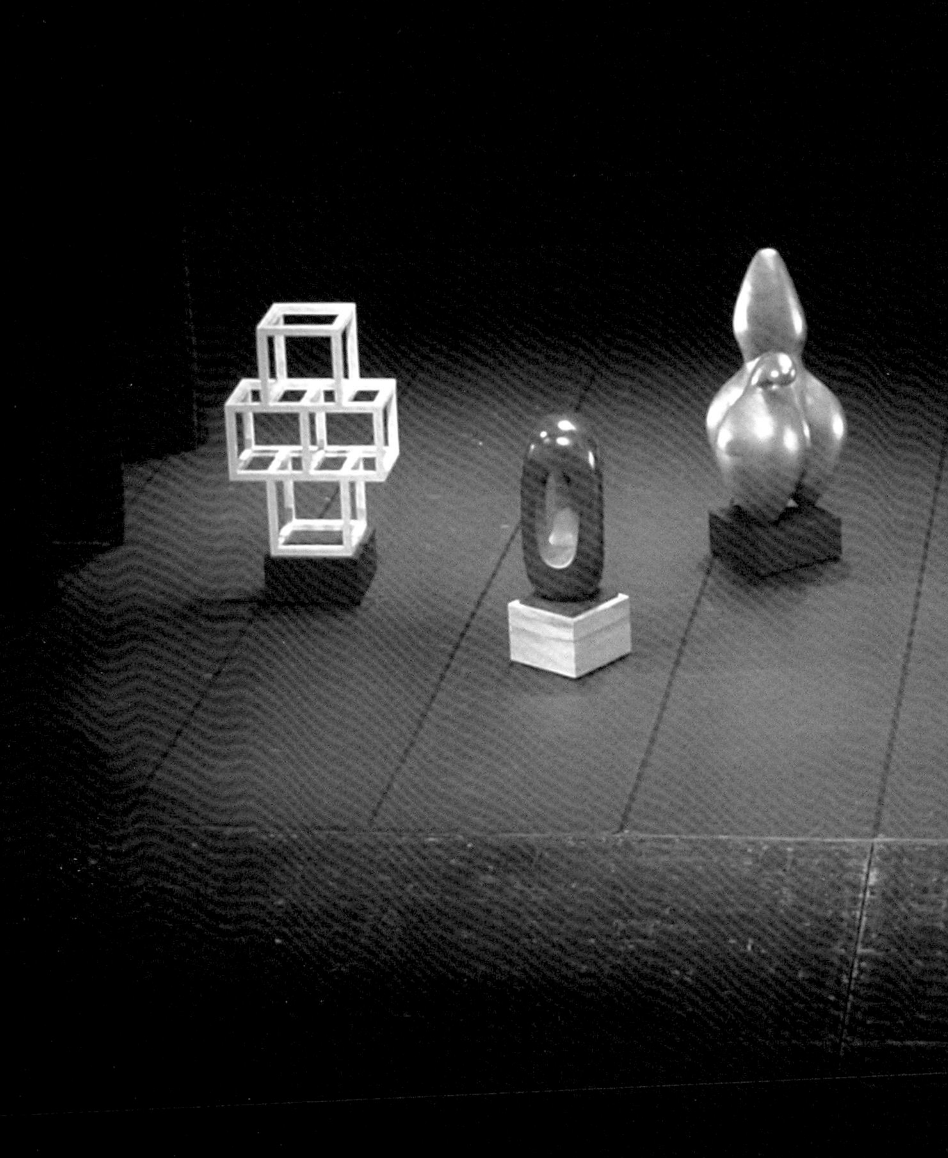

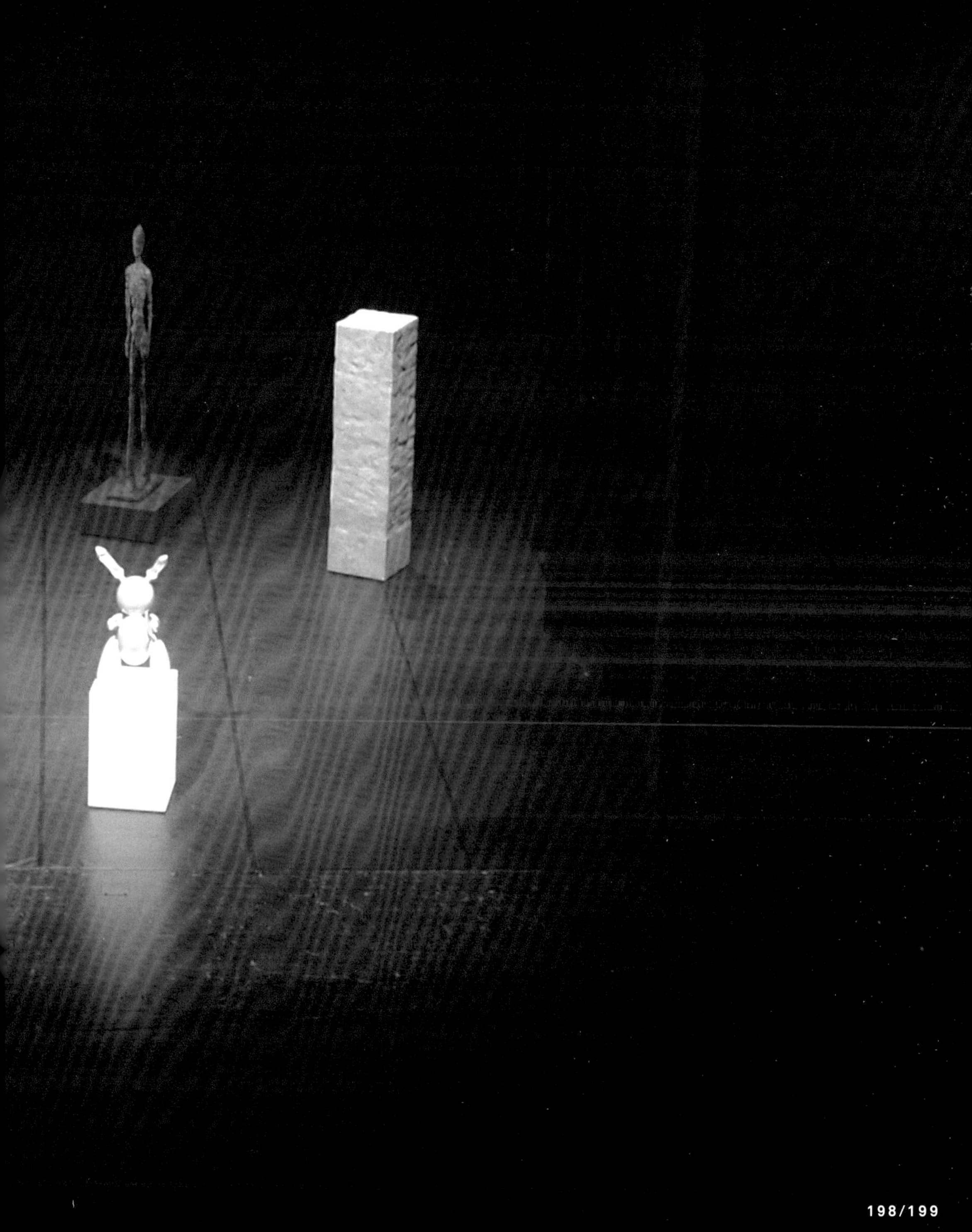

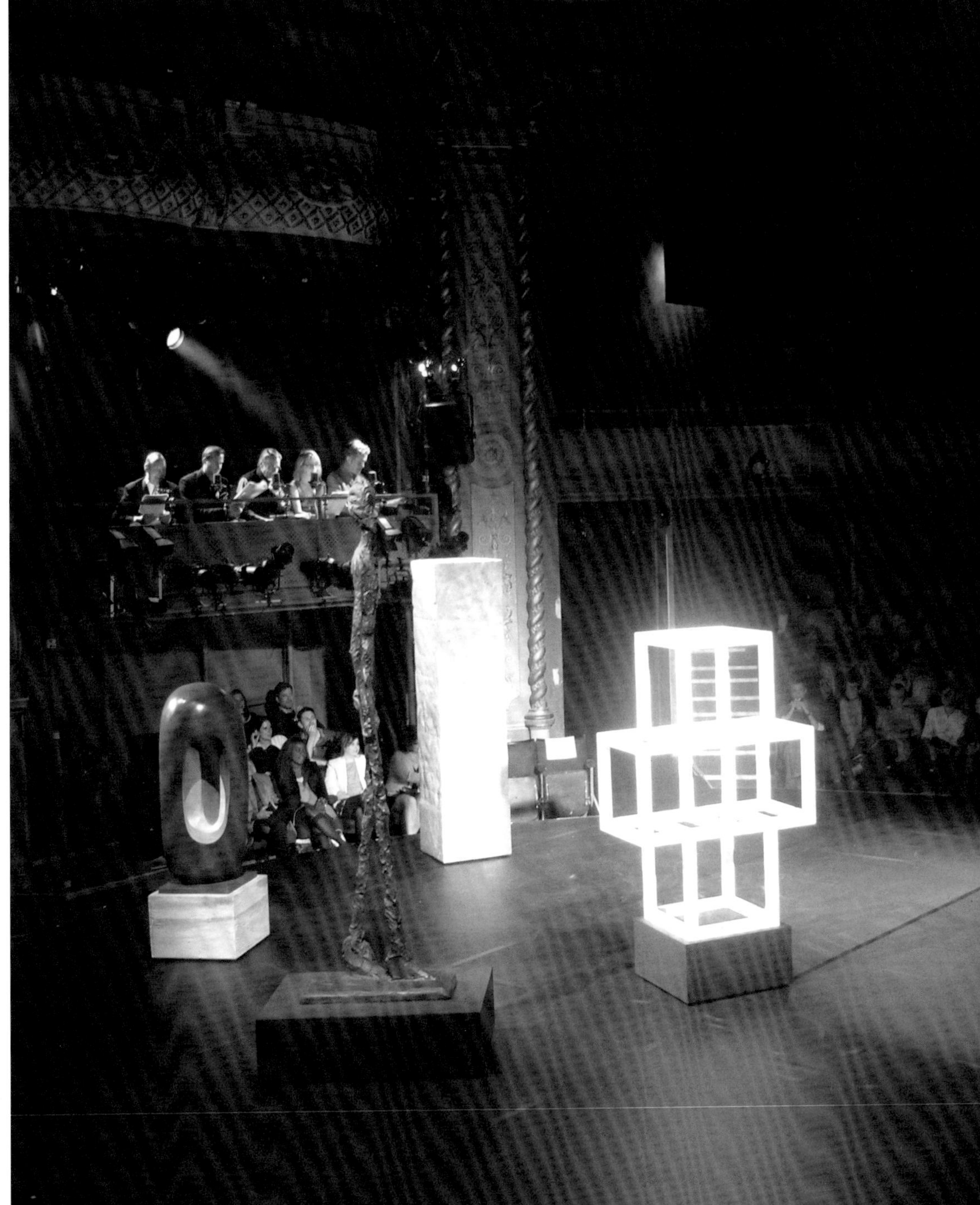

Drama Queens

A PLAY BY ELMGREEN & DRAGSET
WITH TEXT BY TIM ETCHELLS

OUTLINE

Drama Queens is a play without actors. Seven 20th Century superstar sculptures find themselves trapped on a theater stage and out of their usual context. How do they interact with this new environment and with each other? The drama unfolds through a series of clashes and crossovers between the various "isms" and aesthetics which these sculptures represent.

Empty stage. Offstage voices, bumps, cracking and crashing sounds. Multiple voices saying: "Oups, au, I can't see anything! Where am I?"—and so on.

Light comes on slowly. Untitled (Granite) is already onstage. Lurches around onstage alone, moves around a bit as if exploring, then speaks in German and bad English.

UNTITLED (GRANITE): Gott in Himmel. Gott in Himmel. Was ist das? Was ist das? (*moves a bit more*) Was in die Hölle ist das? Wo bin ich? Soll das ein Joke sein? Wer bin ich? Where I am? Hallo? (*calling into the wings*) Hello?? (*and again to the other side*)

CLOUD SHEPHERD: (*enters the stage*) Keep the noise down.

UNTITLED (GRANITE): WAS? What haben Sie gesagt?

CLOUD SHEPHERD: I said no need for shouting. That's not the kind of atmosphere we need. My name is Cloud Shepherd. Who are you?

UNTITLED (GRANITE): Scheiße. Politeness. Scheiße. Where are we?

CLOUD SHEPHERD: (*to the audience as if intent on introducing himself/the event as well as apologizing for Untitled (Granite)*) Okay. My friends... mesdames et messieurs, I'm sorry to...

UNTITLED (GRANITE): (*still moving around a bit, agitated*) Where und fuck are we? Where und FUCK are we? Where und fuck are we?

CLOUD SHEPHERD: It's a theater.

UNTITLED (GRANITE): Scheiße, was ist the point of that?

CLOUD SHEPHERD: A place where... er... where people come to see stuff.

UNTITLED (GRANITE): Was?

CLOUD SHEPHERD: A place where people come to see things.

UNTITLED (GRANITE): What? WAS für things?

CLOUD SHEPHERD: All kinds of things...

UNTITLED (GRANITE): Aggggh. Quatsch.

CLOUD SHEPHERD: That may be so. But for the moment we are stuck here so you had better get used to it.

Elegy III enters in Star Wars robot style; spinning around, stopping, moving, spinning...

CLOUD SHEPHERD: Wow. She moves so beautiful. Like a dream.

UNTITLED (GRANITE): Too romantic.

ELEGY III: Hello.

CLOUD SHEPHERD: Hello.

UNTITLED (GRANITE): Guten Tag.

CLOUD SHEPHERD: I was just explaining that this is a theater.

ELEGY III: I see (*coughs*). I see. And who (*looking at the audience*), if you don't mind my asking, are that lot?

CLOUD SHEPHERD: It's called an audience.

ELEGY III: An audience. I see.

Characters

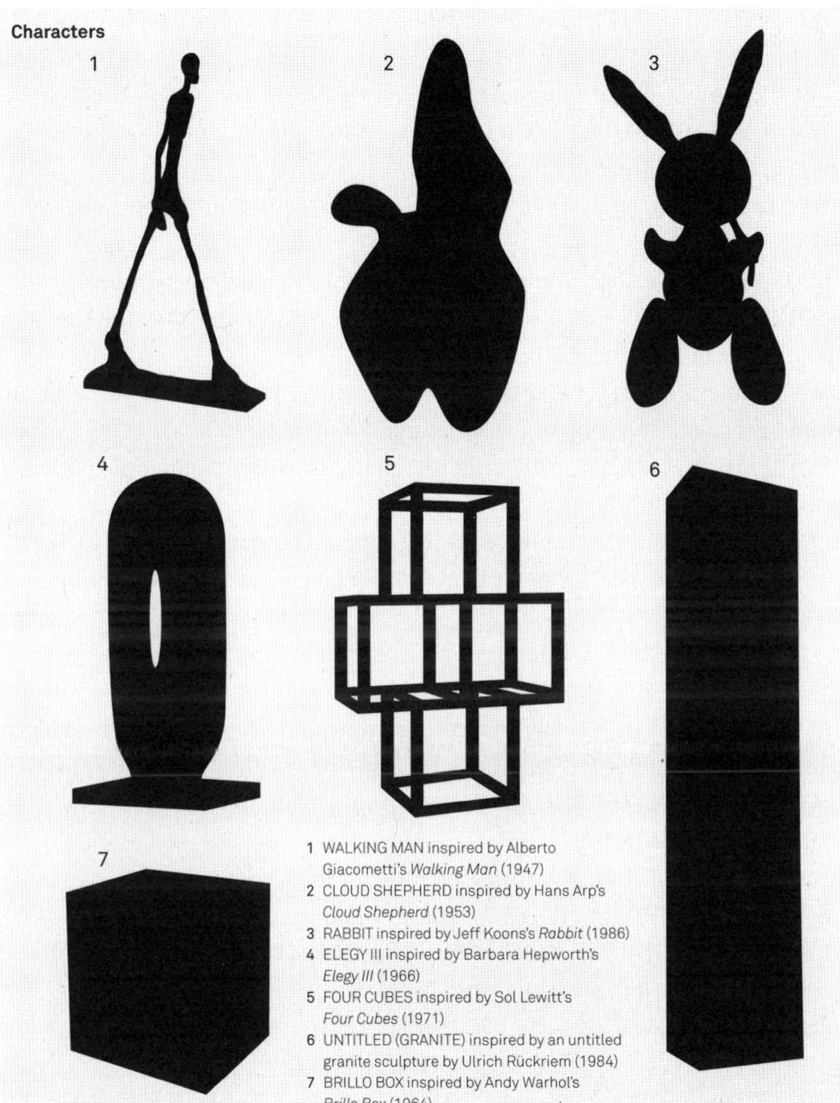

1 WALKING MAN inspired by Alberto Giacometti's *Walking Man* (1947)
2 CLOUD SHEPHERD inspired by Hans Arp's *Cloud Shepherd* (1953)
3 RABBIT inspired by Jeff Koons's *Rabbit* (1986)
4 ELEGY III inspired by Barbara Hepworth's *Elegy III* (1966)
5 FOUR CUBES inspired by Sol Lewitt's *Four Cubes* (1971)
6 UNTITLED (GRANITE) inspired by an untitled granite sculpture by Ulrich Rückriem (1984)
7 BRILLO BOX inspired by Andy Warhol's *Brillo Box* (1964)

UNTITLED (GRANITE): (*just saying the words contemptuously*) "Guten Tag." "Audience." Ha!

ELEGY III: And what, if I might inquire a little further, is an audience?

CLOUD SHEPHERD: Think of it like a visitor to a gallery, only there are lots of them and they all think with one mind.

UNTITLED (GRANITE): (*to the audience, too loud and rude*) "Guten Tag, Audience!"

ELEGY III: Are you sure? But they are all seated! No one walks around?

CLOUD SHEPHERD: Just pay attention. It's like the circus. One laughs, they all laugh. One claps, they all clap.

UNTITLED (GRANITE): Penguins at the Zoo Stinky Fisch für das ganze Publikum! I get the nasty smell of feeding time! Populismus!

CLOUD SHEPHERD: Not really, not like that. Just a group of people with one attention, one intention.

ELEGY III: Are you sure? You're a pretty shaped stranger... nice proportions... but should I trust you? My heart beats a little faster but... Are you leading me on a merry chase?

UNTITLED (GRANITE): Genau! How we can know you're not fooling us all time? How do we know that what you say is for true? How we can trust words?

CLOUD SHEPHERD: Just say something funny and see what they do. They'll laugh alright. You'll see.

UNTITLED (GRANITE): Ich bin NICHT funny. Do ich funny look to you?

CLOUD SHEPHERD: No.

UNTITLED (GRANITE): You think ich look funny?

CLOUD SHEPHERD: No, no. Okay. Doesn't matter.

ELEGY III: He's right. We shouldn't try to be funny. I wasn't born to entertain.

UNTITLED (GRANITE): Wahnsinn. This is Wahnsinn. A fucking insult.

Pause.

WALKING MAN: (*enters*) Hi.

ELEGY III: Hello. My name is Elegy. (*coughs*) Elegy III.

WALKING MAN: Hi—Homme Qui Marche—Walking Man or Man Walking. People find the names easy to switch but for me there's always a little something lost in translation—I still prefer the original—Homme Qui Marche.

UNTITLED (GRANITE): Wahnsinn. He doesn't realize he's a sculpture. Walking Man. Quatsch.

CLOUD SHEPHERD: (*to Walking Man*) Don't worry about this blockhead—I'm Cloud Shepherd.

UNTITLED (GRANITE): Poetic Namen. Absolut Scheiße. I have no name. Ich bin Untitled. Ohne Titel. Ohne Titel. Ganz concrete.

ELEGY III: (*coughs*). No, please don't worry about him at all. So straight-laced the Germans sometimes, so uptight—worse than the Russians or the Japanese, but I digress... Take a seat. Stick around.

WALKING MAN: No thanks. I need to keep moving. I like to walk, I love to walk and walk—you know perambulate and contemplate. That's my thing.

CLOUD SHEPHERD: You're starting to make me dizzy.

Walking Man continues to pace back and forth.

WALKING MAN: The world makes me dizzy again. I thought I got used to its spin.

UNTITLED (GRANITE): Back and forth, back and forth. Stop! Stop! Bitte, bitte.

Walking Man continues.

CLOUD SHEPHERD: It is really starting to get annoying now.

ELEGY III: Yes, stop, stop.

UNTITLED (GRANITE): Halt!

WALKING MAN: Okay. I can stop for a while.
UNTITLED (GRANITE): Danke schön.
WALKING MAN: Even a notorious *flaneur* such as myself needs to rest up on a plinth now and then.

Pause.
In the silence the sculptures' attention is once again on the audience. Maybe one or two of them move to the very front of the stage and "look around" at the auditorium. After some time of silence:

ELEGY III: Don't they wander off and look at something else… these visitors here… ?
WALKING MAN: Not likely.
CLOUD SHEPHERD: No. They're gonna sit there and see what happens.
ELEGY III: Jesus. Does anyone have a cigarette? I find this situation rather intimidating.
CLOUD SHEPHERD: Sorry. No.
ELEGY III: It's just that I'm not used to this. Normally I'm out in the garden all year round. People just pass by. Quite often they don't even notice me. Oh, I love to be outside. I love gardening. I must…
CLOUD SHEPHERD: Don't panic. You'll get used to it.
UNTITLED (GRANITE): Ich will auch OUT. Back to the nature. I want landscape. This is Wahnsinn.
WALKING MAN: I mean days go by sometimes when *no one* looks at me. I'm not even on display the whole time. And when I am, I'm stuck in a corner gallery that I think is too hard to find. I want to move. The light's bad. Depressing. But the only time they move me is to send me on loan. Packing crates. I don't like that, that's worse than here. At times, I've even been in storage. Storage. Can you believe that? Terrible. Terrible. The silence.
FOUR CUBES: (*enters in systematic movements*) I've been there too. In storage. It's no fun at all. Very degrading.

CLOUD SHEPHERD: (*to Elegy III*) Who's this then?

ELEGY III: (*to Cloud Shepherd*) Not another nameless rectilinear structure please... (*to Four Cubes*) Do you have a name? (*cough cough*) (*to Cloud Shepherd*) Let's at least hope he's not as rude as the other square one.

FOUR CUBES: My name is Four Cubes.

ELEGY III: Pleased to meet you.

CLOUD SHEPHERD & WALKING MAN: Hello.

UNTITLED (GRANITE): (*reluctantly*) Hallo.

All a bit embarrassed and quiet. Small movements.

ELEGY III: We were just discussing... various things.

CLOUD SHEPHERD: Yes.

WALKING MAN: Yes. We were.

Silence again.

RABBIT: (*enters at high speed*) Hey. Look, look a Rabbit! Look, look a silver Rabbit! (*Pause.*) You know guys, I think I could really use a bit more reaction here.

UNTITLED (GRANITE): What?

RABBIT: Tell you what we're going to do. I'll go offÐand then come back... and we'll try that whole thing with the entrance all over again. Don't worry folks the Rabbit is here, the Rabbit is in da house! Clap your hands, clap your hands. (*exits*)

CLOUD SHEPHERD: (*to Elegy III*) Good Lord. Some distant relative of mine perhaps—with ears... and the tail...

ELEGY III: (*to Cloud Shepherd*) But rather gaudy. Tasteless.

UNTITLED (GRANITE): Auslanders. Idioten and now Rabbiten. It's not even Easter.

FOUR CUBES: I was just saying that I was in storage...

WALKING MAN: Yes. Even the word sends a shiver... They just come by every few days to check temperature and humidity. They claim I'm too fragile. It's not a normal life. Not a normal life at all. I need the streets, boulevards, I need open spaces.
RABBIT: (*enters again*) Look, look the silver bunny! (*Pause.*) That's better... I guess. Hello, a very good evening to you all and welcome. The Rabbit is in da house. Oh yes! (*A few lame moves around the stage, or on the spot, then he stands still.*)
FOUR CUBES: Hey Walking Man. Don't worry about the Space Rabbit thing. Where do they keep you in storage?
WALKING MAN: Some kind of vault down below the museum... in Switzerland, I don't know for sure. Zurich I guess, or maybe Basel, Geneva, St. Gallen... you name it. They've got museums everywhere. It's dark most of the time. And no one talks to me, no one talks to me. Do you have a clue what that can be like?
FOUR CUBES: Yes. Like I said, I've been there.
WALKING MAN: What about you Cloud Sculpture? Do you have any idea? Any fucking idea at all?
CLOUD SHEPHERD: It's Cloud Shepherd to you, my Little Skinny Walking Boy. Obviously, I'm outside most of the time, herding clouds. The morphing, ever changing clouds.
WALKING MAN: Whatever. I'm talking about loneliness. Isolation. Time alone with your own thoughts. Solitary confinement. The silence. The terrible silence.
FOUR CUBES: You can't call it silence with the sound of that humidification machinery and all the environmental maintenance equipment they have at work down there. Can't sleep in such an environment. That's not silence.
RABBIT: Ha ha. Now the guy thinks he's John Cage. Can we have four minutes and 33 seconds of silence please?
WALKING MAN: Okay. Yes. Whatever. It's not really silence of course. You could go crazy there in storage though, get lost in your own mind.

RABBIT: Can someone please change the subject? It's all getting so very heavy... free uppers to the boring ones. I want to see smiling faces. Come on now. Happy, shining people.
UNTITLED (GRANITE): Ja. Yes. The melodrama is bit thin. Und tearing on the nervous system. Silence would be the preferable. Stille Nacht... Heilige Nacht... ach, egal...
FOUR CUBES: Fellas, now that we've got an audience, I propose we each make a series of numbered statements about art.

The others say nothing, so Four Cubes works to his own invitation.

FOUR CUBES: 1. Art is not rational. It helps us reach conclusions that rationality cannot reach.
UNTITLED (GRANITE): Halt die Klappe! Ruhe! Silence please.
FOUR CUBES: 2. Rational judgments just repeat rational judgments.
UNTITLED (GRANITE): Halt die Klappe, halt die Klappe, halt die Klappe!
FOUR CUBES: 3. Only illogical judgments can lead to new experience.
RABBIT: How many of these statements are you planning to say?
FOUR CUBES: Either 50 or 35. Depends on the situation. 4. Formal art is essentially...
RABBIT: You're not worried that it's going to get just a little bit boring?
FOUR CUBES: Listen Space Rabbit—that hardly matters. It matters that I follow my illogical thoughts rationally and logically. That's going to be point 5.
RABBIT: I see. It's just Rabbit by the way or my real friends call me Bunny in fact, no need for the whole Space Rabbit routine. What do they call you again? I didn't catch your name. I mean, what's your profile?
FOUR CUBES: I'm Four Cubes.
RABBIT: (*high pitched voice, slightly over-eager*) From Ice Cube the rapper and star of critically acclaimed Law and Order: Special Victims Unit—like a joke on that right? Brilliant.

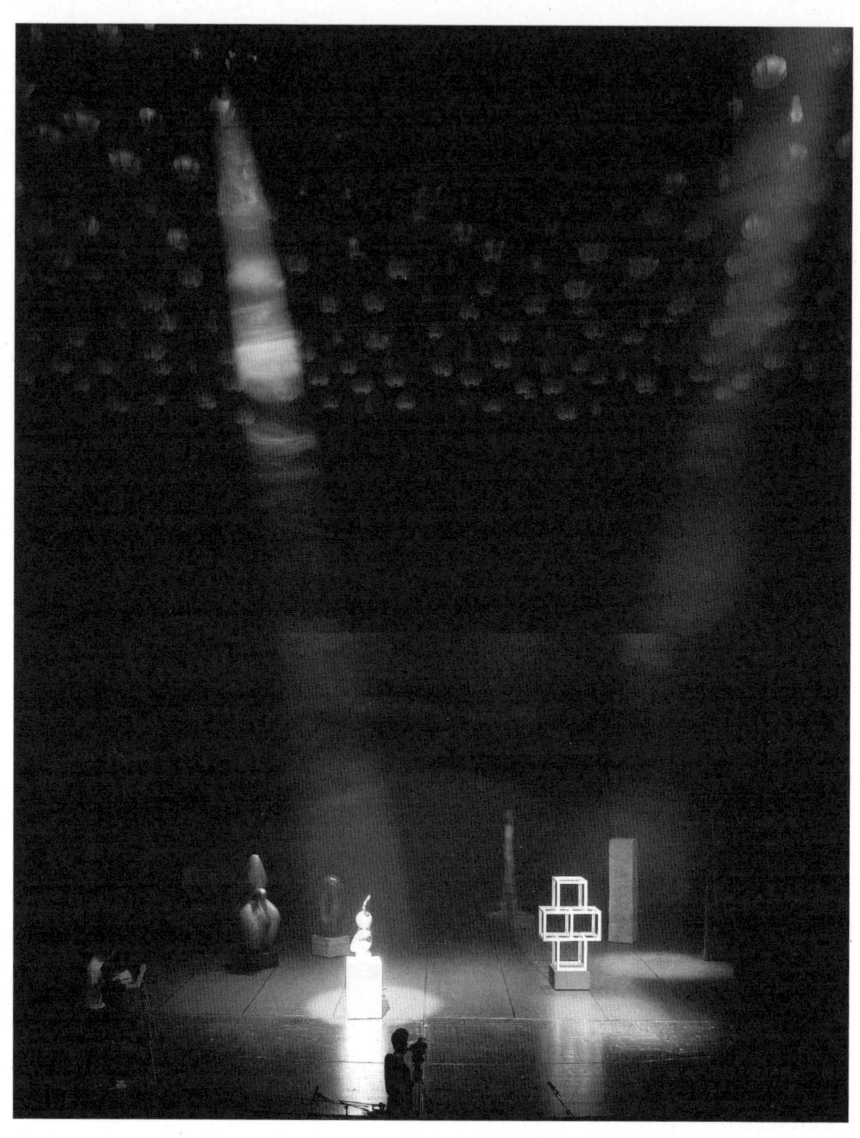

FOUR CUBES: I have no idea.

RABBIT: Or from the Four Seasons, the classic restaurant designed by Mies van der Rohe and Philip Johnson that has been redefining American Cuisine since 1959? You need to book a table months in advance.

FOUR CUBES: I still have no idea. The name Four Cubes comes from the number and kind of geometric forms of which I'm comprised.

RABBIT: Yeah. It's very inventive. My user name is Rabbit, but everyone calls me Bunny. Why not "Two Cubes and One Big Vertical Rectangle?" It's more sexy. You ever think about that, Brainbox?

CLOUD SHEPHERD: Rabbit, there's no need to be so clever, so cynical, or so confrontational.

ELEGY III: I still don't get it with this audience thing. They're just going to sit there? They're not going to move around? They're not going to talk? They're not going to try and touch?

CLOUD SHEPHERD: Not likely.

UNTITLED (GRANITE): (*to the audience, slow, loud and rude as if they did not hear him the first time he said this*) "Guten Tag, Audience!"

ELEGY III: Are we supposed to do something?

RABBIT: Think of them like a bus load of tourists. They came all the way through some museum and what they really want to see is you. Their feet are tired, they're sitting down on some benches, they turned off their audio guides and now they're looking at you. Staring. Waiting. Do something dazzling!!!!! Showtime, babe!!!

ELEGY III: It's vulgar. (*coughs*) Does anyone have a cigarette?

UNTITLED (GRANITE): Halt die Klappe! Shoot up! This is too decadent.

RABBIT: Make 'em laugh, make 'em laugh... (*moving around the stage, from side to side*) Hey, hey over here. Look at that silver bunny! Over here! Now he's over here! Where did he go? Where did he go? He's so fast! He's amazing! Look-at-him-go! Just! Look! At! Him! Gooooo! This is so contemporary, this is so...

UNTITLED (GRANITE): This ist ein totaler insult. Insult total. No dignity.
RABBIT: Can we please get some music? And can we please please do something with the lights? I want Night Fever by the Bee Gees. Donna Summer? Giorgio Moroder? I will survive! Come on, let's do it… How 'bout Grandmaster Flash? Spandau Ballet? You must have some music up there in the sound box.
FOUR CUBES: 32. Banal ideas cannot be rescued by beautiful execution.
RABBIT: Yeah, yeah, yeah. We heard it before. We heard it before. (*Melancholy now, after his burst of energy.*) We heard it before. Death and Storage. That's all there is in the end.
FOUR CUBES: And a set of irreversible processes. Entropy. Decay. Degradation of materials over time.
UNTITLED (GRANITE): Ja. JA. Danke schön Four Cubes. AT LAST speak someone ein bisschen sense in here around. Time passes. We age. In one way we change and in others we stay the same. We watch in silence as the world changes before of us. People come and go but we endure. Watching. Waiting. Betrachten und warten. And mostly silent, until now at least. Mostly silent. I miss the silence. All this talk is so unnecessary, so much too much. Like many good actors I can say more just by the way that I am standing here.

Long silence.
From time to time one of the sculptures moves a little.
Maybe one of them comes up closer to the audience.
In the end it is Four Cubes moving around Elegy III that breaks the silence.
He moves behind her and then to the front and to the side etc. checking out the view through the hole in her middle.

FOUR CUBES: (*to Elegy III*) I can see through you.
ELEGY III: (*to Four Cubes*) I can see through you too.
FOUR CUBES: Yes, we have something in common. May I tell you something?
RABBIT: (*yelling*) There's nothing private on the stage! Don't forget that bus

load of tourists. We're here to entertain. Art could learn a lot from Bono!
CLOUD SHEPHERD: Who is Bono? Is that an artist? Or a sculpture? Or a museum—MOMA, MOCA, BONA, BONO?
UNTITLED (GRANITE): You have nothing understand. Idioten.
FOUR CUBES: (*to Elegy III*) I just wanted to say that I don't like the Rabbit.
ELEGY III: (*to Four Cubes*) You mean the Bunny?
FOUR CUBES: (*to Elegy III*) He's calling himself that sometimes but his real title is just Rabbit.
ELEGY III: Yeah. I know what you mean. I don't like to look at him, it's horrible. You see yourself back, only all distorted.
FOUR CUBES: I noticed that too.
RABBIT: (*still yelling*) They tell you you're great. That you're truly truly NOW, the moment. The fucking Zeitgeist. Studio 54 or whatever. They tell you that you're everything. But in the end it goes. They stop coming. There's something bigger or brighter or more inflatable. Something that kids can climb on or slide down. Or something kids can download or log on to. MySpace. Your Space.
UNTITLED (GRANITE): Bitte. Idioten. Have a bit of dignity bitte. Passage of time is not a thing to be ashamed of. The change gives some wisdom, no?
RABBIT: But... The crowd is so fickle.
UNTITLED (GRANITE): It's okay Rabbit. The crowd does nicht matter. That is was I am trying to say before. The masses are stupid, just look at history...
ELEGY III: (*still speaking about Rabbit*) Thing is it's like you're never really looking at him. You can't really see him at all, you see yourself and the rest of the world, all bent around like a bottomless pool you're going to fall into and...
WALKING MAN: Relax. You know how much he cost that Rabbit? You have any idea what he cost last time someone bought him? You know how much they have to insure that Rabbit for? You know the procedures when they clean that Rabbit and get him all good and shiny like that? You know the kind of

gloves they have to wear and the stuff they have to use? I'm not a cheap trick, me myself, but like Untitled says I'm in the older and wiser department these days.

FOUR CUBES: 34. When an artist learns his craft too well he makes slick art. 17. The artist's will is secondary to the process he initiates. 8. ...

WALKING MAN: (*interrupting*) Is it just my perception affected by all the lights and the confusion or are these numbered statements coming all out of sequence now?

FOUR CUBES: 11. Ideas do not necessarily proceed in a logical order.

WALKING MAN: Four Cubes is a Smart Ass.

RABBIT: Yeah. Somewhere in that stiff frame he's got a real sense of humor. Not as hollow as he looks.

WALKING MAN: You feeling OKAY?

RABBIT: Not too bad. You know it isn't always so easy to be me. Everyone says "where's the silver bunny,""'we want the bunny to do that bouncing thing and get the party started and do the whole like the 1980s—Wall Street—Masters of the Universe—This Boom Will Never End routine." But these days I don't feel like that so often. Sometimes I just wanna stay at home and paint.

WALKING MAN: I understand.

RABBIT: I need to see my banker, my gallerist, my investment manager and my art book editor. I need to see my AA sponsor. And I need to see my agent. There's some sponsorship thing we're trying to figure out. They want to fill me with Helium and float me over Beijing. Something like that, I'm not sure any longer. You have an agent, right?

WALKING MAN: No.

RABBIT: Sure you do. You're modeling for Dior Homme, right?

WALKING MAN: That's not me.

RABBIT: Sure it is. The skinny boy look. So Hedi Slimane. That's totally your thing. I saw you man—on the catwalk, in Milan.

WALKING MAN: Not me.

RABBIT: Sure it was you. We went to that dinner/party thing Victoria's Secret threw for Donatella. Mountains of snow and everything wrapped in black. You were in the bathroom after the main course, bent over the toilet with your head in the bowl "just to make room for some dessert." You're famous, man, so don't deny it. You're the object of desire for all the boys in Paris. Size 26. They all stopped eating last spring. They want to be like you.

WALKING MAN: I have no idea about all this. Like I said—it was not me. Not my scene. I don't have an agent. I don't model for anything or anyone. Not any more. I don't have time for that stuff. Get it? I walk. I think. I look at the world. I walk and reflect.

RABBIT: Whatever. I've been doing some reflecting myself. It's all Death and Storage in the end man, we're all headed to the great padded packing crate in the sky.

UNTITLED (GRANITE): Bring Bier!! I at least should have a drink if I am going to get through this farce. (*yelling*) Was can do ein Mann to get a scheißing Drink in Heir? Wass kann do ein Mann? (*He weeps.*) A rabbit. A whole bunch of abstract rabbits. Mein Gott. I did not deserve this. Ein Bier, bitte !

ELEGY III: I'm no abstract rabbit mister. I was around long before you.

UNTITLED (GRANITE): Aber du bist eine Frau. Ein Frauenskulptur. You are just a hole. Nothing concrete. Female physhjjjj. Four Cubes is the only one who makes a bit of sense here. Arrrgh, scheiß egal. Bier bitte und maybe ein Schnäpschen.

ELEGY III: Don't call me a hole you silly spare phallus. I never understood the German mentality. So rude sometimes.

RABBIT: Yeah.

ELEGY III: I don't think they do boarding schools. All messed up. That might explain their addiction to order. No sense of formal manners. Worse than the French. Worse than you Americans. Worse than the Dutch. Oh. This international relations thing is so tricky. My sister is a guard at the United Nations building in New York—she would have a word or two to say about it.

UNTITLED (GRANITE): Frauen-talk. Blah, blah, blah. Scheiß egal. Vereinte Nationen up my ass. If I must suffer this I at least want to get stoned.
ELEGY III: Okay. I've had enough of this "Frauen-Talkscheiß-egal," mister. How come this show is just one big group of boys and then me? Just starting to wonder if that's a pattern of some kind? (*silence*) Ideas anyone? No?
RABBIT: I hate to break this to you baby, but that's how the world works. You ever check the prices at an auction?
ELEGY III: Why would I? I know how it works. You're pathetic. Great artists and great men mean the same thing around here. It's ridiculous.
RABBIT: Okay. Okay. Think I said the wrong thing. Ladies and Gentlemen, members of the press... I think it's really time for a tune now. We need to kick this into play. Who's on sound? We need some 80s stuff... we need an anthem... a remix... a timeless classic! What about "We are the 'Art' World?" How about that? Brilliant! Look at that Rabbit! Oh Man! He's hilarious Man! (*Laughing hysterically at his own joke.*) He's hilarious! I can't take this anymore. I'm going to throw myself off the stage.
CLOUD SHEPHERD: Don't do that Rabbit. You'd break.
RABBIT: I could do a break-dance. I could vogue. Or I could do that clown dance thing from L.A. that everyone is talking about. I always bounce back. I'm made of stronger stuff than that.
CLOUD SHEPHERD: Is that right?
RABBIT: I'm a version of a cheap and popular toy, cast in a highly reflective tin-alloy substance and shined to perfection. OR put it another way—I'm absolutely dazzling.
ELEGY III: We'd noticed. (*coughs*) Does anyone have a cigarette?
CLOUD SHEPHERD: No, I'm sorry.
WALKING MAN: I have to walk again. He starts to walk, talking as he goes. I dream of the great cities and... er loneliness.... I dream of seeking, walking—seeking and searching ever onwards. They wrote that about me—that I "symbolized mankind himself, always moving forwards, always searching."

ELEGY III: What about women?

UNTITLED (GRANITE): Ja, ja. Alles gut now. Idioten speak. Complains from the Frauenskulptur. Look at yourself! You are nothing but a hole. A lack. Sculptures should be firm und erect. Concrete. I'm still missing the dignity of silence here. The honesty. The simple materials. You are alle so decadent!

WALKING MAN: (*still walking*) They said that I "was a perfect example, that I symbolized certain eternal aspects of human experience, the walk of the thinker, the gatherer, the hunter..."

RABBIT: Will you give it a break, reading out your own press materials?

WALKING MAN: (*still walking*) I'm trying to make a conversation.

RABBIT: We can all play that game.

ELEGY III: They called me soft, and quiet. Some said I was derivative.

RABBIT: They said I was a nothing, an empty gesture, a superficial if kind of clever decoration. Others said that in fact I embodied a devastating critique of the economy of the superficial. They said that from the tips of my ears to the ends of my feet I was a dazzling attack on a whole culture's obsession with wealth, glitz and easy pleasures. Still others thought that I was genuinely charming, that I showed a real and honest sense of fun—a kind of joy without irony that has all but vanished from the world.

ELEGY III: And, what's your own opinion?

RABBIT: I am a silver rabbit, based on the form of a cheap but colorful plastic toy. I am cast in stainless steel, which they call poor man's silver and I am approximately 104 cm high. I just reflect reality on my beautiful skin. That's all there is to it girl. What kind of opinion do you expect me to have about those big questions about symbols and meaning?

ELEGY III: Not much I suppose.

RABBIT: To be honest I'm more interested in them you know, the crowd.

WALKING MAN: Me too. I love the crowd. I love meeting my fellow men on squares and...

RABBIT: Don't make me laugh.

WALKING MAN: What do you mean?

RABBIT: You're not really one of them. You're no man of the people. Too thin, too thoughtful.

WALKING MAN: You aren't a real rabbit. You're a blob. You don't even have a face.

RABBIT: Real whatever. Doesn't matter Thin Man.

WALKING MAN: Bugs Bunny!

RABBIT: You wisecracking elasticized scarecrow.

UNTITLED (GRANITE): Are they going to fight?

FOUR CUBES: Maybe they will yes. Can be good, yeah?

UNTITLED (GRANITE): Ja. I think so. I would like to see that.

RABBIT: I love the crowd and the crowd loves me.

I am showtime. You though—you look like them but there's a difference... something that separates you...

CLOUD SHEPHERD: I put my money on the Walking Man.

UNTITLED (GRANITE): I bet ten Euros on the Rabbit.

FOUR CUBES: Me too. Us rectilinear guys better stick together.

CLOUD SHEPHERD, FOUR CUBES & UNTITLED (GRANITE): Fight! Fight! Fight! Fight!

WALKING MAN: Okay Bunny, okay. I am different—what you say is true in a way.

RABBIT: I know that. You don't need to tell me.

CLOUD SHEPHERD, FOUR CUBES & UNTITLED (GRANITE): (*in the background*) Fight! Fight! Fight! Fight!

WALKING MAN: I am part of the crowd but I'm distant and different because I'm also its observer...

CLOUD SHEPHERD, FOUR CUBES & UNTITLED (GRANITE): Fight! Fight! Fight! Fight!

WALKING MAN: ...a wanderer, destined never to be still. Not one of them, something different yes, something more I suppose. I am sublime! (*to Rab-*

bit) What you say to that?

RABBIT: (*pauses, then*) Nothing.

FOUR CUBES: Disappointing... not really a fight. More like a playground argument.

UNTITLED (GRANITE): That's true. Ja. Ein disappointment. A fight between a steel rabbit and a man made from bronze... Scheiße. That would have been something to see. Heavy metal, ja.

FOUR CUBES & CLOUD SHEPHERD: Yeah. Could have been good. Pity.

ELEGY III: Please. Does it have to be so macho competitive here? So much of a pissing contest? So much "shared showers?" So much all the boys together? You should be ashamed of yourselves.

CLOUD SHEPHERD: Sorry.

ELEGY III: You'll be measuring your penises next. And no one would like to watch that...

RABBIT: (*to Walking Man*) When I said you were different I was just thinking that you are insanely and crazily thin. You really sure about the modeling thing?

WALKING MAN: Yes. I'm sure. That was bound to come up again I suppose.

RABBIT: It's anorexia yeah? You can tell me.

WALKING MAN: No.

RABBIT: Okay. Is it something to do with war?

WALKING MAN: (*impatient exasperation*) No!

RABBIT: Let me have one more guess. I'm good at this. I know lots of stuff. Let me have one more stab at it. Let me think now... Okay, you're thin because...

ELEGY III: The meaning of art is not a proper subject for a quiz-like guessing game.

RABBIT: Why not? You don't think it could be more fun that way?

ELEGY III: It's just not appropriate.

RABBIT: Relax. You know. Frankie Goes to Hollywood. *Relax... don't do it... when you wanna come... when you wanna come...* But still Walking Man, the question is still in the air you know. How come you're so thin?

WALKING MAN: My thinness is best understood as the exterior reflection of an interior state. The reality that art seeks after is more than surface appearances, yes? Reality is more than logic?
CLOUD SHEPHERD: It's true that those of us who came out of the World War grew skeptical of logic.
RABBIT: Oh-oh. (*imitates a siren/warning sound*) Downer-alert! Downer-alert! (*to the audience*) Please Mind Your Heads Ladies & Gentlemen there are Weighty Themes Under Discussion. Take out your bags of popcorn. Check your cell phones for messages. Catch up on your power-napping. Time to get distracted.
ELEGY III: (*to Rabbit*) Really! You should be ashamed of yourself.
CLOUD SHEPHERD: With reason so degraded by the war machine we turned to chance as an answer, and to abstraction. Logic itself seemed to end somewhere in the trenches.
ELEGY III: (*overawed*) What suffering...
FOUR CUBES: 30. There are many elements involved in a work of art. The most obvious are the most important.
WALKING MAN: Am I getting tired or is he saying stuff that isn't even relevant?
UNTITLED (GRANITE): Ich weiß nicht.
WALKING MAN: I'm going to walk, try and get my own thoughts in order again. Anyone want to come with me?
RABBIT: I'll go. I wanna go. Take me with you.
WALKING MAN: Let me think. (*pause*) Okay. I don't want to be unkind but I have to say that I'd feel too strange walking with you. It's not really the atmosphere I want. Walking with a faceless silver rabbit—just not my style.
RABBIT: Okay. I can see it's maybe a bit too *Wizard of Oz* or too much *Donnie Darko*. I'll stay. But listen, Walking Boy—don't blame me when you get bored of your own conversation.
FOUR CUBES: 35. These sentences comment on art, but are not art.
WALKING MAN: (*about Four Cubes*) Jesus. (*to the rest*) Wish me well on my travels.

ELEGY III: Where exactly are you planning to go?

WALKING MAN: Just going to walk around here, you know, in the neighborhood a bit. (*he walks in a circle on the stage*)

UNTITLED (GRANITE): Drama Queen! There he goes.

RABBIT: Hold the front page. Walking Man spotted walking.

ELEGY III: (*with venom*) If you can't say anything nice please try being quiet. (*coughs*) Has anyone got a cigarette?

Silence.

CLOUD SHEPHERD: I'm going to take advantage of the silence and recite a poem. (*to Four Cubes*) You can think of this as a kind of numbered statement from me, okay??

FOUR CUBES: Please, go ahead. I've been waiting for this.

CLOUD SHEPHERD: You might like this Walking Man. Are you ready?

ELEGY III: I like a bit of a poem.

WALKING MAN: Let's hear it then.

CLOUD SHEPHERD: (*clears throat*) "*The feet of morning the feet of noon and the feet of / evening / walk ceaselessly round pickled buttons...*"

(*stops reciting*) No. Wait, I'll start again. That should be "buttocks."

"*The feet of morning the feet of noon and the feet of / evening / walk ceaselessly round pickled buttocks / on the other hand the feet of midnight remain / motionless / in their echo-woven baskets*

WALKING MAN: (*still walking*) I'm liking that. Pretty good...

CLOUD SHEPHERD: *Consequently the lion is a diamond...*

WALKING MAN: (*still walking*) Tell it like it is...

CLOUD SHEPHERD: *On the sofas made of bread / are seated the dressed and the undressed / and the undressed hold leaden...*" (*he stops reciting*).

It's definitely leaden something but I don't remember what. Leaden something? (*to Elegy III*) Any clues?

ELEGY III: Sorry, I can't help. I'm no good with words.

CLOUD SHEPHERD: Shit. I'm forgetting how the middle part goes. But the end goes something like: "*a mouth opens within another mouth / and within this mouth another mouth / and within this mouth another mouth...*"

ELEGY III: Oh... it's so great...

CLOUD SHEPHERD: "*and within this mouth another mouth... / and so on without end / it is a sad perspective / which adds an I-don't-know-what / to another I-don't-know-what.*"

ELEGY III: That's rather beautiful. (*She moves closer to Cloud Shepherd, spins around, she's in love.*)

UNTITLED (GRANITE): Nonsense.

ELEGY III: Don't mind him. You have such a way with words.

CLOUD SHEPHERD: Thanks.

UNTITLED (GRANITE): Nonsense.

ELEGY III: "*within this mouth another mouth.*" So clever.

CLOUD SHEPHERD: It's nothing really. Just something I scribbled.

ELEGY III: Say something else.

CLOUD SHEPHERD: (*shy*) I don't know.

ELEGY III: Please?

WALKING MAN: Yes. (*coming to a halt near them*) Come on. Let's have more.

CLOUD SHEPHERD: I can't perform to order. I need time to find inspiration.

UNTITLED (GRANITE): Warum you halt walking?

WALKING MAN: I'm not sure. I need the sights, the city... I feel trapped up in here. Not even a view out the window. At least in the gallery I can see out on the garden, with the pathways and the little stall selling postcards and T-shirts and coffee cups.

UNTITLED (GRANITE): I feel the same. I miss the outside Natur.

RABBIT: Like I said all along, we need to brighten things up. What we need is a dance.

ELEGY III: Yes. I think that might be an idea. (*to Rabbit*) Please, one moment.

(*to Cloud Shepherd*) Cloud Shepherd, will you dance with me? May I ask that of you?

CLOUD SHEPHERD: Yes, my Elegy III. To dance with you would be an honor.

RABBIT: That's the way. Okay. Okay. (*to the soundbox or offstage*) Are you ready there with the sound? Time for the big bang guys—Four Cubes, Untitled—don't sit there like squares! You're not getting out of this. It's time for a paaaarty! Oh Man, oh Man. You can really trust that silver rabbit to get the dancing started. (*to the soundbox*) Can we have the music pleeeeeaaaaaase?!

Music plays. They dance, some more reluctantly than others. Elegy III and Cloud Shepherd very much focused on each other. Untitled (Granite) getting into it, trying to follow the wilder moves of the Rabbit.

RABBIT: (*as they dance*) Come on—move it! Shake it baby! Get Down! (*some James Brown squeals etc.*)

UNTITLED (GRANITE): Ja! Ja! (*on the beat, in between delighted squeals from Elegy III and Cloud Shepherd*)

The music stops / "collapses" / cuts off brutally.

ELEGY III: (*coughs hard*) Does anyone have a cigarette ?

FOUR CUBES: Oooh, I have never moved that much in my whole entire life.

RABBIT: Really? No way. I love to move. I'm all over the place all the time, I love to dance, to spin like a disco ball.

UNTITLED (GRANITE): Feels gut in fact. So interessant. Not bad. Ich like that.

RABBIT: If you like that Untitled you're going to love the Techno Remix.

UNTITLED (GRANITE): Was it das? Techno Remarks?

RABBIT: The Techno Remix. It's like Disco, but more just the beat, more intense, relentless.

UNTITLED (GRANITE): Ja. Gut. Techno Remarks! We want now the Techno Remarks!

No more music...

RABBIT: Looks like that's it. No more music. The laws about parties are stupid. Everything closes so early. Can't even get started before it's finished. It's not like the 80s. Things are so protected now.

UNTITLED (GRANITE): Scheiße. Maybe we can go somewhere else to find more Techno Dancing Remarks?

RABBIT: Yeah. It's Remix. Remix.

UNTITLED (GRANITE): Ja.

RABBIT: Ja. Maybe later Untitled. I'll make some calls and try to find out what goes on around here. There must be a nightclub somewhere.

ELEGY III: I love to dance.

WALKING MAN: I must say I prefer walking.

CLOUD SHEPHERD: I like to drift, like the clouds. You can call that a kind of dancing.

ELEGY III: (*still beaming love at Cloud Shepherd*) And after the dancing... after the music... there is only silence... only silence.

UNTITLED (GRANITE): Ja.

ELEGY III: (*to Cloud Shepherd*) A beautiful silence that has you in it.

FOUR CUBES: Silence comes as a relief. Just listen again.

WALKING MAN: You can hear time passing.

UNTITLED (GRANITE): The slow decay of the world.

ELEGY III: (*gazing at Cloud Shepherd*) So beautiful...

More silence.

WALKING MAN: Wait? What's that?
CLOUD SHEPHERD: I think...
FOUR CUBES: It's...

Crash. The Warhol Brillo Box falls to the floor. Everyone rushes away to all sides.

Silence as they survey the wreckage.
Some going tentatively close to it, others hanging back.

WALKING MAN: What the hell is that?
UNTITLED (GRANITE): I never saw anything so stupid.
FOUR CUBES: Nice shape, but what the hell is that writing?
ELEGY III: Yes, it's rather queer. It's NOT a sculpture is it? Surely not.
UNTITLED (GRANITE): Ich weiß nicht.
CLOUD SHEPHERD: Does it talk?
FOUR CUBES: Don't think so. Maybe it's injured.
ELEGY III: (*advancing*) Let me see.
CLOUD SHEPHERD: Don't get too close!
RABBIT: It's okay guys. Just a box is all, kind of out-sized.
WALKING MAN: I didn't bring my glasses. Can anyone read what the writing says?
CLOUD SHEPHERD: (*spells it out*) B-R-I-L-L-O... soap pads?! Oh, that's brilliant, we can give the Rabbit a really good shine. Did you order these?
RABBIT: Hey, hey, hey, I've got nothing to do with this.
CLOUD SHEPHERD: You say that but I'm not so sure, I think there may be some connection.
RABBIT: Hey Man, give me a break. First sign of trouble and people always blame the Rabbit. I'm innocent.
UNTITLED (GRANITE): Scheiß egal. Leave him alone.
WALKING MAN: It's okay, Cloud Shepherd. I was watching the Rabbit the whole time when that... thing... came down. This is a strange event, but it's

not his work. He didn't do a thing.

CLOUD SHEPHERD: Okay. (*sighs*) Look—I don't have time for this any more. It's time for me to go. I need to find a way to get back to the heavens. I've got work to do. There are clouds that need moving around.

ELEGY III: Take me with you. Please. Take me with you.

CLOUD SHEPHERD: (*thinks for a moment*) Okay.

Elegy III and Cloud Shepherd leave the stage together.
Some of the others say goodbye.

FOUR CUBES: You think they'll be happy together?

WALKING MAN: Impossible to tell, and pointless to speculate. We'll never know. I'm going for a walk. I think there's an exit to the street back there somewhere. Farewell, my friends, good luck.

RABBIT: Goodbye, Walking Man. No hard feelings.

WALKING MAN: Adieu.

UNTITLED (GRANITE): Auf Wiedersehen.

Walking Man strides off.

FOUR CUBES: I'm off too. You coming, Untitled?

UNTITLED (GRANITE): Perhaps. I maybe wait for the Rabbit and go find Techno Remix.

FOUR CUBES: Okay. See you around. Keep those right angles nice and sharp.

UNTITLED (GRANITE): Naturlich. Gute Nacht.

Four Cubes leaves the stage with systematic movements.

UNTITLED (GRANITE): It's just us two left here now. Shall we find a night-club for dancing?

RABBIT: Sure. Whatever. Let's leave before it's too late.
UNTITLED (GRANITE): Ja.
RABBIT: Just look at it—this place is dead now, with whoever just jumping on stage to get his fifteen minutes of fame. It's over. I'm not gonna hang around and wait for the next big crash.
UNTITLED (GRANITE): What will they do now—that audience—now that the show is over?
RABBIT: Oh you know. They'll move on. Find something else. You know what it's like at these big time art events. They all wanna see something different, they wanna see something new.
UNTITLED (GRANITE): Ja.
RABBIT: They just wanna see something that they never saw before.
UNTITLED (GRANITE): Ja. Ja. Alles same. Alles same.
RABBIT: Alles same. Yeah. Ja. Ja. (*pause*) Let's go. The last one out can turn off the lights.

Rabbit and Untitled (Granite) leave side by side.

UNTITLED (GRANITE): (*offstage*) Zehr gut. Ja. Auf Wiedersehen. Gute Nacht. Auf Wiedersehen.

They leave. Lights fade slowly on Brillo Box.

END

DRAMA QUEENS

A play by Michael Elmgreen & Ingar Dragset
Text by Tim Etchells, www.timetchells.com

FIRST EDITION

Cast (recorded):
Alexandre Partzov: Cloud Shepherd
Mark Coles: Four Cubes
Lucy Coleby: Elegy III
Marek Sarnowski: Untitled (Granite)
James McLean: Rabbit
Johann Schibli: Walking Man

Developed for:
The exhibition "Skulptur Projekte Münster 07"
Performance Dates:
June 16 and 17, 2007

Städtische Bühnen Münster
Neubrückenstraße 63 48143 Münster , Germany

SECOND EDITION

Cast (live):
Joseph Fiennes: Four Cubes
Lesley Manville: Elegy III
Alex Jennings: Untitled (Granite)
Kevin Spacey: Rabbit
Jeremy Irons: Walking Man

Gala in Aid of The Old Vic Theatre Trust
Performance Date:
October 12, 2008

The Old Vic
The Cut, London SE1 8NB, United Kingdom

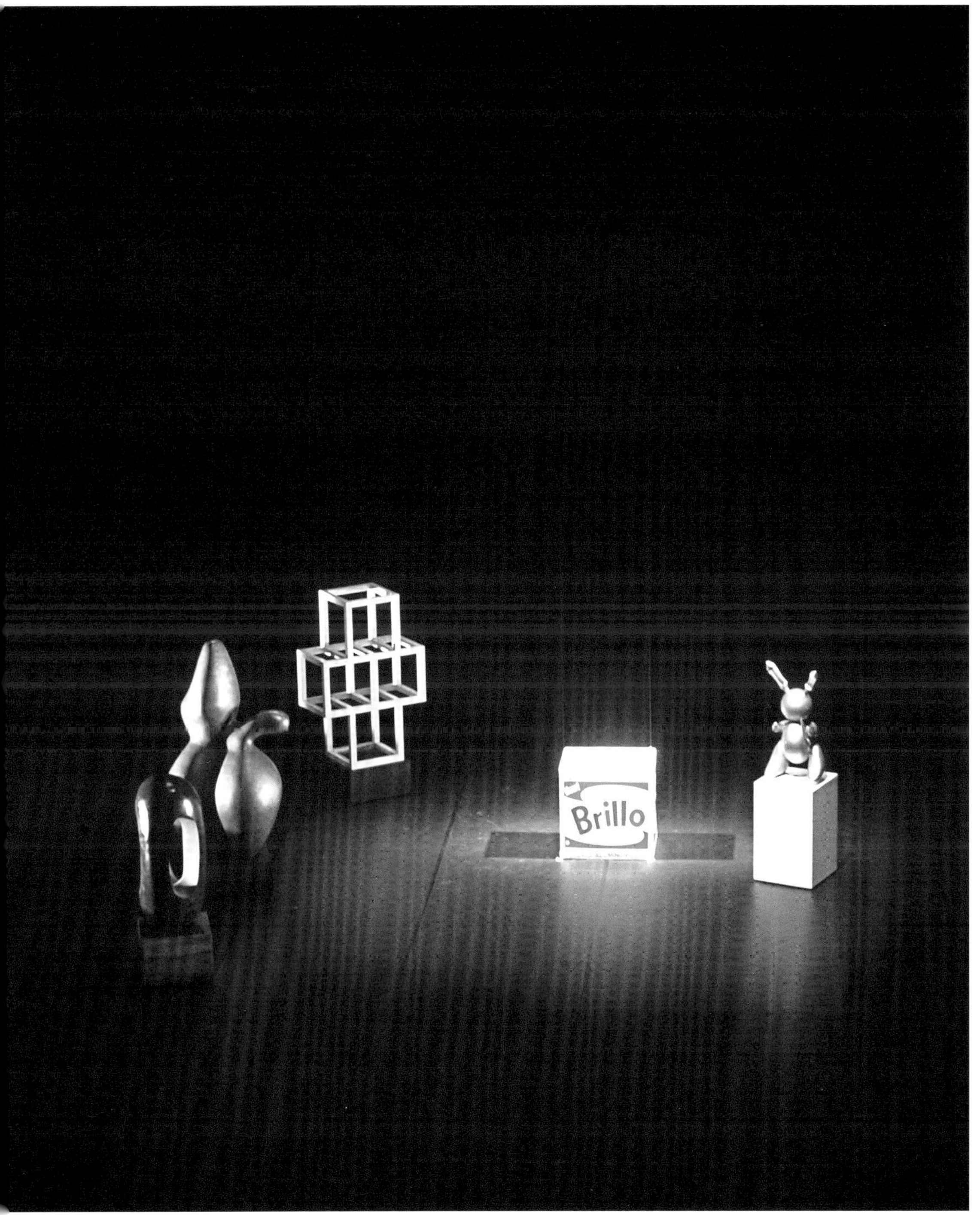
Brillo

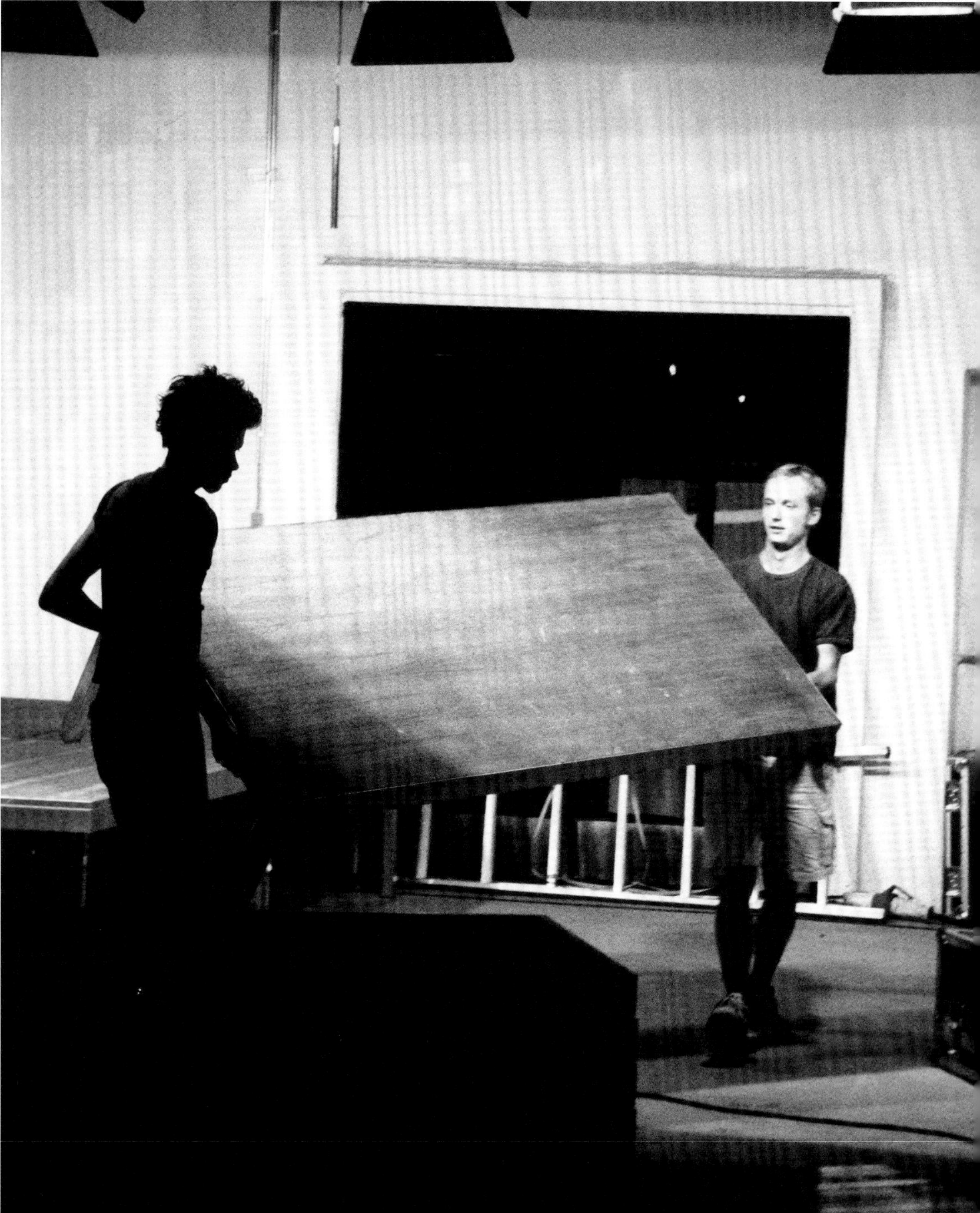

ATERIALS:	*theater stage, lighting equipment, seating*
ERFORMERS:	*theater technical crew*
LOTHING:	*their own*
IMENSIONS:	*variable*
URATION:	*as long as it takes for the crew to de-install and empty the space*
ERFORMED AT:	*Odense Performance Festival, 1998*

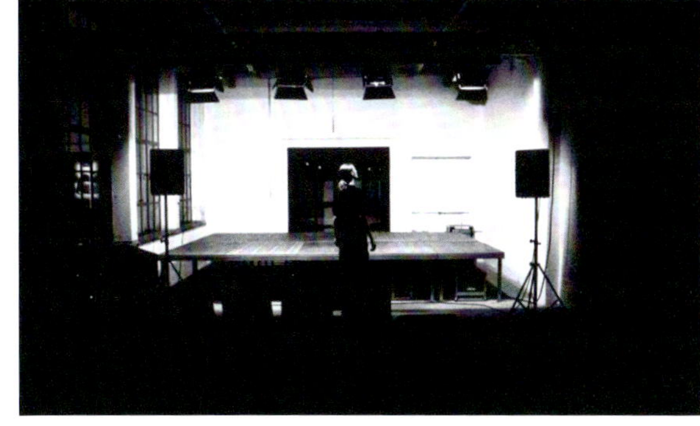

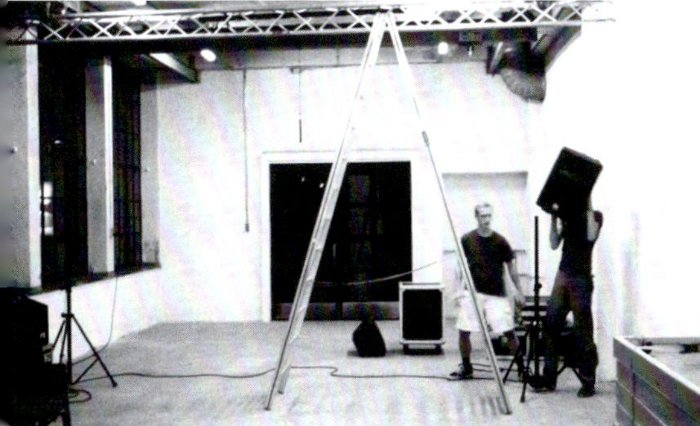

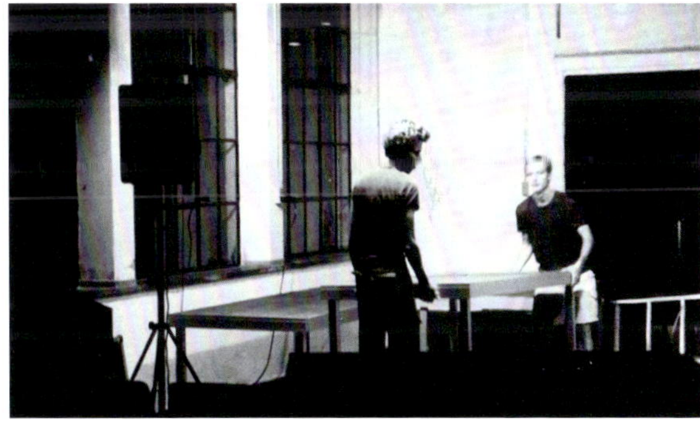

NTITLED
998

—

rformance where the theater stage, lighting equipment, and stly, the seating, are de-installed as the audience arrives.

MATERIALS:	*mixed media*
PERFORMERS:	*five opera singers*
CLOTHING:	*in costume*
DIMENSIONS:	*hydraulic clock structure, diameter: 10 m*
DURATION:	*ninety minutes*
PERFORMED AT:	*Staatsoper, Berlin, 2006; Opéra de Lyon, Lyon, 2006; Théâtre du Châtelet, Paris, 2006*

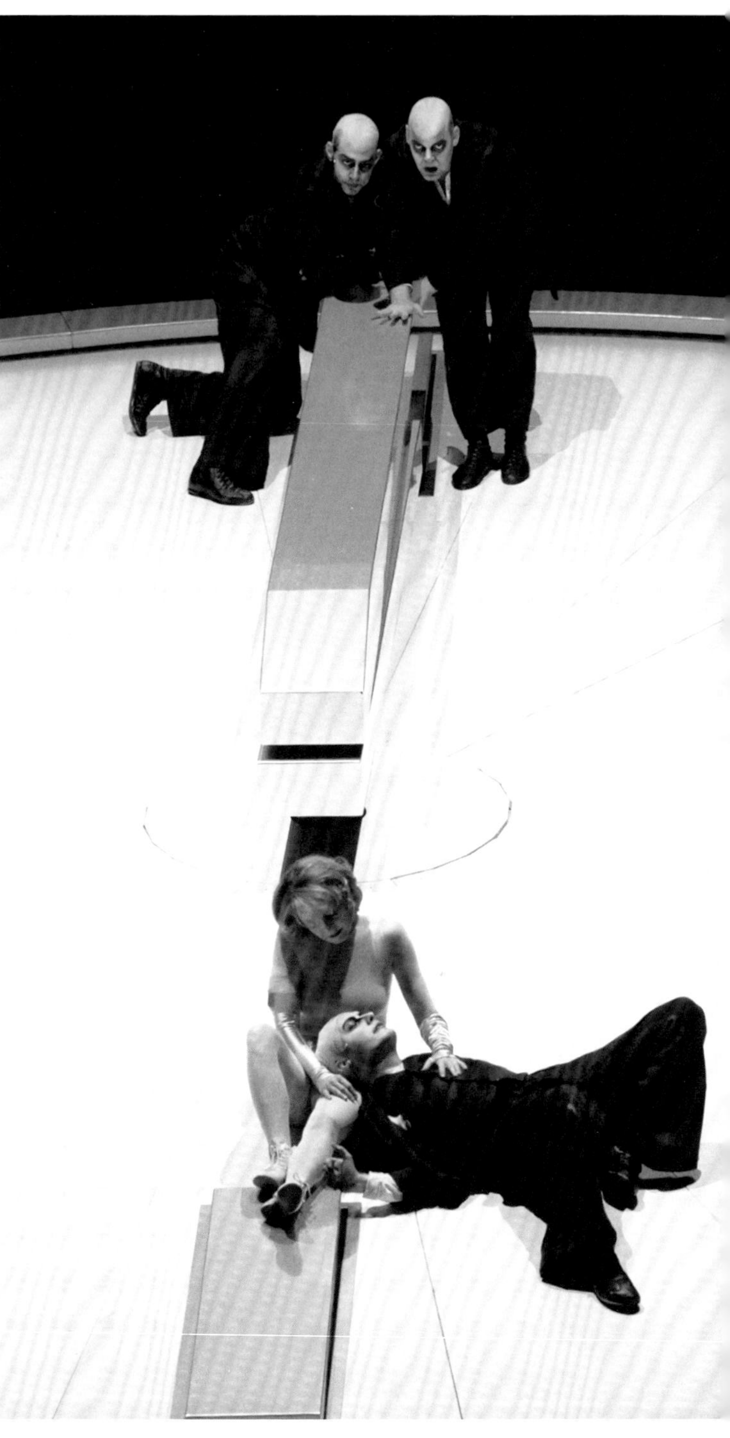

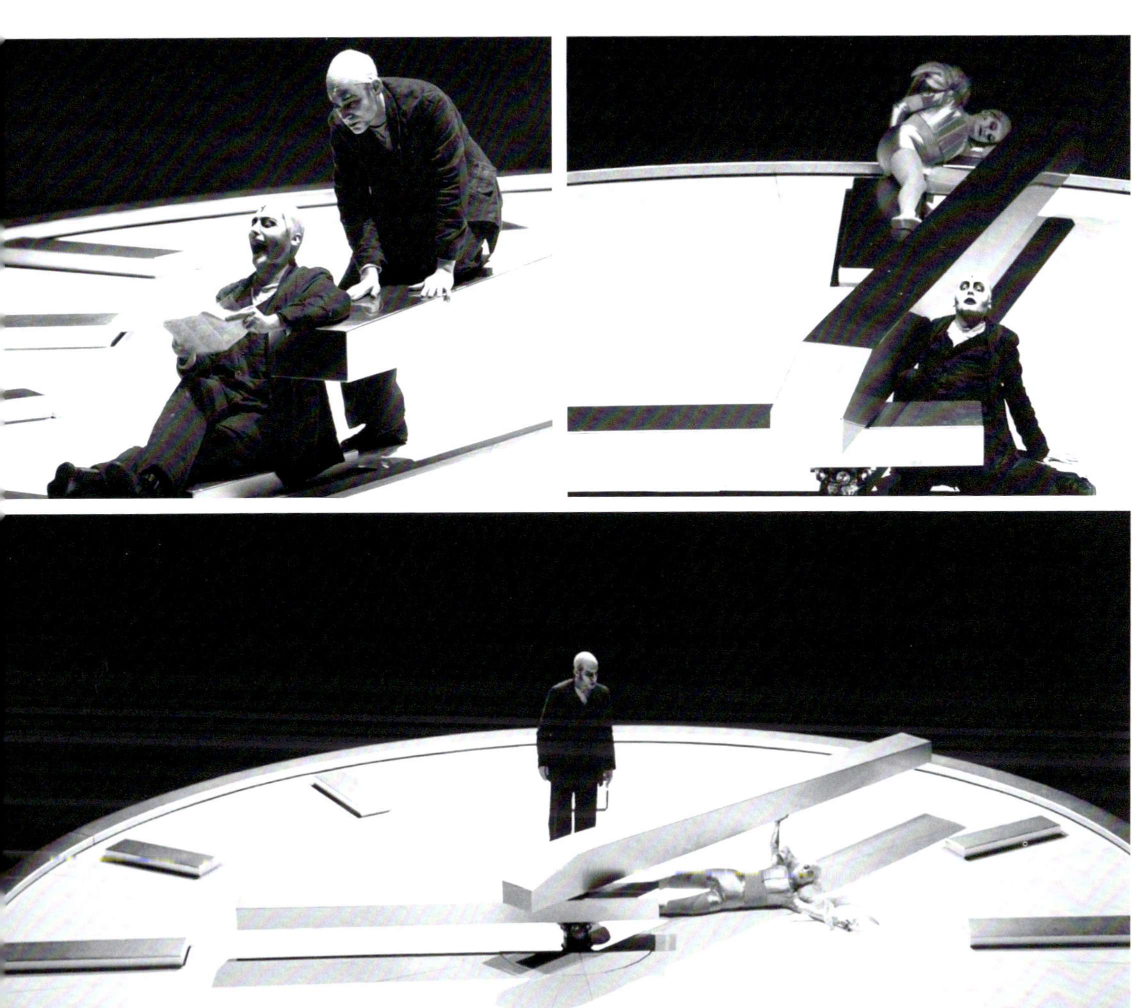

AUSTUS, THE LAST NIGHT
006

tage design for a contemporary opera "in one night and leven numbers" by Pascal Dusapin, produced as a hydraulic tructure in the shape of an oversize clock. The clock's hands ırn, enabling the singers to take a spin on them. The time in-icators were constructed as removable blocks, allowing for ew entrance and exit points and serving as block material for ne performers to build and interact with. The opera was di-ected by Peter Mussbach and performed by five singers with full orchestra.

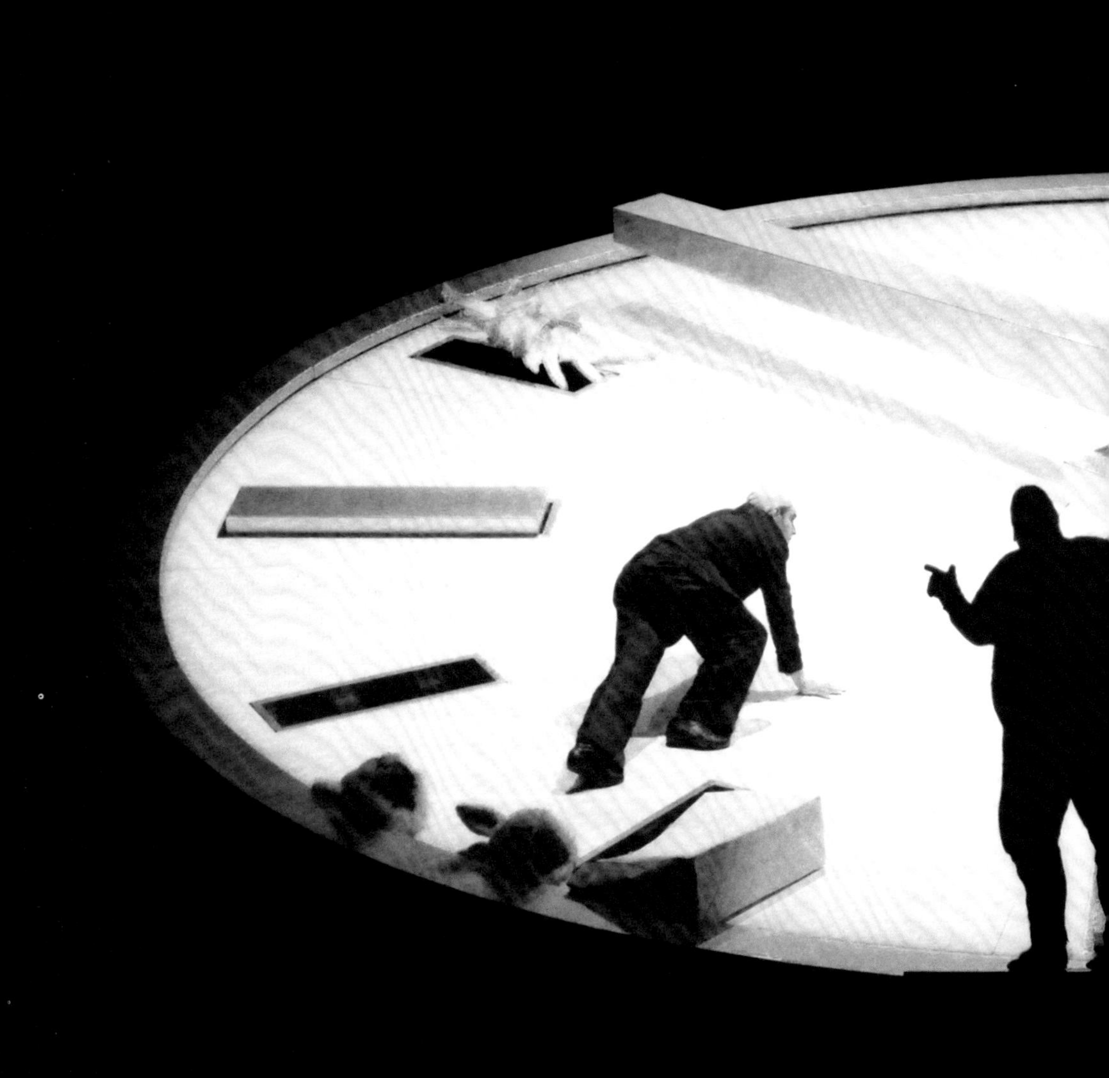

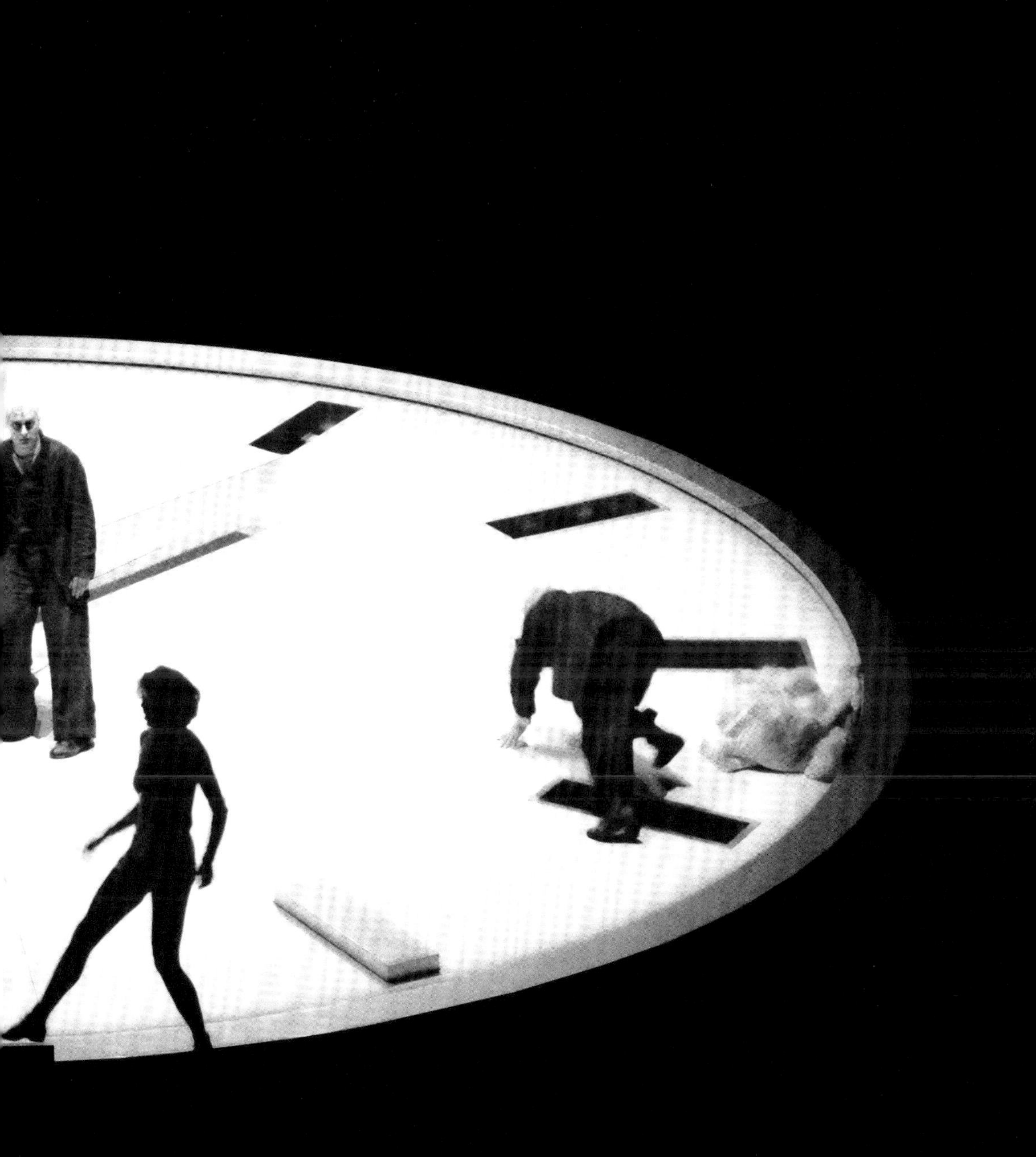

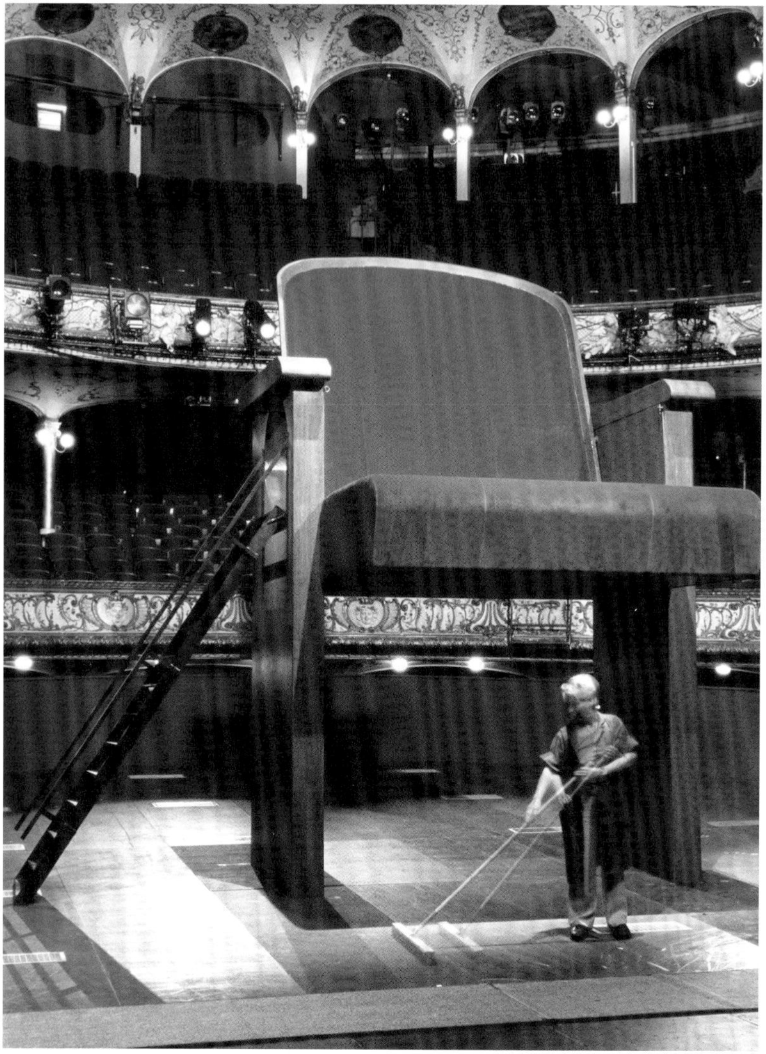

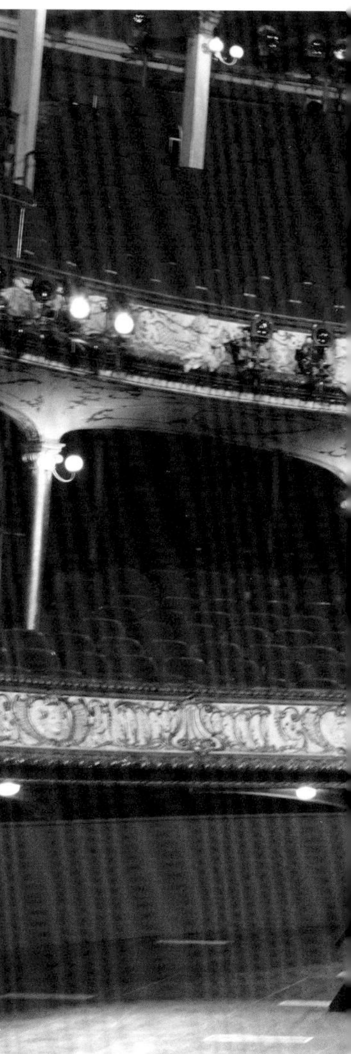

MATERIALS: *wood, velvet, plastic*
DIMENSIONS: *800 x 340 x 220 cm*
DURATION: *weekend event of art projects and stage productions*
EXHIBITED AT: *“Schauplätze 1,” Schauspielhaus Hamburg, 2001*

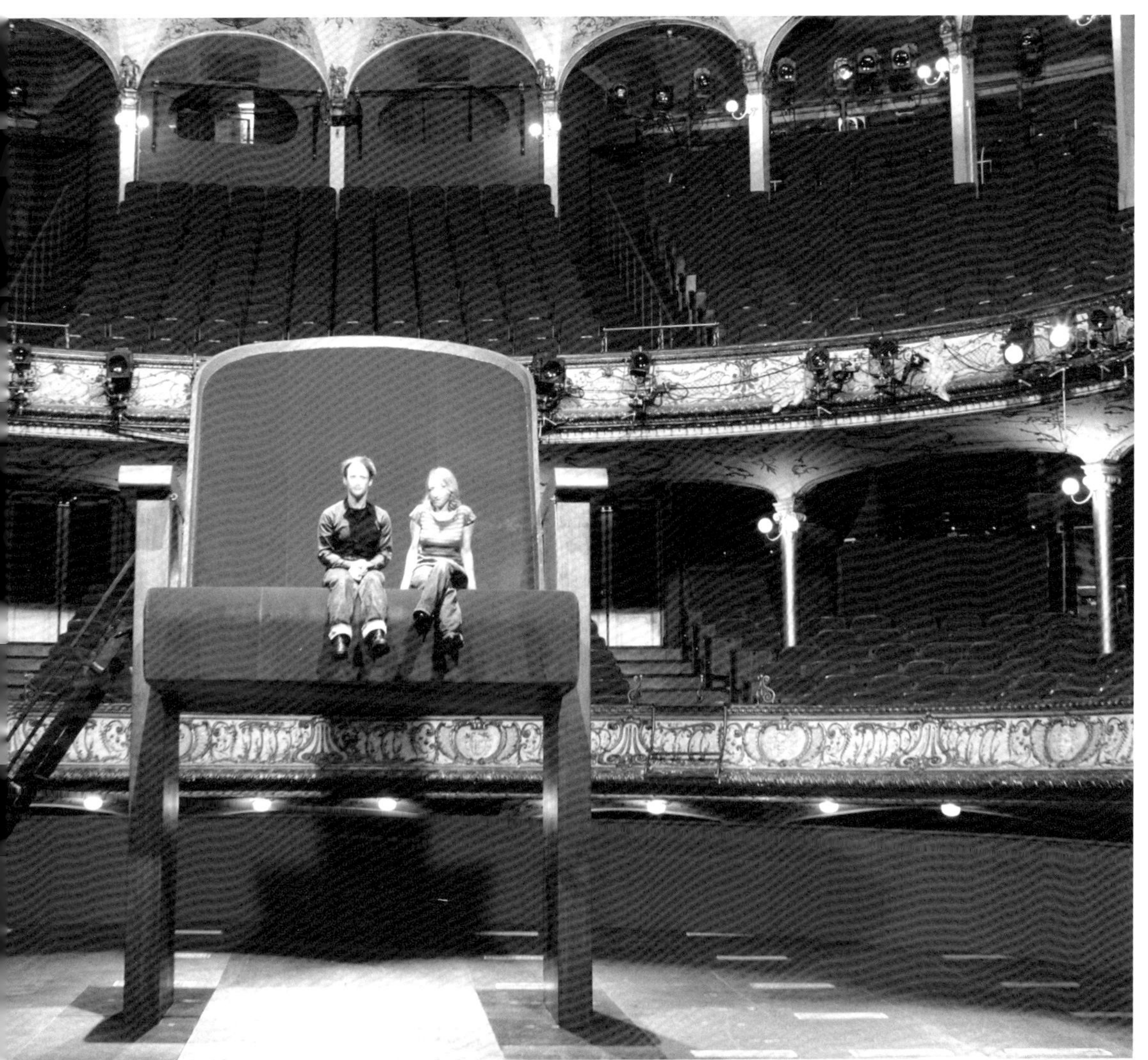

RSTE REIHE (FRONT ROW)
001

l the seats from the theater parquet are replaced by one over-zed replica which can seat approximately fifteen people. The eat is accessible by a ladder on the side.

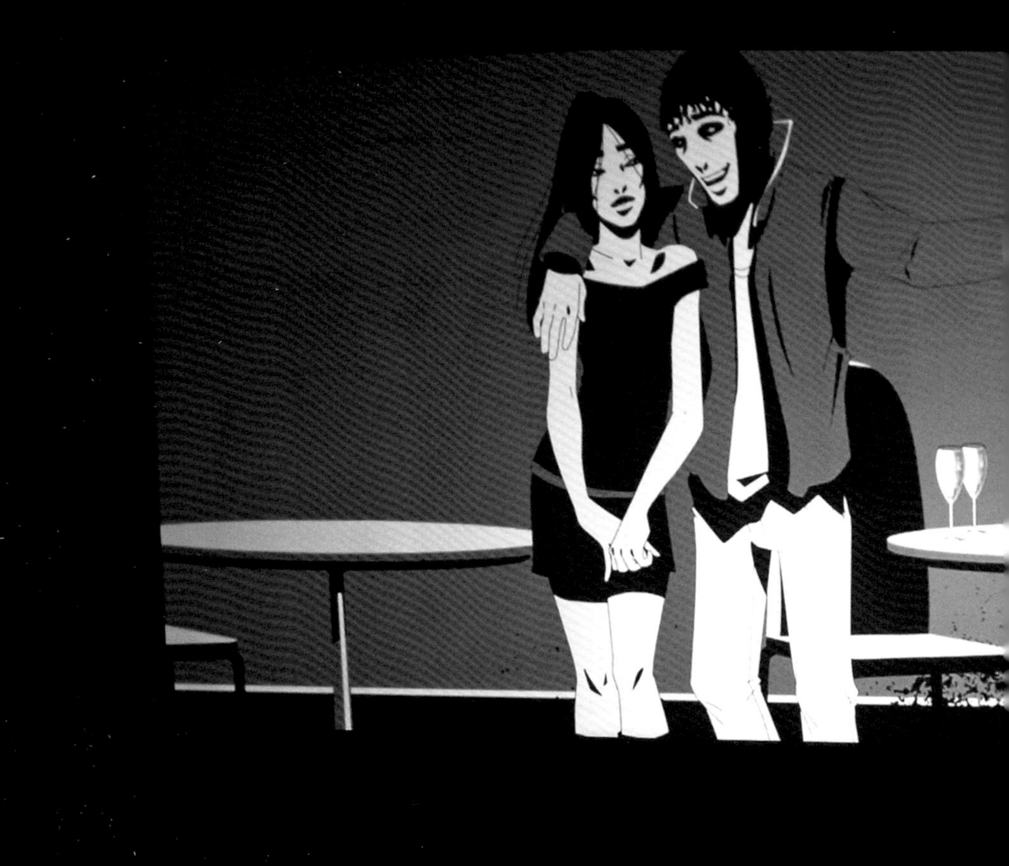

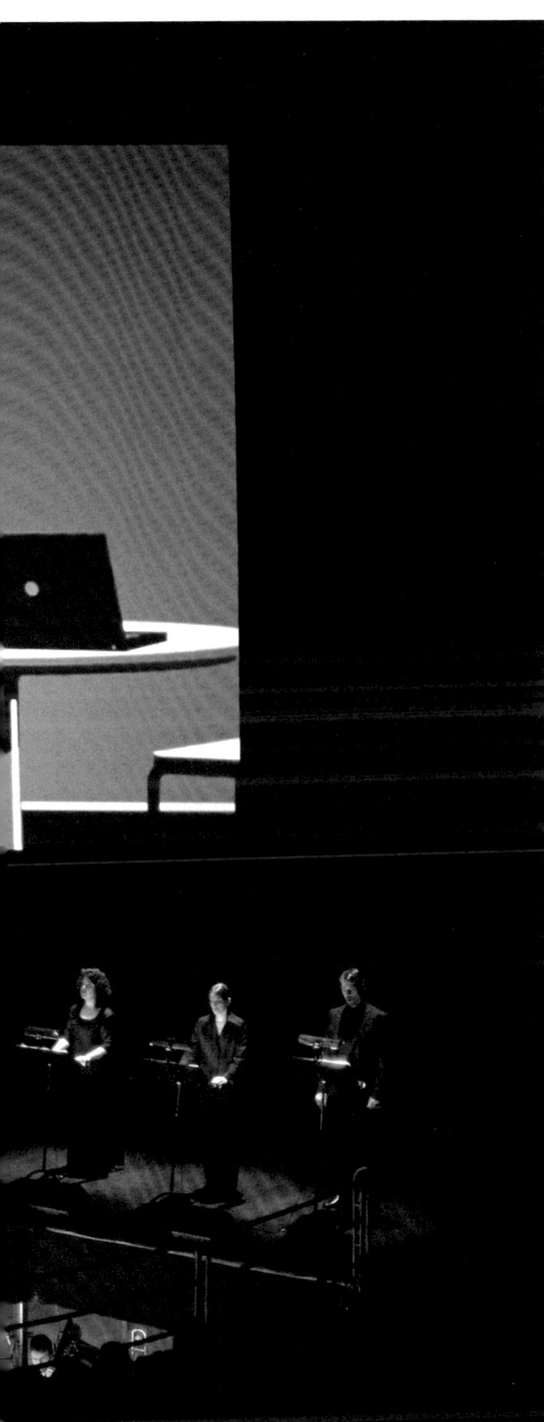

MATERIALS:	*animated movie, three music stands with attached lights*
PERFORMERS:	*two female opera singers and one male opera singer*
CLOTHING:	*minimal black*
DIMENSIONS:	*projection: approximately 9 x 15 m*
DURATION:	*approximately two hours and forty minutes including intermission*
PERFORMED AT:	*Bergen International Festival, 2008*

L'AMOUR DE LOIN
2008

Animated movie accompanied by three live singers and a seventy-piece orchestra for the opera *L'amour de loin* (Love From Afar) by Kaija Saariaho, shown as the opening event of the Bergen International Festival in 2008. Elmgreen & Dragset directed the animated film in collaboration with the film company Fabulab (Copenhagen) and created a contemporary storyline that paralleled Amin Maalouf's libretto, which was based on a Medieval love story, with a failed internet date. Elmgreen & Dragset were responsible for both stage design and direction.

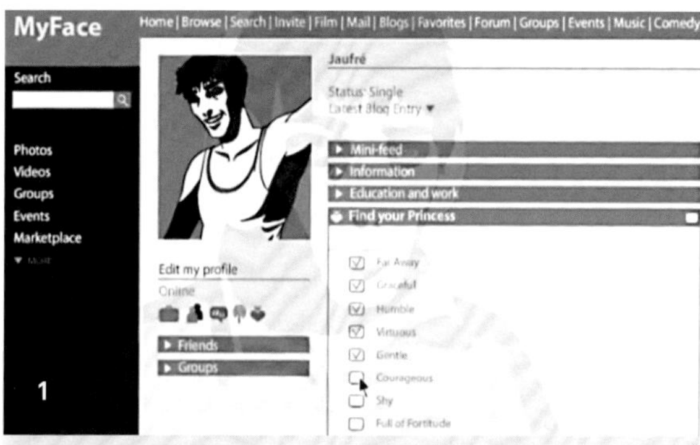

JAUFRÉ: The woman I desire is so far away, so far away, That my arms shall never enclose her.
COMPANIONS: (*mockingly*) Where is she then, this woman?
JAUFRÉ: (*as if in a dream, absently*) She is far away, far, far.
COMPANIONS: Who is she, this woman? What is she like?
JAUFRÉ: She is graceful and humble and virtuous and gentle, Courageous and shy, full of fortitude and delicate, A princess with the heart of a peasant girl, a peasant girl with the heart of a princess, In a passionate voice she will sing my songs...

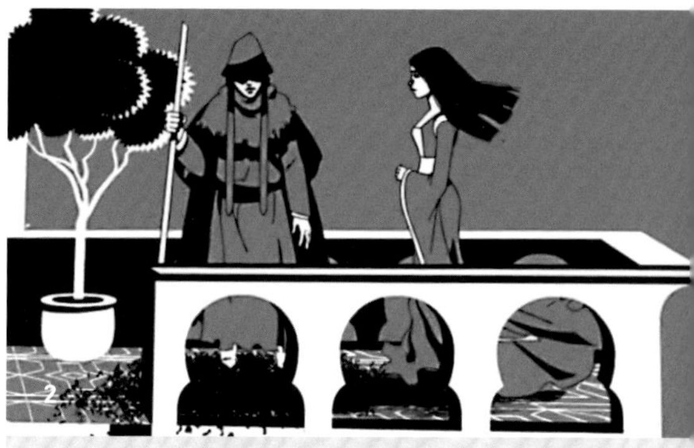

THE PILGRIM: A man sometimes thinks of you.
CLÉMENCE: What man?
THE PILGRIM: A troubadour.
CLÉMENCE: A troubadour? What is his name?
THE PILGRIM: He is called Jaufré Rudel. He is also Prince of Blaye.

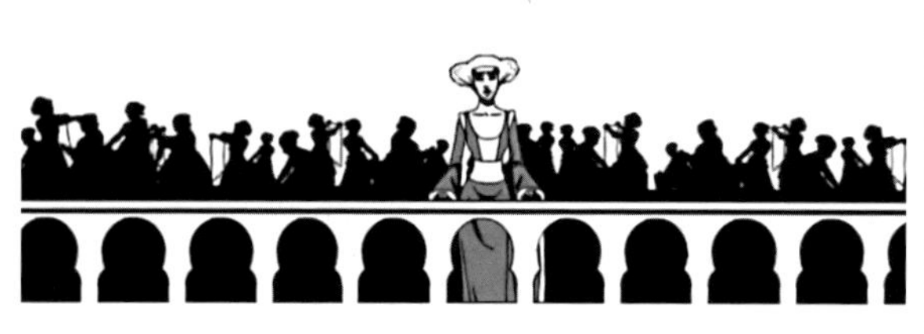

CHORUS OF WOMEN OF TRIPOLI: (*not real singing, but a somewhat chaotic noise of disordered words emerging from the sounds of the port and the sea*)
Countess, look!
In port, on the quay, the ship!
It is here! It is here!
Ja'! Ja'! Ja'!
Pilgrims, flags, and the ship!
The troubadour!
Down there, Countess!
The troubadour!

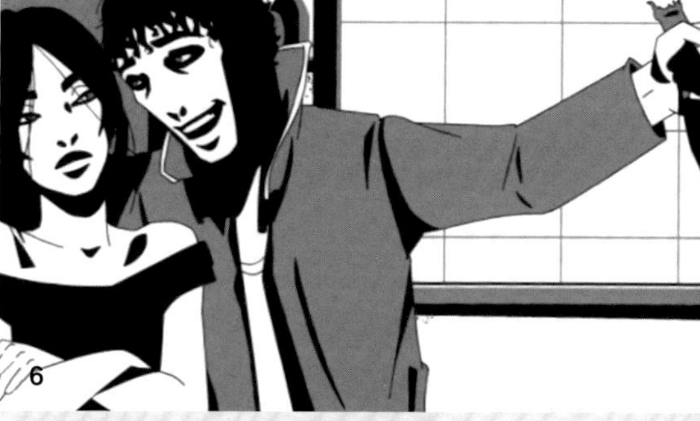

JAUFRÉ: It is you, it is you, it is you!
I would have recognized you amongst all women.
CLÉMENCE: (*bending over him a little*) How do you feel?
JAUFRÉ: Happy... (*He says it very sadly!*) Happy as a man can be whose fate is not a matter of indifference to you.
CLÉMENCE: (*taking the Pilgrim aside*) What does the Arab doctor say?
THE PILGRIM: He says that he will not live beyond dawn.

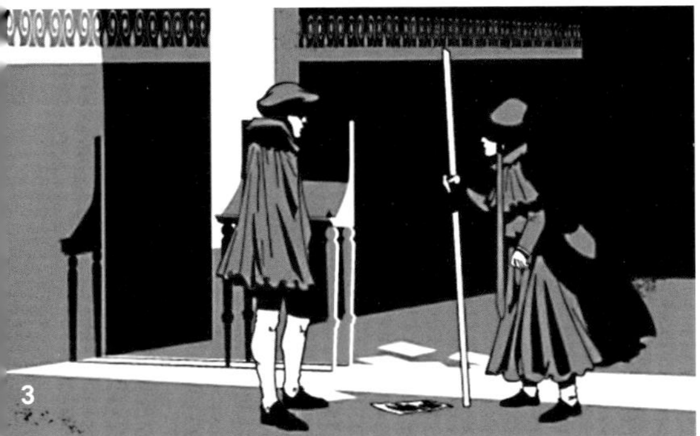
3

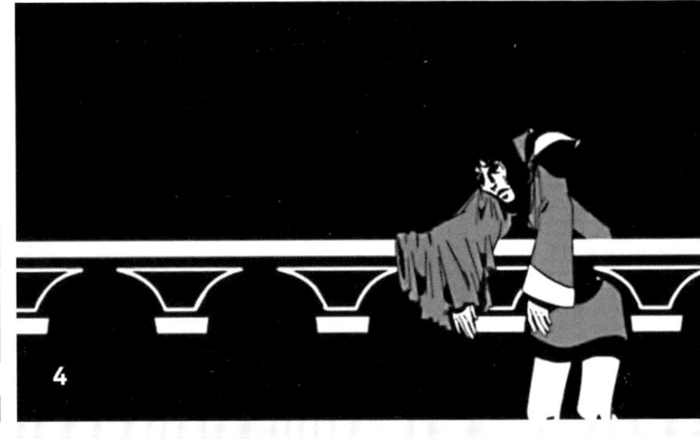
4

THE PILGRIM: (*who has observed him up to this point with a mixture of fascination and pity, and who, after a long hesitation, eventually decides to speak*)
Jaufré, she knows. (*A heavy silence, with all the weight of destiny bearing down on men, then...*)
JAUFRÉ: What did you say, Pilgrim?
THE PILGRIM: I said: she knows.
JAUFRÉ: She knows what?
THE PILGRIM: She knows everything that she should know. That you are a poet and that you hymn her beauty.

JAUFRÉ: I'm afraid, Pilgrim, I'm afraid.
You are the voice of reason, but fear does not heed the voice of reason.
I'm afraid of not finding her, and I'm afraid of finding her.
I'm afraid of being lost at sea before reaching Tripoli, and I'm afraid of reaching Tripoli.
I'm afraid of dying, Pilgrim, and I'm afraid of living.
Do you understand me?
(*Day is rising, but the sea is more and more disturbed. Jaufré is clinging to the rail, his color very pale.*)

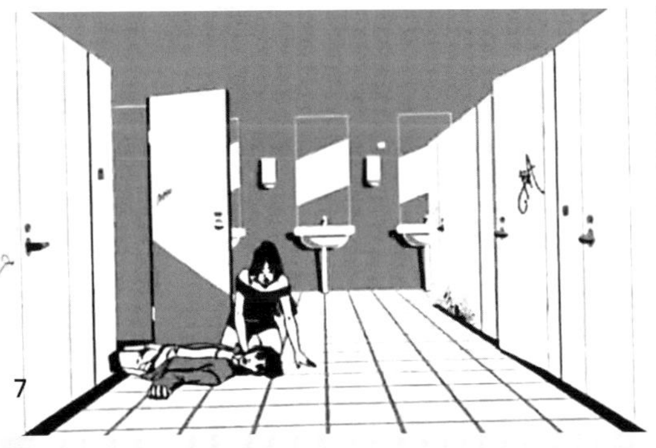
7

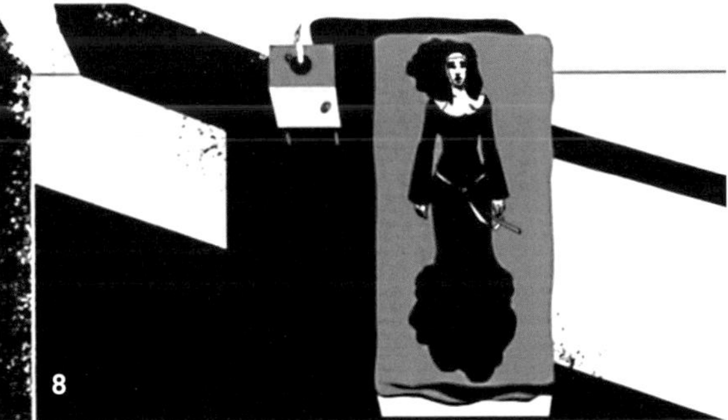
8

CLÉMENCE: My lips close to yours...
(*Their lips brush against one another's.*)
JAUFRÉ: In this instant, I have all I wish.
Why ask life for more?
(*His body goes limp, and he sinks down, motionless. Clémence holds him to her for a moment, her head resting on his shoulder. Then she rises to pray.*)

CLÉMENCE: I no longer deserve to be loved,
I no longer deserve to be hymned by a poet,
Nor held against a man's shoulder, nor caressed.
Tomorrow, after the funeral, I shall go into mourning.
I shall wear a thick linen robe and hide myself away
Beneath a convent roof
Whence I shall never more emerge, neither living nor dead.
I am the widow of a man who did not know me,
And no other man shall ever enter my bed.

MATERIALS:	*stage set: life-size bunk bed with top bunk that can be flipped over, oversize exit sign*
PERFORMERS:	*two main actors (ME and ID): must be similar in age to Michael Elmgreen and Ingar Dragset, similar coloring, similar build; third character (BI, the messenger): female, age 30 - 40*
CLOTHING:	*two main actors (ME and ID): white button-up shirts with thin black ties, black suits (socks for ME, barefoot for ID); third character (BI, the messenger): express mail courier outfit, helmet, big sports sunglasses*
DIMENSIONS:	*minimum stage size: 700 x 1000 cm*
DURATION:	*fifty minutes*
PERFORMED AT:	*Tramway, Glasgow (preview), 2011; Performa 11 biennial, Skirball Center for the Performing Arts, New York (world premiere), 2011*

HAPPY DAYS IN THE ART WORLD
2011

A theatrical performance initially inspired by Samuel Beckett's seminal play *Happy Days* (1961) and Sarah Thornton's book *Seven Days in the Art World* (W. W. Norton & Company, 2008). Partly an intimate look at the struggles of collaboration, creative deadlock, and mid-career panic, the play also expands on Elmgreen & Dragset's tongue-in-cheek satirical take on the contemporary art world as presented in their 2007 stage production *Drama Queens*.

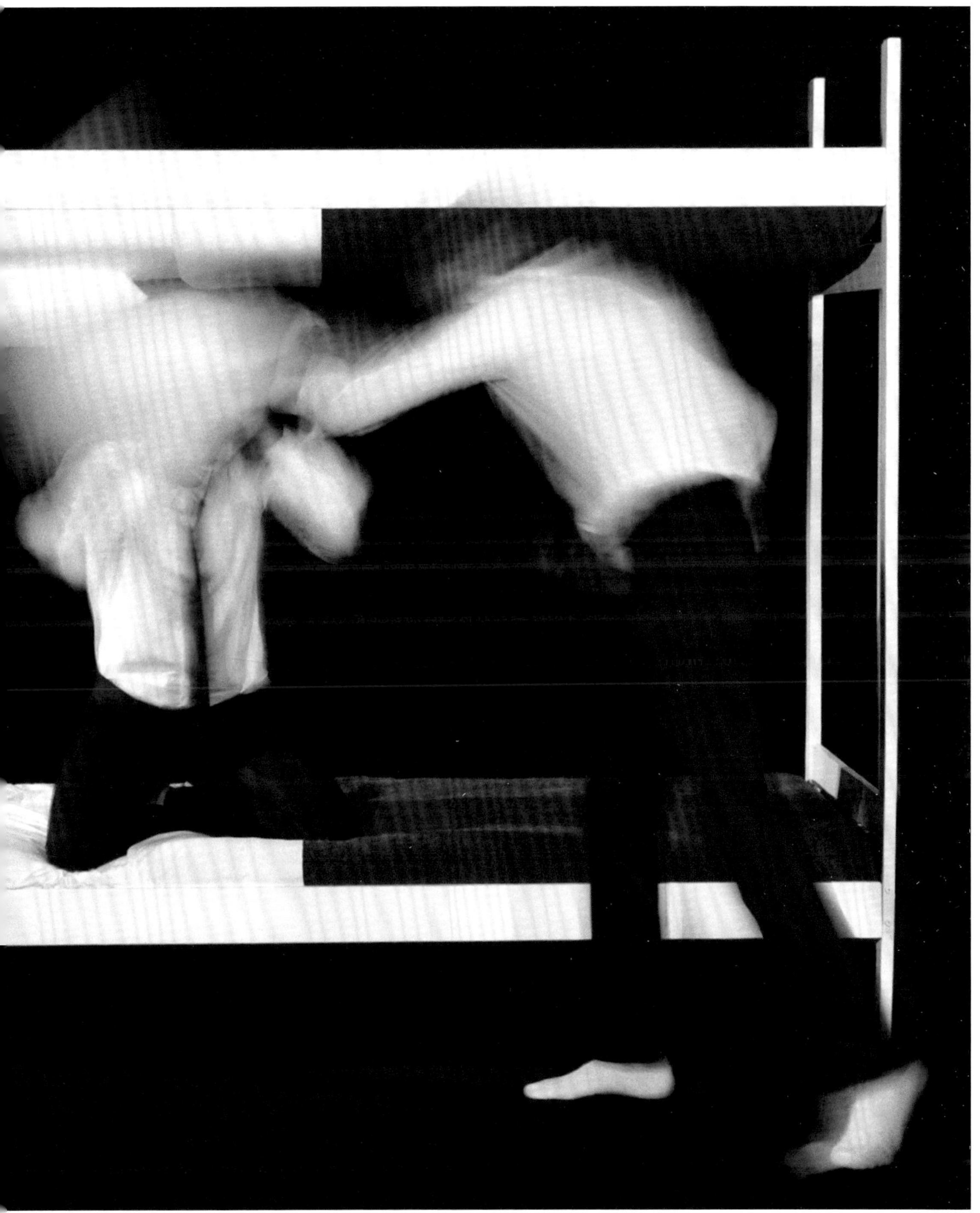

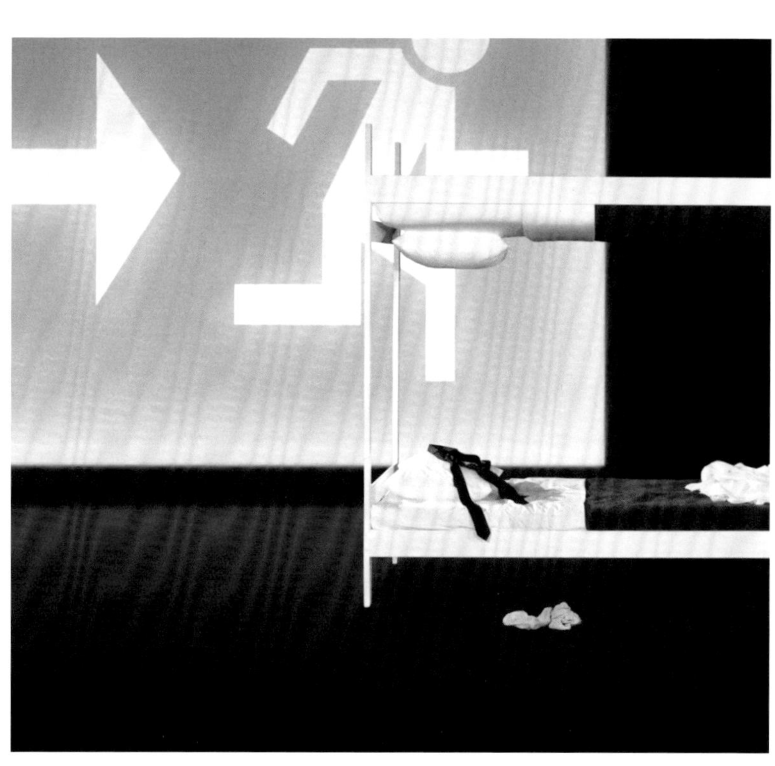

Happy Days in the Art World

A PLAY BY
ELMGREEN & DRAGSET
IN THREE ACTS

This script went to press before the end of rehearsals and may therefore differ from the play as performed at the Skirball Center for the Performing Arts.

Characters:
An artist duo: ME, late 40s and ID, early 40s
An express mail courier: BI, 30s

OUTLINE

Two collaborating artists wake up in a bunk bed. They are uncertain about where they are, but the metal bunk bed indicates they may be in prison. Stuck in this setting and isolated from the surrounding world, they discuss their collaboration, their role in the art scene, and the general workings of the professional art world.

ACT I

Throughout the first act, the two characters are only illuminated by the light from the reading lamps at the head end of the bunk bed. These two lamps come on by themselves, as if on a timer.

ID: (*from bottom bunk*) ME? Are you there? Hello? Hello-o!
ME: (*dreamily/moaning*) Mmmmph, ouuu...
ID: ME! I can hear you! You're up there somewhere! Talk to me!
ME: Achhh, oufff... oh, no no no. Dammit! (*with irritation in his voice*) You woke me up!
ID: There you go! Good morning!
ME: Is it? (*small pause*) I hate mornings. And you just woke me up from a really good dream... Wait a second. What am I doing up here? Where the hell are we?
ID: I don't know. Some hotel probably.

ME: In a bunk bed?

ID: Maybe a hostel then, or a homeless shelter.

ME: Hmm... In my dream we were *successful* artists, we had something *big* coming... something... Aah, let me sleep a little longer, I really need to get back to that dream... mmmmm.

ID: No don't! I'm feeling a bit... lonely... I mean, what shall I do while you dream on? (*with childish eagerness*) I want to be part of it.

ME: You *were* part of it, I already told you. We were these two artists, based in a city where everybody else was an artist too... Berlin I think... a whole city full of artists... and all of them were young artists no matter what their actual age.

ID: (*thinking, massaging his temples*) Are you sure it was a dream? I vaguely remember something similar, only I think it was real. Ough, my head, it's spinning, it hurts so bad... I think we were boyfriends, as far as I... were we? Or are we? Hey —do you love me?

ME: (*dryly*) We don't sleep in the same bed, do we?

ID: Many couples don't. I read somewhere that relationships with separate beds last longer.

ME: Well I'd say we're *not* partners. At least not any longer. I think we're more like team-mates. Team-mates sleep in bunk beds. Or prisoners.

ID: You think we're in prison?

ME: No. Who else sleeps in bunk beds? Backpackers? Boy scouts?

ID: Don't be stupid. We could be brothers! Maybe that's it. I had bunk beds with my brother when we were kids. He was bed wetting every night. Were you? Let me look at you. Let me see your face.

ME: (*pops his head out over the edge of the top bunk*) Oh no. I don't think so.

ID: Why not?

ME: Well what do I look like?

ID: Let me see... hair formerly known as "blond," big blue eyes, muppet face, fair skin, eeh... big nose...

ME: You see? Completely different. No genetic connection.

ID: What do I look like then?

ME: Dark hair, nondescript eye color, wide pointy nose, hhhmmm... muppet puppet face, too but quite a different character... and...

ID: And what?

ME: ...salt and pepper beard...

ID: Ok, that's enough. Salt? You mean gray... or white!? Am I old? I don't even know. Maybe I'm getting senile.

ME: I don't think you're senile—seems a bit early for that. You look like 40 something... something.

ID: But I feel much older. My whole body is in pain, not only my head, also my joints, muscles...

ME: ...bones, guts, back, neck. I know. Stress. Wear and tear.

ID: Nervous exhaustion.

ME: Plus the way I feel I think we might have had a drink or five too many last night. We must have blacked out somehow and ended up here.

ID: That's it! Look, I'm still wearing my clothes! Or are they mine? Why do I wear a suit? There must have been... a wedding... or a funeral. Let me check my pockets... (*He searches his side pockets.*) There's some fluff here!

ME: (*with ignorant voice*) Interesting.

ID: And some grit tangled in the fluff.

ME: (*sarcastic*) Fantastic.

ID: Here, here! A piece of paper... let's see... eh... a phone number... handwritten, but hmmmm... no name... it says, ouph, where are my glasses... 212 614 241... Ring a bell?

ME: New York. 212. Manhattan. Land line. But who uses a landline these days? Let me see... I might recognize the writing... (*ID passes the note up to ME*)
...ok, let's see... hey! You moron. There's something on the other side, something printed. Maybe that's a clue... top corner says... *press release...*

ID: Really? What does it release?

ME: *Us*, I presume.

ID: That would be nice.

ME: But it's completely unreadable. There were more clues about the two of us in the dream I was having than there are on this scrap of paper.

ID: What are you talking about?

ME: My dream. We were artists. Really successful, remember?

ID: Dream on...

ME: (*with accelerated pitch throughout*) Like I said it was Berlin. We were just about to earn a barrel-load of cash: this Ukrainian oligarch, dressed up as a farmer's wife, headscarf 'n all, he-she was coming towards us, crossing a bumpy field, she'd been spit firing through the Polish farmland in a pink Porsche decorated with small butterflies, crossing all of Poland without a single stop just to get to us. We... we were waiting, totally excited at the German border. I could practically smell this shemale monster's aftershave when she opened the door of the car and pushed out the cash—in a barrel. I could see the sun rising behind her big bald head when her hoarse voice declared (*in bad Russian accent*): "I want every object you have in your studio... every single artwork left, everything you've ever made! I want it all!" And I knew we'd be loaded. D'you understand? We were going to be rich and you woke me... idiot.

ID: Well maybe it's good I woke you—sounds dangerous that dream...

ME: You owe me—a whole barrel of hryvnia.

ID: What the hell is hryvnia?

ME: Ukrainian currency. You really ought to know such things. The new world Mr. ID. The new market. The new Art World.

ID: I guess... Are they worth anything, these Hernias, I mean...

ME: Oh, I don't know, a tenth of the euro maybe, an eighth of the dollar, or oops maybe a sixth of a dollar. Changes all the time. One thing's for sure though—as my team-mate and business partner, your waking me cost this enterprise a shitload of money.

ID: You want to calculate it?

ME: OK. Let's say a barrel of hryvnia at... what did I say, maybe one sixth of a dollar... minus some kind of international transaction fee, then deduct production costs, the gallery's 50% share, a recession based 30% discount, transport, insurance and taxes plus the staff in the studio... I think we're down at least a quarter of a quarter barrel-full of US dollars...

ID: (*thinking it over*) Hmmm... a quarter of a quarter?... And... since when did we calculate currency by the barrel? Are we pirates? Smugglers?

ME: It was a dream.

ID: I give up.

ID puts his head down on the pillow and closes his eyes, possibly makes yoga movements.

ME: What are you doing! (*wriggling his legs*) Get up from there. Get up. There's work to do. We have to find out where that dream cash disappeared. Call the galleries, they have a nose for such mysteries. What are you doing! (*wriggling his legs*) Get up from there. Get up. There's work to do. D'you hear me?

ID: Ssshhhh...

ME: Are you telling me to shut up?

ID: Yes, silence, please. I need to focus.

ME: Eh...? What do you think this is—a yoga retreat? A workshop with Marina? Get up now.

ID: Hang on, I forgot that your mind only works visually, sorry... here you go.

ID takes out a "Do Not Disturb" sign from the inside pocket of his suit jacket, lets it dangle from a toe on his outstretched leg and resumes "meditating."

ME: (*stares down at ID in disbelief*) What are you doing?!

ID: I'm trying to concentrate. I need to get in touch with my feelings. Some sort of... Me Time, "The Return of Psychology." Something's coming. I can feel it's going to be big. You just wait... (*ID closes his eyes again*)

Short silence.

ME: You can feel your ass off—just remember your personal emotions don't make the art any better. Wait. Where did you get that sign from?

ID: (*Lowers his leg and sits up slowly.*) (*sighs*) I took it from a hotel we stayed in.

ME: And which hotel was that?

ID: I can't remember. They all look the same.

ME: Look at the back of the sign, maybe there's a logo there, an address, some kind of clue...

ID: (*looks at the back of the sign*) Bitte Zimmer Aufräumen.

ME: What?

ID: Por Favor Arregle La Habitación Ahora.

ME: What?

ID: Please make up my room!

ME: Make up your room! You must be crazy. I'm done with cleaning up after you.

ID: My socks! (*looks under his bed*)

ME: Your socks, exactly!

ID: (*looks down at his bare feet*) They're gone! I've got no shoes, no socks. Where can they be? (*rubs his feet, shudders*)

ME: Who knows? Out there somewhere... in the great darkness.

ID: Don't try to scare me.

ME: Do you know where we are? Do you *know* what happens if we leave these ridiculous beds?

ID: No.

ME: That's what I'm talking about. Since we opened our eyes we've been in serious trouble. It seems like we've ended up in one of our own installations. That's serious trouble, I'm telling you.

ID: I'm cold—it's freezing here. My poor feet.

ME: Maybe the cold is the clue we've been looking for... we must be in the Northern hemisphere somewhere.

ID: (*mildly sarcastic*) That's really narrowed it down. I feel much better now. I'm sockless in Chicago, Copenhagen, Krakow, Malmö, Manchester...

ME: Maybe we really ARE in New York.

ID: What?

ME: Maybe we really are in New York. Like it said on that press release. I'm much more worried about where *we* are than I am about your sodding socks.

ID: I want them back—my socks *and* my shoes. I can't think straight without them.

ME: Your thoughts have never been straight. A queer man's thoughts.

ID: (*slightly insulted*) And now, if you don't mind, I'm going to call for my shoes. (*sounds like he's talking to chickens*) Prada Prada Prada Prada rada rada Prada...

ME: Be careful. We don't know what's out there. You'd better stay close... There might be robbers, rapists...

ID laughs at this. ME gazes at ID's feet as ID carefully tests the ground.

ME: ...used needles on the ground, broken bottles, bits of glass from dropped iPhones!

ID: (*has stopped laughing, in earnest now*) Maybe you're right. Let me borrow your shoes and socks, my toes are like icicles. Then I'll go.

ME: You can't.

ID: Why not?

ME: 'Cause I'm coming with you. I can't let you go out there alone. What if you disappeared?! What would I do here all on my own?

ID: I don't know. But what if we both disappeared? Wouldn't that be worse?

ME: We'd become legends. Mythological heroes. Like that artist who set out in his boat and never came back. Thirty years later everybody still loves him for that row boat trip. Two collaborating artists disappearing is double up. Happy Hour. Double the mystery.

ID: I don't think my socks are worth two artists' lives. Maybe one, but not two. Let

me go alone, please. Stay here, and I'll shout out loud for every 10-15 steps I take. You will answer me and if I can't hear you any more, I'll retrace my steps back.
ME: And what will you shout? What shall I answer?
ID: We need a sort of code. How about I shout VALEEEERIO! And you reply with EVER! EVER!
ME: That's silly.
ID: It's meant to be silly so no, it's not silly. It's a quotation, from someone. Hans Ulrich, I think. He's very clever.
ME: He must be—coming up with stuff like that.
ID: No, think about it. It's reassuring that someone like Hans Ulrich might have foreseen a situation just like this. Someone being lost in the art world somewhere, and then there's a language—a code known only to the people within it —the select few. A catch phrase like that could save a lost soul, someone might hear it echoing out in the terrible darkness and think, "That's one of us shouting down there—I've got to help!"

They are both thinking about this for a bit, while looking about into the dark and in the direction of the audience.

ID: Now give me your shoes.
ME: I'll give you one. An equal partnership. A true artist duo.

ME takes off one of his shoes and one of his socks and lets them drop to the floor next to ID. ID puts the sock and the shoe on.
This exchange goes on as ME continues to speak.

ME: Watch your step, ok?—just remember, if one of us dies, the other won't be worth anything.
ID: Really? Nothing at all?
ME: Of course not. The whole art world will look at the survivor with nothing but pity

in their eyes, they'll just nod silently as they brush past you to get to the sushi buffet.

ID: Bugger.

ME: You wouldn't even be half the artist you are now, and considering you are already just 50% of an artist duo—half an artist, to be exact—there is not much left at all if your partner vanishes. Nothing of worth, neither you nor your art. Everything we've ever made will be meaningless junk.

ID: But the ideas will still be there—the history of the works...

ME: If you disappear, they won't even speak of us, not in the present tense anyway. People might say, (*with the voice of a posh, rich woman*) "Oh, that was terrible, what happened..." or "The two of them were quite interesting somehow, weren't they, not always, but, oh well..." but then they'll hurry on to change the subject to a more cheerful one.

ID: Well, I'm going to change the subject now. At least the trajectory. VALEEERIO!!

ME: Wait, which way will you be going? You can't just set out in the darkness. What if we never see each other again? Is there something we should say to each other?

ID: Yes. It's been lovely. Back in five.

ME: We don't know where we are, remember.

ID: (*looks into the dark, looks to the floor*) Look, there are lines on the floor. Sector red, blue and yellow. Some kind of system. Nothing to be afraid of, just a way of organizing the space. They must lead somewhere, don't you think? A line always goes from one point to another point, unless it's a circle. I'll follow, hmmm... this one, I think, or maybe this one. Yes, this one. Valerio!

ME: Ever... (*sighs*) I guess...

ID sets out into the darkness, following the line that leads straight to the back of the stage. ME is left alone, thinking aloud to himself.

ME: Where could we have been last night? It must have been quite important... When did I last wear a tie? At my own confirmation, I guess, just before I vowed never to wear one again... (*holds up his tattered tie and studies it*) It's... Banana Republic! Well at least I didn't waste the last of my pocket money on this. Who got me into this?... we even wear the same outfit—like some sort of Scandinavian Laurel & Hardy... or Starsky & Hutch or Siegfried & Roy or, oh no... Gilbert & George... terrifying...

ID: (*from a distance*) Valerio!

ME: (*with a tired tone of voice*) ...Republic...

ID: (*louder and longer than last time*) Valeeeeriooo!

ME: (*with despair in his voice*) Never! Ever!

The lights flicker. Blackout. Sounds of ID stumbling around onstage.

END OF ACT I

ACT II

ID: (*echoing effect from far distance*) Valerio!

ME: (*whispers*) Never...

ID: (*a bit closer now*) Valeeerioo!

No answer.

ID: Vaaaaaaleeeerioooo!!!

Suddenly a huge exit sign comes on and floods the stage in greenish-white light. The light reveals that the two characters are in some kind of fenced-in or enclosed environment. ID stands right next to a big light switch on the front left of the stage.

ID: Wow! Just look at it! The United States of America! Look at that sign! Things are so BIG here! Look at it! We're in America! They don't do things in half measures! We're in New York! Maybe Chicago! Detroit! L.A.! Supersize Me Baby! We're saved! Did you hear me? We're safe! We're in New York! We're two happy little worms in the Big Apple! The land of Apple products... Home of the Brave, Land of the Free Market...

ME: (*laconically*) It's a prison.

ID: Exactly! Just like Mike Tyson, Lil Wayne, Lil' Kim, T.I., R. Kelley, Snoop Dogg, P. Diddy, Ol' Dirty Bastard, OJ Simpson, Wesley Snipes, Robert Downey Jr., Charlie Sheen, Martha Stewart, Bernie Madoff, Dominique Strauss-Kahn, Lindsay Lohan... The list could go on. We'll be famous. Aren't you happy?

ME: What's there to be happy about? I'm stuck here with you, there seems to be no way out.

ID: We can get lawyers... celebrity lawyers. Our galleries will pay won't they?

ME: Face it—this place could be anywhere: prisons are like Ikea... or museums. Same format around the globe. They have prisons in Russia, Mexico, Honduras, Cuba—Guantanamo Bay—... and in... China!

ID: Okay, okay, I get it—there are prisons everywhere. There are Starbucks on every street corner and there is a Gagosian in any city with more than two billionaires. But I just know we're in New York. I can feel it in my bones.

(*looks towards the graffiti on the exit sign*) Look! Look! There's graffiti over there! Further proof! Look at it—that's authentic graffiti alright—might even be from the 80s... yes... just think, Giuliani himself might have tried to remove it, the color's gone but you can still make out the outline.

(*goes closer to the smudged, almost washed out graffiti*)

You see! That's raw communication—the beginnings of Art itself, fresh from the caves—the traces of a message from one person to another, clear proof of individual freedom not granted to you by anyone other than yourself... Let's see. I can see an F, the first letter is definitely an F. It could be an E, but I think it's an F. Next one O. No, U. F... U.

ME: Fuck you.

ID: Don't speak to me like that. I need to concentrate. F. U. O or C. F. U. C... Hmmmm. The last letter... no, it's impossible to make out. There's another word. O, this is definitely an O, yes, and then there are two E's, I think...

ME: FUCK OFF. It says FUCK OFF for God's sake. Welcome to New York. Fuck off. Simple as that. You've always had a tendency to brush over any humiliation. Even when you've been fucked over in the worst possible way. You have to stop believing that people want anything good for you—especially in the art world. It's cruel and competitive, and people only want the best for themselves.

ID: But... this message was never meant for me. Nobody knew I would end up here. The message might even have been ironic in the first place. Like a mate saying "Oh, sod off" or (*in US accent*) "Give me a break, man" in an affectionate, loving sort of way.

ME: Whatever. I do wish we could get the fuck out of here though. Is that light switch all you found? No exit, no hole in the fence over there?

ID: I don't know your highness. I'll take a look, shall I?

ID goes over to the fence and studies it for a bit, tries shaking it, knocking on it, maybe jumping on it. Does he try to climb it? He stops, facing the audience, and his eyes follow the fence up to the top, he gazes up into the air. ME follows ID's movements and gazes with his own eyes from his top bunk.

ID: Can you see the stars?

ME: Nope.

ID: Me neither. Not a single star out there. (*looking towards the audience as if he were on a ship*)

ME: It's cloudy. The stars are still there, don't worry.

ID: I wonder what time it is though. We must have slept for a while and it's still dark out there.

ME: Yes. And I'm so hungry I could eat my tie. What are we supposed to do for food here? Can you hear the sounds my stomach is making? (*makes rumbling, squeaking sounds*)

ID: Don't be such a moaner. If you come down, we can do something fun and you'll forget about being hungry.

ME: No, no, no. Just listen to my stomach. It's like three Finnish noise artists are performing in there.

ID: Don't be silly.

ME: I'm serious. Where is that Thai soup kitchen when you need it? You know I'm so hungry I wouldn't even mind being at one of those little champagne charity buffet things right now. Just think—a teeny weeny Swedish meatball on a toothpick to help save endangered penguins on the melting poles, or a better yet a nice piece of raw fois gras dipped in organic white chocolate to raise money for...

ID: Listen. If it's true we're in New York, we're gonna have to be anorexic. The jet set here doesn't eat. At least no carbs, no protein and no fat, meaning no cheese, no rice, no meat, no chocolate, no... eh, caffeine...

ME: Stop! I want a fat old skool politically incorrect chunk of beef right now!

ID: If you come down, I've got breakfast ready.

ME: Eh... I didn't think there was any food here.

ID: I've got half a pack of LifeSavers in my pocket.

ME: Why didn't you tell me before? Were you planning on keeping them to yourself? Did you eat half the pack on your own, perhaps?

ID: I didn't touch them. I thought... I was planning to save them in case of an emergency. Then it occurred to me that being stuck here is a kind of an emergency and I thought maybe we could have one. *Together.*

ME: Show them to me! I'm not coming down if this is just a trick. I'd rather suffer in bed.

ID: A trick! Why would I want to trick you to come down. You can stay up there as long as you like so far as I'm concerned. I quite like you up there, in fact. I've got the whole floor to myself. I can choose exactly where to stand and sit at any point during the day.

ME: There is no day. It's not even night. As far as I can see there is only a big black void like an endless darkened auditorium filled with a bored, exhausted and invisible audience.
ID: Quit the melodrama. We don't need your moods here. Of course it's day. It's just a dark day.
ME: Show me the LifeSavers.
ID: Okay, I'll show you. (*shakes the lapel on his jacket*) Can you hear them? All those little delicious things just waiting to save our lives.
ME: I can hear them. Now come over here and help me down.

ID positions himself so that ME can ease himself down onto his shoulders. ID carries ME on his shoulders, runs a bit. ME shrieks, wants to be put down.

ME: Stop! Where are you taking me?
ID: Where should I be taking you? We might be stuck here forever. Maybe I'll carry you for the rest of our days. Let's turn this into a durational performance. Or a gay version of Linda Montano and Tehching Hsieh tied together for a year.
ME: Give me those bloody LifeSavers!
ID: OK, OK.

ID lets ME down.

ID: Here you go.

ID hands the pack of "LifeSavers" to ME.

ME: Thanks.

ME opens the package greedily and puts one "LifeSaver" in his mouth. Tastes it, first happily for an instant, then disapprovingly.

ME: Doesn't taste like anything. (*tries chewing*) Ow! Shit, my tooth! What is this!
ID: A button.
ME: A button! Are you mad? Are you planning to kill me?! Buttons! I'll show you buttons!
ID: (*laughing, jumps around like a boxer or a jester*) Are you going to button me down? Want to see my belly button? Want to punch it? Punch my face? Is it a face off? Or do you want me face down? Want to see my real face? Let's face it—we're fucked! We fucked it up, somebody fucked us over, I can't be fucked, fucking fuck, fuck-face, shit-face, shit hit the fan, I give a shit, eat shit! That's all there is! (*collapses, weak now*) I didn't want to be alone down here. So, I told you I had LifeSavers in order to get you down. I'm sorry.
ME: (*looks a couple of times from the button in his hand to ID*) I could have lost my teeth. This button could have got stuck in my throat, together with my teeth. Made me choke. Or the sharp edges of my teeth could have slashed my jugular vein from the inside of my neck.
ID: Come on.
ME: Blood gushing out of my mouth as I thrash about on the floor in my last, painful death throes. 30 seconds and it's Game Over. All thanks to your fake LifeSavers.
ID: Drama queen!
ME: I saw my life flash before my eyes. It was terrifying.
ID: You're making too much of it.
ME: Don't talk to me.
ID: How about this—I've got a joke for you.
ME: Go on then.
ID: How many conceptual artists does it take to choke on a LifeSaver?
ME: None.
ID: How did you know?!
ME: Too obvious. All conceptual... they're satisfied with the idea. No object—no choking. No lives saved.
ID: Okay, okay, what about this one: What do you call a whole group of curators

in front of an artwork?

ME: I don't know.

ID: Unemployed.

ME: Funny. Curators could say the same about artists though.

ID: Not at all. Curators are more dependent on artists.

ME: I'm not so sure. They are few—we are many. Curators can pick and choose, forget and discard as they please. As an artist it's one day you're in, the next day you're out. Auf Wiedersehen. Adieu. Scram. It can take years to get back inside... if ever.

ID: But curators are multiplying! There're hundreds of new ones every year—breeding, interbreeding, graduating. Before long they'll outnumber the artists. We'll be selecting them! We'll visit their offices, look at their credentials, ask them about old ideas and new ideas. We can take forever with our selection processes then change our minds, put them in spaces they don't like or make them share space with other curators they can't even stand. We can force them not to talk about the artworks, or make them write three different press releases, and then censor them all in the end and...

ME: Don't get too excited, we might not be around long enough for that to hap...

A mobile phone starts ringing and interrupts the conversation. Both men go quiet, look at each other, dumbfounded. The sound level of the phone constantly increases during the following conversation, until it has reached an almost unbearable level.

ID: Is that your phone?

ME: I think it's yours.

ID: It's got your sound.

ME: Yours sounds the same.

ID: So why don't you get it!

ME: You get it!

ID: I've lost mine.

ME: I've lost mine, too.

ID: So how come it's ringing?

ME: You tell me!

ID: This could be our way out. Check your pockets—I already went through mine. No phone.

ME: (*reluctantly brushes over his pockets*) Nothing! I told you it was gone.

ID sighs, starts crawling along the front "fence" as if he's got a whiff of where the ringing cell phone might be. After a little while he stops, reaches a hand out through the fence, and grabs a black phone lying on the floor.

ID: (*excitedly*) I found it! I've got it! AAMMEERRIICCA!

ME: Then get it! Press the green key!

ID: There is no green key!

ID becomes increasingly fiddly and nervous during the outburst that follows from ME.

ME: Then press the top left one. I can't stand this ringing any longer!

ID: I've never seen this phone in my life. It's not yours or mine!

ME: Just press any key! A key! The key! The keys! All of them!

ID drops the phone to the floor and sits down on it. The ringing is muted, and ID lets out a sigh of satisfaction.

ME: Pffff... Thank you.

ID: (*with a smirk on his face*) It's hot.

ME: Hot?

ID: Warm—and vibrating. Aaaah...

ME: That's disgusting. Get off that phone. Get off it right now!

ID: Okay, okay.

ID lifts his rear end off the phone several times—each time, the phone starts ringing again.

ME: Please, just answer it! It might be important. They might be calling from America.

ID: I thought we were *in* America.

ME: We don't know that. I'm telling you, they're calling from America!

ID: This still looks like America to me!

ME: Everywhere looks like America!

ID: Not China.

ME: Here we go again. China looks more like America than America does.

ID: I'm telling you, they're calling from China!

ME runs over to ID and grabs the phone just before he sits down on it again. ME presses the answering button. ID slowly does the yoga "dog position" during ME's phone conversation.

ME: Hello? Hello? (*short silence*) Oh, hello. Speaking. (*short silence*) ...oh, you know, we're just having some creative time here... no-no, always busy...he-he-he... no-no, this is a good time... (*longer silence*) ...Aha. (*silence*) ...Mhmm... (*longer silence*) ...Oh, hundreds, hundreds... Great. Yes. We'll have that sent to you... Well then, thanks for calling... no problem... Auf Wiedersehen... tschüss... cheers... ciao... ciao...

ID: Who was that? Where was it from?

ME: Germany. Didn't catch the name. Doctor something. Someone from Dokumenta.

ID: Really?

ME: Really. (*chucks the phone over the fence*)

ID: What did you do that for? What did he want? Or was it a she?

ME: A she.

ID: So—what did *she* want?

ME: Nothing. The usual. Names. Bright young things. A list of new, interesting, Berlin-based artists.

ID: Oh. We're based in Berlin!

ME: Yes, but we're not 20-something. We're middle-aged, mid-career, middle class...

ID: ...and in the middle of nowhere. (*small pause, then excited*) Together we're almost a hundred years old!

ME: If you are almost a hundred and suddenly dragged around in the limelight you need to be female... You need to be Bourgeois.

ID: I'm not that old and I'm not having a mid-life crisis. Quite the contrary. Everything is going perfectly well. Given the circumstances I couldn't be happier!

ME: Just like every other Norwegian. You lot would just sit up there on your mountains of oil and smoked salmon and watch the world burn down to the ground around you. "Couldn't be happier!" Only a deeply depressed person in a state of complete denial would say something like that.

ID: (*misanthropically*) Maybe you're right. (*then more optimistic*) But we are getting older! If we muddle through for a decade or three more, we might be really hot stuff!

ME: It's so great to be stuck here with you. You really are unbearingly unbearable.

ID: Cheers! Fancy another LifeSaver?

ME: Sure. Whatever.

ID: I'll give you another color this time.

ME: What does it matter? It's not going to taste any different—they're buttons.

ID: Still. It'll be a change from the last one. It's white, it's bigger, and it's more or less rectangular...

ME: Please take one as well—with any luck it'll shut you up for a while.

They both sit sucking on their buttons for a while.

ME: Why do you carry those buttons around?

ID: Eeeeeh... No particular reason, really, just...

ME: Come on, nobody does anything without reason these days. Tell me now.

ID: I sew them onto things.

ME: What?

ID: I sew them onto things.

ME: What things?

ID: Ooouph... airport waiting lounge seats... towels... door mats... scaffolding plastic covers... leaves on trees in parks... bits of scrap lying around... flags flapping in the wind outside stores...

ME: But why?

ID: I needed a hobby.

ME: No, you didn't! Your hobby is your work, and your work is your hobby. You've been sewing buttons onto things behind my back! I thought we were col-la-bo-ra-ting!

ID: I just felt like being a bit creative.

ME: Creative! So you'd call it art as well?

ID: Well... a kind of street art, perhaps. Urban craft, or something. I don't care... Craftiti, you know?

ME: Ridiculous.

ID: Really, it was only to pass the time, being bored...

ME: But you had your BlackBerry! There was no reason to be bored anywhere—you were always connected!

ID: I know...

ME: If you hadn't been so busy sewing buttons on random objects you'd probably still have your BlackBerry!

ID: I know, I know. I'm sorry, I didn't mean to... You can have the rest if you want. I promise you—these are all the buttons I have left. (*hands over the "LifeSavers" packet*)

ME: What about the ones in your jacket? And trousers?

ID: I... are you serious?

ME: Yes, deadly.

ID: Okay, I guess...

ME: Tear them off.

ID: Well...

ID tears all the buttons off, hands them to ME who puts them in the "LifeSavers" packet.

ME: Good. Now, that's over.

ID: Yes.

ME: No more intriguing little independent solo sewing projects for you.

ID: No.

ME: One focus, one goal.

ID: Yes. We're absolutely the same now.

ME: Same same but different... Look, I think I'm going to get back into bed.

ID: Me too.

ME: What?

ID: I think I'll get back into bed too. There wouldn't be anything much to do out here on my own.

ME: Do as you please, I'm not the boss around here.

ID: I know that. We're the same.

ME: Almost.

ID: Should we switch beds?

ME: Why on earth should we. They're almost identical too.

ID: But...

ME: What difference would it make?

ID: I just thought...

ME: ...Don't think too much. It only makes people unhappy.

ID: But you said before...

ME: (*as he moves towards the beds, followed by ID*) Never mind what I said before —the good thing about art is you can say one thing one day and another the next. Nobody minds.

ID: That's why nobody takes art seriously anymore.

ME: That's missing the point. Flux is where the freedom lies.

ID: Quite the philosopher tonight aren't you? What else is going on in that tired looking head of yours?

ME: Nothing. Just leave me alone.

ID: Come on. What would we do without each other? I'm glad we met. Aren't you glad we met? Just think if we hadn't bumped into each other way back then in that hideous club in Copenhagen... what was it called again?

ME: After Dark... downtown Copenhagen...

ID: What a place to start a lifelong collaboration. I can still hear Yazz singing "The Only Way is Up, Baby-y..."

ME: Ouch, ouch. Promise not to mention that in company.

ID: OK. Your secret is safe with me.

ME: Good. Keep it that way. Or I'll tell people about your juggling fire spitting career.

ID: You wouldn't...

ME: Of course not.

ID: OK.

ME: I'm exhausted.

ID: Me too.

ME: Can you help me up to the bed?

ID: No problem.

ID automatically cups his hands for ME to step up into the top bunk. They both lay back, similar movements, fold hands behind heads.

ME: Goodnight.

ID: Goodnight.

Short pause. ME sighs. Short pause. ME sighs again.

ID: What are you thinking?

ME: Nothing. You?

ID: Nothing. Just...

ME: What?

ID: Remember the first work we made together? The performance where we both wore knitted skirts...

ME: Really?

ID: Yes, when we both wore those knitted skirts and then we unraveled them slowly off each other's naked bodies.

ME: We actually did that?

ID: Don't make out you don't remember. There are photographs. You can't deny it.

ME: We should do it again some time.

ID: In public?

ME: Maybe not.

ID: Oh yes, I will put it in the planner! (*pause*) Oh, I miss the wall planner. How sad is that. I miss the dots, I do, I like the different colored dots for different projects. I can't get oriented without them.

ME: Don't panic. Try to think. Visualize. As an artist you're meant to be good at that kind of thinking. Focus on where are we now, where are we... and how do we move on from here. Think!

ID: I'm thinking...

ME: Get a clear picture... fix it in your mind... and now tell me what it is.

ID is snoring. Before long ME too is snoring.

END OF ACT II

ACT III

During the blackout, one can hear a ring tone with the first bars of the song "One" by U2 (instrumental) and then a whispering voice-over by BI (the messenger). When the light comes on ID is sitting on top of the exit sign. ME is still in the top bunk.

BI: (*voice-over with a lot of reverb*) "...It's too late tonight to drag the past out into the light..."

ID: (*from the top of the exit sign*) ME! ME! Help me! I'm stuck!

ME: What the fu... What are you doing up there? Come down from there straight away and help me down!

ID: How can I? I'm stuck I said.

ME: But... why... how did you get up there?

ID: I have no idea. I might have been sleepwalking. I got into bed and then... I don't know what's going on... this place is getting stranger. Am I going crazy? Am I? Am I? Don't feel you have to answer that.

ME: You always wanted to be on top of things. Now there you are. Top of the pops.

ID: What?

ME: Up where you belong...

ID: Help me down.

ME: ...enjoy it as long as you can. But don't forget: your position is just a consequence of the structures which *we*—society as a whole—have agreed upon. Remember? Foucault and the Powerless Structures. If you want to get down from there, rethink those structures.

ID: Bastard.

ME: Use your imagination and there might be a way out.

ID: I don't know who you're talking to.

Short pause.

ME: I want to go home.

ID: Home is the place you left.

ME: I've had enough. I can't stand this limbo any longer. I don't care, just put me on the next long haul flight... dump me in monkey class next to a sweaty, snotty, snoring, obese Bible Belter on coach any time! I promise never to complain again —not about delays, the scrutiny of the security, the denied access to the business lounge, the worst of Hollywood played out in miniature on the seat-back screen, the bullying at immigration, the taxi driver's detours... I love it! I've always loved every bit of it! I want it back, I want to get down...

ID: I can't! You help me down!

ME: Great.

ID: I mean I can't fix this mess for you. I wish I could. But I can't.

ME: Like I said—great. You're a friend indeed. A friend in need is a friend indeed.

ID: I'm sorry.

ME: Don't say sorry. You're fired!

ID: What?!

ME: You're sacked, made redundant, your services are no longer required.

ID: My services? But... I'm not a servant. I'm not serving anyone.

ME: Exactly! You're not serving, as in "serving no purpose."

ID: You can't fire me for serving no purpose. That's what artists do.

ME: Then you don't do it well enough.

ID: While you do it only too well—turning every purposelessness into a self-fulfilling purposefulness! I can't stand it any longer. I quit!

ME: But... you can't quit!

ID: Why not?

ME: 'Cause there's no way out. No place to go.

ID: I haven't signed anything.

ME: You signed up for it—you signed all the artworks we made together: your name next to mine. That should count as a deal. Quite a deal, as our dealers would say.

ID: They were just artworks, certificates, not exactly certified contracts or holy matrimonies. Those papers were like wedding certificates signed in Las Vegas.

ME: We spent all of our adult life together, making those works—they're the proof of our existence the last many years!

ID: We sold the proofs.

ME: But not all of them!

ID: Maybe so. It's just that...

ME: The works we sold all have better homes now and others are cared for by the authorities: they're in state-run institutions, safe and sanitary municipal buildings... antiseptic white spaces resembling mental institutions.

ID: That's good isn't it?

ME: No.

ID: But it's more social... more, eh, Scandinavian? More democratic.

ME: Art has never been democratic. Democracy is something Presidents speak about just before they launch an air strike on a third world country. Democracy is something for teenage bloggers.

ID: But Facebook...

ME: Are you an idiot or do you work in advertising? Facebook is *not* democratic. And neither are big museums.

ID: But if more people get to see the art...?

ME: Audience size has no impact on the significance of an artwork. How many people watched Chris Burden get shot in the arm? Five? Ten? The whole thing lasted a second, but the image stands out in history.

ID: The history of art, that is. A lot of other people got shot with much greater impact on the world... Franz Ferdinand—the Archduke of Austria, John F. Kennedy, Malcolm X...

ME: History is just material.

ID: Really?

ME: Yes. Just like reality.

ID: Reality can always be altered.

ME: Only by drugs.

ID: But also by art. It's a quick shot, a short high and then a looong downer.

ME can't get his words out, laughing uncontrollably.

ID: What are you laughing about?

ME: High art! High art! People off their heads on high art! I like that. Art for the sake of getting high!

ID: (irritated) For God's sake.

ME: Whose?

ID: For God's...

ME: He's dead. Nietzsche killed him.

ID: We're past post all that. God is more googled than Nietzsche. Post post mortem.

ME: It's all a big loop.

ID: A big long downer.

ME: A slump. A trump. A bump. A rump. An end.

ID: Let's hang ourselves immediately!

ME: Right now? Do you think it will work?

ID: We can always try. We use our ties, just make a noose and attach it to the edge and then... snap!

They each make a noose.

ME: Go ahead.

ID: After you, sir.

ME: No, no, you first.

ID: Why me?

ME: Because you are heavier than me.

ID: And so what?

ME: If it can hang you, it can hang anything.

ID: Then how can I be sure that you hang yourself too?

ME: Because I promise.

ID: But... why don't we do it at the same time?

ME: Because there's a chance that the tie can't hold your weight. If we both go at the same time and you fail, I'm fucked. And you'll survive—meaning you'll be fucked too. Murphy's law. Understand?

ID: I... I... So, what do we do?

ME: Nothing. It's safer.

ID: Yes, let's hold out here a little bit longer. Let's enjoy it while we can—the peace and quiet... of this place, I mean.

They enjoy the silence for a while, until the roaring sound of a (not visible) helicopter fills the space above them. They look up and at each other, agitated, frightened, they shout unfinished questions at each other. A big, voluptuous woman (BI) dressed in an express mail courier outfit (including helmet) enters the stage by rope from above. She is blind and wears big sports sunglasses. (Alternatively—if flying a person from above proves difficult, the messenger can come in from behind the exit sign.)

BI: (*stands mid stage, listens for sounds, holding a letter above her head*) Just Relax, it's SpedEx! SpedEx delivery! We move the world.

ME and ID look at each other, dumbfounded.

ID: Who are you?

BI: (*moves a bit left*) There you are! So we are! SpedEx! If you could sign here please.

ME: We haven't ordered anything.

BI: (*moves a bit right*) There you are! So we are! SpedEx! If you could sign here please!

ID: Who's it from?

BI: (*moves a bit left*) There you are! So we...

ME: Excuse me, do you know what time it is?

BI: SpedEx. Always on time!

ME: I see, or day? Could you tell us what day it is?

BI: Day to day, sir. Overnight.

ID: Or possibly where we are?

BI: Coast to coast! Worldwide! Signature please.

ME: Okay, come over here and I'll give you your signature.

BI: Express! Yourself with us! (*rushes about blindly without finding ME's spot immediately*)

ME: (*guiding her*) Over here... no, no, yes, getting warmer... no, yes, hot hot hot, almost there now... that's it, a little bit to your left...

BI: Left and right! Up and down! Always on the spot!

ME: Right on. Stay there! Just stay exactly where you are, that's good...

ME eases himself down onto BI's shoulders.

BI: Me! Your modern mule!

ME tries to grab the letter, but BI is protecting it.

BI: Signature, sir! I need your signature! ...signature! ...sign here!

BI has ME in a headlock. Keeps repeating: "Signature, sir! I need your signature! ... signature! ...sign here!" etc. ME responds with "I can't see! I can't sign—I can't see!") ID jumps down from the top of the exit sign and tries parting them. BI gets ID in a headlock. Keeps repeating: "Signature, sir! I need your signature! ...signature!" ID says "I can't breathe! I can't breathe! Help! Let me go!" Now ME tries to part the two, but quickly gives up. He hits BI in the face and knocks her out.

ID: What did you do that for?

ME: I just switched her off. Don't you see. No human could act like that.

ID: You didn't seem to mind the way she acted for while.

ME: She came on to me.

ID: Probably. She was blind. And now she's dead.

ME: No—look! She's moving.

BI (*groans long and loud... then silent*)

ID: Scary.

BI: The trans... (*moans*) Given to the... (*moans*)... given... given that the...

ME: Here we go.

BI: Give. Given the.

Given the transformation of the image in a digitalized reality and with it the waning of affect and corresponding to what we now know, or think we know as a new and as yet unseen configuration of politics, desire, space, social space and economics, and given a new set of co-ordinates in the relation of knowledge and information or social mediatics, in short the field of infomatics, and in long, at the same time, always hungry, always knowing that the potential for art—as art—to be socially and politically critical has not been fully but only partly negated in post-post-modern society, and knowing or thinking or thinking and knowing at the same time that the relationship between artistic production and socio-political commentary has undergone a kind of mutation, mutilation high speed rotation or oration or some type of dubious transformation translation transmediation strangulation Lacan and Derrida that, nonetheless Rancière, nonetheless anyhow, nonetheless or overmore, moreover, there exists from this now, this particular now a kind of... There exists a kind of... there exists a kind of... MOMA, MOCA, MUSAC, León, Kunsthalle Zürich, Serpentine Gallery, MCA Chicago, Tate Britain, Tate Modern... And given what we know, and what history has taught us Butler and Kristeva... and given that... and given that... and given the other, the other and the other's other... and given that there exists a 13th Street Subway Station derelict somewhere in 2004, and continuing with the siting or sighting of a Prada boutique in a Texan desert in 2005, immobile, sand-locked and ending with, or not ending with or pending bending with the insertion of institutional spaces within the architecture of a public... Bonami, Serrota, David, Enwezor... Qatar and Hong Kong as the new destinations and so many names lost in translation... and Klaus... Klaus... And given that celebrity has exchanged credibility and that the credit crunch seems to have no further influence on the art market, and still the fact is that for every female artist there are dozens of male ones high on testosterone, crash tests, testing the patience of their audience and do they never get tired in their eyes, the audience, morphing into endless mutations, mute, mutilated, MOCA, MAXXI, MOMA, MACBA, Marfa, mama, papa and mmmmph, mmmm, MOTHERFUCKER; I'm your sister and we are many and we're one big family and you're the one, baby, so Happy New Year, I wish you many, many happy days...

BI collapses and falls silent.

ID: Now she's dead. Those were some pretty strange last words for a courier.

ME: Must have swallowed a really heavy art catalogue.

ID: Or ingested an online guide. What a way to go...

ME: Doesn't really matter.

ID: We killed someone.

ME: Does that mean our work should change? Get better maybe?

ID: No. It means we should go to prison.

ME: Right... We *are* in prison, aren't we?

ID: I feel sorry for her. There was something sad about that, towards the end. Don't you think? Something? I feel a little...

ME: Don't get melancholic. Please. We don't need that. Come on—let's open that letter.

ID: We should sign first. She would have wanted that.

ME: I guess we owe her that final tribute.

They both sign the electronic signature gadget, ME first, then ID. While ID signs, ME opens the letter and reads it to himself.

ID: Who's it from? What does it say?

ME: Wait.

ID: OK.

ME: It's from Achilles Anastasius Stefanolopolus chief curator Nancy Spector.

BI: Ughhhh...

ME: Looks like the messenger is alive.

ID: That's good news... But who is the letter from?

ME: Like I said. It's from Achilles Anastasius Stefanolopolus chief curator Nancy Spector.

ID: The name is too long—what were they thinking? Is it a man or a woman? It's totally confusing.

ME: It's simple—the name of the person who gave money for the title of the curator... and then the name of the curator. Genderless. Guggenheim. Which again is the name of the person who gave money to the museum where the curator works.

ID: Guggenheim? That's... What does she write?

ME: She's coming by for a studio visit.

ID: Oh shit. Shit, shit, shit. Merde de l'artiste. SHIT.

ME: What?

ID: We have NOTHING to show her!

ME: We've gotta come up with something.

ID: But we've got nothing here. There's... just those two beds.

ME: The bunk bed?

ID: No one's made a queer work on boy scouts...

ME: How do you know?

ID: I don't know but I'm sure...

ME: I'm not so sure... So many bad boy artists in New York alone... surely...

ID: OK. Come on—just think. There has to be something.

ME: What about the fence?

ID: Too much of a statement.

ME: The shoes?

ID: No works about Prada.

ME: The shoes and the fence combined?

ID: No.

ME: Shoes and fence and bed?

ID: No.

ME: Is this our agreement? I have ideas and you tell me if they're good enough? Since when was that how this works?

ID: Don't know.

ME: We have to think of something.

ID: I know, I'm thinking.

ME: (*panicking*) Nancy InSpector doesn't wanna come here and see no nothing. We've got to do something.

ID: I know.

ME: Doesn't even have to be finished. We can call it a work in progress. Works in progress are progressive.

They both look around the space, searching for inspiration.

ID: (*running through the checklist of what they have discussed*) Bed—No. Fence—No. Shoes—No. LifeSavers. Absolutely no.

ME: The messenger?

ID: Combined with the fence somehow?

ME: No.

ID: Combined with LifeSavers?

ME: No.

ID: Just the messenger.

ME: Strong... in a way.

BI: (*moans*)

ID : Too morbid. Not the kind of thing we'd do.

ME: We did a dead collector, floating in his pool, remember?

ID: Yeah. The dead messenger would be a repetition.

BI: (*moans*)

ME: Back to the beds. There's something...

ID: Let's push them to the middle. We need more space.

ME: Art needs room to breathe.

ID: Right.

ME: If nothing comes up we do a stereo version of Warhol's "Sleep."

They go around and attempt to push the beds from behind. After a short struggle, the top bunk suddenly flips over and remains upside down.

ID: Oopsy daisy. What happened?

ME: It flipped!

They walk around the bunk bed, looking at it.

ID: Just like that. It flipped...

ME: That's it!

ID: You think so?

ME: Yes. I think so.

ID: What about a title?

ME: We can get to that later.

ID: OK. But what do we do with the messenger?

ME: We should get her a doctor.

ID: Or a glass of water? Maybe after the studio visit.

ME: She's still mumbling. As if she wants to tell us something urgent.

ID: (*sits down on the bottom bunk*) I think we're done now. Don't you?

ME: (*sits down next to ID on the bottom bunk*) Pretty much. We just have to wait here for Nancy.

ID: What time did she say?

ME: She didn't say a time.

ID: Let's wait then.

ME: It's getting dark.

ID: It does sometimes.

Pause.

ID: You sure she knows where we are?

ME: I think so.

ID: OK. We'll wait then.

ME: Yes?

ID: We'll wait.

ME: Nothing more to add.

The lights fade out except on BI.
Music (solo cello or electric guitar playing "One" by U2) starts and BI rises up and starts singing the song with a grand and booming voice.
Song ends and lights off.

END

HAPPY DAYS IN THE ART WORLD

A play in three acts by Michael Elmgreen & Ingar Dragset

Script: Elmgreen & Dragset
Script advisor: Tim Etchells
Director: Toby Frow

Cast:
ID: Joseph Fiennes
ME: Charles Edwards
BI: Kim Criswell

Production manager: Hester Chillingworth
Stage manager: Veronica Berg
Lighting designer: Nigel Edwards
Sound designer: John Avery

A Performa Commission
for the Performa 11 biennial

Preview Performance Dates:
October 21 and 22, 2011

The Tramway
25 Albert Drive
Glasgow G41 2PE
United Kingdom

Performance Dates:
November 1 and 3, 2011

Skirball Center
for the Performing Arts
New York University
566 LaGuardia Place
New York, NY 10012
USA

May 23 to June 4, 2012

Bergen International Festival
Norway

Comissioned & Presented by:
Performa

Co-presented by:
Skirball Center for the Performing Arts

Supported by:
Outset Contemporary Art Fund, Royal Norwegian Consulate General in New York, Consulate General of Denmark in New York, Office for Contemporary Art Norway, Danish Arts Council Committee for International Visual Arts, Arts Council Norway, The American-Scandanavian Foundation and Producers Circle members Victoria Miro, Emmanuel Perrotin, Galleri Nicolai Wallner and Massimo De Carlo

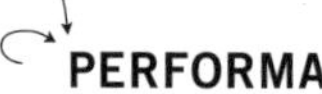

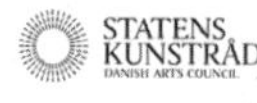

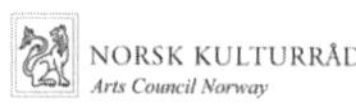

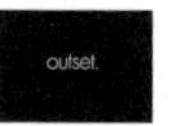

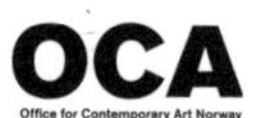

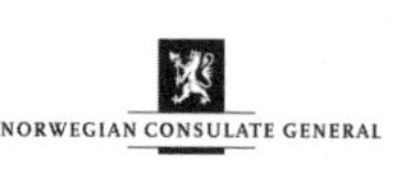

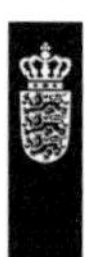

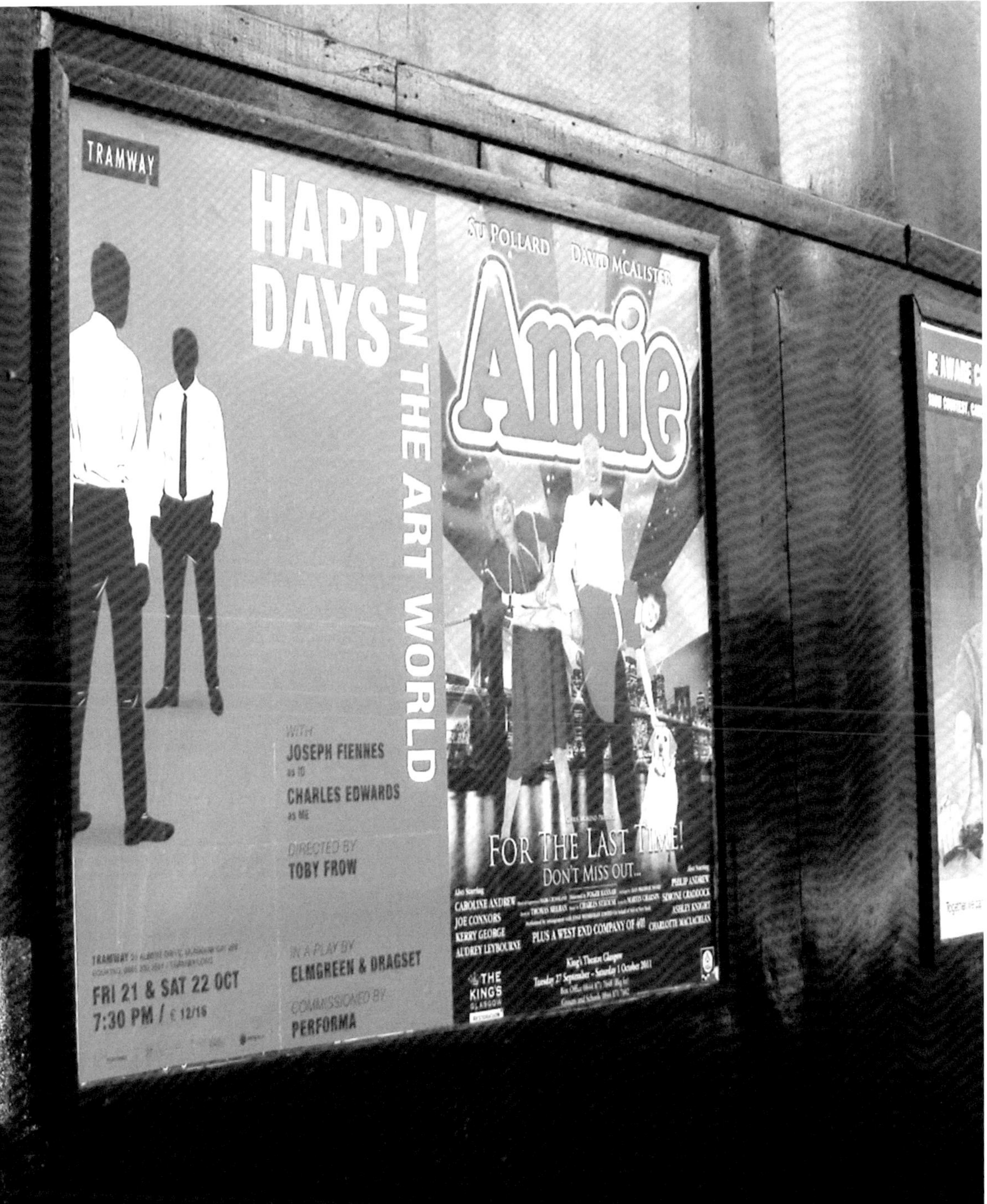
TRAMWAY
HAPPY DAYS
IN THE ART WORLD
WITH
JOSEPH FIENNES
CHARLES EDWARDS
as ME
DIRECTED BY
TOBY FROW
IN A PLAY BY
ELMGREEN & DRAGSET
COMMISSIONED BY
PERFORMA
FRI 21 & SAT 22 OCT
7:30 PM /
SU POLLARD
DAVID McALISTER
Annie
FOR THE LAST TIME!
DON'T MISS OUT...
Also Starring
CAROLINE ANDREW
JOE CONNORS
KERRY GEORGE
AUDREY LEYBOURNE
PHILIP ANDREW
SIMONE CRADDOCK
ASHLEY KNIGHT
CHARLOTTE MACLACHLAN
PLUS A WEST END COMPANY OF 40!
King's Theatre Glasgow
Tuesday 27 September - Saturday 1 October 2011
THE KING'S GLASGOW

ARON BETSKY is the Director of the Cincinnati Art Mu-um and a critic of art, architecture, and design. He is the uthor of a dozen books, including the forthcoming *What Modern* (W.W. Norton, 2012) and his collected essays will e published by RMIT Press this fall. His blog *Beyond Build-gs* appears twice a week at architectmagazine.com.

—

A BLOM is a Professor at the Institute of Philosophy, lassics, History of Art and Ideas at the University of Oslo. former music critic, she also works as an art critic, con-ibuting to *Artforum*, *Parkett*, *Afterall*, *frieze*, and *Texte zur unst*. Her recent books include *On the Style Site: Art, Social-y and Television Culture* (Sternberg Press, 2007); *The Postal erformance of Ray Johnson* (Sittard, 2003); and *Joseph Beuys* yldendal, 2001).

—

OSELEE GOLDBERG, the founding director and curator f Performa, is an art historian, critic, and curator whose ook *Performance Art from Futurism to the Present*, first ublished in 1979, pioneered the study of performance rt. Former director of the Royal College of Art Gallery in ondon and curator at The Kitchen in New York, she is also e author of *Performance: Live Art Since 1960* (1998) and *aurie Anderson* (2000), and is a frequent contributor to *rtforum* and other publications. In 2010, she received the gnes Gund Curatorial Award from Independent Curators nternational, and in 2006 the French government named er Chevalier of the Order of Arts and Letters. Since 1987, oldberg has taught at New York University. In 2004, she ounded Performa, which launched New York's first perfor-nance biennial, Performa 05 (2005), followed by Performa 7 (2007), Performa 09, (2009), and Performa 11 (2011).

—

ENS HOFFMANN is a writer and exhibition maker based in an Francisco where he is the director of CCA Wattis Insti-ute for Contemporary Art.

—

SHANNON JACKSON is Director of the Arts Research Center at University of California, Berkeley, and the Richard and Rhoda Goldman Chair of the Arts and Humanities. Past publications explore the relationship between performance and social reform (*Lines of Activity*), between performance and the disciplines of higher education (*Professing Performance*), and most recently, between performance and contemporary art (*Social Works: Performing Art, Supporting Publics*). Jackson is currently at work on a book about new media performance to be published by M.I.T. Press. She has published numerous articles and catalogue essays, sits on a variety of boards, and has organized a range of artist residencies in Northern California.

—

ANDREA KROKSNES is an art historian, curator and art critic. Since 2001 she has been senior curator for contemporary art at the National Museum of Art, Architecture and Design, Oslo, Norway. She graduated with a master in "Kulturwissenschaften" from the University of Lüneburg, then studied art history and criticism at the State University of New York in Stony Brook, writing her Ph.D. thesis on Visual Culture and contemporary art. Kroksnes has also worked as a lecturer at the University of Lüneburg and at the art academies of Oslo and Bergen. In recent years, she has published a number of catalogues, edited books and written essays for specialist journals and compendia on the conjunctions of contemporary art and Visual Studies.

—

LARS BANG LARSEN is an art historian, curator and writer. He has co-curated exhibitions such as *Pyramids of Mars* (2000-2001), *Populism* (2005), and *A History of Irritated Material* (2010). His books include *Sture Johannesson* (2002), *The Model: A Model for a Qualitative Society, 1968* (2010), and *The Critical Mass of Mediation* (with Søren Andreasen). The booklets *Kunst er Norm*, *Organisationsformer* and *Spredt væren* ("Art is Norm," "Forms of Organisation" and "Dissipated Being," 2008-2010) have appeared in Danish. Lars wrote his Ph.D. at the University of Copenhagen about psychedelic concepts in neo-avant-garde art.

—

IMPRINT

CONCEPT:
Michael Elmgreen & Ingar Dragset
EDITOR:
Anita Iannacchione
DESIGN & LITHOGRAPHY:
Anja Schiller
STUDIO ELMGREEN & DRAGSET:
Jan Sauerwald, Sandra Stemmer, Katrin Dölle,
Nils Garup, Elmar Vestner
TYPEFACES:
Arnhem (by OurType, Fred Smeijers)
Akkurat (by Lineto, Laurenz Brunner)
PAPER:
BVS matt, 150 g/m²
Recy Star Natur, 90 g/m²
Invercote G 350, 350 g/m² (Cover)
PRINTING & BINDING:
Druckerei zu Altenburg GmbH, Altenburg

This catalogue is published on the occasion of the premiere of *Happy Days in the Art World*, a Performa Commission for the Performa 11 biennial in New York City, which also features the first-ever retrospective of Elmgreen & Dragset's performances.

PERFORMA

Elmgreen & Dragset would like to extend a big THANK YOU to:
all performers, technicians and assistants, institutions, galleries, organizers, curators and writers who have made their performance work and this catalogue possible.

PUBLISHED BY:
Verlag der Buchhandlung Walther König, Köln
Ehrenstr. 4, 50672 Köln
Tel. +49 (0) 221 / 20 59 6-53
Fax +49 (0) 221 / 20 59 6-60
verlag@buchhandlung-walther-koenig.de

Bibliographic information published by the Deutsche Nationalbi liothek. The Deutsche Nationalbibliothek lists this publication in t Deutsche Nationalbibliografie; detailed bibliographic data are ava able on the Internet at http://dnb.d-nb.de.

DISTRIBUTED BY:
Switzerland
AVA Verlagsauslieferungen AG
Centralweg 16
CH-8910 Affoltern a.A.
Tel. +41 (44) 762 42 60
Fax +41 (44) 762 42 10
verlagsservice@ava.ch
—
United Kingdom & Ireland
Cornerhouse Publications
70 Oxford Street
GB-Manchester M1 5NH
Tel. +44 (0) 161 200 15 03
Fax +44 (0) 161 200 15 04
publications@cornerhouse.org
—
Outside Europe
D.A.P. / Distributed Art Publishers, Inc.
155 6th Avenue, 2nd Floor
USA-New York, NY 10013
Tel +1 (0) 212 627 1999
Fax +1 (0) 212 627 9484
eleshowitz@dapinc.com

ISBN:
978-3-86335-099-4

PRINTED IN GERMANY

PHOTO CREDITS:
Carla Åhlander (20 left, 33-37, 54-57, 71, 75, 78, 82-84/85) Arken Museum of Modern Art, Ishøj (58 top; bottom left) Anders Sune Berg (126/127) Kathryn Bradl (281) Till Briegleb (25 right) Thor Brødreskift (20 right, 102-105, 130-131) Marine Castoriano (66/67) Ken Cheong (180 middle and bottom, 181) Elmgreen & Dra set (16 right, 26 right, 58 bottom rigth, 59, 106-107 top, 152, 157, 159, 170-172, 177, 180 top, 182-185, 203, 230-231) Elmgreen & Dragset / Fabulab (240-241) Galle Struts, Oslo (42-43, 47, 49) Aline Gwose / Michael Hering (26 left 114 top, 115) Leif Hansen (64-65) Pez Hejduk (68-69) Klosterfelde, Berlin (108-109) Komisch Oper Berlin / Joreg Reichardt (194/195) Kunstnernes Hus, Oslo (Cover, 38-39) Pablo Leon de la Barra (188-189) Didier Leroi | www.vernissage.tv (128-129) Kirste Lilli (162-165) Jannes Linders (13 left, 116/117) Matthias Lindner (16 left) Armin Linke (135, 160/161) Paulina Magdalena Markowska (147) Cameron McNee (13 133) Burkhard Meltzer (85 right) Roman Mensing (196, 197 top left and right; bottom left, 210) MUSAC (186-187) Musée d'Art Moderne de la Ville de Paris (40-4 Museum Kunst Palast, Duesseldorf (90-92, 95-96, 98-99, 101) Old Vic Theatre (197 bottom right, 200) ONUK (118-119) Overgaden, Copenhagen (50-51) Proje Haersalongen (52-53) Bent Ryberg (16) Jan Sauerwald (166-169) Schauspielhaus Hamburg (236-237) Anja Schiller (13 right) H.Ch. Schink / Punctum Fotograf (70, 72, 81) Helge Skodvin (238-239) Studio Blu, Torino (86-89) Tate Bankside, The Old Power Station in action. © Tate, London 2011 (107 bottom) Tot en m ontwerpen (120-125, 155) Elmar Vestner (25 left, 114 bottom, 158/159, 198/199, 229, 242-244) Ruth Walz (232-235) 10th Havana Biennial (178-179)

COVER IMAGES:
Front: *Untitled* (1996), Kunstnernes Hus, Oslo
Back: *The One & The Many* (detail, 2011), Museum Boijmans van Beuningen, Submarine Wharf, Rotterdam

TEXT CREDITS:
L'amour de loin. Original French language libretto © Copyright 2002 Amin Maalouf. English language translation © Copyright Amin Maalouf. All Rights Reserved. International Copyright Secured. Reproduced by kind permission.
BBC News – Screenshot (19.06.2003) / Pictures by Armin Linke